THE PARADOX
OF RELEVANCE

THE PARADOX
OF RELEVANCE

ETHNOGRAPHY AND CITIZENSHIP
IN THE UNITED STATES

Carol J. Greenhouse

UNIVERSITY OF PENNSYLVANIA PRESS

PHILADELPHIA

Published by
University of Pennsylvania Press
Philadelphia, Pennsylvania 19104-4112
www.upenn.edu/pennpress

Printed in the United States of America on acid-free paper
2 4 6 8 10 9 7 5 3 1

Library of Congress Cataloging-in-Publication Data
Greenhouse, Carol J.
    The paradox of relevance : ethnography and citizenship in the United States /
Carol J. Greenhouse.
        Includes bibliographical references and index.
        ISBN: 978-0-8122-4312-3 (hardcover : alk. paper)
    1.   Anthropology—Political aspects—United States—History—20th century.
        2. Ethnology—Political aspects—United States—History —20th century.
        3. Social structure—Political aspects—United States—History—20th century.
        4. Citizenship—United States—Philosophy.   I. Title.
GN17.3.U6 G74 2011
323.60973 22
                                                                2010047526

CONTENTS

PROLOGUE

The dominant political art in the United States of the 1990s was a new language of liberalism keyed to the market as the most promising arena for social justice. It emerged in the 1980s as a language of opposition—honed against grassroots demands for the renewal of federal civil rights remedies, as federal courts began to curtail the broad access to law that the landmark legislation of the 1960s had offered. But between 1990 and 1996, the discourse of the new liberalism—neoliberalism—gathered a powerful bipartisan consensus in the U.S. Congress and as an electoral platform. Rights did not disappear, but the shift of discourse had weighty consequences. It involved a massive reorientation of federal services and governance in relation to the private sector, as the government retooled social security from public safety net to personal responsibility. The new consensus did not speak for everyone, but the political spectrum narrowed in ways that made alternatives appear to be moot (Goode 2001: 365). The new Congressional majority moved swiftly to redefine (by restricting) the legal standards that defined discrimination. In the name of efficiency, they terminated key welfare entitlements, and imposed heavy constraints on immigration. In the name of liberty, they recast antidiscrimination measures as *reverse* discrimination. In the name of security, they crafted measures to counter unregistered immigration with a system of fines and deportations. All of these developments had major consequences for the significance of identity.

This book examines the makings of the new federal discourse from the standpoint of its circulation in an unexpected quarter: the anthropology of U.S. cities, where—below the radar of policy making and media commentary—the old liberalism and its iconic bond between identity, society, and security sustained anthropologists' sense of problem and professional practice. Among anthropologists, the 1990s saw a revival of the community study in the ethnography of the United States—a classic genre in U.S. sociology and anthropology, but with a difference this time. As in the past, these were monographs grounded in long-term fieldwork; however, this time, the empiricism of the community study functioned preeminently as a literary trope—lending the concreteness of the page to the contradictions between neoliberalism's insistence on individual responsibility and the actuality of the new constraints that made marginalization a permanent status for some classes of immigrants and citizens.

This book is about the community studies of the 1990s, since they make so readily visible the discursive knot connecting U.S. lawmaking and identity. I focus particularly on three related discursive strands: the racialization of class, the gendering of difference, and the marketing of culture. These associations and their interrelations made *culture* a potent and polyvalent keyword in the public sphere, including academia. The strands of that knot also connect anthropology to other genres and disciplines—notably sociolegal studies and literature—as the mutual implications of citizenship, subjectivity, and experience readily jump disciplinary and institutional bounds. Such interconnections are this book's main subject matter—for the most part evident through the patternings of authors' interpretive choices and textual practices. In this sense, the book is as an exercise in "thick description" (Geertz 1973)—rematerializing the practice of cumulative ethnographic reading around the historical specificity of ethnographers' writings. Though the book is about the past, it is not a history or a genealogy—or comprehensive in any bibliographic sense. Publication is a poor guide to the genealogy of ideas, since at a minimum most academic books have long prequels in oral form, if not also in other written forms. As discussion tacks back and forth between close readings and more general discussion, I focus on texts that are especially telling in the sense of offering explicit accounts of their own textual and theoretical practice—illuminating of the period yet without being typical. I do not claim that every work from the decade mirrors the ones I have chosen here, nor should my critical contextualization in the period be read as critique of the scholarship as such. My concern throughout is with how state-centered notions of identity and social life enter unbidden into ethnographic discourse.

Hovering between the narrative conventions of monograph, memoir, epic, and novel, U.S. community studies of the 1990s not only tell stories of community experience, but also—in the process—question the American individualism of the late twentieth century: hero or remainder? self-made or abandoned? local subject or global object? opportunity or waste?[1] Cast as ethnographic accounts of cultural experience in place (which they also are), they make such questions inescapable—and, while overtly celebrating cultural pluralism and the American Dream, they also make plain the fictions in the myth of the free market (cf. Polanyi 1957). In distinctive ways, through its literariness, the ethnography of the United States in the 1990s demonstrates the connections between empirical significance and democratic implication.

This sense of purpose and positioning—of writing *for* communities engaged in an "unfinished business of struggle and negotiation" (Pels 1997: 164)—involved complex entanglements and effects. In structural terms, via borrowings from diasporic and postcolonial fiction, ethnographers transposed a discourse of postcoloniality to the U.S. landscape. In the process, they reinforced the tacit framing of ethnographic projects in terms of a national state (see Cattelino 2010b: 277–278): as a system of over-rule and cultural domination, as addressee through its proxy (the reading public), and, more subtly, in the temporality of the work—that is, keyed to the political present. Through these channels the very writtenness of these U.S. monographs imports an implication of federal power into the process of social description via cultural critique aimed at the new (neo)liberalism.

In relation to the debates of the day, community studies, as written, tend to position their authors as mediating figures. The discursive and analytical constraints of that mediation are broadly evident. In this book, as we explore the discursive context of the new community studies in policy debates and other developments, we shall see how ethnographers crafted their texts in ways that bridged often sharp divisions over the meanings of citizenship and equality, as well as the nature and limits of law's power—as if to hold in place an idea of political possibility not spoken for in media arenas. In part, their agility in this regard was due to the small scale of their studies. Depictions of neighborhoods, community cooperation, intimate spaces of family life, and individual narratives furnish these accounts with imagery that resonated as fully with the right as with the left. The texts are guided by what appear to be several key templates of relevance constructed around themes of inclusion, exclusion, and movement. At the same time, the terms of social description in the monographs evoke literary figurations of identity, aspiration, and the search for justice; these images circulate back and forth across genres and institutional settings. The literary, the legal, and the ethnographic are inseparable in these works, for reasons this book explores in detail—but their convergence in ethnography corresponded to no available political space.

Capping two decades of national political hardening against "dependency" and rights-based remedies to social problems, the main legislative contests over federal social policy in the 1990s were in the areas of race discrimination, welfare, and immigration reform. As ethnographers of "the new poverty" noted at the time, the policy discourse acknowledged neither the cumulative systemic effects of income inequality, nor the prejudice and structural forms of discrimination that reproduce it (Garland 2001: 81–82; Morgen and Maskovsky 2003: 318; see also Wacquant 2009: 76–109). Instead, the new federal discourse racialized class in "a new regime of disappearance" (Morgen and Maskovsky 2003: 319)—conflating gender, race, and poverty (Morgen and Maskovsky 2003: 322; Mullings 1997, 2001; Susser 1996: 422–426, 1998: 220). *Culture* was an expedient and flexible rubric for this elision in policy discourse—constructing inequalities as the result of learned behaviors on the part of individuals socialized to *dependency* as a lifestyle. More than a euphemism, the elision of race and culture both sustained a broad stage for negative stereotyping (wily yet vulnerable women, lazy yet aggressive men) and set inequality beyond the reach of the law.[2] That distancing of law from the status contingencies of identity became central to rationales for new legislation curtailing access to law in employment discrimination, welfare rights, and immigration.

In rendering culture negatively in this way—as social pathology targeted for social engineering—politicians and policy makers were making a calculated response to social movements for whom culture was both historical affirmation and a current call to commitment. Looking back across the 1990s, anthropologist Leith Mullings writes that "the resurgent turn toward culture is in part a reaction to the failures of liberal integration; in part a consequence of the state-sponsored destruction of the left; and in part a challenge to apologists for inequality who attribute the cause of increasing poverty to the culture of African Americans" (Mullings 1997: 189). She also reminds us that the appeal to culture was not merely a response to those developments, but also "the continuation of a long tradition of activist social scientists" (Mullings 1997: 189). Indeed, just as colleges and universities—pressed by scholars and students—began to open to those theoretical traditions in the form of ethnic cultural studies programs, *multiculturalism* became a new keyword for a widespread assault on identity politics, as well as what some influential commentators saw as the excesses of U.S. diversity and cultural pluralism.

As the term *culture* jumped from the social sciences to national politics and back again via social movements and cultural studies, it became integral to the mainstreaming of neoliberalism and, at the same time, an object of contestation and anxiety among social scientists—and in particular ways for anthropologists. Anthropology's ownership claim with respect to the concept of culture never asserted a monopoly, but it has involved a claim to priority in the dual sense of purpose and pedigree. During the same years when partisan politics over federal social policy were reworking the meanings of race, culture, class, and the individual, the numbers of anthropologists engaged in U.S.-based research surged (Moffatt 1992). These can be understood as broadly related developments. A half-generation earlier, the U.S. anthropological profession had resisted U.S. ethnography on a variety of grounds (analyzed by Varenne 1986; see also Greenhouse 1985). By the late 1980s and 1990s, resistance was no longer overt but, with varying degrees of nuance, still evident in terms of epistemology, politics, and ethics—as is especially clear in the book reviews discussed in the next chapter.

The growth of U.S. ethnography occurred largely in a disciplinary space apart, as is also evident from the ways ethnographers address their imagined audiences. Commentators at the time (whose sentiment is well captured by Moffatt 1992) ascribed the growth trend to shortfalls in research funding for fieldwork overseas, or to local politics in countries unfriendly to U.S. anthropologists. Perhaps, but these factors do not account for the nature of the new work, its authors (not all of whom were from the United States), nor the extent to which new theoretical questions in the discipline made the United States particularly fruitful as an ethnographic location just then.

In the 1990s, many of the books about the United States published by anthropologists took the form of community studies in urban neighborhoods marked by poverty and ethnic segregation. Their literary qualities are highly patterned, and those patterns are in turn deeply resonant with the cultural forms that comprise their subject matter. This book details the recursive relation between genre and politics that was characteristic of this body of literature. Two preliminary observations are in order. On one level, these ethnographic accounts are conspicuous for their understatement, as they deploy standard methods to investigate the life conditions of people suffering from various forms and degrees of prejudice and neglect. On another level, they also show something of the constraints in the profession—institutional avoidance of partisan politics, ambivalence with respect to the ethnography of the United States and urban anthropology, and the silence over race, among other things. In the anthropology of the United States in the 1990s, these issues had to be faced, and the texts bear the imprint of patterned indirection, made legible by authors' narratives of their own choices (and sometimes struggles) with respect to objectivity, engagement, and professional responsibility. From these accounts, we can consider that U.S. anthropology was not wholly an artifact of disappointment as borders and foundations closed down, but an affirmative attraction for scholars who were drawn by these challenges.

Race was central to the politicization of neoliberal ideology, notably in the way the rights critics (including those who advocated terminating entitlements) drew on a particular image of African American urban poor as a driving rationale for disembedding the federal government from the social sector—while at the same time denying any race prejudice. Race was in sharp contention as a theoretical concept among academics, and their contests were inseparable from deep political divisions over access to law and entitlements in other settings. The differential impact of a decade or more of neoliberal reform was evident by the 1990s—in the restructuring of labor, widening income gaps, rising poverty, de facto resegregation of cities, and massive social displacement. In metropolitan areas such as New York and Los Angeles, large communities of new migrants sought a place in the United States as they retraced in reverse the routes of U.S. military and corporate investments (Sassen 1988: ch. 3; see Passel and Fix 1994). Cities, which had been the crucibles of New Deal liberalism, now suffered from the return of nineteenth-century laissez-faire politics amidst steep income gaps and other differentials of social condition (Bender 2002: 181–183; Susser 1998).

Anthropology's so-called postmodern crisis was related to the collapse of New Deal liberalism in the 1990s. As culture became a proxy term for race in the public sphere, some anthropologists moved away from both terms—discrediting them as essentialisms incompatible with modern understandings of history and the constitutive effects of experience on identity. In anthropology, too, then, culture became politicized as theoretical object and as a core element of methodology. The critique of culture was the centerpiece of the hotly debated but misnamed *postmodernism*—misnamed since it emerged in anthropology not as an "ism" but as a broad array of critical, methodological, and literary experiments with and for ethnography. Ethnographers' experiments were keyed to the knowledge demands of engaged scholarship in a world widely perceived as forging new forms of power and vulnerability. Urban decline made these vectors highly visible, as the withdrawal of public services combined with rising property values left many individuals and families homeless or in substandard living conditions (Susser 1996).

In the 1990s, cities were still new as ethnographic locations for anthropologists—traditionally set off limits by a pervasive methodological skepticism on the grounds of their complexity and scale (Canclini 1995:

743; Low 1996: 1).[3] For ethnographers working on U.S. cities at this time, the major refrain is social marginalization and suffering (Susser 1996: 427). Another is the "murk" (Bourgois 1996: 249) and "incoherence" (Strauss 1990) of the ideological nexus that shapes the social fields of the urban poor—their overexposure to political crosscurrents arising directly from the centrality of urban margins within the dominant discourse of social policy (Bourgois 1996: 249; cf. Schneider 1999).[4] The anthropology of the United States in the 1990s was preeminently urban anthropology, and from its new beginnings looked to urbanism as a theoretical location where the traditional distinction between science and engagement could be productively suspended.

It was not engagement as such that was controversial, but a particular kind of engagement. As heirs to Franz Boas, anthropologists have always embraced the correction of negative cultural stereotypes as integral to their purposes as scientists. In the milieu of the 1990s, reversal of cultural stereotypes became a consistent motif in the new monographs—particularly where these concerned groups that had been singled out by politicians as evidence of pervasive cultural pathology. But anthropological authors of community studies—performing their discipline's traditional value neutrality—did not address themselves directly, at least in print, to the debates of the day. Anthropological authors who sought to make their cultural critique explicit did so by reaching beyond the discipline for textual strategies that would guide readers toward appropriate associations and conclusions—borrowing (knowingly or not) from other genres that were also responses to current developments. In particular, they reached into the motifs of the civil rights movement for a construction of the individual subject and the ambivalent powers of law. They reached out to theories of narrative emergent from the expressive genres of third-world feminism, *testimonios*, and feminist jurisprudence.[5] And they reached out to fiction—in particular novels in which the internal narrative declares itself aligned with social justice. The literariness of the community studies is enmeshed in the narrative genres of national and transnational liberation movements of the 1980s and 1990s, and this makes the politics of genre salient as entrée to cumulative reading.

The corridors of Congress and anthropology departments were spaces apart, yet connected by shared conventions for eliding race, class, and gender within broader notions of citizenship and social value. Those conventions amounted to a new discourse of citizenship, a new federal subjectivity—an imagined self-made liberal subject whose primary identity could be *national* and whose entitlements could be limited to his or her expected return on investment (i.e., as income and taxation). Urban ethnographies literalized the new federal discourse and in the process revealed its limits—and, as already noted, at the same time revealing certain limits within the discipline itself. The most prominent effect of the segregation of the ethnography of the United States within the discipline was a misreading of U.S. neoliberalism as the definition of globalization, and the particularities of U.S. identity politics as if the template of a global multiculturalism. The case of anthropology's engagements in the United States in the 1990s thus makes visible both the punishing selectivity of neoliberalism as it was realized in key areas of federal policy, and the channeled circulation of rubrics of *identity* across superficially disparate disciplines and institutional settings.

The Call for Relevance

In the 1990s, anthropology as a profession and discipline was at odds with itself, uneasy with a pervasive mood of crisis over postmodernism (Thomas 1991: 306). A history of postmodernism in U.S. anthropology would begin earlier, in the 1980s, the early debates unfolding around issues of canonicity, multiculturalism, representation, coloniality, and cultural studies (Michaelsen and Johnson 2008: 4; see also Amsterdam and Bruner 2000: ch. 8, esp. 218–225; Eller 1997; Fischer 1991; Turner 1993). In the 1990s, these concerns became more pressing—contested as priorities and challenged from several directions at once. The sharper tonalities of that second decade hint at some underlying periodization—not simply the effects of an accumulation of disagreements or an exhaustion of collegial patience. The underlying issues included the mainstreaming of neoliberalism and the pernicious public climate around culture and difference made evident in legislative debates during the first years of the 1990s.

As academic debates over postmodernism reached a fevered pitch in the mid-1990s, anthropologists began to worry in public about the survival of their discipline. "What is the future of anthropology?" James Peacock asked the audience at his presidential address at the American Anthropological Association in 1995. His answer presented three possible scenarios. The first would be "extinction"—"Gotterdammerung. We go up in flames." The second would be to "seek refuge in our enclave"—as "living dead." The third, the theme of the rest of his speech, would be "a flourishing redirection of our field into a prominent position in society" (Peacock 1997: 9). To save ourselves, he said, "we must focus on things that matter most, but we must also emphasize those things that concern humankind, not just the academy" (Peacock 1997: 10).

None of these fates materialized. The discipline ultimately flourished in fresh directions, neither on wholly new ground nor from positions of retreat or prominence. Producing neither Gotterdammerung nor Kuhnian paradigm shift, the turmoil of the 1990s gave way to other conversations, questions, and debates. Indeed, one implication of the very notion of paradigm shift is that multiple paradigms are simultaneously legitimate, any question of dominance being unanswerable except in specific circumstances. Anthropology's internal divisions had been highly visible, some departments reconfiguring (even divorcing) along lines of conflict, but similar debates cut breaches into the boundaries of the humanities and social science disciplines. Anthropology was the avant garde, its problems signaling a deeper crisis in the human sciences, as debates over basic questions of methods, meanings, and stakes became inescapable, for a time eluding containment. Peacock's address to anthropologists spoke to the profession as it was in 1995, but his words captured that wider sense of crisis along the horizon of ethnography and cultural inquiry.

The crisis was most manifest in overt conflicts over basic questions of method and theory in ethnography—the rationales for conducting field research, for collecting and analyzing field data, the nature of ethnographic data and the prospects for comparative analysis, and the value of ethnographic inquiry itself, among other things. For some anthropologists, the value of ethnography was precisely its value-neutrality; for others, it was its critical engagement with contemporary social issues.[6] These disagreements were widely experienced as epistemological debates, that is, debates over the nature of knowledge and truth. At the time, positions on these and other questions tended to polarize around commonsense notions of science and politics as antithetical foundations of knowledge.

In retrospect, it was not the differences between science and politics as modes of truth-seeking that were at issue; rather, it was the other unresolved questions and antagonisms that held these positions apart. The export of ethnography as a mode of inquiry from anthropology to adjacent disciplines in the humanities and social sciences expanded the intellectual centers around anthropology in cultural, ethnic, and gender studies. At the same time, universities were downsizing, straitened by economic pressures and the new "audit cultures" (Strathern 2000). The new audit culture treated colleges and universities as service industries—requiring mission statements as if they were service contracts, refashioning students as consumers and clients, valorizing teaching as productive labor as over against research, except where research could be shown to have a clear public interest in relation to policy or profitability.

Audit measures also established standards for rates of productivity, making these the basis for departmental resources and in some cases, accreditation. As public funds for higher education receded, "soft money"—grants from foundations and business—became increasingly important to core missions. In a discipline as wide and varied as anthropology—spanning arts, social sciences, and natural sciences across its four subfields of sociocultural anthropology, linguistics, archaeology, and bioanthropology—such pressures could and did produce powerful crosscurrents. The science-politics debate within anthropology was an extension of a situation outside of anthropology in which academia and the conditions of intellectual life were increasingly subject to new forms of power and value. A debate over ideas is the essence of academic life; what ailed the canary in the mine was not the loss of epistemological consensus but the claustrophobia that resulted as institutional pressures (both internal and external) straitened the means and ends of collegial exchange.

One symptom of that claustrophobia was a discursive impasse within the ethnography of the United States during the decade of the 1990s. By *discursive impasse* I mean a pervasive and persistent inability to continue a conversation across lines of opposition where there is no agreement on the terms of debate. A discursive impasse is sometimes manifest as silence, sometimes as an abrupt shift of terms; it can also be a potent political tactic, fracturing or redirecting opposition to create the illusion of consent (Greenhouse 2009a). Under other circumstances, a discursive impasse can be productive creatively, sustaining novel associations and active partnerships. Anthropology's discursive impasse in the 1990s was a redirection of the political debates in the U.S. federal policy field that developed around the calculated incompatibility of rights-based and market-based policy approaches to equality. As neoliberals and conservatives in Congress broke their opposition, oppositional discourse intensified in the academic fields most closely implicated in the new federal discourse of culture and identity. Those years of highly public debate had major implications for the mutual significance of race, class, culture, and the individual in the public sphere—and so not surprisingly with broad effects on core concepts of the human sciences and academics' textual practices.

In the 1990s, anthropologists' neighborhood studies were keyed to the widespread interest within the discipline in transnational and globalization. These were widely understood as transformations of anthropology's subject matter, as locales lost their theoretical cache as social and cultural micro-cosms and became interesting instead as localized instances of global "flows" (Appadurai 1990). Anthropologists attached new importance to the diversity within cultures, to their indigenous voices, to the dialogic and relational aspects of inquiry, to diverse standpoints within the ethnographic scene (particularly women's perspectives), as well as new attention to history and reflexive accountings of their own interpretive authority. These innovations also posed textual challenges—in particular to the "meta" perspective of the traditional omniscient narrator, and to narrative structure that emphasized form and function over agency and meaning. The literariness of anthropology was already a subject in itself (see Clifford 1989; Clifford and Marcus 1986; Marcus and Cushman 1982; Marcus and Fischer 1986; Lavie, Narayan, and Rosaldo 1993). Novel subject matter entered where grand theory exited, particularly in relation to the institutions of what were still at the time called "complex societies." All of these practices and concerns are mainstream now, but they were innovative then, and, in disciplinary terms, politically marked. The controversies then rampant tended to encamp over science versus art, empiricism versus interpretivism, behavior versus "talk" and symbols, truth versus subjectivity, and so forth. The conventional rendering of these tensions as traditionalism versus postmodernism politicized creativity in ways that tended to encode methodology and engagement with wider significance in relation to other more fundamental divisions in the society at large.

The new literariness of anthropology and other social sciences made the conservative politicians' weighty play with the language of liberalism accessible ethnographically. Congressional hearings—some of them now fully televised in real time on the new medium of cable—became pitched contests over the fate of rights, in the process reworking the language, imagery, and meaning of the nation's history, the public good, and personal testimony. Any social description could be politically charged. Politicians were keen to demonstrate the social legitimacy of their positions with carefully choreographed sessions with witnesses—some experts, some ordinary citizens. Sociolegal scholars looked to law as the encompassing expression of social and cultural diversity; authors of fiction looked away from law for their idioms of social ordering and self-knowledge. Anthropologists, even where law is not within their field of vision, seemed to take up some of these formulations in the ways they organize their narratives and address readers as members of the public. Law was seemingly everywhere, mainly—as theorized by Durkheim—as society's sign. Thus rights were redundant for neoliberals, and indispensable to neoliberalism's critics. It was in the community setting where these competing visions of security could be made clear in theory and in practice, and where the airy indeterminacy of political speech could be brought to the ground—hence the prominence of the community study as an ethnographic genre shaped by the tensions between the form and contents of the American Dream.

Not Alone in the City

The mutual implication that public relevance would enhance theoretical consensus was strongly felt in anthropology, but not in anthropology alone. The most proximate case, just a few years earlier, is that of sociology. The president of the American Sociological Association, Herbert Gans, used the occasion of his presidential address in 1988 to call his colleagues to revitalize their discipline through research and writing relevant to the general public. The call to "public sociology" shaped the modern discipline (Haney 2008: vii).[7]

It is perhaps not surprising that anthropologists working in or on the United States took up the community-study approach in response to their own concerns with relevance. Somewhere between a motif and a method, the *community* focus gave these 1990s works something of the form of the classic community studies of the 1930s, 1940s, and 1950s, notably by Lloyd Warner, and even more so, the urban ethnographies of the 1960s by Elliott Liebow, Carol Stack, Ulf Hannerz, and others. The more recent wave of community studies combines the self-conscious sense of experimenting with anthropology's limits that pervades the first wave (e.g., Lloyd Warner's essay on Memorial Day, or his book, *The Living and the Dead*), with the even more conspicuous cultural critique of the second wave (e.g., Elliott Liebow's indirect critique, in *Tally's Corner*, of the Moynihan report's analysis of African American masculinity). The first wave was written during the years of the New Deal and war—and this body of work can be read as among the literary genres that contributed to the public discourse of the United States as a national *society*. The second wave was also written in a time of crisis—one that put the notion of a national society to the test with major civil rights legislation in Congress and a series of landmark opinions from the U.S. Supreme Court in the 1960s.

These first- and second-wave community studies gesture toward the nation, but they do so in different ways. For Lloyd Warner, it was immigration and the expansion of capitalism—from Yankee City ownership to New York City, for example—that were in the background of the project. In Yankee City and Jonesville, Warner showed that while individual upward mobility was central to the popular discourse of capitalism, it was in practice strongly hedged both by the claims of family life on individuals and, more strongly in Warner's accounts, by the moral value attached to key signs of class identity—race preeminent among them. He used the term "caste" for the widest differential in the likelihood of success for the two groups he symbolized with categorical labels as black and white. His descriptions of actual social life emphasized a wide spectrum of ethnic identities (not just "blacks" and "whites") as well as individual opportunities for success across the full spectrum; however, his analysis and usage of terms make it clear that in his view *race* is the key sign—a form awaiting content—that is the template of difference and makes moral meaning of it in ways that transcend local particularities. *Community*, then, is the scenario of a problematic organic solidarity—a Durkheimian image that is explicit in Warner's work on the United States—as people actively wrestle with the contradictions between civic equality and social status in a period of massive economic and social restructuring.

For Elliott Liebow, too, the context is national—he declares this in the opening and closing pages of *Tally's Corner*—but the content is local. It may seem obvious that this should be the case, since the allusion of the particular to the general is embedded in ethnographic practice; however, it is not obvious how this should be done, and to what ends. In *Tally's Corner*, the action is worked mainly around a few men—men with names, intentions, and memories, men who know each other and together make a parlous community of mutual support and respect. It is a study of persistent poverty among African American men in a Washington, D.C., neighborhood.

The men on Tally's corner understand their own situations—and understand them well. Liebow does not ironize their points of view; rather, he conveys them as valuable knowledge. It is the findings of the Moynihan report that he ironizes—stepping back at the end of the book to deliver a powerful epilogue on the urgency of community empowerment and participation in the development of federal social policy. Like Warner, Liebow examines the connections between race and class, but he does so close up—where structural questions morph expansively into issues of personal authority and agency and their collective effects. This is part of his point: the focus on race and class is vividly keyed to national policy debates over civil rights at the time, but Liebow's attention to the actualities of experience on one street-corner in the nation's capital insists on the relevance of local knowledge to political community. *Community*, then, is framed by the federal more than the national—and as a political location in tension with the federal rather than (as for Warner) as an automatically constitutive or generalizable part of the whole. Liebow refuses to generalize on the basis of race and class, withholding generalization where democracy has failed to provide for active participation. Though not explicit in his account, a Weberian strand emerges in his attention to the ways political communities are taken up by the state—and accordingly, the ambiguity democracy presents as between popular justice and absolutist authority (see Weber 1954: 356).

By the 1990s, much had changed. In the background of Liebow's work was a massive legislative agenda in the U.S. Congress; there was no further major civil rights legislation for a generation, until the Democratic Congress sought to wrest a new agenda from the George H. W. Bush administration in 1990. With the Americans with Disabilities Act as a rehearsal of sorts, the Civil Rights Act of 1990 was put forward by Democrats explicitly as the corrective to a decade of limiting conditions set by the U.S. Supreme Court in the area of anti-discrimination in the employment context. These bills are discussed in detail in Chapter 3. The civil rights bill would have affirmed employers' obligations to account for their hiring practices in relation to business necessity, and to provide individual plaintiffs with information relating to their own job category. After extensive and highly publicized debate, the bill passed but failed on a presidential veto—on the grounds that employers might be led by the threat of lawsuits to establish quotas on the basis of race and gender. This was one claim put forward by the opponents of the bill, and the burden of proof provisions were stripped from the successor bill that passed the following year as the Civil Rights Act of 1991.

The other claim opponents used effectively was that the legal conditions for individual opportunity were already well established—and that persistent poverty only showed the consequences of a cultural pathology of dependence in some sectors. The testimony of expert witnesses made plain the reference to African Americans and Latinos—men in particular. That logic—though absent in the president's veto statement—prevailed as the basis for the Clinton administration's welfare reform legislation in 1996. The politicization of culture as the pathology of poverty was central to the mainstreaming of neoliberalism in the 1990s—not only because it challenged discrimination as integral to systematic disadvantage, but also because it shifted attention to individual opportunity rather than collective status. The same logic—constructed as "individual responsibility"—became the banner for immigration reform (also in 1996). *Culture* became a keyword in contention—in prevailing conservative usage as the foil for *the individual*, and uncoupling *race* from *class*. Prominent liberals decried the excesses of identity politics and multiculturalism, and sought correctives in community deliberation rather than rights. This is where the third wave enters.

For the most part, ethnographic work on U.S. cities published in the 1990s involved new immigrant groups living in urban ethnic enclaves. The iconography of the public policy debates over civil rights and welfare—which mainly featured African American urban poor—were in the background, but the narrative organization of these works is consistently patterned around the new discourse. This sort of indirection was prominent and possibly necessary, given the high stakes debates within the profession at the time with respect to science and objectivity—and to which some authors refer. The controversies over postmodernism in full gear, most scholars who wrote in the community-study vein made a conspicuous performance of their methodological classicism—not only by adopting the community study as their model, but also by bracketing their texts with prologues and epilogues that made their personal intentions clear, including their struggles to remain scientific in relation to the circumstances they faced in the field.

In monograph after monograph—many of them set in New York City, among Puerto Ricans in East Harlem, Haitians in Brooklyn, Brazilians in midtown Manhattan, African Americans and Chinese in Queens, Salvadorans on Long Island, and so forth (cited in the main text)—anthropologists took their openings from the new public discourse that took *culture* as its euphemism for the damaging hold of the past or pathology on individuals. Turning their lenses the other way, anthropologists presented culture as communities of meaning, sustaining individuals in their efforts to live the American Dream on behalf of those they love. They are above all pleas for tolerance; written as if for general readers, these are American stories even more prominently than they are anthropological accounts.

The monographs are written with a pervasive tone of irony, particularly where they juxtapose liberalism and intolerance. As we shall see, this particular contradiction is sometimes explicit in the authors' own statements. But the ethnographers also perform that irony—not just commenting on contradictory values, in other words, but also holding the ethnographic focus on the experiential connections between difference and disadvantage for the people among whom they studied. The performance of irony in this sense draws implicitly on readers' awareness of a public rhetoric that increasingly championed the market as the guarantor of equality and made *culture* a euphemism for the social pathology of a racially marked underclass.

Perhaps the main finding in the ethnographic accounts from this period overall is the extent to which social and economic participation is overdetermined by race and ethnicity. This refrain and the evidence for it are striking. The contradictions between systematic constraints on the ethnographic ground and the idealization of opportunity among conservatives and the new liberals were the primary context for—literally, the pretext for—U.S. ethnography in the 1990s.

But between pretext and main text, however, there was a wide space to cross. The narrative organization of 1990s ethnography was standardized by what appears to have been a commonly felt impulse to push back against the limits of anthropological practice as to value-neutrality with evocations of literatures of engagement. They drew important critical and poetic repertoires from the resources (then new) of diaspora and postcolonial fiction, sometimes venturing into their own experiments with genre. Genre counts for a great deal in decoding these works. Ethnographers—consciously or not—drew on the textual and rhetorical templates of new social movements and minority literatures in crafting accounts of their own positionality, as well as in their constructions of authorship and voice, their use of narrative, and figurations of identity. Their approach gendered difference in ways that mediated between the new federal discourse and new feminist voices in literature and sociolegal studies.

As liberalism edged progressively away from the strong public sector investment in reform and social service toward an endorsement of privatization and libertarianism as a substitute for "big government," this ethnographic space widened—and the monographs acquired a patterned quality. The community studies—with notable exceptions (Roger Sanjek, Steven Gregory)—are not studies of actual community processes, but rather localized accounts of a general state of affairs. This gives them their patterned emphasis on stigma and marginality. Most authors took up *community* primarily, it seems, to ironize cultural misrecognition of U.S. minorities and the failures of global capitalism.

From a literary and rhetorical standpoint, ethnographers' attention to U.S. communities reflected a dual concern with life conditions at ground level, and with the capacity of the federal government to deliver on its promises of equality to the previous generation. To the extent that such textual strategies run ahead (or just askew) of actual prospects, ethnographers of the time also draw heavily on the textual strategies and poetics of voices for reform from arenas outside the state. The very structure of U.S. ethnographies reflects the tensions within the polity at large, as well as the literary movements that have been among their primary modes of articulation. Indeed, the monographs are in a very real sense shaped by their position "between" the new mainstream neoliberal discourse valorizing market principles and the critiques of law's limits that pervade the fictional works. This proved to be an impossible position corresponding to no available political location, and community studies have once again faded from fashion.

The discursive power of the community study tradition's episodic dominance as a practice of localizing broader national and even global concerns is to be found in the details of everyday descriptions. This is not to suggest that anthropology's long enchantment with the village study in other contexts (national and colonial) is irrelevant to the development of U.S. ethnography; rather, it is to suggest that this history had a particular salience in the U.S. context that resisted relinquishing, given "community's" new idealization among neoconservatives, republicans and progressives as the ideological arena of democratic deliberation and social action. Indeed, as the civil rights era brought the federal government into direct confrontation with state and local officials, the localism of American ethnography became an extension of *federal* claims for jurisdiction—and with it, particular forms of federal modernism and moral life.

U.S. community studies are always in some sense "about" federal power (or its lapses) even when the books are overtly addressed to other concerns. Indeed, the literariness of U.S. ethnography is indispensable to its meaning. The community study of the 1990s is ultimately about democracy, modernity and the state as the qualifying contexts of opportunity, practical action, and personal meaning. Reading them together illuminates a critical juncture in the history of American liberalism. In some ways, it is the illumination of a jeweler's bench, trained on the life forms—forms of political life—suspended in textual amber. Those life forms are nourished by the image of a liberal democracy in which an electorate might yet be stirred by the facts of impoverishment and exclusion, and moved to attend to the needs of the newest and most vulnerable populations.

Read cumulatively, the works show how American communities at the margins were—by their very costing out in the name of national security—

central to an understanding of U.S. global power. This enfolding gesture—the hallmark of postcolonial anthropology (Kearney 1995: 551)—could be read as a gesture toward sociocultural anthropology at large, although it was not read in this way at the time. U.S. ethnography remains a case apart, but missing anthropologists' work in the United States in the 1990s means missing the centrality of race—or rather, the denial of racism—to the mainstreaming of neoliberalism as well as modern forms of federal power.

And read cumulatively, the 1990s community studies also gesture toward the critical potential that the idea of *culture* retains in relation to democracy in the broadest sense of the term—not through relativism or representation so much as through problems of contradiction and consciousness. This is perhaps their strongest connection to the community studies of the past— their insistence on identity as socially produced (anything but self-made). Yet the very protean quality of community in these more recent works is, in the aggregate, also a vivid reminder of the dispersal of the contemporary public sphere around issues of inequality and need, and correspondingly, the potentially extreme vulnerability of individuals for whom the need for community is real, and that the earlier works prepare us to see.

Thick Reading

While it might seem that such terms as *culture* and *identity* were neutral analytic terms for social scientists or technical argot for members of Congress, a cross-reading of government texts and academic works of the time shows them to be thickly and mutually coded for particular lines of opposition, and long historical trajectories of discursive displacement. The anthropology of politics and law sooner or later confronts a particular version of a problem that Johannes Fabian calls the "dematerialization" of writing—a "fascination" with signs, symbols, and representations (1992: 82). Fabian proposes a corrective in the form of a disciplined reflexive reading. The 1990s are well suited to such a project, since political spokesmen and academics alike were producers and consumers of a discourse of identity the implications of which both claimed but neither could control. The reflexive reading in the present volume is intended to foster an informed alertness to the ways anthropology's textual practices registered that political struggle, particularly in relation to genre, narrative, and realism.

Ethnography's literariness became an object of struggle and an icon of political struggles beyond the discipline—and in a seemingly direct relation to the extent that the new federal discourse deployed the keywords anthropology shared with liberation movements to rein in rights. The interpretivist analogy between culture and text imports key liberal democratic norms into ethnographic reading practices: the claim to the mutual substantiation of local knowledge and legal knowledge (Geertz 1983), the generality of power in discourse (Foucault 1978: intro.), the totalizing of "articulatory practice" as discourse (Laclau and Mouffe 1985: 105), the tacit equation of representation and recognition (Clifford 1989; Kaplan and Kelly 1999) and the constitution of national community through print media (Anderson 1983). Each of these issues aligns reading—our readings as observers, that is—with a priori judgments of political subjectivity (whether individual or collective).

Benedict Anderson's thesis has been particularly influential in this regard, although its specificity is often submerged in a neutralizing and universalizing formulation of reading (Rutherford 2000: 312). As Rutherford argues, a reader's sense of "imagined community" is neither an automatic nor general function of reading, but a particular linkage between specific reading practices and content, and specific projects of national citizenship. Reading high state texts—in our case, mainly transcripts of Congressional hearings—represents a particular twist on this issue. The risks of dematerialization are as pressing in relation to the official texts of state offices as they are for texts of other kinds. Anthropologists have discussed the ways states use a variety of techniques to manipulate knowledge and assert their own legitimacy and efficacy: statistics (Briggs 2004 and Paley 2001), conventions of scale (Briggs 2004; Strathern 1995), organizing metaphors of encompassment and spatialization (Scott 1998; Ferguson and Gupta 2002), temporality (Greenhouse 1996; Nugent 2002), figuration, hegemony, and discursive fracture (Greenhouse 1997, 2005, 2009a)—among other things. Often taken as enunciations of general attitudes or consensus, government documents can be more productively read as intertextual forms that have survived the competition among competing interests and political positions (see Riles 2001). In the Congressional transcripts discussed in this book, race, gender, and the general image of an underclass functioned in this way—sustaining a sense of substantive contact with vulnerable communities through narrative even as the state withdrew from key areas of the social sector for victims of discrimination and the poor. In the academic works discussed most closely in subsequent chapters, race and gender also have important textual functions beyond what might seem to be their descriptive power. Rewritten as culture and community, they expose—precisely via this path of indirection—the myth of color-blind opportunity. In this sense, race and its proxy, cultural identity, function literarily as a key piece in the political competition over discursive control.

Laclau and Mouffe (2000: 104–114) argue that discourse is ever-contingent on the conditions of its own remaking. Drawing on Foucault, they propose that discourse therefore always resists the absolutes of "fixity" and "non-fixity" (2000: 111). But this very formulation suggests the conditions under which contingency might become subject to various forms of temporary suspension in the way language circulates through state processes from sources in moral communities outside the state (see Corrigan and Sayer 1985). This is the essence of hegemony—the echo effect that nullifies the oppositional force of expression. Elsewhere, I have called this effect "discursive fracture" (Greenhouse 2005, 2009a). Discursive fracture is a political tactic aimed at creating a situation in which irreconcilable differences cannot but speak each other's language—thus cutting antagonists off from the oppositional force of their own speech. The works in question in this book show the diffuse effects of discursive fracture, as well as the importance of cross-genre improvisation in strategically countering its effects. For anthropologists, the paradox of relevance arose from the effectiveness of the tactic of discursive fracture that conservatives made integral to the new federal discourse by using the language of the old liberalism (identity, inequality) to spell its demise.[8] In that situation, anthropologists' efforts to counter the hegemony of the new discourse through the authority of ethnographic knowledge necessitated novel forms of creativity.

Some of those innovations were available as re-imports of the concept of culture from adjacent human sciences. The broad circulation of *culture* among emergent humanities communities in the 1980s (at that time still framed as *movements* rather than *fields*)—law and literature, cultural studies, gender studies, ethnic studies, subaltern studies—had by this time furnished the term with a critical democratic resonance against patriarchy, coloniality, orientalism, and other forms of hegemonic exclusion through their associations with social movements (see Amsterdam and Bruner 2000: ch. 8; Fraser 2009: ch. 3; Michaelsen and Johnson 2009: ix; Williams 2004; Wing 1997). Where anthropology's internal critique of culture targeted the double essentialism that historically associated culture and race (Abu-Lughod 1991), colleagues in adjacent fields—though alert to that critique—had a different history with the concept, as the rallying cry for identity-based social movements. In the 1990s community studies that are the subject of this book, culture functions dually—as the hallmark of classic sociocultural anthropology and as a discourse of resistance against the universalizing claims of globalism, coloniality, and other forms of hegemony. At the time, the latter associations were not directly available to anthropologists from within their own discipline, given its classic reservations regarding political engagement as a form of bias; however, particularly as anthropologists and colleagues in other fields increasingly asserted the value of their discipline in terms of giving "voice" to others, they became available through the literariness of a shared craft. Judging by their texts, ethnographers asserted the relevance of their work in part through meanings of culture and forms of literariness associated with these postcolonial- and rights-oriented social-and-scholarly movements—which is to say, for want of a better term, postmodernism.

With the definitive end of New Deal liberalism and the aftermath of the attacks of September 11, 2001, the older, more tender notions of security that had been the warrants for the community-study revival in the 1990s no longer had the same counter-hegemonic valence of just a few years before. The community study has once again receded from fashion, and ethnographers are more likely to declare their alliances directly, out loud. Transparency is the new objectivity. The point of the present project is not some belated diagnosis of what went awry within anthropology during those years, but the observation that—in the American context *then and now*—state discourse is integral to disciplinary practices of social description and debate. If for this reason alone, the need for creative freedom grows with ethnography's urgency—once it is understood that what makes anthropology relevant as useful knowledge is not the use to which it is put by powerful institutions, but the knowledge it offers to willing imaginations to think beyond them, to other kinds of knowledge, powers, needs, and futures.

Everyone whose work I discuss in the following pages went on to write other things, keyed to their ongoing engagements. Ethnography flourishes on U.S. ground and elsewhere, intellectually sustained by the ever-changing creative demands of relevant scholarship and substantive collegiality.

CHAPTER 1

Relevance in Question

By the 1990s, the term *postmodernism* had become highly coded as a critical touchstone across the human sciences. Reading the reviews of the time, one quickly gains the sense of a discipline divided between those who saw so-called postmodernism as a diversion from the real work of anthropology, and those who saw it as its corrective. Methodology thus became a roomy basket for a host of questions about other things. Anthropologists writing about the state of the discipline in the United States at that time read postmodernism as posing challenges to the privileged place of "exoticism" in anthropology (Thomas 1991: 206), the reification of culture (Lugo 1994: 462), old essentialisms (Lamphere et al. 1993: 274), the sometimes punishing hold of positivism (Wax 1997: 21) and the conventional limits of ethnography (Clifford and Marcus 1986; Marcus and Fischer 1986). In such usages, postmodernism was in this sense a political rhetoric, drawing substance from debates within the profession—and iconic form from antagonisms in broader debates over priorities, stakes, and responsibilities beyond it. Such developments were not limited to Americans writing about the United States. Peirano (1998), Abélès (1999), and Ramos (1990) note the extent to which new anthropologies were emerging "at home" elsewhere—the inflections of those critical engagements keyed to their national contexts and ethnological traditions.

Book reviews and other critical literature of the time are vivid evidence of the patterned ways references to postmodernism featured rhetorically. Their main function appears to have been to consolidate anthropology's critical discourse around methodology, especially along an axis that (purportedly) divided long-term or intensive fieldwork from ethnography of other kinds.

What is striking in the reviews of the 1990s is that this critical discourse circulated more or less independently of the specific content at hand. Such usages are often casual, without specification or reference, coloring questions of approach with the shades of value and tradition. For example: "In a world in which studies of gay and lesbian populations tend to be haunted by queer politics and postmodern sensibilities, . . . the tried and true brand of social anthropology—the kind that benefits from long-term, intensive fieldwork— has a lot to contribute" (Lewin 1996: 932). Praise for an author's fieldwork often takes the form of an indirect critique of postmodern ethnography—for example, "This is no drive-by ethnography" (Lawless 1996: 908). Sometimes it is Marxist political economy that emerges in positive light against the foil of deconstruction: "This book provides a synthesis of urban social issues in a climate permeated by the deconstruction of Marxism" (Attinasi 1996: 171). And in yet another context, dualism is deployed to underscore the praise for an author's detailed evidence and blunt argument: "It may not please interpretivists and postmodernists but . . ." (Shankman 1996: 889).

When reviewers want to draw attention to a book as shallow or unconvincing, they frequently single out its reliance on texts as the cause of its "depthlessness"—as if textual studies are self-evidently one-dimensional or lacking crucial effort (Strauss 1997: 363; Schmidt 1994; Park 1996). At least in part, such criticisms rest on the absence of a "native" interlocutor, as in Michael Moffatt's commentary on Elizabeth Traube's analysis of a popular film: "What . . . is an anthropologist doing publishing an article in a journal of anthropology about the meaning of certain cultural artifacts which is based on no ethnographically rooted evidence of what these artifacts mean to 'the natives'?" (1990: 372–373). Text- and narrative-based ethnographies came in for a particular version of this critique, as if their attention to literariness somehow sapped ethnography of its engagement and "thickness."[1] Reviewers at the time tend to refer to this literariness mainly as a sign of the author's position on anthropology itself as *either* science *or* politics. Gewertz notes the drifting quality of that critical horizon in her own experience: "Formerly, I taught against a sociobiology that explained cultural differences in what I considered politically suspect terms. Lately, I have begun to counter a textual analysis that reveals these (and other) terms for what they are, but in an involuted manner, obscuring, it seems to me, much of political significance" (1991: 977).

What is striking in the reviews of the 1990s is the way a discourse of critical evaluation circulated more or less independently of the specific content at hand. Some of postmodernism's codings were keyed to internal struggles that were concrete and consequential. Within the academy, some of these involved issues of generational, racial, and gendered hierarchies in the profession; others, issues of resistance to everyday practices of erasure and prejudicial constraints on what might count as legitimate scholarship. These issues frequently mixed. The other side of the so-called postmodernists' challenge to ethnographic authority was their readiness to identify with their own research subjects (the "natives") and to project that identification into their own professional milieus, that is, their own subaltern status within the discipline (Said 1978; Asad 1973). Revision of the longstanding assumptions that had stabilized the roles of observer and observed became visibly undone, and anthropologists caught up in these new relations experimented broadly with their knowledge practices and claims to authority. As George Marcus wrote at the time: "The most important political struggle in which American academics engage is within their own establishments and over the forms of knowledge itself" (1991: 125).

The crux of such experiments was a series of textual strategies aimed at unsettling the "fixity of a distinction between 'native' and 'non-native'"—yet without erasing *difference* understood as "shifting identifications amid a field of interpenetrating communities and power relations" (Narayan 1993: 671, 682). "Enacting hybridity" (Narayan 1993: 671) called for new forms of writing. Indeed, the signature of the politics of the new anthropology was its textual ethics—"ethnographic writing" that "moves away from unified representations of culture and . . . produces more complex, or multiply-inflected, cultural objects" (Harding 1994: 276). Postmodernism (so called) was reflexive in the sense of incorporating the conditions of knowledge production within the ethnographic frame, a reflexivity imagined as offering a bridge between "our expert public sphere" and "the modern public sphere" beyond the academy's walls (Reddy 1993: 161).

The folding of "inside" and "outside" into one political field was crucial to the new multi-sited research: "The conventional 'how-to' methodological questions of social science seem to be thoroughly embedded in or merged with the political-ethical discourse of self-identification developed by the ethnographer in multi-sited research. The movement among sites (and levels of society) lends a character of activism to such an investigation" (Marcus 1995: 113). Continuing, Marcus is careful to specify *activism* as the agency he sees as inherent in an anthropologist's professional persona rather than in a cause or movement:

It is not the activism claimed in relation to affiliation with a particular social movement outside academia or the domain of research,
nor is it the academic claim to an imagined vanguard role for a particular style of writing or scholarship with reference to a posited ongoing
politics in a society or culture at a specific historic moment. Rather, it
is activism quite specific and circumstantial to the conditions of doing
multi-sited research itself. It is a playing out in practice of the feminist
slogan of the political as personal, but in this case it is the political
as synonymous with the professional persona and, within the latter,
what used to be discussed in a clinical way as the methodological.
(Marcus 1995: 113)

The identification of ethnography with feminist activism implies an understanding of ethnographic critique as a feminine relation (even when performed by men). Feminist theory made knowledge practice a critical site of
engagement even when it was not acknowledged as such (as famously noted
by Mascia-Lees et al. 1989). Postmodernism also authorized more personalized expressions of reflexive analysis of and discursive opposition within the
profession (i.e., in workplaces and other locations of professional practice)
(Visweswaran 1994; Weston 1998). Such engagements were critically received
by some as beyond the bounds of ethnography. Contemporary accounts show
the extent to which enacting a personal identification with one's research subjects could be problematic, even professionally fatal. For example, Lutz (1990)
notes the erasure of women's work, citing as evidence the disparity between
the proportion of women's authorship and rates of citation to their publications. Similarly, she notes the strong feminist presence at professional anthropology meetings as compared to their neglect in overviews of the field.

Contemporary accounts also reveal a pervasive sense of risk among scholars who felt marked by their commitments. Traube's response to Moffatt's
"disciplinary reaction" (quoted above) analogizes his critique to the "fantasy
of a disciplinary community under attack" and the self-righteousness "of the
right-wing patriot" (Traube 1990: 374). But it was not only methods that
could put a scholar at risk; subjectivity and subject matter were also potential
vulnerabilities. Recounting the origins of her study, Lewin explains in detail
her concern to present her original research proposal to potential funders in
a way that would deflect attention from her interest in lesbian motherhood.
In her proposal, her project title referred only to *single* motherhood: "As a
lesbian, I felt a special obligation to focus my energies on a 'lesbian project'; at

the same time, I was concerned, not without reason, that my fledgling career might prove to be a casualty of this kind of commitment" (1993: xv). Williams (1997: 223) confirms that assessment, pointing to "rampant homophobia" in anthropology and professional taboos on the subject of homosexuality at the time: "Faculty in anthropology departments . . . dissuade students from studying homosexuality, and vote against hiring and tenuring scholars who publish gay-positive books. Anthropological journals publish few essays on homosexuality, and granting agencies seldom fund ethnographic research on the subject."

The issues that were, in those years, at once so disruptive and divisive tend to be read (now as then) as a two-sided conflict between the "ancients" and "moderns" (Stewart and Harding 1999: 300), "fashion-seekers" and "old-time religion" (Sanjek 1992: 999), tradition and innovation, positivism and postmodernism, materialism and interpretivism, as Oedipal intergenerational struggles, or as democratic upheaval as the academic profession changed shape around new categories of participants and new commitments (feminism, African American studies, cultural studies, and new social movements, among others). For those who remember what departments and conferences felt like then, the binarism of such renderings might be a reminder of both the exhilaration of new intellectual communities and the dread of antagonisms in which collegial relations and professional futures might be at stake. But reducing the creative efforts of the time to such binaries understates the range, form, and substance of anthropologists' experiments, as well as their seriousness of purpose. As they played out in the United States, such intellectual tensions were not merely two-sided.

The End of Liberalism

Thinking back to a context at once cerebral and visceral, it is pointless, now, to ask whether it was one or another element that mattered most—any more than one can settle on singular causes when a personal relationship runs awry. Of more enduring interest and ongoing relevance is the question of what it was in the milieu of the 1990s that made those positions such ready ground for antagonism. Just a few years earlier, in the 1980s, the novelty of postmodernism was exhilarating or vexing, depending on one's point of view, but it was still epistemology—not yet the grinding machine of division that it became. The question of why postmodernism became toxic rapidly spills over the edge of theory into other aspects of experience, and thus into a time and space that includes our own. Paul Stoller captures this temporal slipperiness in his celebratory review of Ivan Brady's collection, *Anthropological Poetics*, drawing a passage from Roy Wagner's opening essay: "A Cartesian scientist aims to discover what is there; the surprise of poetics is that it is here. The industries of Cartesian science have labored to make the time of creation interminably long; the surprise of poetics is that it is now." Stoller continues: "The surprise of this volume . . . is that it *is* now. It is now that anthropologists . . . must return to poetics, to re-center themselves, to confront the challenges of ethnographic subjectivity and representational politics" (Stoller 1992: 508; Wagner passage quoted from Brady 1991: 39). Stoller's "now" suggests an important insight: that the tensions of the time were less in the methods of anthropological practice than in the subject matter itself. The immediacy of its knowledge demands pressed the discipline against its previously settled limits in the field and in writing.

The immediate surround—the now—for American academic debates over subjectivity and representation in the 1990s involved several pressing national public policy debates that significantly reshaped the mainstream political and media discourse of identity and citizenship. The civil rights legislation of the George H. W. Bush years—the Americans with Disabilities Act (ADA) and the Civil Rights Act of 1991—revealed the extent to which even a Democratic Congress was prepared to accept neoliberal principles that valorized markets over rights as the basis for equality. President Bush's nomination of Clarence Thomas to the United States Supreme Court was ultimately a highly public display of liberals' political vulnerability. President Clinton was elected in 1992, but by 1994, when the Democrats suffered devastating losses in the mid-term elections, the Congress was once again in conservative Republican hands. The fact that "liberal" and "conservative" became the vernacular antimony of partisanship is one indication of shifting alliances across party lines, particularly as a bipartisan consensus emerged around the termination of federal welfare entitlements—crucial as both cause and effect of the mainstreaming of neoliberalism in the United States. The major legislative achievements of the Clinton era—ending federal entitlements in welfare and tightening borders against unregistered migrants—were passed with bipartisan support, signaling a major shift in national politics that confirmed the neoliberal consensus central to the political mainstream. In that context, the transnational cosmopolitanism and multicultural pluralism so prominent in anthropological conversations (Clifford 1994: 328; Traube 1996: 129) —not to speak of the liberalism inscribed in anthropology's inherited notion of *society* itself—emerged in new light as oppositional discourse. These issues are discussed in the following chapters. For now, let us observe that the sea change within anthropology came in part from without, in the world of events. Without having sought an active political engagement, anthropologists in the United States found themselves positioned against the major national political currents of the time. While the theoretical effervescence of the 1980s had provided anthropologists with theoretical choices, these new developments now pushed scholars to reconsider the boundary—long written into the canons of their professionalism—between their political lives as citizens and their professional lives as scientists. Defining the profession as inherently political was more an acknowledgment of a pervasive situation than it was a solution to a particular problem.

But there was more than this, in that the channel through which the new mainstream flowed was sculpted by language that borrowed conspicuously from the identity politics it was calculated to oppose. Between 1990 and 1996, the Congressional debates over civil rights, welfare, and immigration reworked the discourse of identity, insistently uncoupling *race* from *class*. As we shall see, the winning position asserted a reading of recent history to the effect that civil rights law had already effectively provided the legal tools for equality—and that the persistence of poverty was the result of a cultural pathology expressed as welfare dependency and other ills. The term *culture* was prominent in public debates as the negative antithesis of upwardly striving individualism—throwing back to minoritarian social movements and their allies the very keyword of their political community but with a valence antithetical to their purposes. Ultimately the debates attached the state's logo to a now-familiar fusion of nation and capital (and its figuration in the citizen-consumer) that made the older liberalism out to be tantamount to an attack on the tax-paying public, even an assault on equality itself. The 1996 immigration debate—like the welfare debate, the culmination of years of public controversy—similarly valorized a Malthusian approach to limited good through an imagery of assault on taxpaying citizens, portraying the status quo as a threat to U.S. national security (Schneider 1998: 86; Chock 1991, 1994, 1999; Coutin 1996, 1999).

Those who defended entitlements as consistent with the federal role in social security were made to appear ludicrous, nostalgic, unrealistic, or lacking in substance. Their vision of a national society such as had emerged with the New Deal and again quickened during the civil rights era was made to seem abstract (academic in a negative sense) in comparison with the concreteness of the dominant position. That position was lent substance by some social scientists' testimony about incentives and dependency. These debates and outcomes showed neoliberalism to be anything but liberalism with respect to the poor and new immigrants, in the sense that the fullest application of neoliberal principles involved strong elements of surveillance, regulation, and social engineering. The traditional liberal positions were vulnerable to caricature as out-of-date in relation to the competitive demands of the new global economy. Drawing on simple correlations and anecdotes, opponents of entitlements portrayed joblessness as a moral status that, particularly for men, was also linked to criminal behavior. Young women and their children might be the most proximate victims of such men (Chock 1996; Susser 1998), but the real victims were said to be "the taxpayers."

Shifting the language of rights to the idiom of property—and to taxation as expenditure—was integral to the repositioning of neoliberalism from partisan ideology as general common sense. As ideology—that is, as a program actively produced and promoted—neoliberalism was initially a partisan response to federal regulation of the 1960s and early 1970s (Harvey 2005: esp. intro. and ch. 2): "Neoliberalism is in the first instance a theory of political economic practices that proposes that human well-being can best be advanced by liberating individual entrepreneurial freedoms and skills within an institutional framework characterized by strong private property rights, free markets, and free trade. The role of the state is to create and preserve an institutional framework appropriate to such practices. . . . There has everywhere been an emphatic turn towards neoliberalism in political-economic practices and thinking since the 1970s" (Harvey 2005: 2). The so-called Reagan Revolution popularized neoliberalism, now sloganized as "getting the government off our backs." Its popularization was inseparable from the ways in which globalization was politicized and domesticated as a foreign threat during the Reagan-Bush years (Aman 2004: ch. 1). Signs of its emergence as a popular discourse were the relative ease with which any improvement of the alignment between neoliberal principles and institutional functions could be defended as a necessary step toward efficiency, the connection between efficiency and national security drawn together as means and ends, and the rapid diffusion of privatization and contracting out as principles of good government. But neoliberalism as discourse extends far beyond the instruments of governments and markets. The privatization of government disperses political life, and the marketization of social value makes consumption its prominent index and confirming sign. Both the means and ends of membership, neoliberalism as discourse reconfigures political subjectivity around consumption, literally and figuratively reworking social bodies—and with these effects, the conditions of ethnographic practice (Coombe 1996: 218; Greenhouse 2009b; Richland 2009: esp. 171–172).

The dominant discourse—by which I mean dominant in the U.S. Congress and as a winning political gambit—took up and accelerated the circulation of already-available stock images and logics. *Culture* and *the American public* became prominent phrases in contention—culture becoming a euphemism for race and the public recast as investors (that is, taxpayers) and shareholders. These were the years when divided government (i.e., the executive branch and the Congressional majority held by different parties) was at its most contentious: major social legislation became heavily coded for contests over the power of the separate branches within the federal government. In short order, the Americans with Disabilities Act, the Civil Rights Acts of 1990 and 1991, the Personal Responsibility and Work Reconciliation Act ("Welfare Reform Act") of 1996, and the Illegal Immigration Reform and Immigrant Responsibility Act (IIRAIRA) of 1996 emerged from Washington, D.C. This package of legislation was composed around the core principles of neoliberalism—welfare reform and immigration reform being conceptually linked not only in their common discourse of dependency and personal responsibility, but also in barring unregistered migrants from public assistance as a welfare cost-saving measure (Stepick 2006: 395).

These were not the only issues that absorbed the public in the question of the significance of culture. These were the also the years of the first Gulf War, the Thomas hearings, the violence in Los Angeles, and ethnic cleansing in the former Yugoslavia and Rwanda. This was the era, too, of the end of apartheid in South Africa, a ceasefire in Northern Ireland, the reunification of Germany, and the end of the Cold War—the emergence of discourse of globalism in which culture, widely imagined as a singularity, was implicitly antimodern in its exclusivity. It was in this milieu that anthropologists turned in significant numbers to ethnography in the United States, largely in defense of positive meanings of culture that had been lost in the political contests of the day. The "condensation" (Hall's term [1985: 93]) of vernacular discourses of social description around neoliberal principles also became an opening for ethnographers. In the 1990s United States, anthropologists returned to the classic community study, critically localizing national and global concerns such that neoliberalism's dissociation of racial identity and class status could be informed and challenged in empirical terms.

As the federal legislative initiatives filled the airwaves and newspapers, the spectacle made highly public not only the official validation of a particular line of analysis, but also a performance of control that obviated opposing discourses. That combination of discursive uptake and control were the essence of its hegemonic force.[2] In this context, social description became (or perhaps, became more obviously) a political act. Social scientists' testimony colored in the main lines of each reform bill, but the main lines of argument were already in place. By its very nature, the social science evidence, primarily anecdotal and statistical, stopped short of offering conclusive evidence of motivation and intention, or causation; those interpretive elements came from the committee members. The major bills effectively deployed racial, class, and gender stereotypes, including details of character, motivations, sexual appetites, and health status—for example, in the immigration debate, the connection some reformers drew between immigration and contagion (Schneider 1998, Chock 1991; see also Segal 1996; Stewart and Harding 1999: 292). The bipartisan support for these measures showed that the era of the national society—which had lasted from the New Deal through the Great Society—was now over, without political force within the institutions of federal government.[3]

In this context, its keyword taken and its most immediate public audience on the wane, anthropology was caught "beside itself."[4] In its new politicized proximity to *race*, the category *culture* became theoretically suspect (Abu-Lughod 1991), just as *race* had been discarded by progressive cultural anthropologists on essentialist grounds. The anthropological critique of culture as essentialism—that is, as a proxy for race—came at precisely the juncture when mainstream media and politicians were deploying *culture* as a euphemism for race in connection with persistent poverty among urban African Americans and Latinos.

In the increasingly claustrophobic political space of that period, the critique of the category *race* put those anthropologists paradoxically on the side of the new conservatives, for whom racial equality required the erasure of racial categories—along with the special federal scrutiny legally mandated in race discrimination claims. U.S. anthropology was being positioned by events—to some extent in spite of itself—as an oppositional discourse, but without a conceptual language to articulate its new relevance. That language could not be overtly political, given the established profession's insistence on value-neutrality—as pervades the reviews. Instead, it became methodological and epistemological, as anthropologists rendered increasingly sophisticated reflexive and historical accountings of the constitutive effects of power on identity, status, and agency, particularly in regions of the world formerly colonized by European powers. In short, as postmodernity beyond anthropology provided anthropologists with new subject matter, postmodernism became increasingly charged as a touchstone of internal debate within the discipline—the slippage between subject and object sustaining its intensity.

The Politics of Relevance

This was the context in which appeals for anthropology's reconciliation and renewal began to circulate as calls for commitment (see Peacock 1997; Weiner 1995). Some anthropologists celebrated the progressive sophistication of their field by contrasting it with other disciplines. For example, the keywords and images of the public policy debates of the 1990s are targeted explicitly if indirectly in this review of a volume on ethnicity edited by two psychologists: "The arguments utilized in this book to explain the subject matter under study—ethnicity—follow a 'developmental perspective' from psychology that, in one way or another, still includes such discredited anthropological notions as enculturation, acculturation, assimilation, adaptation, and culture contact, all of which enjoyed heyday status in the 1940s and 1950s . . . thus, it is difficult for the postmodern, poststructuralist, or post-1960s 'practice theory' reader . . . to take the book seriously" (Lugo 1994: 462, in-text references omitted; see also Keita and Kittles 1997: 542). Among anthropologists and colleagues in adjacent fields, the old lexicon was replaced by new terms for new questions about the locations and relations of identity—"the contact zones of nations, cultures, and regions: terms such as *border, travel, creolization, transculturation, hybridity,* and *diaspora*" (Clifford 1994: 303). But discredited though it may have been among anthropologists, the old lexicon circulated widely and powerfully as very much a current lexicon elsewhere. Such discursive crosscurrents sustained a "consciousness of conceptual transition" (Brightman 1995: 510). The "performative deployment of these . . . phonological shapes" featured prominently in an intradisciplinary politics over the question of their novelty (1995: 510), their implicit concept of culture, and the differences between power and its representation in discourse (see Sangren 1995: 5). Clifford suggested optimistically that "it is now widely understood that the old localizing strategies—by bounded *community,* by organic *culture,* by *region,* by *center* and *periphery*—may obscure as much as they reveal" (303). Widely understood, perhaps, but only on the near side of a discursive gulf where anthropologists might listen in vain for a voice in their conceptual language coming from the opposite shore, where public policy was being made by federal officials who seemingly understood otherwise.

In the gathering context, the calls for relevance could only make more pressing the question of what relevance could actually mean in practice. Ethnographers conducting their research in poor neighborhoods, for example, stressed the non-correspondence between policy options and the interests of activist groups among the poor (see, for example, contributions to Goode and Maskovsky 2001). The fact that *relevance* was presented as a *mediating path* in relation to anthropology's internal debates implied that anthropologists had only themselves to blame if the public overwhelmingly communicated through other channels.[5] In retrospect, this accusation misses the mark. It was politics that abandoned *society* as social—the basis of social security— and failed the people with whom anthropologists most readily identified, that is, minority communities at the social margins.[6]

As it was, under the pressures of the time, the issue of relevance was taken up in ways that tended to reinforce the lines of intradisciplinary debate. For some anthropologists, political developments on the national scene sharpened the sense in which ethnographic discourse was itself a political field. Marcus and Fischer write: "Embedded in . . . modernist choices is a goal of cultural criticism of the anthropologist's home society" (1986: 71). It is in this context that Marcus and Fischer turn to poetics, positionality, and narrative (both realist and fictionalized) as relevant issues for ethnographers (74–76). Fiction, they suggest, is an expedient archive of "indigenous commentary" and "autoethnography"—"as similar literatures [are] in our own society" (74). And fictionalized ethnography, they suggest, is an appropriate response to the ethical imperative of concealing identities (75). U.S. ethnographies deploy each of these strategies, among others, in highly elaborated form.

Among the genres of experimentation that Marcus and Fischer assay are "psychodynamic ethnographies" (48–54), "realist ethnographies" (54–57), "life history" (57–61), "ritual" (61–64), "dramatic incident" (64–67), and— closest to their own concerns—"modernist texts" (67–73). The latter category, characterized by documentation of "the eliciting discourse between ethnographer and subjects" and by the intention "to involve the reader in the work of analysis" (67), contains the kernel of their larger argument regarding ethnography's potential as a medium of "cross-cultural juxtaposition" and "epistemological critique." That dual project requires both ethnographic discovery of the outside world and a reflexive critique of an interior world of cultural assumptions and conventional practices.

Marcus and Fischer frequently turn to the ethnography of the United States as a foil—doubling and inverting the category of Other—so as to highlight reflexive connections between anthropology and the world stage:

> In the United States, [the crisis of representation] is an expression of the failure of post–World War II paradigms, or the unifying ideas of a remarkable number of fields, to account for conditions within American society, if not within Western societies globally, which seem to be in a state of profound transition. This trend may have much to do with the unfavorable shift in the relative position of American power and influence in the world, and with the widespread perception of the dissolution of the ruling post-war model of the liberal welfare state at home. (Marcus and Fischer 1986: 8–9; paragraph break omitted)

In this sense, the ethnography of the United States emerges for Marcus and Fischer as a productive transnational complication in anthropology's routine practices—specifically, the complications posed by thick epistemological challenges in attempting to ground a point of view simultaneously in the near and the far, the local and the global, "them" and "us."

This is the context in which the United States emerged as a location for anthropologists interested in developing a reflexive basis for cultural critique and riposte, even as their own research took them elsewhere. In this way, ethnography's reflexively attuned literariness opened up an interpretive space where a distinction between anthropologist-as-ethnographer and anthropologist-as-citizen could be suspended and reworked, yet without challenging the classic exceptionalism that excludes the United States from anthropology's terrain. Varenne (1986) analyzes the classic resistance to U.S.-based work in the U.S. anthropological profession on the grounds of "excessive diversity" in the United States (see also Greenhouse 1985). By the late 1980s and 1990s, resistance was no longer on methodological grounds but, with varying degrees of nuance, on grounds of epistemology, politics, and ethics—as is especially evident in book reviews. DaMatta, for example, compares one book favorably to what he claims is the more usual case when "natives study natives." The norm, he contends, is "confusion and narrowness" since "an epistemological limitation [is] bound to arise" whenever ethnography takes place under conditions of cultural proximity (1991: 1006). "The proof of the pudding," he says, "is more studies of America by Americans" (1005). The risks to the quality of scholarship in merging the identities of observer and observed is a frequent theme in reviews (e.g., Proschan 1995; see also Moffatt 1992: 206, 208–210). Other reservations are framed in terms of potential theoretical and ethical distortions in work "at home" (see Battaglia 1995 on "selfing" and Gewertz, already cited [1991: 977], on political (ir)responsibility).

The tone and presuppositions of knowledge in such reviews suggest that they are directed primarily to American anthropologists as fellow citizens whose main professional "fields" are elsewhere. Indeed, the United States is polyvalent in this sense. The United States is not the location usually associated with anthropology, yet—especially for American scholars—it is experientially fundamental to its critical discourse and sense of political stake in relation to identity and other aspects of social description and analysis.

In the U.S. ethnography of the 1990s, the ethnographic subject, in this very sense, is always *dual*—agentive in his or her own milieu and, through the ethnographer's agency, a figuration of American dilemmas. The ethnographic *relation* thus bears a heavy performative load, at once ethical and political. Ethnographic authority is predicated on specific forms of alliance in the field situation and at home. But so, too, is ethnographic *authorship*. Anthropology's literariness—its writtenness—was as much a function of the new disciplinary consciousness as its research practices. In particular, anthropology's new literariness was calculated to bridge the distance between the foreign and the familiar—no less for overseas fieldwork as for research "at home." Seen in this light, the renovation of ethnography as literary practice is just the other side of its relevance as scientific practice in the context of then-new forms of globalization and transnational experience.

The critical thrust of the call to rework ethnographic writing around new standards of authority and representation entailed a vision of social life itself as an endless political field (cf. Foucault 1990; Donald 1996). As influentially framed by Marcus and Fischer, the transformative interplay of ethnography and literature rests on assumptions as to the potential universality of access to literary expression, and the extent to which such access was within reach as a precondition of agentive, self-representing subjects and the more collective forms of social transformation they might enable.

Following the arc of this premise, access to the means of expression is the essence of literature's transformative potential, through ethnography, for politics: "We can escape the alternative of populism and conservatism, two

forms of essentialism which tend to consecrate the status quo, only by working to universalize the conditions of access to universality" (Bourdieu 1990:
388; emphasis omitted; cf. Anderson 1993). The literary turn in anthropology was in this sense deeply indebted to the postcolonial literary criticism
and feminist theory of the time. Marcus hints at this connection in his reference to the potency of "distaff voices" and "the sheer power and influence
of ideas from the margins toward the putative center or mainstream" as two
main "source[s] of transformation" in the task of "remak[ing] the disciplines"
(1991a:126; cf. Ashcroft, Griffiths, and Tiffin 1989: 31, 174–177; Enslin
1994: esp. 537–538).[7] For U.S. scholars, the postmodern turn was a double
maneuver—looking outward but from critical vantage points embedded in
the new neoliberal consensus in U.S. politics.

Geographies of Relevance: Relocating the United States

Drawing the margins into the center through writing and reading was presented as both a means and end of anthropologists' alliances with social
movements and other communities, including other disciplines (see, for example, Morgen and Maskovsky 2003: 323ff.; Susser 1996: 412).[8] Those inter-
relationships became a new object of inquiry and debate—inquiry and debate
conceived as direct participation in a creative, dynamic, and heterogeneous
expressive field (Laclau and Mouffe 1985; Stoller 1992; Tsing 1994; cf. Feldman 1994; Rafael 1994).[9] But, as the journals made plain at the time, this
was not an answer to the question of relevance, only another way of framing it. Thus the same scholars who advocated these moves wrestled with the
practical and ethical implications of their own positionality vis-à-vis those
wider engagements from a variety of perspectives: relative to native voices
(Narayan 1993; Segal 1996), the intricate "conversions between exclusion and
empowerment" (Tsing 1994: 280), "cross-class and cross-culture interaction"
(Bourgois 1996), public culture (Ortner 1998)—among other areas in which
a subject/object distinction could no longer be clearly drawn.

A related dilemma evident in the journals was that anthropology's "shift
to the here and now (or to recognizing the hereness and nowness of everything)" made the question of the discipline's "distinctive contribution"
problematic, since "anthropology [is] only one voice, one entry, within an
enormously complex and multivocal universe of 'public culture'" (all quoted
phrases from Ortner 1998: 433). But the parentheses eliding the "here and
now" with the "hereness and nowness of everything" seems to put the stabil-

ity of these categories beyond question (Coronil 1996). More fundamentally for our purposes, they bracket what is perhaps the most paradoxical of the challenges of positionality at the time: the rejection of the privileged distinction between observer and observed, yet still alongside a defense of anthropology's value primarily in terms of "the Other" (see Traube 1996: 128–129).[10]

For some anthropologists, this paradox is precisely the conceptual and ethical location of ethnographic innovation. Fernando Coronil, for example, seeks "room for a decentered poetics that may help us imagine geohistorical categories for a nonimperial world" (1996: 52). For Anna Tsing, the paradox of positionality is the essence of anthropology's potential for renewal in a dialectical gambit at the margins—its participation in the "uncanny magic involved in imagining the local in the heart of the global" (1994: 280), where the terms of oppression and empowerment might be one and the same, forcing ethnographers to "attend to the political-cultural specificities" through which "the local is created as a site of powerlessness" (1994: 280; cf. Feldman 1994: 406).

Tsing locates the ethnographically generative "margins" at a fold where the field of *discourse* is—in practice—selectively doubled, partially unlayering analytic and critical registers. The divergence between them points to some conceptual strain in holding together the critical "here" alongside the analytic "hereness" of other ethnographic locations. The critical register encompasses the officialized discourse of the new right coalition, evident in some authors' explicit references to the neoconservative and neoliberal inflections of U.S. policy discourse at the time. The function of such references is primarily to establish a "here and now" as a context for analysis, though not as a focus of analysis in itself. When references are deployed this way, they consistently appear in the framing sections of the article (for examples, see Ortner 1998: 423; Page 1997: 99–111; Peacock 1997: 11; Stewart and Harding 1999: 289, 292).[11] Such framings are rich resources for rereading, since it is in introductory and/or concluding paragraphs that the conventions of textual form call for contextualization but also offer room for authors to exercise some creative license in doing so.

This textual topography positions the emergence of the United States as familiar terrain, though more usually as "modernity at large"—to borrow Arjun Appadurai's phrase (1996)—than as institutional locations or processes that compel interpretation. For example, in the introduction to the essay quoted above, Tsing sets the stage this way: "Attention to marginality highlights both the play and constraint of subordinate social positions. In the United States, for example, minorities are marginalized by exclusion from the assumption of being ordinary—and often the jobs, housing, or political opportunities that 'ordinary' (white) people expect. At the same time, minority cultural and political movements are launched from reinterpretations of these same exclusions. Related processes make political struggles over cultural marginalization lively all over the globe" (1994: 279–290). Having moved from "here" to "hereness" in this passage, textual form then requires some transition before Tsing can move on to her analysis of experiences in South Kalimantan. She accomplishes this by setting aside "the rhetoric of U.S. political struggle" as insufficient "to understand the complex conversions between exclusion and empowerment that are key to what I call the marginal"—insufficient due to the "*easy intelligibility of power*" in the U.S. case, relative to the interpretive demands of those other situations (1994: 280; emphasis added).[12] On the one hand, the defense of the transformative value of anthropology's critical reflexivity tacitly projects the *United States* as the producer of a global discourse of modernity, against which the local is to be retheorized as resistant and apparent. On the other hand, the defense of anthropology's empiricist traditions tacitly project *science* globally, rendering the local as a site where imagination and experience are held to be commensurate with the real.

The force ascribed to U.S. or western hegemony by some scholars associated with the postmodern turn was challenged by others who advocated anthropology's return to "latent culture" as a necessary corrective to "postmodernist polemicism" (Dominy 1993: 331; cf. Carrier 1991). But the intelligibility of power—rendered as self-evident in typical formulations of the United States—is also contested more broadly as a theoretical question about the nature of power and its availability to ethnographic arts. This framing underscores the extent to which the paradox of positionality shapes this question along the same discursive fold where critical and analytical registers partially diverge.

The divisions within the discipline over postmodernism were not first and foremost epistemological debates (notwithstanding their conventional framing in such terms). Rather, cleavages ran along the fault lines where the question of anthropology's global relevance ran ahead of disciplinary conventions limiting truth claims to local knowledge. Notwithstanding anxieties as to the risk that "tangible people" might be erased from ethnography (Borneman 1995: 670) or that the "public" no longer exists (Stewart and Harding 1999: 292), there was strikingly little debate over field methodology or the value of ethnographic specificity. Indeed, it may have been the broad consensus on these points that contributed to making "the local" into "a trope for ethnographic specificity" (Nassy-Brown 2000: 349). Be that as it may, the more contentious issue was the question of what specificity signifies from an interpretive standpoint. The relevance of the local to anything else (and with it, of anthropology to anything else) was ambiguous in a way that made questions of agency contingent on the limits of empiricism. Is agency necessarily subject to an empirical test? Is it agency if it hasn't won? If nothing changes? To be sure, these questions have not gone away.

Importantly, while Marxist and Foucauldian theorists argued about the nature of state power, they framed the question similarly as an interpretive problem arising from beyond the immediate ethnographic milieu—its putative non-appearance at the level of description belying its urgency. For scholars who reckoned their debts primarily to Foucault, discourse accounts for power and its internalization as knowledge. For scholars who reckoned their debts to Marx, Foucauldian discourse merely represents power—"real" power being something else. For Stephen Sangren, to take a leading example, the problem with Foucault is the lack of a difference between "the real operations of power and the ways in which power is represented in social institutions and discourses" (Sangren 1995: 5). In ascribing power to discourse, Sangren contends, "Foucauldian power assumes demiurgic, demonic properties (sometimes named 'the state')" (Sangren 1995: 4). Arguing for a stronger distinction, Sangren makes *ideology* the key to ethnographic "realism," on the grounds that "there are social realities that exceed our representations of them" (21). He continues: "Emphasizing the local specificities of social life, especially the multiplicity of 'sites' of its contests and contestations, ought not to be viewed in opposition or as an alternative to an attempt to comprehend encompassing coherences. To do so is to attribute to a useful acknowledgment of the limits of realist social analysis and of our abilities to entirely comprehend social life the unwarranted status of a descriptive or explanatory principle of social life itself" (21). Ensuing debates over the limits of empiricism made techne—the craft of anthropology—an object of epistemological and moral debate, most stridently in relation to the locations of political struggle (see Comaroff and Comaroff 1997: ch. 1; see also Lederman 2007).

Rethinking the Impasse

For our purposes, the point of this story is not to assess the careers of those antagonisms as such but rather to venture onto the zone of their non-meeting—to borrow an image from Ellison (1995: 311) and Hall (1985: 103). The question of what holds these positions apart is—by now—more interesting than their differences since it points to a missing figure in the field of debate—that is, minority identities emergent from new local/translocal relations. Ethnographic accountings of local social life necessarily took into account the production of the local—identity in place emerging as a potent figuration of political agency, perhaps even in global terms. Such ethnographic connections, where critical reflexivity and ethnography engage the same field, and where symbolic associations are subjects of political contestation in the field, would not resolve past or future conflicts within anthropology but would clarify their stakes. Indeed, more importantly, they would illuminate emergent ethnographic questions about the contemporary contingencies of political agency in showing the ways the discourse of power works simultaneously through identity and life conditions. As Corrigan and Sayer famously write: "The enormous extent of [state] power cannot be understood unless state forms are understood as cultural forms, state formation as cultural revolution, and cultural images as continually and extensively state-regulated. A central dimension . . . of state power is the way it works within us" (Corrigan and Sayer 1985: 199–200). The new work at this time connected the discursivity of power and identity to anthropology's knowledge practices—bringing together the two sides of the impasse noted by Hall (1985: 103).

Hall's reference is to a break in the theoretical terrain of identity and ideology, that is, between Foucauldian theories of subjectivity—posed as questions of "the constitution of subjects" and "how ideologies interpellate us in the realm of the Imaginary"—and Marxian theories of class—posed as questions of "ideology and the reproduction of the social relations of production": "As a result of treating those two aspects in two separate compartments, a fatal dislocation occurred. What was originally conceived as one critical element of the general theory of ideology—the theory of the subject—came to be substituted, metonymically, for the whole of the theory itself." As a result, Hall writes, there has been "considerable theorizing" on issues of subjectivity, but on questions of ideology and social reproduction "nothing. Finito! . . . The two sides of the difficult problem of ideology were fractured in that essay, and . . . since then, never have the twain met" (all quoted phrases are from

Hall 1985: 102). Keeping them apart, for Hall, is the unresolved theoretical question of the state (92–93).

For American anthropologists in the 1990s, that zone of non-meeting was very close to home, in the form of raging public policy debates over civil rights, welfare, and immigration. In the United States, the two sides of Hall's impasse converged palpably in the daily headlines as these policy debates unfolded. Rights debates in these contexts made *race* prominent in public discourse—race understood not only as a population category, but as an analytic at the crux of any possible conception of the relationship of power, knowledge, and identity in the United States. The importance of race as an analytic was a major theme among anthropologists writing about the United States at the time. Their publications encompass the social and political histories that made race central to the knowledge practices of anthropology and other disciplines[13]; to the legalities of kinship and partnership;[14] to basic forms of social security;[15] and to local and translocal communities of identity, memory, genres of expressivity, and collective mobilizations;[16] to state practices in the making of urban and national space.[17] Race exerted a discursive hold on literal and figurative forms of representation (Gates 1989; McKeever 1999) and concomitantly on the discourse of American federalism (Stone et al. 1991: 471–472)—and in turn (via the Commerce Clause as the basis for federal powers in civil rights law enforcement) on the conditions of consumer capitalism and the meanings of property in the United States.[18] The stakes in the struggle for racial equality shape the meanings of culture even now.[19]

"It is difficult to imagine any public debate more appropriate for [the] anthropology of the future than that associated with the issue of 'race,'" Mukhopadhyay and Moses wrote at the time (1997: 517). Yet on issues of race, they observe, anthropology has become "silent," "rarely called upon and even less often heard in the often-tumultuous contemporary public discourse on race" (517; also Lieberman 1997: 552). For anthropologists, the discrediting of *race* as a cultural determinant had been definitive (see Gregory and Sanjek 1994). It was successively displaced by *culture* and *discourse* (Handler 1998) or euphemized as *ethnicity* (Harrison 1995: 48), yet its essentialism remained, tainting the new contents of that old form (see Visweswaran 1997: 609–610).

The assumption as to the universality of race obviated attention to the specificity of the connection between race and the U.S. state, that is, the distinctiveness of the federal U.S. state's entwinement through race and racial experience. Cattelino's analysis of recent ethnographic writing about the United States suggests a context for this omission in the disciplinary tradition that divides Native Americans and settler experience from other ethnographic projects in the United States (2010b). Without recognition of the specificities of the American state with regard to race and state power, the domestic context was retrievable only to the extent that it could be claimed as a particular instance of a universal situation. In an earlier era, race had stood in for that relation—as the instance of a generalized human condition. During the period covered by this study, that choreography remained in place, now with distinction between global and local as a proxy universality of sorts. To some extent, gender could displace race as the "essential difference" (borrowing from Stepick 2006: 393), since—for many American feminists at the time—the distinction between male and female was thought to be universal. Be that as it may, as globalization entered the national political discourse, Congress took up *identity* to cancel the implication of collective entitlement and empowerment. Ethnography and politics were in this sense locked in a contest over the literariness of identity—apart from and to some extent unbeknownst to each other.

The closest association most anthropologists had with political struggles involving race then under way in the United States was not directly through their fieldwork, but through their collegial encounters in campus debates over multiculturalism and cultural studies. "Perhaps our greatest 'failing' in the mid-1980s," Michael Fischer wrote in his five-year review of *Anthropology as Cultural Critique*, "was to underestimate the furor within the American polity that the challenges of this post-1980s world would face in the politics of the early 1990s" (Fischer 1991: 527). His reference, capturing a refrain in the anthropological literature of the time, was to the way anthropology's disciplinary space tightens uncomfortably "when a powerful right-wing challenge to the expansion of the American university curriculum threatens on the one side, and, from the other side, the overenthusiastic demands for particularistic cultural representations and 'identity politics' to be made part of the required . . . curriculum" (527; emphasis omitted).

In a similar vein, Peacock's call for relevance also cites the threats of competition from adjacent fields: "Within the academy we are fighting against fields such as law, policy studies, and education which contest our claim on internationalism, diversity and cultural analysis, often beating us in the game of applicability" (1997: 10). But the distrust of multiculturalism was a different matter, underscoring the extent to which the demands of self-identified racial and ethnic communities within the United States awakened some anthropologists' traditional resistance to public political commitments—resistance recast as an objection to an *excess* of representation. This same objection was a tenet of new (neo)liberal theorists at the time, central to their call to extirpate government from identity politics by reforming welfare and reining in the legal remedies that they identified with the "new" rights of the civil rights era (discussed in the next chapter). It may seem easy, now, to recognize anthropology's battles in their American inflections as a chapter in those wider struggles, but this was not clear at the time (Dirks 1998: 15). Their construction as epistemological debates tended to conceal the extent to which they were political battles in the more usual sense of that term.

In retrospect, the relevance of the United States in ethnography's theoretical terrain is not as some cultural geography to be filled in, but as conceptual ground where issues of subjectivity and power converge in a distinctive way. The convergence has broad implications for the relationship of anthropology (and other human sciences) to public life. To miss the distinctiveness of the U.S. historical experience in relation to settlement, enslavement, Indian removal, borders, and the ongoing constitution of federal power is to miss the way race and state power enter social description through the very significance of what it means to be *present*. That missing conversation shaped ethnographic genres in the United States—as evidenced in the monographs about U.S. communities in the 1990s.

For the most part, the ethnography of the United States has not been configured around the problem of domination, but rather of contradiction. This configuration is what gives the ethnography of the United States its prevailing tone of irony in relation to issues of access and distribution of resources, as well as with respect to waning participation in representative government (Rodgers and Macedo 2009). In *The Dialectics of Enlightenment*, Horkheimer and Adorno (1997) point to the stakes in political community when "surplus production" becomes a false coin of equality. Their suggestion illuminates how—in the context of the expansion of the U.S. economy in the 1990s—*race* was caught at a conceptual crossroads. Horkheimer and Adorno argue that race materializes the contradiction—that is, lends contradiction a human form—between excess production on the one hand, and growing need on the other. The reproduction of poverty from the midst of affluence together with the denial of that contradiction points to the ways the concept of culture is complicated by its functions in diverse, even antithetical milieus. The artful experiments in U.S. ethnography during this period are perhaps above all gestures toward contradictions such as these, as well as a deep ambivalence over the power of law to create social change. For Horkheimer and Adorno, it is art that restores the social content of representation, marking resistance to the proposition that "justice is subsumed in law" (1997: 16). "The blindfold over Justitia's eyes," they write, "does not only mean that there should be no assault upon justice, but that justice does not originate in freedom" (1997: 17).

The *now*ness of that observation is all around us.

CHAPTER 2

Templates of Relevance

The raw material for this book comes from textual resources that contributed to shaping the revival of anthropological community studies of the 1990s. The community studies were keyed to a particular formulation of a national society and its implicit warrant for federal action—and in this sense the book offers a reader's guide of sorts to the themes and tenor of the times. In context (as discussed above), this means that it is also necessarily an inquiry into the relationship between disciplinarity and aspirations to social justice—a reflexive project of rematerializing reading (Fabian 1992) via a decoding of key signs, symbols, and genres (see also Boyarin 1992 and Rutherford 2000: 312). This chapter presents the principal encodings at work in the community studies of the 1990s—ones the genre was well suited (I will not say calculated) to animate for readers. I call these "templates of relevance" since those signs and their deployments would have been readily recognizable to contemporary readers as references to the major social policy issues of the day in stock images and ordinary language.

To ask how ethnography makes its object in the United States means asking how *the United States*—specifically, the idea of U.S. federal power—pervades practices of social description. Even the most basic elements of sociological description (in the broadest sense of this phrase) in the United States—individual, community, locale, state, and nation—echo key terms of social theory from deeply rooted practices of federalism: citizenship, membership, jurisdiction, nationalism, and, perhaps most broadly, an equivalencing of structural statuses into subjective identities (e.g., of individuality into individualism, national origins into ethnic groups). Such exchanges are not only in one direction. As we shall see, legislators also borrow from social science—and sometimes from social scientists as witnesses—to aid in promoting or popularizing their policy designs with claims of their scientific (i.e., rational and nonpartisan) merits as social engineering. Methodological questions in social research are in this sense never very far from a discourse of democratic citizenship. This means that popular discourses of the nation's social life—that is, how people talk about "American society" as problems, solutions, or social fact—are strikingly close to the discourse of citizenship grounded in law, broadly speaking (Greenhouse 1986, 1994, 1998). It also means that social theory easily misses the profound significance of the American state in social life, since some of the key terms of that engagement are pre-coded in the notion of social life itself (Greenhouse 2002, 2009b).

States and state power are routinely written into social science—even a social science professedly dedicated to value-neutrality—through the concepts of individual, community, and culture that are also (conversely) integral to the social legitimacy of federal law. In the works in question here, race, culture, and gender cover and displace each other in ways distinctive to modern civil rights advocacy in the United States. The possibility of those displacements was the focus of intense political competition in the country at large—since at stake was the question of whether the United States had fulfilled the legal requirements of universal equality. In the 1980s and 1990s, conservatives pressed the courts and Congress to roll back key elements of the liberalism that had prevailed from the New Deal through the Great Society of Lyndon Johnson's era—"great society" being a reference to John Dewey's *The Public and Its Problems*. Conservatives now sought to restrict access to law by raising the bar for civil rights claims, campaigning against welfare, restricting immigration, decrying the identity politics under the rubric of "multiculturalism," and in general curtailing federal powers from social sectors. The referendum on the Equal Rights Amendment timed out at the ballot box in 1993. The increasingly virulent campaign to reverse *Roe v. Wade* (the U.S. Supreme Court case recognizing women's right to reproductive choice) was to some extent part of this same project—as advocates for reversal (such as dissenting justices in subsequent court challenges to *Roe*) saw that prospect as an opening to broader limitations on the powers of federal courts relative to the powers of state legislatures. Race and gender entered the 1990s, then, already thickly coded for formulations of federal and state powers and sharp struggles associated with contests between them in broad arenas of personal rights.

This was the context in which anthropologists returned to the study of the

United States, taking up themes of community, identity, social mobility, and urban dislocation—issues where classic sociological traditions intersected with current public policy concerns: multiculturalism, affirmative action, immigration, welfare, globalization, and the state of the nation's "social fabric," among other issues. These templates of relevance pervade the ethnographic accounts of the time. Reading these works cumulatively yields an understanding of how the emergent conditions of neoliberalism affected the lives of the ethnic poor and middle class in U.S. cities—as well as the conditions of ethnographic practice.

Ethnographers in Between

Navigating the sense of crisis in the world beyond academe (not to speak of within it) on the one hand, and the straits of positivist social science on the other, most anthropologists who wrote about the United States did so from within the discursive registers of their profession. But judging by the texts themselves, this was apparently not enough. As we shall see, they also borrowed carefully (if not always intentionally) and in a patterned way from other genres made adjacent by the political contests over rights—all sides emphasizing individual agency but from within contested visions of community and social security. From the right, anthropologists borrowed the idioms of community and individual choice that were the main features of the new neoliberal consensus. From the left, they borrowed the complexities of gender, class, and race as repertoires of identity—and above all, as rationales for the explicit theoretical association of writing with the surrogacy of voice. Cleaving to the middle road, they held out no promises or policy solutions, but nonetheless held onto the idea of federal power as the nation's active principle. This was simultaneously a formulation of globalization—given the extent to which neoliberalism was embedded in global capitalism as its organizing principle, giving rise to a resurgence of identitarian revindications (Comaroff 1996).

In the 1980s and 1990s, U.S. cities became prominent locations where these national/global crosscurrents were visibly tangible, and, in related but different ways, so did colleges and universities—where ethnic and cultural studies were developing new curricula on literatures, cultures, and histories of North American minorities. The cities were targeted as federal laboratories for the management of all manner of social ills—persistent un- and underemployment, poverty, female-headed households, teen pregnancy, drug marketing and drug abuse, illegal immigration, and scarce credit and other obstacles to minority participation in business as well as welfare dependency. The shift from judicial arenas to legislated "solutions" retained the federal government at the center of race and class relations, and cast the social construction of upward mobility as a matter of good administration of pliant subjects.

As liberalism was readapted to its "neo" forms (Comaroff and Comaroff 2009), social policy and democratic theorists alike turned to neighborhoods as the proving grounds for their visions of democracy. But poor urban neighborhoods were in the process of becoming yet poorer, and social conditions worsened relative to the suburban white middle class just as they became more prominent as icons of the new liberal theorizing about the promise of civic republicanism and community deliberation for the future of democracy—the very contradiction envisioned by Horkheimer and Adorno cited in Chapter 1. In the universities, chronicling these conditions and their effects on ordinary men and women became a diffuse multidisciplinary effort, as ethnographic methods were taken up well beyond their disciplinary origins in anthropology, and came back to that discipline in new form, with new resonances. The anthropology of the United States entered the conversation on the ground at once intensively theorized and politicized, and at the same time materially neglected or altogether overlooked.

Within anthropology, the impulse to enter the conversation reverberated with older anthropological and sociological traditions in mid-century (from the Lynds and Lloyd Warner to Elliott Liebow and Carol Stack), and the new work in important respects seemed a deliberate echo of those straightforward accountings of the social effects of inequality on American citizens. But this time, the traces of that earlier hopefulness as to a legislative movement, directly addressed to the voting public, could only be ironies—given the extent to which the rescrolling of civil rights law seemed to spell the end of that era. Anthropologists navigated the pressures arising from the neoliberalization of the universities and the conservative retrenchment against cultural and ethnic studies by emphasizing the overtly anthropological aspects of their work—their engagement in the field, the long tradition behind their subject matter and approach, the rigor of their methods, the neutrality of their authorial position. In effect, their performance of disciplinarity was deeply coded, seemingly aimed at reengaging a broad national public.

Paradoxically, perhaps, anthropology's chapter at that moment in the history of social science has been much written and rewritten in the form of many monographs, but little read. Its authors—mainly American anthropologists—

addressed themselves primarily not to fellow anthropologists, but to fellow citizens about their own country. The stories they told were—are—about what was happening to racial and ethnic minorities in U.S. cities in the 1980s and 1990s. In most cases, their studies were set in the context of urban communities where most residents were poor or struggling to hold on to the lowest rungs of middle income, even falling below the income levels of their parents (Massey and Denton 1993; Omi and Winant 1994; Newman 1999). In many cases, they involved new immigrants or the children of immigrants, drawn to the United States in the 1970s and 1980s along routes first opened the other way by U.S. business and military ventures (Sassen 1988).

Anthropologists "at home" were also writing about people who identified themselves as members of what were by the century's end more settled minority groups—children of older diasporas, African Americans, Asian Americans, Puerto Ricans. Like anthropologists writing about people anywhere, these accounts are small scale, close to the ground, trained on the details of everyday life and on the resources of knowledge and sensibility people bring to questions—cosmic or mundane—about the world around them. Like ethnographic studies anywhere, these show readers how people make sense of things, build lives with others, make do with what they have, and make the hardest choices for themselves and their families. These books also show how people live with prejudice and disappointment, and, in particular, they dwell on these as ironies of neoliberalism and globalization, in the guise of the American Dream.

A particular form of critical interplay—sometimes contradictory—between textual form and content emerged as a signature characteristic of ethnographic "community studies" in the 1990s. It is as if ethnographers, seeking to expand the constraints of their professional discourse, made a point of demonstrating its limits, performing democratic contradictions by shifting across various registers not ordinarily included in anthropological texts. I must say "as if" since, in fact, I make no claims as to authors' motives or intentions beyond what they write in their books. In the climate of the times, genre was both a literary and political register in specific ways; therefore, an analysis of the politics of genre in relation to ethnography's literariness is a productive historical and reflexive route to questions of the contemporary conditions of political agency.

Intensely engaged, ethnographers of U.S. cities produced dozens of monographs during the decades of the 1980s and 1990s. This surge in attention and publication was noteworthy, particularly given anthropology's axiomatic association with foreign fields. In 1992, Michael Moffatt opens his review article synthesizing "ethnographic writing about American culture" with the observation that "anthropologists have done more research in the United States in the last dozen years than in the entire previous history of the discipline—far more, perhaps twice as much" (1992: 205). In the same passage, Moffatt finds the causes of this relatively sudden increase in ethnographic interest in the United States (at least among its authors) to be strikingly ambiguous. Among the possibilities, he cites "heightened interdisciplinarity and genre-blurring all through the social sciences and humanities, postcolonial critiques of First-World/Third-World distinctions foundational to an older anthropology, [and] new forms of older concerns about relevance and application" (Moffatt 1992: 205). He also points to "declining transnational access and funding" as factors in the homeward turn—a nod to the convention that sets the United States outside of anthropology's stereotyped self-image, but neglecting the fact that not all ethnographers of the United States are American. Beyond the arithmetic advantage of drawing the United States into anthropology's field of vision, Moffatt finds no particular theoretical gains in U.S. anthropology for anthropology itself.

In retrospect, so-called American ethnography was positioned at a juncture where key questions about the discipline of anthropology and the state of the nation were mutually in play, in theory and practice. Not all ethnographic writing about the United States took the form of community studies, but that body of work makes especially clear the complexities of sustaining cultural and disciplinary critique at that historical moment. Its textual forms make plain a core vision of the nation as a crucible of justice. Superficially straightforward, these texts are masterpieces of indirection, borrowing their beauty from the poetics of diasporic and indigenous literatures, and their claims to relevance from political debates of the day over federal law reform. Their theoretical interest is in the substance of their cross-referencing between state power and identity—accessible primarily through the works' literariness (narrative organization, style, figurations, and voicings). Their historical interest is in their response to a political discourse that works against cultural diversity in the name equality.

Within anthropology, the sense of the nineties as a distinctive period was due partially to national developments, but also, and perhaps even more fundamentally, to what was broadly viewed as a transition toward globalization. Anthropologist Mary Steedly, a specialist in Southeast Asia, captures the sense of the times in her review essay on the "the state of culture theory":

> For many of us who have maintained long associations with one or more parts of Southeast Asia, this is a time of uncertainty. There is a growing sense of confusion, as if we had somehow lost our ethnographic footing. . . . In the 1990s, the Southeast Asian "economic miracle" made computers, satellite dishes, cell phones, and fax machines commonplace. Air-conditioned shopping malls replaced street markets; Kentucky Fried Chicken and its like-named clones were a fast-food vanguard for culinary Americanization, soon to be followed by McDonalds, Pizza Hut, and Planet Hollywood. Isolated villages tuned into CNN or MTV or StarTV. For middle-class city dwellers, having a car or a computer was no longer a sign of social prominence but an ordinary necessity of life. (Steedly 1999: 423–433)

Anthropologists returned from fields everywhere, it seemed, that had been restructured by the local effects of new global institutions and transnational practices (some of them U.S. exports) in the broad spheres of politics, economics, and development.[1] The return of anthropology to U.S. fields should be seen as an *extension* of those projects, not (as implied by Moffatt 1992) their *diversion*. The global frame is everywhere around the community studies that are the focus in this volume—once one learns to read them as localized studies of global social displacement and devaluation, and as consequences of the entrenchment of neoliberal hegemony at home.

The transformation of cultural anthropology in response (in part) to globalization gave anthropologists interested in the United States a new freedom to pursue their interests, easing the conventional exceptionalism around the United States. One theoretical consequence of these developments was a broad critique of the concept of culture (see Abu-Lughod 1991). But the critique of the culture concept within anthropology was simultaneous with its reemergence as a rallying cry outside of anthropology. All over the world, it seems, anthropologists found the concept of culture coming back at them, as the contested banner of national and subnational political claims.

The implications of those claims resonate well beyond the regions of their articulation. For example, in the same essay quoted above, Steedly presents the complications of culture in broad terms: "Culture is increasingly viewed by Southeast Asianist anthropologists as an attribute of the state—as an object of state policy, an ideological zone for the exercise of state power, or literally a creation of the state—whereas the state itself is comprehended in ways analogous to totalizing or superorganic models of culture" (Steedly 1999:

433). Similarly, Andrew Apter's assessment of the postcolonial, post-imperial dilemmas of Africanist ethnography is specifically keyed to the critiques of African scholars, yet in terms that implicate the discipline at large. In the following illustrative passage, Apter engages the work of social anthropologist A. Mafeje, paraphrasing his central argument: "Caught in the double bind of either reproducing colonial reifications or losing the ethnographic referent in self-reflexive confusion, anthropology has become a lost cause for postcolonial African scholars. . . . [He] proposes a way out of the anthropological double bind by replacing the anthropological concepts of 'society' and 'culture' with revised concepts of 'social formation' and 'ethnography'" (Apter 1999: 589–590; notes omitted).

For anthropologists interested in the United States, as engaged by these developments as their colleagues working elsewhere, the turn to U.S. communities was—in this context—anything but a return "home" (cf. Peirano 1998). The theoretical charter that would authorize any simple claim to knowledge as a "native" was by this time irreversibly shredded. Less so, perhaps, were the prospects of a cosmopolitan anthropology and an anthropology for public consumption that would include the United States. But more fundamentally, given the texts in question, the ethnography of the United States that developed in the 1990s responded to these broader critical trends by reappropriating the concept of culture—both for (and with) the communities in question, and against the mounting nationalist/nativist discourse in U.S. political arenas. Ethnography was calculated (in this case, this is the right word) as an answer to the conservative right's tactics of erasure and delegitimation of difference (see Stewart and Harding 1999: 292; Kaufmann 1999: 439; Sarat 1998). Whether this counter-discursive maneuver was successful—or could be—is a question beyond the scope of this book.

Globalization at Home

For some anthropologists, defending anthropology's relevance was their answer to its internal crisis. But their appeals to relevance involved more than an affirmation of ethnography's value as useful knowledge in relation to the problems of the day, or as a basis for some competitive advantage as colleges and universities began to downsize under economic pressure. It also implied a hierarchy of knowledge, indexed to policy relevance. The surge of ethnographic writing about U.S. neighborhoods and public institutions in the late 1980s and 1990s was selective, clustering thematically around the social imagery of the main public policy debates of the time. These images were in plain sight, in the debates over rights, entitlements, and immigration gathering pace and partisan force in Washington, D.C. Directly and indirectly, community studies were localized studies of discarded promises, unexamined premises, and unintended consequences of federal policy making with respect to minorities and the urban poor (see Sanjek 2000: 368). These developments made culture contentious in a particular way—pitting group interests against equality, multiculturalism against democracy, and dependency against government efficiency—each of these terms being borrowed from the enduring political slogans of the time. Anthropologists responded by making values, aspiration, and constraint the major themes of their cultural community studies.

These issues were interconnected substantively, and, as policy talk, by a discourse in which the keyword *culture* featured cynically and prominently: as the root of persistent poverty and dependency in the inner city, and as the false coin of *multiculturalism*. Ethnographers of (or rather, in) the United States in the 1990s countered this discourse—albeit for the most part tacitly, performing their critique rather than addressing the issue directly. Their ethnographic explanations targeted the negative stereotypes of immigrants and the poor, as well as contradictions between culture (understood negatively as pathology or excessive diversity) and citizenship (understood positively as individualism). The templates of relevance amounted to a defense of difference, and more broadly, a critique of the contradictions between the emergent public policy discourse and older liberal conceptions of the citizen and the public. In the context of the debates of the day, attaching even the most general positive meanings to culture among minority and new immigrant urban poor had the resonance of a counter-discourse. For U.S. ethnographers working in areas implicated in these policy domains, no overt political critique was needed to affirm the usefulness of anthropology, at least for a willing reading public. Narrative form loosely paralleled conversion narratives, and stock images—readily recognizable from literature, law, and American mythology—were carefully honed to convey the message.

As the 1990s approached, the self-conscious sense of the moment as a millennial transition was strongly marked by the end of the Soviet empire and the worldwide expansion of capitalism in a neoliberal mode. The hallmark of the end of the Cold War was global capitalism—widely imagined by theorists and politicians as a new world order (to borrow President George H. W. Bush's phrase) to be run mainly by and for the private sector, on terms written to streamline the competitiveness and profitability of world trade. The preeminence of the private sector in this scenario seemed to valorize the vision neoliberal reformers had promoted for decades: global governance through the market, as the warrant of freedom. Writing at the time, David Held asked ironically: "Has the West won? Has liberal democracy finally displaced the legitimacy of all other forms of government? Is ideological conflict at an end?" (Held 1992: 14). Held's question (in one version or another, from many quarters) was very much in the wind in those days—and not always ironically—as a comment on the new terms of global governance and the future of the nation-state, as well as "the character and form of modernity itself: the constitutive processes and structures of the contemporary world" (Held 1992: 14).

Globalization came to anthropology first as an expansion of the question of trade, as a way of registering the theoretical implications of "cultural flows"—Appadurai's (1986, 1990, 1996) influential phrase—in the movement of people, ideas, and goods. Perhaps because of that emphasis on consumption and exchange, "the global" became a general reference to the sphere of the foreign, in contrast to "the local" as its constitutive element. The alignment of national governments around new global institutions such as the World Bank and the International Monetary Fund masked the extent to which local communities—including the United States—were not merely parts of the whole, but reconstituted in it, and transformed. The refrains in the United States and elsewhere were the widening gap between haves and have-nots, declining public support for a social service sector, outsourcing, new idioms of accountability (shareholder value, profitability), decaying infrastructure, and other shocks associated with the monetization of social value. Far from being the end of ideological conflict, globalization shifted the centers of such conflict to zones redefined as the social margins. In the United States, these developments were most prominent in cities—where new immigrants and the expanding ranks of the poor struggled to find housing, credit, and employment, and where municipal offices administered the human consequences of those reallocations from dwindling social service budgets.

Anthropologists working in U.S. cities approached these conditions as outtakes of globalization—migration, restructuring of the economy and labor, and other forms of unsettling. Read as exposés of globalization's hidden costs, these monographs refuse the new canons of visibility that were redefining the urban landscape at the time (analyzed in depth by Harvey 1989 and Sassen 1991) —turning their backs on the new skyscrapers associated with the global financial industry and corporate headquarters, and exploring instead the side streets and urban margins, where ordinary people—including the ordinarily poor—struggle to make ends meet.

In the 1990s, as globalization yielded unprecedented personal capital for those fortunate enough to touch it, the American Dream also yielded new forms of disappointment and resentment—arising from maldistribution in a time of plenty, rising immigration in a context of tightening borders, new involvements of the private sector in public services and democracy deficit (see Aman 2004; Gregory 1997). In cities—especially New York—radical contrasts of fate and fortune were (are) to be found in adjacent blocks. Anthropologists' community studies take such contrasts as their backdrop, a curtain to be opened onto neighborhood stages where the ethical and pragmatic dilemmas of global capitalism play daily as intimate dramas.

These accounts revive a place for the nation—if only as a position from which to address the reading public and conjure the relevance of ethnographic inquiry in democratic terms. The idea of the nation in this sense—collective social needs understood as warrants for federal power—was not new; it was the legacy of Franklin Roosevelt's New Deal. But the New Deal notion of the nation as a public proved to be short-lived in the United States. The tension between democracy and state power was debated in the abstract as a contest between liberty and equality—and concretely as the antithetical positions of free market and rights advocates. Left-leaning liberals and progressives debated the efficacy of rights amidst broader fields of disadvantage and vulnerability. Conservatives and centrist liberals advocated for social justice without the compelling force of the federal government.

Theodore Lowi maintains that it was the Kennedy era that yielded a fully national state through its innovative use of federal power to enforce civil rights. Evoking the Kennedy years, Lowi writes that "the federal government . . . discovered that there was national as well as state police power . . . involv[ing] the federal government in direct and coercive use of power over citizens. Washington policy-makers could no longer hide from themselves the fact that policy and police had common roots" (Lowi 1979: 273). Under John F. Kennedy and even more so under Johnson, the federal government became national government, involved as a "presence in all areas of social and economic endeavor" through new powers of regulation and redistribution (Lowi 1979: 277). The "federal presence" involved controversial interventions in state and municipal jurisdictions aimed at the enforcement of new laws intended to curtail race discrimination, poverty, and other forms of inequality. The federal presence also involved unprecedented call-ups of the National Guard, FBI, and army surveillance of civilians, and conspiracy trials in response to urban violence, radicalism, and street crime.

The federal commitment to civil rights not only altered the public's consciousness of the nation but also, concretely, the scope of federal powers. The paradoxical twinning of civil rights and the legitimation of federal police powers (in the form of mobilizations of the National Guard) suggests the necessity of complicating the popular narrative of liberalism's rise and global transcendance, or indeed of neoliberalism as the immediate successor to liberalism. For Lowi and others, the period of the 1960s was already "the end of liberalism."[2] Liberalism, indeed, had failed to achieve equal rights for citizens. Throughout its heyday and "most of American history," political scientist Rogers Smith writes, "lawmakers pervasively and unapologetically structured U.S. citizenship in terms of illiberal and undemocratic racial, ethnic, and gender hierarchies, for reasons rooted in basic, enduring imperatives of political life" (Smith 1997: 1). Race and gender, so deeply embedded in the discourse of federal power, became conceptual icons of federal jurisdiction in local affairs. In this new context, identity and diversity were coded as potent political keywords, transcending the singularity of a group's experience as instances, instead, of minority status in relation to the nation.

The new terms were widely taken up as rubrics of representation in the human sciences. It is perhaps difficult now to reconstruct that moment in the early 1980s when the term *identity* was new in the public and professional gathering spaces where such issues were discussed (the periodization is from Rouse 1995). It is also difficult, now, to reconstruct the depth of need for a rubric of alliance against the strong backlash unleashed by the civil rights landmark legislation and its implementation. It is difficult in part because the challenge came in terms that are now everyday parlance—the language of costs, profitability, and value for the taxpaying public. That social security was ever the dominant idiom may strain belief for anyone too young to remember those days.

Even as it waned from public prominence, a vision of democracy articulated and implemented through the federal government by a willing national public remained crucial to the very notion of society in the United States. That vision was central to the ethnography of the United States in the 1990s. The ethnography of that period preserves the record of the condition of American cities as viewed from the neighborhoods where urban working poor—most often, in these accounts, ethnic or racial minorities—struggled

to retain any sort of foothold within globalization. By virtue of its close attention to the situations of minority urban poor, the work is also a critical record
of the political moment when the liberal politics of the civil rights era gave
way to other visions of state power and the public. In this sense, the work
exposes the integument of neoliberalism in negating the value of communities, as the monographs detail the vitality and vulnerability of poor ethnic
neighborhoods facing various forms of disempowerment and abandonment.

The ethnographies based on community studies in the 1990s are profoundly shaped by political unease—as anthropologists hold onto cultural
inquiry as relevant knowledge for a public that seemed to have diminishing
interest in it, or patience for it. As anthropologists carved out some space
for maneuver between the competing claims of partisanship and scientific
neutrality, the problems they faced were compounded as their ethnographic
agendas crossed those of community organizations, identitarian social movements, and activist struggles.[3] The era when anthropologists undertook to
explain "natives" to others was over, yet the persistent public associations of
culture with pathology, and cultural diversity with racial and ethnic conflict,
presented ethnographers with an ongoing challenge from which they could
not easily or entirely withdraw.

Identity and the New Liberalism

Among the questions that dominated their debates was whether a multicultural society could sustain the conditions of liberal democracy. In the 1960s,
"liberalism" had meant an activist federal government responding to popular
demands for equality (Gordon 1982: 284–285). Conservatives and neoliberals appropriated the term "liberalism" and used it against old liberals, constructing a Hobson's choice between individual equality through the market
and special group rights created by an activist federal government.

Philosopher Ronald Dworkin maps the terrain succinctly from his neoliberal perspective:

> Liberalism shares the same constitutive principles with many
> other political theories, including conservatism, but is distinguished
> from these by attaching different relative importance to different
> principles. The theory therefore leaves room, on the spectrum it de-
> scribes, for the radical who cares even more for equality and less for
> liberty than the liberal, and therefore stands even further away from

the extreme conservative. The liberal becomes the man in the middle, which explains why liberalism is so often now considered wish-washy, an untenable compromise between two more forthright positions. (Dworkin 1984: 60)[4]

For Richard Posner, too, "liberalism is fuzzy at the edges" (1995: 26–27) but Posner—a legal academic serving as a judge on the seventh federal circuit Court of Appeals—develops his point less as a critique of principles of state power than as a logistical problem of their applicability: "Liberalism is in tension with democracy. . . . Liberalism implies the limited state, but democracy implies majority rule—and majorities are often willing to coerce minorities. Yet . . . by placing government under popular control, democracy reduces the power of the state to infringe liberty; and liberty is a precondition of informed and uncoerced, and hence authentic, democratic choice" (Posner 1995: 25; note omitted). Echoing popular assumptions of the day, Posner associates popular democracy with "inane" excesses of law, presumably arising from the regulation associated with the enforcement of civil rights laws and other aspects of public administration (1995: 26).

Michael Sandel, a political scientist, sees liberalism as incapable of producing the conditions of liberty in a diverse society:

> Our public life is rife with discontent. . . . The main topics of national debate—the proper scope of the welfare state, the extent of rights and entitlements, the proper degree of government regulation—take their shape from the arguments of an earlier day. These are not unimportant topics; but they do not reach the two concerns that lie at the heart of democracy's discontent. One is the fear that, individually and collectively, we are losing control of the forces that govern our lives. The other is the sense that, from family to neighborhood to nation, the moral fabric of community is unraveling around us. (Sandel 1995: 3)

For Sandel, liberalism is about individual rights: "Since people disagree about the best way to live, government should not affirm in law any particular vision of the good life. Instead, it should provide a framework of rights that respects persons as free and independent selves, capable of choosing their own values and ends" (Sandel 1995: 4). But liberalism, he says, "is a recent arrival, a development of the last forty or fifty years" (1995: 5). It cannot by itself bring about the conditions of liberty since liberty depends on "something more" than "sharing in self-government" (1995: 5). He defines the principles and preconditions of republicanism:

> To deliberate well about the common good requires more than the capacity to choose one's ends and to respect others' rights to do the same. It requires a knowledge of public affairs and also a sense of belonging, a concern for the whole, a moral bond with the community whose fate is at stake. To share in self-rule therefore requires that citizens possess, or come to acquire, certain qualities of character, or civic virtues. But this means that republican politics cannot be neutral toward the values and ends its citizens espouse. The republican conception of freedom, unlike the liberal conception, requires a formative politics, a politics that cultivates in citizens the qualities of character self-government requires. (Sandel 1995: 5–6)

There was no obvious place for anthropologists to enter a conversation framed by these positions. From the standpoint of ordinary usage of the term "liberal," any of the statements just quoted would seem to be an example of Orwellian "double think" since for liberals in the vernacular sense of the term, the claim for equality was not about negative rights (i.e., freedom from government imposition) but positive entitlements to opportunities and services. Posner's separation of liberalism and democracy goes farther than Dworkin's, implicitly faulting liberals for putting democracy at risk. Sandel goes the farthest, all but specifying new claimants and new immigrants as a danger to the American social fabric.

For the most part, anthropologists did not participate directly in the public debates over the cultural future of the U.S. democracy—at least not as media commentators, political consultants, or expert witnesses before Congress. In his scathing attack on the state of university education in the 1980s, Allan Bloom made a wry virtue of anthropologists' alienation from the prevailing discourse:

> Anthropologists have tended to be very open to many aspects of Continental reflection, from culture on down, to which economists were completely closed . . . ; they have tended to the Left . . . and to be susceptible to infatuations with experiments tending to correct or replace liberal democracy. Economists teach that the market is the fundamental social phenomenon, and its culmination is money. An-

thropologists teach that culture is the fundamental social phenom-
enon, and its culmination is the sacred. . . . The disciplines simply
inhabit different worlds. . . . The anthropologists have no . . . influence
beyond the academic world but have the charms of depth and comprehensiveness, as well as the possession of the latest ideas. (Bloom
1987: 362–363)

That said, it is all the more striking that anthropologists continued to press
their case in terms that (to borrow from Bloom) implied that the "culmination" of their work would be legal change at the federal level. By the 1990s,
the obstacles to civil rights legislation involved questions of protection for
business profits, and the political struggle had moved primarily to the private
sector—to issues of credit and housing, for example. The surge of ethnography in the 1990s followed the pathways of that expansion of the private sector
in the aftermath of the Reagan-Bush years, but—with a few notable exceptions (some of them discussed in Chapter 8)—making all the more apparent
the paradoxical nature of their localism.

What was the liberal democracy implicit in anthropology's U.S. projects?
Anthropologists' main concerns were not with democracy or governance
on location, so to speak, but with ethnography as a resource for challenging
the emergent neoliberal discourse in its associations of cultural diversity as a
threat to deliberative democracy. Anthropologists' allusions to federal legality
verge on an invocation of "the sacred"—in a sense well captured by novelist Darryl Pinckney's fictional narrator's past-tense reference to the Supreme
Court as "Lourdes" (Pinckney 1992: 309). Historian Alan Brinkley commem-
orates slain activist Allard Lowenstein's idealism in terms that also evoke the
positionality of much 1990s U.S. ethnography:

> He believed in the possibility, and necessity, of fighting for social
> justice while defending the nation's basic institutions. And he insisted,
> too, that there was a liberal ideal of freedom and equality to which
> everyone could and should aspire; that the claim of American democ-
> racy to transcend the particularism of racial, ethnic, and social groups
> was not rhetoric but, potentially, a reality. . . . It is hard to imagine
> him flourishing amid the fragmented cultural politics of the 1980s
> and 1990s, in which liberalism self-consciously shed the crusading
> idealism that, to Lowenstein, was its most important and redeeming
> quality. (Brinkley 1998: 246–247)

These elements are vital common threads across the ethnography of the 1990s: the faith in social solidarity, the possibility of achieving social justice through existing political institutions, the compatibility of liberty and equality, and the transcendent power of liberal tolerance, the expressions of faith in federal state institutions (if only to hold them to account), the capacity of democracy to avert tragedy—among other things. Ethnographers rarely expressed these commitments in so many words, but they are implicit in their choice of subject matter and their textual conventions of narrative organization, localization, and figurations of cultural identity.

This was the tenor of the times. In the major (and deeply prescient) U.S. ethnography of the 1970s, *Americans Together*, Hervé Varenne (1979) responded to this catch-22 by showing individualism and community to be corollaries, and demonstrating, too, the limitations of local conceptions and practices of "community" as a basis for collective action.[5] Yet by the late 1980s and 1990s, it was clear that neoliberal critics and conservative allies had constructed an unbridgeable polarity between individuals and communities as rights bearers, once communities were defined as collective victims of discrimination, as defined by race. Sandel's vision of a republican alternative—emblematic of wider cultural commentary in elite public intellectual circles—set the bar even higher by stipulating diversity as a form of social disorder, at least until it could be tamed with common public values.

The contest between liberal individualism and republican community posed an impossible choice for anthropologists interested in the conditions of American democracy at its margins. Tied to both positions by the proximity of Durkheimian notions of society to Deweyan notions of democratic culture, anthropologists were likely to be predisposed to find merit across the board—a promising scenario from which to introduce an ethnographic perspective into the public debate, as a disinterested but relevant resource for multicultural citizenship.

Ethnography Redux

As the public climate grew more conservative in the 1990s—with increasingly strident resistance to identity politics—a new discourse emerged around keywords such as *community* and *culture*, but with new meanings that positioned these terms antithetically to the legitimacy of rights demands. The new conservative discourse gained ground as a centrist mainstream, and culture acquired increasingly polarized meanings as both a name for Americans' putative common orientations and, on the other extreme, for a pathology of dependency iconically associated with African American urban poor.

This doubleness and the intensity of conservatives' attention to discourse in their mobilization efforts in part accounts for the rise of discourse-oriented anthropological studies in the 1980s and 1990s, as well as their tendency to begin *in medias res* as responses to a point of view constructed a priori as mainstream or—to capture the power valence—elite (see, for example, Rouse 1995). Caught between a national political culture that was moving to the right, and a profession that was more or less by comparison relatively left, ethnographers took their cues from the social movements around them (see Gregory 1997), turning to the rhetorical templates of classic 1960s liberal pluralism and sociological positivism to navigate those turbulent crosscurrents.

In the course of its revival in the late 1980s and 1990s, U.S. ethnography never abandoned the assimilationist and nationalist framings of their precursors earlier in the century, but they did rewrite them—as chronicles of exclusion on the basis of race and ethnicity, and as intellectual warrants for a democratic liberal pluralism based on understanding and acceptance (if not active embrace) of cultural diversity. The compression of the signs and symbols of federal power and multicultural nationalism was central to these works. But this also raised a contradiction, in that such accounts of difference had to be cast as apolitical in order to count as serious scientific research— and it was only as scientific research that anthropologists could, for the most part, aspire to make a difference from the midst of always-precarious careers. As we shall see, it is this contradictory aspect of the federal/multiculturalist compression that yields the dominant literary features of the works: their narrative form, their techniques of localization, their figurations of cultural identity, and above all the story lines that constitute their claims to relevance. It is also this aspect that constitutes self-conscious literariness as a democratic discourse, embedded in performances of everyday sensibility rather than technical expertise.

For anthropologists working on the United States, the new global discourse within anthropology was a fertile resource for articulating some of these elements—albeit, for the most part, in a highly coded way. In the case of the United States, anthropologists' debts to postcolonial and subaltern movements is evident primarily in the subtle transformation of the ethnographer to the role of narrator, as well as in specific features of literariness in their narratives. The new U.S. ethnographies drew heavily on first-person testimony and vernacular speech, both as evidence and as vehicles for analysis in the registers of indirect discourse. The influence of postcolonial and sub-altern studies, evident more as discursive osmosis than by direct reference, appears to have been especially useful in relation to the problem of narrating the ethnographer's standpoint in relation to his or her field (i.e., as a physical community), and in constructing the ethnographic present as a transitional moment. Indeed, all over the world, spokesmanship was reclaimed out of lib-eration movements, and anthropologists "were supposed to support 'indig-enous' peoples in their struggles, to help the latter achieve the modernization that the legacy of colonialism—a perfidious combination of an ideology of modernization and a strategy of exploitation—denied them" (Pels 1997: 164). Anthropologists, though working "at home," consistently resisted privileging their "at home-ness"—emphasizing instead the social distances that trump the physical geography of near and far, even when they are writing about their own city (for example, Philippe Bourgois and Karen McCarthy Brown, discussed later).

The primary form of social distance at the core of the U.S.-based works is a racial, ethnic, or class divide self-consciously crossed by the ethnographer, discovery formulated as the transit from visibility to familiarity to fellow-ship. Except for ethnographic works specifically devoted to U.S. law or reli-gion, virtually all the ethnographies of the 1990s were about ethnic or racial difference—a trend that hints at the way race and ethnicity encode significant scalar jumps even when they involve highly localized accounts. By definition, difference cast in these terms can never be local or small scale, but always points across borders to national and—for anthropologists in ways distinctive to their discipline—transnational spaces. As we shall see in more detail later, in this regard, the substitutability of ethnicity and gender for race hints at the enduring traces of anthropology's race concept (as entailing pre-national origins and transnational significance) that continued to govern the textual functions of identity long after race was dismantled in theoretical terms. This long shadow of meaning was cast in part by the salience of race, nationality, and gender in contemporary debates over rights and federal powers.

In some ways, crossing the color line (to borrow from W. E. B. Du Bois here) is the point of the works, as authors invite readers to identify with them as they model an anthropologically informed imaginative openness to neigh-bors whose differences mark them as literally or figuratively alien. *Difference*, in the process, is restored to its relational meaning rather than an attribute of individual identities. But the lines of difference also have other functions in the works: doubling back as a comment on the value of anthropology in contemporary society, and even more so, as a critical comment on contemporary society itself—construed in these works as the federal government and its figuration as American public. By virtue of crossing the line, then, anthropologists may fulfill the traditional expectations of making the strange familiar, as well as the more contemporary demands arising from the critical and reflexive discourses swirling within anthropology and the human sciences at this time. Crossing the line of difference, then, functions as a warrant of *relevance*—in the process soldering localized content to national and transnational frames.

Indeed, it is through the works' literariness and their claims to relevance that professional practice remains fused to "state-craft" (Pels 1997: 165). By defining "relevance" in terms of democratization and public policy at the federal level, however indirectly, anthropologists commit themselves to a particular optic—that is, a perspective at once that of an outsider and an advocate. The tensions between these authorial positions suffuse the works' narrative organization and content—narrative functioning as evidence of both the constitution of moral communities through culture, and liberal affirmation of the inherent value of self-expression. Those are themes for subsequent chapters. For now, suffice it to say that in the United States no less than elsewhere it can be said that anthropology "precariously straddle[s] a world of paradox and contradiction in which notions of race [are] universalistically shunned at the same time that they particularistically [help] constitute the nation-state's civilities" (Pels 1997: 165).

At the same time that *relevance* is an opening for anthropology, it is also a constraint—since the mainstream public discourse of relevance is narrowly construed around the federal mandate for assuring social security. In the decade of the 1990s, that mandate was under considerable pressure, and the language of social policy was increasingly dominated by terms of accountancy—literally, costs in relation to value added. Anthropology brings a lush intellectual tradition to social problems, but at this time its traditional solution—the conversion of difference to a social asset—lay outside the gathering currents of the neoliberal mainstream. For this reason, the search for solutions may import into anthropology an alienated conceptual vocabulary that I refer to as a *discourse of solutions*.

Within anthropologists' texts, evidence of the pressure to define "solutions" through ethnography for the most part registers as discursive pressure—the fulfillment of the requirements of narrative form—rather than an undertaking as such. The named solution is *understanding*; the rest is left to the reader. Thus the pressures of relevance fully expose anthropologists to the contradiction between universalist constructions of rights and their increasingly stringent costing out in the American scene at that time. In the 1990s, rights had become expensive—for example, retrofitting businesses and public facilities to improve accessibility, or exposing business to liability on grounds of discrimination. The costing out of rights, and the compression of the political spectrum around neoliberal reform, meant that anthropologists' efforts to appeal to the public confronted multiple ironies.

Ethnographers as Uneasy Liberals

The ethnography of the United States is essentially a liberal discourse, but it is also a critical discourse—revealing both the discursive limits of liberalism and liberalism's untapped potential under conditions of emergent neoliberalism in the 1990s. Anthropologists framed this ambivalence not in terms of policy debates but rather as a question of stakes—a question of democracy's future, tested by difference. They demonstrate (in the aggregate) pervasive political dislocation for ethnic and racial minorities, even for those who participate fully in the social and economic life of their communities.

The most important tenets anthropologists shared with liberals (whether or not *as* liberals) were a positive understanding of the diversity of American society, a contextual approach to social problems such as joblessness and social dislocation, and a tacit faith in the transformative effects of social knowledge—as well as the infinite capacity of citizenship to accommodate difference. The value of social description, in other words, is based on the premise that it actively contributes to the production of democracy by providing a willing public with the basis to take each other into account as they articulate their own preferences in the public sphere. As social science, the monographs were about local situations, but as literary works, they were—are—animated by a "poetics of relation" (Glissant 1997).

At the same time, it is worth stressing that ethnographers' participation in this liberal vision reached its peak (judging from the volume of publication) twenty to thirty years after the civil rights movement and Great Society. Earlier works were few but deeply influential as models of U.S. ethnography—most importantly, *Tally's Corner* (Liebow 1967), *Soulside* (Hannerz 1969), and *All Our Kin* (Stack 1974). Those works analyze the causes and consequences of inner-city poverty among African Americans. James Q. Wilson's evocation of liberal social-science scholarship in the 1960s conveys the critical thrust of these works (though without referring to them directly):

> Liberal scholars in the 1960s argued that cultural values do not ultimately determine behavior or success. Rather, cultural values emerge from specific social circumstances and life chances and reflect one's class and racial position. Thus, if underclass blacks have limited aspirations or fail to plan for the future, it is not ultimately the product of different cultural norms by the consequence of restricted opportunities, a bleak future, and feelings of resignation resulting from bitter personal experiences. Accordingly, behavior described as socially pathological and associated with the ghetto underclass should be analyzed not as a cultural aberration but as a symptom of class and racial inequality. (Wilson 1987: 14; notes omitted)

By the 1990s, neither the structural conditions nor the terms of debate had changed, except for hardening.

The classicism of the community-study format highlights the global context of anthropology in a particular way. In their writing (keyed to the nineties even when the research was conducted earlier), anthropologists approached communities for their own sake, but also as condensations of the place of the United States in the world. This telescoping is a hermeneutic maneuver predicated on racial or ethnic identity as its principal sign—identity being explicitly a sign of disparate origins. Issues involving new immigrants were important in their own right in these works, but ethnic identity—with its implication of global mobility—also functioned synecdochically, miniaturizing the world at large. The texts draw heavily on "localizing strategies" (Fardon 1990) and literary conventions of realism to evoke the empirical accessibility of global experience. In this sense, textually, ethnic identity (and as we shall see later, gender) functions as a literary device for jumping scale, while also engaging local specificities. Thus, there is not as much difference as one might imagine between ethnographic accounts grounded in "the local" and those grounded in the emergent discourse of globalism as it played out in policy debates.

Ethnographic work on U.S. cities published in the 1990s mainly involved new immigrant groups living in urban ethnic enclaves. This means that the contexts most directly implicated in the iconography of the public policy debates over civil rights and welfare—African American urban poor—were approached ethnographically only indirectly. As early as 1970, Wilson writes, "it was clear to any sensitive observer that if there was to be research on the ghetto underclass that would not be subjected to ideological criticism, it would be research conducted by minority scholars on the strengths, not the weaknesses, of inner-city families and communities" (Wilson 1987: 15). The force of the elision of race and ethnicity was felt within anthropology at the time as an erasure of race, but even so, the prevalent theoretical status of race at the time was such that—notwithstanding those compelling critiques—any ethnic community could stand in for the general category *race*. As already noted, the concept of race—though unmoored from its biological determinisms—was largely marked as nonwhite, thus retaining its generalizing implications of distant origins, alienation, and adaptation; ethnicity stood in for these literary functions of race in relation to the new community studies.

As ethnographers of the United States turned to the policy debates of the time as the self-evident relevance of their work, they also—crucially—defended ethnography as science. This was largely a defense by demonstration—a performative defense constituted complexly and primarily through the community as foil for the national state. The reliance on terms of policy debate already in general public circulation imported into anthropology's textual practices the textual and rhetorical forms of the civil rights era. Anthropologists drew on formulations of individuality, identity, community, and society that were—and are—specifically keyed to those legal and political struggles. In the 1980s, those struggles were ripe for renewal. The Reagan and Bush administrations were ideologically committed to rolling back federal intervention in the civil rights area, and to setting limits on access to law for potential plaintiffs by narrowing the grounds on which civil rights claims could be litigated. The conservative backlash confronted identity-based social movements with increasing restrictions on access to law, and a widespread disparagement of law as a means of resolving social conflict as well as so-called "identity politics."

No simple summary can do justice to the complexity of that social history; I can do no more than gesture toward the historical background to the double-sided relationship—at the level of signs—between federal power and the everyday realities of communities at the social margins. For anthropologists, the hermeneutics of identity emergent from federal-level identity politics set up a series of synecdoches—worlds within worlds: any singular difference could stand in for all difference, any failed community pointed to national failure. The templates of relevance sustained a textual practice in which the federal was evident in the local, since federal and local amounted to two sides of the same question—that of democracy's present and future. Here again, the difference of scale between localized ethnography and larger-scale studies is only superficial—since it is the embedded attention to national political discourse that does the work of enlarging the scale around even the most personalized ethnographic accounts. The scalar claims are implicit in the literariness of the works, as well as their focus on the particulars of global displacement.

From a literary and rhetorical standpoint, ethnographers' attention to U.S. communities reflected a dual concern with life conditions at ground level, and with the capacity of the federal government to deliver on its promises of equality to the previous generation. In the next chapter, we examine key legislative debates, showing how the literariness of public debate on some of these same issues shifted consensus away from strong public-sector investment in reform and social service toward privatization and marketization substitutes for "big government." As the ethnographic space widened between the older liberalism and the new political mainstream, the monographs acquired a patterned quality (discussed at length in Chapter 4). The very structure of U.S. ethnographies reflects the tensions within the polity at large, as well as the literary movements that have been among their primary modes of articulation. To the extent that such textual strategies ran ahead (or askew) of current prospects, ethnographers also drew heavily on the textual strategies and poetics of voices for reform from arenas outside the state. As we shall see, those evocations from other genres predominate at the monographs' margins—prologues and epilogues—where an author has more license for creativity and personalized statements of purpose.

No Place Like Home

Against the backdrop of anthropology's new breadth and theoretical sophistication in the 1990s, the community studies of U.S. ethnic neighborhoods might have seemed to be an eddy of methodological traditionalism. Moffatt is dismissive on this score: "Despite the great interest in textual experimentalism in anthropology in the last decade, most of these domestic monographs are conventionally written. Ethnography and relation-to-subjects is confined to the beginning or end of a book; the bulk of the text consists of impersonally written, monologic descriptions variously mixed with various theories, interpretations, or styles of analysis" (Moffatt 1992: 212; notes omitted). The critical interest of these works was hidden in plain sight. In the rest of this book, we explore the ways genre worked critically in relation to the key terms through which the new political mainstream made identity central to market-based social reform.

As public debates over civil rights and welfare entitlements made clear, the U.S. political spectrum enfolded toward a new center in the 1990s—a market-based centrism that, for the most part, no longer had its former narrow partisan associations with the Reaganite wing of the Republican Party. The mainstreaming of neoliberalism is echoed, in varied ways, by the monographs—particularly in their renderings of identitarian communities against the foil of their mis- or underrecognition by the public at large. The public is represented by readers whom authors, for the most part, address directly—but it is not constituted by them alone. The reading public becomes a discursive stand-in for a *national* public—and, metonymically, the federal government. This metonym is a critical assertion in itself, regarding the contemporary state of democracy in the United States.

The codings that would situate these monographs in relation to the trends of the times are to be found in their literariness: their form and narrative organization, their deployments of voice, their sense of problem, their ironies and occlusions—and their participation (at the level of signs) in a federal subjectivity that positions anthropological knowledge as a knowledge relation among citizens, their mutuality signified by—and, pragmatically, through—the federal government. The legibility of this chain of signs is predicated on the significance of identity and difference in relation to specific federal powers. Sustaining that legibility for readers across the text carries the pen past the page containing information, reminding them of what they know from the registers of their own experience—imaginative and otherwise—with state power. It calls on the literary techniques of storytelling, and the powers of fiction (Aretxaga 2003: 401). Walter Benjamin writes: "It is not the object of the story to convey a happening per se, which is the purpose of information; rather, it embeds it in the life of the storyteller in order to pass it on *as experience* to those listening" (Benjamin 1968: 159; emphasis added). With direct political engagement barred (as antithetical to scientific neutrality) for the mainstream profession, relevance called for art.

This was the context in which anthropologists—drawing on their methodological traditions—returned to the "community." But the function of location in these works extends far beyond the actuality of place or the specifics of context. By the close of the decade, roughly half of the monographs about the

United States involved one of New York's boroughs. But read through these templates, New York City is not just a location for ethnographic study, important in itself as an urban environment with distinctive qualities. Rather, the city emerges as a localization of broader concerns regarding the United States and globalization. New York is almost always (and only) presented as a global city—a synecdoche for the global conditions wrought by neoliberalism, and hinting at other globalisms and alternative futures.[6] The neighborhood also has literary functions—establishing the groundwork, so to speak, for a claim to realism in the text, and containing the imperative for description within workable limits.

A quest for solutions tends to align text and context discursively such that the neighborhood is explicitly metonymic of social problems on a national, and even global, scale (for example, Liebow 1967 and Bourgois 1995, discussed in Chapter 5). This is a distinctive feature of these works; it is neither obvious nor automatic that ethnography should be written or read in this way. Even where policy questions are not so near to page, anthropology's concept of culture does its own work of rewriting local situations as but instances of wider currents of time, place, and meaning. Moffatt writes that no U.S. anthropologists (in 1992) are theorizing "cultural hegemony as a . . . productive way of restating . . . old debates about *an* American culture versus 'pluralism' or 'multiculturalism'" (Moffatt 1992: 214). It is safer to say that this was, in fact, the *only* subject of these works—even excessively so, overspilling the limits of ethnography's conventions of genre, recoded and packed into the books' formal features.

The localizations of U.S. ethnography sometimes double as legalisms, derived from the legal conventions of jurisdiction or other aspects of law. Towns and city wards, for example, are legal entities, not just social locations. But such legalisms are not limited to questions of place; they are even more pronounced when the community in question is delimited by the effects of past or present legal action. For example, "Japanese Americans"—widely dispersed physically—are constituted *textually* by Takezawa (1995) in relation to the reparations movement consequent to Japanese and American citizens' internment during World War II. Latino and Asian communities are *textually* configured around their immigration status (e.g., Freeman 1989; Welaratna 1993; Margolis 1994; Leonard 1992; Chen 1992; Mahler 1995). In modern anthropology, African Americans come to the page as agents of rights struggle—over civil rights (Wagner-Pacifici 1995) and property rights (Gregory 1998 and Williams 1988). The poor are shown to be effective agents of their own interests within constraints that impede the paths out of poverty (Morgen 2001; Morgen and Maskovsky 2003). In some cases, it is the legalities themselves—including abuses of legal power—that figure importantly in the constitution of the cultural subject (e.g., Coutin 1996, 2000; Chavez 1991; Heyman 1999). Ethnographic studies of law use and attitudes toward law in the United States in this period emphasize communities' orientations toward legal institutions as expressive of the meaning of community itself (Greenhouse 1986; Greenhouse, Yngvesson, and Engel 1994; Merry 1990; Yngvesson 1993).

Importantly, most of these examples involve *federal* law—Executive Order 9066 and the Reparations Act of 1993, border and immigration controls, and civil rights law. The exceptions involve policing—by definition municipal agencies in the United States—and the public-private partnerships involved in struggles over land use and gentrification. In all of these works, the risks in misrecognition and the stakes in equality of access to law (i.e., in terms of democratic participation and access to legal remedies when grievances arise) are prominent themes. In this respect, American Indians are perhaps iconic of legal misrecognition, providing the ethnography of the United States with a discursive and literary template, even if the anthropological literature on native American cultures is conventionally excluded from accountings of the ethnography of the United States (Cattelino 2010b). The exclusion of American Indians from the ethnography of the United States both reveals and conceals their critical connections though coloniality, sovereignty, and federal power.

State institutions outside of law making—most prominently schools— also become, in anthropologists' texts, multicultural locations structured by the politics of federal law at the time—as microcosms of the *nation's* diversity and metaphors of its multicultural prospects. Peshkin's (1991) ethnographic study of one California suburban high school's efforts at multiculturalism is presented in this way. His metaphorical reference to strangers and friends in the book's title refers loosely to "descent and consent" (Sollors 1986: 6, 259ff.)—the relevance of ethnicity in the reproduction of families and political power (especially state power): "A friend is someone who may be considered—without necessarily being—a suitable mate for one's child or a suitable candidate for political office; a stranger is someone who is not" (1991: x). As an ethnographer of education, Peshkin is drawn to Riverview High School (RHS, a pseudonym) by the fact that the school's administration, like the Riverview community, is committed to multiculturalism. Like the community, the school has no clear ethnic majority: "I was interested in learning about educational ethnicization, that is, how far the school had gone, if at all, in making decisions based on ethnicity" (9). Anticipating his conclusion in the prologue, he deems Riverview "a bright spot" in the national picture (x).[7]

All in all, the connection of ethnographic practice to federal law is everywhere, but for the most part everywhere silent—taken for granted in the relevance accorded *cultural identity*, the efficacy of the works' literariness, and their thematic focus on issues of values, aspiration, and constraint at the cultural margins of U.S. globalism.

CHAPTER 3

Texts and Contexts

The public policy issues that dominated the Congress in the 1990s were shaped on the one hand by the rhetorical appeal of the New Deal and the Great Society, and on the other by the political appeal of neo-liberalism. The new keywords were *efficiency* and *competitiveness*, as market values suffused debate over government programs and accordingly—in material ways—the meaning of citizenship. The old New Deal liberalism and the new (neo)liberalism were farthest apart over the question of the relationship between social security and equality, and the connection between them as means and ends. When these were set up as trade-offs against profitability in the new environment of global economic competition, neoliberalism prevailed. In the 1990s, neoliberalism became mainstream, both cause and effect of public policy debates over civil rights, welfare and immigration in the first half of the decade.

A full account of those legislative initiatives that would extend far beyond the chambers that produced the texts considered here—mainly transcripts from Congressional hearings and floor debate over what became the Americans with Disabilities Act of 1990 (ADA), the Civil Rights Acts (CRA) of 1990 and 1991, the Personal Responsibility and Work Reconciliation Act of 1996 ("Welfare Reform Act") and the Illegal Immigration Reform and Immigrant Responsibility Act of 1996 (IIRAIRA). IIRAIRA was in some ways the twin of the welfare-reform bill, not only in their common keyword—responsibility—but also in their discursive reliance on a calculus of taxpayer burdens. Both bills targeted immigrants as drawing excessively from public coffers, and the calculation of savings to the federal government in terminating welfare entitlements included estimates based on new exclusions of unregistered immigrants and their children from federally funded social services (Stepick 2006: 395). In a sense, one can look to the immigration bill to see what neoliberalism looks like without citizenship—at least to the U.S. Congress at that time.

The transcripts of the hearings and floor debate show the nature of the rhetorical contests and controls that successively reinforced the discursive impasse between rights-based and market-based liberalisms. The makings of that impasse were not in some inherent antithesis between rights and market freedom, but in the concerted construction of discursive opposition (as if they were polarities) along lines of political antagonism extending well beyond Congress and the federal government. Discursive opposition is everywhere (in any context) a principal register of political control, as the alignment of language and authority open, limit, or altogether foreclose the range of anyone's freedom of action. To be sure, other registers include direct action such as violence and other forms of coercion and exclusion; however, even these in their most extreme forms are not separate from the forces of social judgment and denial that find expression in words.

For our purposes, the rhetorical impasse over rights and entitlements is relevant in precisely that sense—as the legislative process (among its wide-ranging functions and effects) linked highly material stakes to particular keywords. That horizon was where terms such as *equality* and *opportunity*, keywords in the civil rights and welfare rights movements, were retuned to their denial—and so to highly public stakes for African Americans, the poor, and other historically disadvantaged groups. That discursive retuning—the repeal of meaning, so to speak—became the horizon for the new ethnographic engagements with the United States that are the subject of this book.

The rhetorical challenge for politicians and witnesses before the committees was to sustain the values of the New Deal and Great Society programs while curtailing or terminating the government's role in relation to discrimination claims and welfare. That challenge was not met all at once. Initially, debate focused on the nature and limits of federal responsibility for law enforcement, as in the context of the Americans with Disabilities Act (ADA): is there a limit, critics asked, to the expense businesses should undertake to accommodate people with disabilities? In the context of the subsequent debate over race and gender discrimination in employment, though, the key terms had shifted to individual responsibility. In response to the Civil Rights Act of 1990, critics asked: is there still a need to support individuals in their efforts to enter into the marketplace for opportunity? With the veto of the act, and its replacement by the Civil Rights Act of 1991, the answer to that question was officially no. The theme of individual responsibility became the dominant motif of the debate over the Welfare Reform Act of 1996. Under that same banner in the same year, immigration reform tightened borders and sharpened administrative controls.

In the space of just a few years, Congressional action reworked the discourse of the old liberalism, fusing rights to costs, uncoupling race and class within a federal discourse of relief, and terminating entitlements by reworking the distinction between individual and collective cultures as a moral distinction between responsibility and pathology. This point is not merely about the chronology of the hermeneutics of political persuasion or the situation of powerful institutions in a broad mediascape (Appadurai 1990) linking government and consumers. Through the Congressional testimony and debate over these measures, specific constructions of personhood, partnership, and citizenship became hegemonic, and written into law and administrative practice. As they worked their effects on actual communities, they also reworked discourse—in the process selectively taking up and valorizing particular images and story lines associated with chronic poverty in the United States (especially negative stereotypes about African American and Latino men). Indeed, one could begin such an analysis anywhere—in novels, monographs, the hearing room, or in any number of other locations, including the street. This implication is one of state hegemony—its echo chambers reverberate with discourse pirated from scenes of private life (see Greenhouse 2005). I begin with the hearing room, then, not because discourse flows "down" from the government, but because it acquires high visibility there. It bears emphasizing that the literariness of social description is everywhere, not just in books conceived as art.

Civil Rights and the Costs of Equality

In 1989, a liberal Congress was pitched for a partisan contest with the conservative administration. Partisan divisions within Congress ran deep. The last years of the Reagan administration had seen the Iran-Contra hearings and the defeat of the Bork nomination in 1987. The controversy over the Bork nomination put the judiciary in a bright spotlight as the object of highly public partisan contention. But the confirmation process was not the only lightning rod for partisan politics within the federal government. Those partisan divisions were also, importantly, divisions among the branches of government, specifically over the expansion or containment of federal powers, as these were indexed to civil rights and welfare entitlements. The contests took the form of debates over costs and profitability for American business in an increasingly transnational (global) economic order. The Civil Rights Act of 1990 was vetoed by President Bush, passing the following year in a different form—as discussed in the next section. But that outcome is relevant here, too, since the long process of committee hearings on the ADA contained auguries of that failure, notwithstanding its easy passage with bipartisan and administration support.[1] The proposed safeguards for people with physical and mental disabilities were already guaranteed in forty-five out of the fifty states, and the bill had numerous cosponsors from both sides of the aisle. But the outcome in a sense belied strong underlying divisions, reflected in the record of the hearings, as to what constitutes civil rights and appropriate remedies in a market-driven environment.

Like the proponents of the Civil Rights Act (CRA) of 1990, passed later that same year, the proponents of the ADA evoked the Civil Rights Act of 1964 as their refrain. The invocations of the earlier law were broadly celebratory—notwithstanding the awkwardness of the constructed parallels between "race" and "disability." Congressman Moakley's statement in committee, as he presented the bill, is an example:

> As you know, Mr. Chairman, the Civil Rights Act of 1964 prohibits employment discrimination on the basis of race, color, religion, sex, or national origin, but provides no protection for disabled workers. Handicapped individuals share a host of deprivations very similar to deprivations directed toward minority groups which are now protected under the CRA. Realizing the parallels between disabled individuals and minority groups, I strongly believe that the best way to combat flagrant discrimination is through a remedy which has proven successful in the past, the Civil Rights Act of 1964. (U.S. House 1987: 3)[2]

Advocates of the ADA presented their support in terms of a range of identifications with specific experiences of disease and disability, with other groups who had historically experienced discrimination (e.g., Jews), and with universal issues such as old age. These opening statements in support of the bill were rhetorically keyed to other minority groups or to women. For example, Senator Tom Harkin (D-Iowa) said, "Today under our Nation's civil rights laws, an employer can no longer say to a prospective employee, 'I will not hire you because of the color of your skin, or because you are a woman, or because you are Jewish"" (U.S. Congress 1988b: 8). In some cases, these associations involved intertextual allusions to the slogans of other social movements, for example, Congressman James Jeffords's (R-Vermont) invocation of "one simple right, the right to control their own lives, to make choices and to choose" (U.S. Congress 1988b: 20). Senator Kennedy drew the widest circle:

> I think, as you listen to those who have spoken today, you realize that there probably has not been a family in the country that has not been touched by some form of physical or mental challenge. . . . I bet if you go across this country, there really is not a member of a family or an extended family that has not been touched.
>
> This legislation will become law. . . . There is a movement and it is alive and it is growing. And it should grow.
>
> This legislation will become law. It will become law not because of the people up here, although all of us want it to become law, but because of you all across this Nation, in the small towns and communities, in the plants and factories all across this Nation, that are really challenging this country to ensure that we are basically going to have an even playing field and we are going to eliminate the barriers that keep people out, so that people can become a real part of the American dream. (U.S. Congress 1988b: 17)

The allusions to the legislative agenda of 1964–65 were highly literal. For example, Sandra Parrino, chairperson of the National Council on the Handicapped, said in her testimony: "Martin Luther King had a dream. We have a vision. Dr. King dreamed of an America 'where a person is judged not by the color of his skin, but by the content of his character.' ADA's vision is of an America where persons are judged by their abilities and not on the basis of their disabilities; 36 million Americans, our Nation's largest and no longer silent minority" (U.S. Congress 1988b: 27). Congressman Tony Coelho (D-California) later set the figure at 43 million, noting, "That is a tremendous political force" (U.S. Congress 1988b: 36).

Reverend Jesse Jackson, president of the National Rainbow Coalition, spoke in favor of the bill, comparing the rights struggle of people with disabilities to that of the students in Tiananmen Square, and closer to home, the protest against the appointment of a hearing person to the presidency at Gallaudet College earlier that year (U.S. House 1989a:31). (The comparison between Gallaudet and Selma was drawn by participants in the protest; see [U.S. Congress 1988b: 4].) Congressman Donald Payne spoke for the bill on behalf of the Congressional Black Caucus—in an eloquent statement equally in support of the Civil Rights Act of 1990, by then emergent ("We must again place America on the right side of history with the passage of this omnibus civil rights statute" [U.S. Congress 1989a: 15]). The many other statements in this vein from Congressmen, Senators, and witnesses drew explicitly on the making of the Civil Rights Act of 1964, invoking the reality of justice, the urgency of inclusion, the practical benefits—political and economic—of extending full employment rights and other rights to people with disabilities. Those had been the arguments in 1964: here, those principles were marshaled for service in both the ADA and the imminent Civil Rights Act of 1990.

Principle and pragmatics were compatible lines of argument only so long as these cost issues were beyond question. Advocates minimized costs, balancing them against overall gains to the economy—as civil rights advocates had in 1964. For example, a sympathetic Congressman Martinez raised the cost issue on the first day of the hearings, in the opening question to Congressman Moakley, referring to "hav[ing] heard on several occasions . . . that the cost would be prohibitive to providing access for these handicapped workers" (U.S. House 1987: 5). Moakley replied: "Well, actually we wouldn't expect an employer to build a certain type of entranceway to hire one employee in his plant. There might be a little cost of moving a desk from here to there or a machine, to give a certain entrance, but, Mr. Chairman, if you look at the overall picture, there would be $1 billion more in the economy"—and he continued, elaborating the consequent reductions in welfare costs (U.S. House 1987: 5). As in the earlier era's contests over the CRA of 1964, the defenders of the ADA argued (in the words of Congressman Moakley): "The contributions of disabled workers would clearly benefit our economy" (U.S. House 1987: 13).

But precedent and principle were repeatedly confronted with costs questions. The repeated appeals to 1964 as the promise of universal rights now threatened to make any implementation of this new law seem uncontrollably expensive. Awkwardly, congressmen and witnesses sought to insert some distinctions within their earlier all-inclusive circles of potential beneficiaries. Congressman John LaFalce (D-New York), chair of the House Committee on Small Business, put it this way: "But there is a difference, is there not, in the type of discrimination? . . . If you are discriminating against a woman or if you are discriminating against a minority, it is usually not going to involve the issue of expense on your part, is it? For some reason or another, you just do not want to deal with women or do not want to deal with minorities. . . . You are talking about the will, and you are talking about the mind really discriminating" (U.S. House 1989b: 29). Kenneth Lewis, representing the National Federation of Independent Business, sought to introduce some distinctions: "When I was attempting to study this bill, I was informed there are over 900 different disabilities the bill addresses. We need to have a definite understanding of what type of disabilities that we need expect provisions made for readily available accommodations" (U.S. House 1989b: 42). Another witness, Les Frieden, professor of rehabilitation at Baylor College, responded immediately: "Please forgive me as I do not intend to offend anyone, but there are over 900 shades of black and brown, and the law says you cannot discriminate on the basis of color" (U.S. House 1989b: 42). To this, Congressman Jim Olin (D-Virginia) interjected:

> I do not know. There are innumerable numbers of different types of disabilities. It would be endless, obviously. They are the same variety as we have people. But nevertheless there are some big categories that you are certainly going to want to be sure are covered such as putting a seat behind a post for a disabled person. Certainly you would not want that done. If that can be defined a little bit better or some kind of limits put on this, I think that you would find the business community much more amenable to trying it out for awhile and see how it works. (U.S. House 1989b: 42)

Indeed, the expansion of the democratic appeal to identify people with disabilities as "everyone" raised (for some) the specter of endless litigation against businesses. Olin continued: "You do not want to end up in court all of the time. You do not want a great controversy. You want people to work out reasonable solutions" (U.S. House 1989b: 42). Joseph Dragonette, representing the U.S. Chamber of Commerce, encouraged this line of conversation, drawing a line between productive discussion of pragmatics and lofty talk of rights: "When you start using words like practical, that makes sense. It makes sense to me a lot more than words like undue burden or readily achievable. . . . Now let's specify those things that we can in the bill to make it understandable and workable for business. I mean this is not an opposing kind of thing" (U.S. House 1989b: 42–43). But the problem of fusing promise to practice—that is, of fusing democratic inclusiveness to costs—produced some awkward syntax. While improvised speech, especially under stress, is likely to produce infelicities, my interest in these crumbling sentence structures is in the way the fractures isolated significant key terms and/or stopped phrases short of lending full expression to the idea that equality should be limited by cost considerations—as in this passage from David Pinkus, testifying for a small-business interest group:

> You brought up the term *full and equal* and Mr. Frieden talked about the Astrodome. I agree that putting seats behind the posts is not within the spirit of what we are trying to achieve here. But when you say full and equal, this is one of the terms that we feel should be deleted from the bill. Because full and equal to me in relation to the Astrodome would mean that you have to provide all of the seats on the 50-yard line to accommodate wheelchairs. *I mean you can carry some of these terms.*
>
> *Full and equal.* The term full is a pretty broad definition, and it is not really defined. If you leave that up to the courts, some day somebody is going to say that means that every seat in the movie theater needs to accommodate disabled people. I am not sure that is what we are doing, or I am not sure that is what you are looking for either, and we just need to clarify that. (U.S. House 1989b: 43; my emphasis)

As the democracy rhetoric confronted costs considerations, the fulsome invocations of citizenship and equal rights became more condensed. They crumbled to mere key phrases—especially the phrase "full and equal" drawn from the 1964 act and in play again in this context. For Congressman LaFalce, the cross-pressures arising from the universalistic appeal to democratic inclusion entailed in the 1964 law and the various current special interests yielded this lament (tellingly built on the rhetorical opposition of an able body and disabling legislation):

> I want to assure you that every fiber in my body wants to see passage of a bill. But also, I have had such bad experiences with so many other laws. I do not trust anybody these days. I do not trust other Members of Congress or other committees because they come in and they say, oh, yes, we have thought of all these things, and then all of a sudden it is a law and you say, my God, I was relying upon you and you did not think about the most simple, basic elementary things. . . .

Sure enough, once the law is being implemented there are a million and one horror stories. Unfortunately, this has more often been the rule than the exception with legislation. . . . People do not want to be opposed to legislation that will deal with discrimination. (U.S. House 1989b: 55)

Caught between a precedent that was beyond question and a set of challenges on the cost question, LaFalce could only lament the law itself, and lawmaking (of which he was a part). This scissoring was precisely what scored the risks that eventually defeated the Civil Rights Act of 1990. Later, in the context of the civil rights bill, Senator Orrin Hatch (R-Utah) seemed to share this sentiment, ruing the power of the very words *civil rights*:

This bill is well intentioned. I know that. I want to resolve discriminatory wrongs. I want to . . . be progressive in doing what should be done in these civil rights areas. But I think we have got to think this through before we . . . just do it because we put the term civil rights on a bill and everybody rolls over and plays dead around here. Besides, you go on television to debate it, and the one side says, "Well, this is a civil rights bill." Then the reporter turns to me and says, "Well, how come you're against civil rights?" And I have to explain two semesters of civil rights law in seven seconds. It is a little difficult to do. (1990: 144–145)

Meanwhile, the ADA passed. The costs questions were handled with a series of phase-ins, limits on retroactive lawsuits, and adjustments of the requirements to the scale of the business in question.

The broader partisan debate over separation of powers created a context in which democratic universalism could not be answered by the costs question. Instead, it was consumed by it—leaving the speakers' syntax in a shambles, and the efficacy of legislation itself explicitly in doubt. One can literally—and literarily—hear the rights discourse yield to a market discourse in the following exchange between James Turner, acting assistant attorney general in the U.S. Department of Justice Civil Rights Division, and Congressman Olin:

Turner: Certainly, Mr. Chairman, there will be costs associated with this law. There are costs associated with not having this law that

> are at least as expensive. . . . To see wasted human resources is a
> very significant cost for our country.
>
> *Olin:* I'm not arguing that point. Excuse me for interrupting you. I
> am talking about the potential of huge economic consequences
> and the need for putting some kind of a ceiling on that so we
> understand to what extent we are going to expect enterprises,
> public enterprises to respond to situations that they will be
> faced with.
>
> *Turner:* I think that is true. The language that you quoted, the full
> and equal enjoyment of the accommodation or the facility, was
> drawn out of Title II of the Civil Rights Act of 1964. That has
> never—
>
> *Olin:* I think that is a non sequitur all by itself. It is probably
> impossible to achieve that.
>
> *Turner:* It may be.
>
> *Olin:* Even as much as you might try. (U.S. House 1989b: 59–60)

In this passage one can hear the production of a certain silence—here, literally cutting off the testimony of a witness at the critical juncture where he
presumably would have defended "full and equal" as worth the cost. But also
in more fundamental ways—in moments such as these where the discourse
of universal equality confronts the discourse of the market—silence marks
the place where their irreconcilable differences are masked as trade-offs,
that is, problems of management. In the 1960s, equality had been free, in
market terms—even efficient, as dual accommodations were merged for an
integrated citizenry. In the context of the 1990s, though, rights had become
expensive—burdening profitability with social limits that were intolerable to
the expanding (and ultimately bipartisan) Congressional consensus around
neoliberal principles.

Equality as Negation

In 1990, Edward Kennedy, as chair, opened the Senate Committee on Labor
and Human Resources, announcing a project of reclaiming for the Congress
a civil rights agenda that had been led off course (he claimed) by a conservative Supreme Court: "When the Court misinterprets the legislative intent of
Congress, Congress can correct the mistake by enacting a new law. And that
is what we intend to do" (U.S. Senate 1990: 1).[3] But that is ultimately what they

failed to do, ultimately unable to protect the burden-of-proof element of the legislation from attack as a covert program of racial quotas in employment. In the discrimination context, *burden of proof* refers to the assignment of responsibility for demonstrating the merits of either the employer's practices of hiring or promoting, or the merits of the discrimination claim—depending on how the burden of proof is assigned.

The U.S. Supreme Court had recently decided *Wards Cove Packing v. Atonio* in a way that reassigned the burden of proof from employers to candidates. Previously, it was employers who had been responsible for proving that their practices were not discriminatory, by demonstrating that the pool of successful minority employees matched the proportion of minority candidates (unless *business necessity* warranted otherwise). Now, the Court revised this requirement on the grounds that it would create a quota system—shifting the burden of proof to the candidate. In the debate over the Civil Rights Act of 1990, the connection between the assignment of burden of proof and quotas was explicit from the beginning. In his opening statement, Senator Kennedy referred to the effects of *Wards Cove*:

> In *Wards Cove*, the U.S. Supreme Court unwisely and unfairly shifted the burden of proof . . . from employers to employees. By shifting the burden, the U.S. Supreme Court has made it far more difficult and expensive for victims of discrimination to challenge the barriers that they face . . . Chief Justice Burger was right in *Griggs* in 1971, and Congress should restore the *Griggs* rule in 1990. Two decades of experience are clear. The *Griggs* rule does not lead to quotas, and never has. It is a mockery of civil rights and the fundamental principle of equal justice under law for opponents of this legislation to raise the false hue and cry of quotas. (p. 2; paragraph break omitted)[4]

Senator Orrin Hatch, ranking member of the committee, responded. Where Kennedy had referred to restoration of civil rights, Hatch cast the new bill as an "overhaul [of] the American legal system" (p. 4). Where Kennedy spoke of fundamental principles and access to law, Hatch saw "a litigation bonanza for lawyers" (p. 4). Senator Hatch's main objection to the bill was that it would make employers more vulnerable to lawsuits: "The only way to avoid being sued is to house [sic: *hire*] solely by numbers, to use quotas for hiring and promotion. . . . Hiring the most qualified applicant may no longer be an acceptable defense to a charge of discrimination. . . . There ought to be a right to hire the most qualified applicant. . . . [The same sections] conflict with the fundamental principle that one is innocent until proven guilty. . . . We must not legislate by label" (p. 4).

In the ensuing statements by members of the committee and witnesses, advocates and critics alike invoked the civil rights landmarks of the 1960s as a baseline reference. For example, Senator Howard Metzenbaum (D-Ohio) introduced *Brown* this way: "Since 1954, when the U.S. Supreme Court issued its landmark *Brown v. Board* decision, women and minorities have been able to look to the U.S. Supreme Court as a safe haven for the protection of civil rights. I am saddened that, some 35 years later, that safe haven for women and minorities has been closed. . . . We must tell the U.S. Supreme Court in no uncertain terms that turning back the clock on civil rights protection is unacceptable" (pp. 8–9).[5] Senator Strom Thurmond (R–South Carolina)— cosponsor of the administration's bill countering S. 2104—was more general in claiming that "much progress has been made in our Nation to ensure that any individual will not be discriminated against in employment opportunities or adversely affected on the basis of race, color, religion, sex, or national origin, in keeping with the precepts of Federal statutes" (p. 10). For Shirley Hufstedler—former federal appeals court judge and Secretary of Education under President Carter—the 1960s were also the baseline but its horizon was still in view: "We still have a long way to go. . . . Take a look at the plantation economy in *Wards Cove*. It looks very much like the Old South did before the Civil Rights Act became effective" (p. 30).

The rhetorical common ground in the Johnson era legislation cast important segments of the debate as judgments of history itself—as we shall see, a discursive turn that simultaneously offered a language of collective responsibility. Thus the leading witness for the bill was William Coleman, an African American lawyer in private practice, formerly Secretary of Transportation under President Ford. His opening statement looked back to the history of slavery, but in terms that borrowed from the very current lexicons of the ongoing immigration debate as well as the conservatives' emphasis on the role of the private sector:

> Black Americans today seek in our own country precisely what brings thousands of new immigrants to our shores every year, to achieve the dream of being fully integrated into the society.
>
> From the beginning, . . . even when slaves were forbidden to learn to read or to seek jobs of their own choosing, blacks understood that

a good education and decent job were the keys to full participation in our democratic society. Blacks recognized from the beginning that education and employment remain the essential tools by which black Americans can avoid, for themselves and for this great Nation, crime, inadequate housing, insufficient medical care, poor government in the community, high rates of illegitimacy and illiteracy, and all the other evils which shamefully are still visited upon blacks in our country in greater proportion than upon whites.

And I think that is why it is very appropriate that this legislation is before this committee, because part of this is trying to help blacks achieve those conditions that everybody else in this room thinks is part of the American way. (p. 13)

But Glenn Loury, a member of the faculty at Harvard's Kennedy School of Government, turned the question of responsibility and proportionality the other way, to "blacks" who, "despite the long-term upward trend," remain in poverty for reasons that (in his view) exceed the scope and efficacy of civil rights legislation:

In the case of blacks, the relative labor market gains of individuals have not been matched by comparable gains in the resources available to families. This is because the proportion of families headed by a single parent has risen dramatically among blacks during the same period in which individuals' earnings have improved. As well, the percentage of black children residing in households in which only one parent is present has risen sharply. . . . More generally, the emergence of what some have called an "urban underclass" has been noted in many of our cities. Blacks are disproportionately overrepresented in this population, where the problems of drugs, criminal violence, educational failure, homelessness and family instability are manifest. It is my conviction that these problems constitute the most important and intractable aspect of racial inequality in our time. Unfortunately, these problems are unlikely to be mitigated by civil rights legislation, because they do not derive in any direct way from the practice of employment discrimination. (p. 77)

Loury was a witness on these same issues in the hearings on the Welfare Reform Act five years later, when the construction of the "underclass" became relevant again as the framework for that legislation, as we shall see in the next section. In strategically securing the fate of this bill, as well as the welfare bill, the compartmentalization of race into individual and collective referents was crucial.

Loury is highly critical of so-called culture of poverty arguments, and of social legislation that steepens the vulnerability of the poor (see Loury 2001). In the context of the CRA of 1990, however, the committee used Loury's arguments to subdivide the discourse of race—setting apart the "individuals" who were in a position to benefit from labor market gains, and those others, always referenced collectively as "blacks," who could or would not. Ultimately, the compromise bill tacitly accepted this discursive distinction, reconfiguring *race* as the attribute of an individual, to be *erased* by civil rights—as opposed to the underclass that by dint of social and psychological pathologies were outside the law's reach. This discursive shift—crystallized in the CRA bill's critics' position on the burden of proof issue—was ultimately important to the mobilization of bipartisan support for the new welfare law, as the disparate impact of that legislation could by then be presented as race-neutral, targeting *cultural* problems rather than minority individuals or racial communities. Loury himself rejected the culture-of-poverty concept in its modern racialized formulation, lamenting the rightward trend in the politics of welfare (2001: 450, 453).[6]

The crucial legal issue in relation to the CRA was not the meaning of race but the question of the burden of proof. Yet the one was wound around the other in the question of how the fact of discrimination should be established, and by whom. Advocates of the CRA of 1990 read *Griggs* as putting that burden on the employer—just as (from the standpoint of agency) *Brown* and the CRA of 1964 put the burden on school boards and others responsible for public facilities. In the CRA of 1990, advocates sought to restore that assignment of responsibility; indeed, the subtitle of the bill was "to amend the Civil Rights Act of 1964 to restore and strengthen civil rights laws that ban discrimination in employment, and for other purposes."

Critics, on the other hand, saw the bill as a fishing license for plaintiffs and their lawyers—acknowledging the pervasiveness of disparate impact of hiring practices but also denying the relevance of those statistics in relation to *individual* hires. Thus the bill's critics conceded the appropriateness of assigning the "burden of production" (i.e., the legal requirement to produce evidence relating to hiring practices) to employers, but not a corresponding burden of persuasion (i.e., to show that the evidence was not due to discrimination). In arguing that the burden of persuasion should rest with the plaintiff, they raised three related issues: shielding employers from lawsuits, maintaining equal rights (i.e., for those who would be victims of "reverse" discrimination), and preempting the quota system that (they argued) would be the inevitable result of the CRA's language allowing discrimination only when it was consistent with business necessity.

These positions render *equality* differently. Advocates saw equality as a criterion of collective social judgment, and so sought to make employers responsible for making equality integral to their business practices. Critics saw equality as a criterion for judging individual motivation and merit—apart from larger patterned effects—and so sought to shift the burden of proof to individual candidates for hire or promotion. In this they eventually succeeded. Importantly, there was no dispute over federal power as such, as there had been in the earlier generation's civil rights contests. Still, the debate over the CRA of 1990 referenced federal power in notably different ways. The bill's advocates sought to widen direct access to federal power on behalf of potential plaintiffs; its critics sought to limit it. Advocates looked to federal law as a statement of national interest; critics looked to federal law as an instrument of regulation (restricting employers in the management of their businesses). Advocates constructed the law as key to mobilizing collective attitudes around a commitment to equality; critics recontextualized access to law in a context of responsibility and incentive.

In short, the bill's advocates defended it in terms of its anticipated effects of empowering plaintiffs to act on their own behalf. Its critics attacked it as a disincentive for individual responsibility—just as they did later in the welfare reform debate in relation to federal entitlements. In other words, advocates presented federal power as a means to particular collective ends; critics presented it more abstractly as an element in a larger moral and sociological discourse of individual responsibility. In that discourse, the very appeal to federal assistance was tantamount to a disqualification, except under the most blatant circumstances, given their premise that the law was sufficient to allow motivated individuals of appropriate moral caliber to find their own pathways to opportunity. But more fundamentally, the critics' opposition to the bill's construction of burden of proof rested on nonlegal factors, primarily their assumption that employers would seek to avoid liability by establishing racial quotas. This factor was the basis of their claim that the bill was itself discriminatory—as well as the basis of the president's veto (as recorded in the veto message dated October 22, 1990; see Congressional Record 1990).

At stake in the conflicts over burden of proof (or persuasion) was the question of whether a pattern of hires disproportionate to the pool of candidates was evidence of discrimination, and under what circumstances. The critics of the bill did not object to the CRA's requirement that employers provide data to account for disproportions (disparate impact), and advocates of the bill never claimed that disparate impact should be treated the same as intentional discrimination. This position was not always easy for the bill's critics to sustain, given the tendency of production requirements (i.e., the obligation to provide information) to spill over into persuasion requirements (the rationales for the practices that yielded those statistical profiles). For the bill's proponents, the link between the two requirements was precisely what they sought to reinforce, accusing attempts to distinguish them as a misreading or misunderstanding of existing law. On the first day of the hearings, Coleman's colloquy with Senator Hatch—occasionally punctuated by calculated moments of collegial jocularity—concentrated on the question of the impact of *Wards Cove* on *Griggs*. For Coleman, there was no question that *Wards Cove* overturned *Griggs*: "I am making the statement to you and I wish you would ask them, that nobody can read *Wards Cove* without coming to the conclusion that it overruled *Griggs*" (p. 15). Later, they sparred at length over this question, Coleman and Hufstedler ultimately urging Hatch to read the relevant documents again. "Well, I will be interested in reading that," the senator replied, adding, "Well, we will sit down and chat" (p. 66).

When the witness table was turned over to the bill's critics, the exchanges turned once again to the impact of *Wards Cove*. And once again, the colloquy was led by Senator Hatch—in an exchange with Charles Fried, a member of the faculty at Harvard Law School and former solicitor general under President Reagan. Fried disagreed with the day's first panelists in their assessment that *Wards Cove* had produced hundreds of failed complaints that would have succeeded under the *Griggs* standard. For Fried, those outcomes reflected a backlog of cases that a clarification of *Griggs* made ripe for resolution. "*Wards Cove* did not change the law, did not overrule *Griggs*," he said, "it focused it and clarified it where there was confusion before" (p. 86).

At issue in the burden of proof debate were two main themes. One was the standard to which employers would be held in accounting for their hiring practices. Should they be required to show that their hiring practices were essential from a business standpoint or—a looser standard—consistent with business necessity? Fried took the position that the Civil Rights Act of 1990 introduced a new, more stringent standard than *Griggs* and that this standard placed unreasonably heavy burdens on employers:

> *Senator Hatch.* There are other parts [of the bill] that I think are objectionable, but nothing as serious as this particular new standard. And you agree it is a new standard.
>
> *Mr. Fried.* The way I would put it is it doesn't too much matter what you say about how heavy the employer's burden is, just make it a burden which is clear and specific and not just this amorphous endless list, and that it is reasonableness, not "essential," which really that is an enormous innovation and very serious.
>
> *Senator Hatch.* In the law that is a very important word, and that did not exist prior to *Wards Cove*.
>
> *Mr. Fried.* I don't believe so. (pp. 86–87)

This position was later taken up by the witness from the Justice Department (see p. 110), speaking for the administration, and other critics of the bill.

The other main issue was related to the objection critics took to what they regarded as an impossible standard. Here, again, Hatch and Fried developed this point in their public dialogue:

> *Senator Hatch.* Now, you indicated that if this law passes in its present wording, including the definition of business necessity a [*sic*] meaning essential to effective job performance, that employers are just going to have to protect themselves and hire on a proportional or quota basis.
>
> *Mr. Fried.* Well, I believe that common sense would do that, because how are they going to defend themselves? Plaintiffs' lawyers are very aggressive. They come in, they show the numbers are wrong, and they can point to an endless list of practices, and there is no defense.
>
> *Senator Hatch.* But what if they cannot hire by quotas? What if they cannot hire by proportionality?
>
> *Mr. Fried.* Because the people aren't out there?
>
> *Senator Hatch.* That's right . . .
>
> *Mr. Fried.* Well, the thing that troubles me is that by talking about essentiality, you are telling every business, nonprofit

> organization, school, museum, hospital, that the Courts will
> decide what the essential way to run their business is.
> *Senator Hatch.* That's right.
> *Mr. Fried.* . . . That is a very serious intrusion. (p. 87)

At the time of the hearings on disparate impact, the keyword was "essential" but the version of the bill that passed the Congress some eight months later included a somewhat softer standard. The language of section 4(k)(1)(A) defines "proof" this way: "An unlawful employment practice based on disparate impact is established under this section when—a complaining party demonstrates that an employment practice [or group of practices, as in 4(k)(1)(B)] results in a disparate impact on the basis of race, color, religion, sex, or national origin, and the respondent fails to demonstrate that such practice is *required by business necessity*" (emphasis added). Following President Bush's veto, the CRA returned to the Senate for a vote on the veto override; after blistering debate, the override failed to carry by one vote (66 yeas to 34 nays; U.S. Senate n.d.a).

Proponents of the CRA of 1990 returned to redraft the text primarily to meet the administration's objections to its definition of burden of proof, deemed (in their view) to set too high a standard. In his veto message, the president had characterized the very debate on this point as evidence that the bill's standard was illegitimate: "The very fact of this dispute suggests that the bill is not codifying the law developed by the Supreme Court in *Griggs* and subsequent cases." In the CRA of 1991, that passage was revised. Whereas the 1990 bill referred to the effects of hiring practices, and allowing them where they are not *required* by "business necessity," the new bill shifted the standard to an individual's agency in directly *causing* disparate impact: "An unlawful employment practice based on disparate impact is established under this title only if—a complaining party demonstrates that *a respondent uses a particular employment practice* that *causes* a disparate impact . . . and the respondent fails to demonstrate that the challenged practice is job related for the position in question and *consistent* with business necessity" (section 105(a); emphasis added).

The CRA of 1990 also specified employers' responsibilities for the effects of their hiring practices even if a discriminatory practice was not the only one that produced the result in question. Section 5(a)(1) reads: "Except as otherwise provided in this title, an unlawful employment practice is established when the complaining party demonstrates that race, color, religion, sex, or national origin was a motivating factor for any employment practice, even though other factors also motivated such practice." This section was dropped altogether from the CRA of 1991.

The debate over the CRA of 1990 is rich evidence of the extent to which political opposition found expression in rights debates at that time, in a way that advanced neoliberalism and consolidated its bipartisan support. As the administration hardened in its opposition to the bill, its proponents were driven to compromise in a way that set business interests as a trade-off in relation to civil rights remedies.[7] Senator Hatch was explicit in this regard: "I want to do what is right for minorities in this country and women in this country, and, frankly, for everybody. I really want to do what's right for small business in this country, too, and this bill could have a devastating impact with that one standard [of proof] on small as well as large business in this country" (p. 87).

The president, too, seemed to have business in mind in his reference to the prospect of litigation if CRA of 1990 were allowed to stand. In his veto message, he held up the specter of "years—perhaps decades—of uncertainty and expensive litigation," adding: "It is neither fair nor sensible to give the employers of our country a difficult choice between using quotas and seeking a clarification of the law through costly and very risky litigation." Representing the CRA as reverse discrimination allowed the bill's critics to gloss their defense of business interests under the rubric of equal rights—but as the president's language suggests, the implication of a trade-off between rights and business was never far from the surface. The ADA had occasioned debate over the necessary costs associated with civil rights, and the debate over the CRA went farther, focusing not only on costs (in terms of requiring the hire of underqualified personnel, or groundless lawsuits) but presenting business interests as the civil right of the majority—that is, as the true basis of equality.

This is the context in which the rewriting of *race* in relation to rights involved significant discursive shift. In defeating the original formulation of the burden of proof in CRA of 1990, the administration also defeated a vision of history in which the civil rights era had provided sufficient gains for further progress—albeit with vigilance. Thus, the fact that minority individuals could find opportunities for upward mobility trumped the status of the so-called underclass—accordingly rewritten as (literally) an outlaw culture. In the process, race was written onto individuals as a characteristic the public significance of which should disappear. Without the individualization of race, its disappearance could not be proclaimed—or defended as a measure of equality. The color blindness of the critics' position was a double negative—the mark of difference relative to (unmarked) whiteness, the difference valued when it makes no difference. This principle discursively uncoupled race and class and, as well, the individual and culture. The debate over welfare reform deepened and clarified these reformulations.

Ending the National Society

The terms of the Congressional consensus on welfare reform were set with the passage of the Personal Responsibility and Work Reconciliation Act of 1996 (colloquially known as the Welfare Reform Act of 1996).[8] This legislation had been in process for years, through many successive proposed bills, since the end of the George H. W. Bush administration.[9] The bill that finally passed modified the Social Security Act and twenty-two other laws after fifty-eight hearings involving twenty-three committees, subcommittees, select committees, and task forces in both chambers—thirty separate hearings in 1995 alone—as well as extensive floor debate.[10] Its passage was among the first fruits of Congressman Newt Gingrich's "Contract with America," instituted as the Republican Congressional agenda after the devastating Democratic defeat in the mid-term elections of 1994. As the process gathered force and drew more public attention, the hearings themselves became highly public—calling on long lists of witnesses, as many as seventy in one day, speaking for five minutes each, and even longer rosters of submissions to the record. The process put competing visions of state and nation before the public and, as we shall see, the incommensurability of their discursive framings was made amply evident. The transcripts make a rich resource for anyone interested in the crosscurrents of the time. In my own examples below, I draw primarily from the most prominent hearings on welfare reform by the House Ways and Means Committee, since these dealt with appropriations, and were held under the rubric of the "Contract with America"—based on the platform that had swept Republicans into the majority—in January and February 1995 (U.S. House 1996). I also draw on the Senate Finance Committee's wrap-up hearings (U.S. Senate 1995).

The Welfare Reform Act ended a series of programs that had evolved out of the New Deal, including Aid to Families with Dependent Children (AFDC), food stamps, federal job training programs, and other assistance to needy families. It replaced those programs with block grants to the states, where their distribution of funds would be subject to state law under new federal guidelines. Those guidelines restricted eligibility to two years, after which work would be mandatory; parents under the age of eighteen would not be eligible. These were the main features among extensive provisions aimed at reducing federal expenditure and improving what its proponents saw as the flawed incentive structure of the old welfare system.

But the revisions to assistance programs were not the only consequence of the welfare reform legislation of the 1990s. The public debate over welfare put into direct competition two competing theories of poverty. One looked to the behaviors of the poor, especially African American urban poor, identifying the prominence of female-headed households as a major social ill, as well as teen pregnancy and persistent joblessness. The other looked to the status of the United States in relation to the global economy, taking into account the deepening of poverty as a result of the restructuring of the economy, heavier economic pressures, and loss of political support for the poor. One witness, Thomas R. Carper (then governor of Delaware), acknowledged the political difficulty of reconciling these different accounts in strikingly familistic terms: "We started off [in Delaware] with a democratic position on welfare reform and in the end we voted in two options, a democratic plan which was maybe on the love side of the tough love scale, and then we had a Republican plan, which was probably on the tough side of the tough love scale, and we really didn't have an alternative to do anything in between" (U.S. House 1996a: 19).

The Clinton welfare program gave the discursive victory to those who constructed welfare as an element in the larger problem of family life, bracketing U.S. poverty as a pathology rooted in a particular culture, and setting it apart from whatever the globalization was becoming. Those brackets were racial—that is, the welfare pathology was made out to be the problem of the African American community in particular, an association of long habit following the reception of *An American Dilemma* (Myrdal 1995) and the so-called Moynihan Report (U.S. Department of Labor 1965). In adopting this assessment, they made rising rates of poverty the consequence of the Johnson administration's "war on poverty"—a point of contention in the hearings. For example, in his testimony before the House Ways and Means Committee, Robert Rector, then senior policy analyst at the Heritage Foundation, drew a correlation between increased federal spending on welfare and rising rates of poverty:

> What we see on the chart is that starting at the high point in 1950, about a third of the population was poor. The red line charts constant

dollar welfare spending. During the fifties the spending was at the bottom of the chart. You can barely see it. But during the fifties and early sixties, the poverty rates plummeted. . . . Poverty fell from 30 to 15 percent of the population while welfare spending remained at a tiny level. Then something happens. In 1965 the spending takes off and begins to explode. But the poverty rate stops falling. It kinks over and basically remains unchanged for the next 30 years, bumping up and down a little bit. It is higher today than it was in the midsixties when the war on poverty began. (U.S. House 1996a: 64)

Michael Horowitz, then senior fellow at the Hudson Institute, followed Rector on the panel, and drew this connection between the American dream and poverty: "The American dream is not working for those who need it most. Nothing matters more for us as a nation than to recapture our magic for those people. . . . The manifest failure of *welfare programs, which have perversely increased poverty in almost direct proportion to the growth of federal programs waging their Great Society 'war' on it,* imposes a moral obligation on all of us to seek new answers and new approaches" (U.S. House 1996a: 83; emphasis added).

Like others who shared his view, he focused his criticism on the system of entitlements that would guarantee "independent incomes" (a phrase ordinarily associated with the nonworking rich) and "homes of their own" (drawing on the argot of the middle-class American Dream) to "unmarried sixteen year old mothers" and their "lost-at-the-start families" (U.S. House 1996a: 84).

Others tried to correct the correlation, recontextualizing it in the emerging global economy of the time, and attempting to defuse its partisan associations. For example, in dialogue with members of the committee and other panelists, Robert Greenstein, then executive director of the Center on Budget and Policy Priorities, sought to uncouple the causal link others drew between federal spending and poverty:

I think this whole discussion is offbase. I will tell you whether they are liberal or conservative, there are very few economists who would subscribe to this analysis. During the period that poverty is going way down, we had a booming economy. We had rapid rate growth. We had high rates of productivity growth.

The very point on the chart where poverty stops going down,

around 1973, this has been written by economists of all persuasions, is the point at which wage stagnation sets in and productivity growth in this country stops growing forward at a substantial rate. . . .

You go to Wall Street and ask people if they think the Food Stamp Program or the AFDC Program rather than trends in the international economy and others are the reasons for the 20-year slowdown in the rate of productivity growth in the U.S. economy. People will look at you like you are a little bit offbase. These are fundamental issues that relate to the larger economy. (U.S. House 1996a: 128)

Moments later, he attempted—unsuccessfully, it seems—to recontextualize the association between welfare and illegitimacy when a member of the committee, John Ensign (R-Nevada), called on Greenstein again, testing him—and interrupting him to insist on his personal *opinion* when he opened his response as a summary of available research:

Ensign: Do you think that the illegitimacy rate in this country has gone up in any small part due to the welfare state?
Greenstein: This is a matter on which there is a great deal of research and the—
Ensign: What is your opinion on that?
Greenstein: My opinion is that the bulk of the research is . . . that there may be an effect from welfare here, but if there is, it is relatively modest. We find illegitimacy rates rising as rapidly among women with more education, people in other countries with different social welfare systems. In particular, I would note that if AFDC were the driving factor, then we would have expected as AFDC benefit eroded, as they have in the last 10 or 20 years, then rates of out-of-wedlock births would have slowed or gone down and they didn't. (U.S. House 1996a: 129)

Indeed, at several critical junctures, committee members and witnesses negotiated (sometimes sparring) over the question of whether and how the "technical literature" or "studies" supported particular claims as to causal links between welfare and certain behavioral demographics. The hearings frequently revolved around talk of, and displays of, numbers—levels, rates, comparisons, correlations. Proponents of the bill often relied on simple correlations (as in the example cited above), anecdotal evidence, or so-called common knowledge. For example, asked by Dave Camp (R-Michigan, ranking member on the House Subcommittee on Human Resources) if he could "tell me why the rate of illegitimate births rose sharply in the late eighties," Glenn Loury (an economist) responded: "Mr. Camp, no, I can't. I am not aware of any analysis that has specifically, in the technical literature, that has specifically addressed that question, nor can I think offhand of anything that has changed in the environment of the late eighties to which one could attribute" (U.S. House 1996a: 163).

Later, Camp rephrased the question: "Would you agree with the statement that welfare subsidies sustain illegitimacy?" This time, Loury replied: "Yeah. The statement is true almost by definition" (U.S. House 1996a: 163). In the same panel, Camp asked William Bennett (former drug czar): "How has the current welfare system contributed to the rising crime rate and drug abuse in America?" Bennett's response referred to presumptive common knowledge: "Well, Mr. Camp, I think any police sergeant in the country will tell you the day the welfare checks go out is a big day for drug buys. That is just the way it is. That is just the way the world works, and it has been in the drug literature" (U.S. House 1996a: 163).

Critics of the bill challenged these assessments by offering findings from different studies (on the grounds that they were better social science), by reversing the direction of causality in the proponents' correlations, or by recontextualizing the statistics in relation to broader economic and social trends (e.g., recontextualizing poverty rates in relation to wage levels, not just welfare expenditure).[11] For minority (i.e., Democratic) members of the committee, this sometimes put them at risk of reversing roles with the more powerful witnesses for the majority. In an exchange with William Bennett, for example, Harold Ford (D-Tennessee) challenged Bennett's account of "the social science evidence" for a causal link between welfare and illegitimacy. "According to the most respected social scientists," Ford said, "just the opposite is true . . . Poverty and decay are the surest roads to illegitimacy." He went on to cite low rates of *intentional* pregnancy on the part of teens (U.S. House 1996a: 163–164). But Bennett interrupted him at that point: "What is your question, sir?" and then twice more interrupted Ford to challenge his (Ford's) line of questioning.

Other critics of the bill presented their arguments in nonnumerical terms, drawing on the language of values and national traditions for appeals in terms of collective responsibilities for the poor, the idea of the nation, or the long tradition of federal sponsorship of social security. For example, witness

Lawrence Mead, from Princeton's Woodrow Wilson School, invoked citizenship as he concluded his argument in favor of retaining welfare as a federal program: "Welfare . . . is one of the ways in which we operationalize what citizenship means. That is of the highest national importance. It is for Congress to make decisions about it rather than turning this over to the States" (U.S. House 1996a: 264). Katherine McFate, a social scientist, made a detailed argument to show that devolving welfare to the states would likely sharpen "regional and racial inequalities" (U.S. House 1996b: 1092). Other witnesses took up more specialized appeals, for example, on behalf of children and their mothers.[12] But in the environment of the hearings, at least inside the committee chamber, such statements were never dispositive; the partisanship built into the committee structure—with partisan solidarity in full force in those opening weeks of the new Republican Congress—precluded any effective challenge. Moreover, the plethora of committees involved with the welfare-reform issue gave members considerable scope in cutting off discussion of some of these more wide-ranging appeals on the grounds of the specificity of their charge, and deference to other committees' jurisdictions.

In the heated partisan milieu of the hearings, order occasionally broke down as minority members fought against perceived cuts into their time or as members of the audience interrupted the proceedings. But these were exceptions as the committee proceedings increasingly took on the qualities of a choreographed performance. The majority's discursive control was evident in the difficulties witnesses faced if they wished to linger in gray areas. Those who attempted to argue over the quality of a study (e.g., the exchange between Ford and Bennett cited above, or U.S. House 1996b: 1071), or who took a position in favor of reform that did not *also* ascribe to the existing welfare system the full range of social ills targeted by the majority, were quickly pulled back into line. For example, political scientist James Q. Wilson supported welfare reform but not the correlation between AFDC and illegitimacy, on the grounds that rates of illegitimacy were rising worldwide, and that they were higher in the United States than in countries where welfare payments were higher. But his attempt to uncouple a causal connection between money and behavior in favor of cultural approaches quickly drew a censorious response from Jim McCrery (R-Louisiana) on the grounds that culture went beyond the committee's jurisdiction: "Unfortunately, some of those things aren't within the power of this Subcommittee. The welfare program is, though." McCrery then spoke for Wilson, retrofitting his testimony to the dominant discourse: "And so I am going to take the liberty of saying that you . . . agree with me that at least this would be a positive step toward fighting the problem of illegitimacy in this country. And if you disagree, I will give you a chance to say that" (U.S. House 1996a: 166). Wilson did not correct the Congressman, but used his remaining interventions to advocate support for program experimentation—while deferentially referring to the politicians' overt discursive control as warranted by their specialized expertise: "I don't know how to write bills. I am an ivory tower professor" (U.S. House 1996a: 173).

Given the security of the political controls over discourse, it was not damaging to admit ignorance, even on key points. For example, there was no discernible consequence when Congressman Ford elicited a confession of ignorance from a witness who had linked intentional pregnancy among unmarried teenagers and welfare:

Ford: I just want to make sure that you would not try to suggest that all of the intentional teen pregnancies are welfare recipients.
Witness: No. I think a large percentage of them are. I do not know what that percentage is, but, no, I am not suggesting that. (U.S. House 1996b: 1284)

Similarly, committee members who overreached in seeking to buttress the majority's position seemed to suffer no embarrassment. For example, the following exchange between Senator Bob Packwood (R-Oregon, and the committee chair) and Senator Tom Harkin (D-Iowa, and a congressional witness) took place during the Senate Finance Committee's wrap-up hearings, after Harkin described an Iowa workfare program, advocating it as a potential model for federal legislation. Packwood changed the subject, seeking a connection to the teen pregnancy issue:

The Chairman: Just a quick question. . . Do you know, or can you tell, if it is having any effect on illegitimacy?
Senator Harkin: I do not know the answer to that question.
The Chairman: What I am curious about is whether there is a relationship between jobs and job availability and legitimacy or illegitimacy. I do not know either.
Senator Harkin: I do not know the answer.
The Chairman: All right.
Senator Harkin: We do not have the research on that. (U.S. Senate 1995: 7)

But for those who sought to de-link behavior and welfare, skepticism regarding the correlations advanced by the majority witnesses was reconstituted and delegitimated as *ignorance*. For example, Senator Moynihan (D-New York) acknowledged the division of opinion over the reform proposals, only to dismiss the opposition as a "parallel view" of the problems. The colloquial phrase in this context (like the more usual "parallel universe") implies that the critics are bent on denying the obvious. Ventriloquizing, he caricatured the doubts of those who did not accept a causal connection between welfare and family structure and in the process subjected Wilson to yet another rescripting: "A parallel view has been that, what we call the welfare system is simply a fall-out of the change in family structure in our country. It is not at all clear why this has come about, and even less clear what we might do to change it. . . . James Q. Wilson, who is a dear friend and colleague . . . and [who] would associate himself with conservative thinking in most matters said, in testimony before the House, 'We are told that ending AFDC will reduce illegitimacy, but we do not know that. It is, at best, an informed guess'" (U.S. Senate 1995: 2).

The discursive discipline that kept social debate focused on numbers made it easy to shift frames into issues of cost. The scale of federal expenditure on welfare in absolute terms as well as relative to other federal budget categories were dominant themes. One supportive witness, for example, presented a chart comparing welfare expenditures to the United States defense budget, projecting a widening gap (in favor of welfare) over the next five years (U.S. House 1996a: 74). While a direct trade-off between social security and national security was not a major explicit theme, the implication was pervasive—if only in the continual references to damaged masculinity and the consequent vulnerability of women and children in the inner city. But there were also more specific implications that welfare imposes undue burdens on U.S. viability in global economic terms (as a drag on U.S. competitiveness), or depletes the value of federal expenditure by saddling it to poor returns on investment. Other risks, too, hint at the global frame of reference as the backdrop for the neoliberalization of welfare reform (i.e., downsizing the federal government in favor of states and the private sector). Those risks were presented in highly emotionalized language, using terms that were strikingly militaristic—perhaps playing on the metaphor of the Johnson administration's "war on poverty"—and global in their referents. For example, William Bennett referred to a "rapid and massive collapse of family structure" as being "without precedent among civilized nations" (U.S. House 1996a: 157) and later adding: "Look at the body count. . . . Whatever you do, don't stay the course" (U.S. House 1996a: 167). Senator Rick Santorum (R-Pennsylvania) referred to the Supplemental Security Income (SSI) as "killing people... We are giving them money to do what? To stay drug-addicted and alcoholic for the rest of their life" (U.S. Senate 1995: 16). For Senator Alan Simpson (R-Wyoming), the risks were cosmic: "There is an interesting prayer which is, I believe, embraced by most faiths which begins with, Our Father, Who art in heaven. Now these people that we hear the statistics on do not even know what a father is." He then drew a connection to the bombing of the federal building in Oklahoma by a domestic terrorist: "Then you see something like Oklahoma City come along, and what is the emphasis? It is on prayer and religion, care and nurture. Somewhere in there that has failed" (U.S. Senate 1995: 50).

"Welfare" went forward explicitly as a project in social engineering, based on the premise (recast as Congressional "findings" in the law's text) that the state's interest in the welfare system was primarily as a powerful force, molding positive behaviors in relation to work and family life. As Dave Camp said in committee: "We want to send a strong signal from the Federal Government that taxpayers are no longer willing to provide a comprehensive package of public benefits to young men and women *who violate social convention by having children they cannot afford*" (U.S. House 1996a: 134; emphasis added). The opening lines of the enacted bill, announcing the Congress's findings, are not about welfare, but about a wide ranging set of propositions and correlations:

> The Congress makes the following findings:
> (1) Marriage is the foundation of a successful society.
> (2) Marriage is an essential institution of a successful society which promotes the interests of children.
> (3) Promotion of responsible fatherhood and motherhood is integral to successful child rearing and the well-being of children. (U.S. Congress 1996: 6)

The Congress then devotes two full pages to the statistics of teen pregnancy: "An effective strategy to combat teenage pregnancy must address the issue of male responsibility, including statutory rape culpability and prevention. The increase of teenage pregnancy among the youngest girls is particularly severe and is linked to predatory sexual practices by men who are significantly older" (U.S. Congress 1996: 7). Next, it takes up child health, and finally, two paragraphs on young criminal offenders—here, as elsewhere, comparing rates and seriousness of crime among the children of single-parent and married-parent families. The three pages of findings culminate in a resolution: "Therefore, in light of this demonstration of the crisis in our Nation, it is the sense of the Congress that prevention of out-of-wedlock pregnancy and reduction in out-of-wedlock birth are very important Government interests" (U.S. Congress 1996: 8). The measure passed handily, with approximately half of the Democrats voting with the Republicans in both chambers.[13]

Neoliberal Subjects Without Citizenship

The politicization of immigration is the other side of the "ideal of citizenship" as it has evolved legally around concerns with naturalization and eligibility (restricted by race until 1965)—and culturally around tensions in the field of identity (Urciuoli 1994: esp. 20, 27). Urciuoli's analysis of "the evolution of the citizen" and the "model ethnic" implies the extent to which debates over immigration might be heavily charged for legal migrants as well as for the native born. Citizenship and respectability converge in ways that complicate any neat connection between citizenship status and status in other senses of the term. Such complexities were evident in the debate on immigration reform in the 104th Congress. As welfare reform moved through Congress after the 1994 mid-term elections, Congress also took up immigration reform with President Clinton's support—passing the Illegal Immigration Reform and Immigrant Responsibility Act (IIRAIRA) in 1996. IIRAIRA was a selective composite of numerous House and Senate bills on different aspects of legal and illegal immigration, and eventually passed in both chambers as part of a defense appropriations bill (Public Law 104-208).

Phyllis Chock's pioneering ethnographic work on immigration reform has followed Congressional "myth-making" (Chock 1991) in hearings and floor debate since the legislative initiatives of 1975.[14] These eventually became law as the Immigration Reform and Control Act (IRCA) of 1986, subsequently revised by the broad Congressional effort that became IIRAIRA (Chock 1991, 1994, 1996, 1999). Although Republicans in the 104th Congress favored strong checks on immigration, IIRAIRA was not part of the Contract with America; it passed with bipartisan support.[15]

IIRAIRA involved hearings in numerous committees, reflecting the varied discursive trails that converged in its making. One set of premises made unregistered immigration a national security issue, conflating *illegal aliens* with *criminal aliens*.[16] That side of the bill involved hearings on border controls, judicial processes associated with deportation, and executive power relative to deportation (e.g., enhancing the discretionary powers of the attorney general with respect to deportation). Another set of premises echoed the welfare bill's concerns with dependency. A third premise flipped the dependency discourse—with the claim that unregistered immigrants posed a particular economic threat to African Americans. The assumption was that migrants would sell their labor below market value, displacing African Americans at the bottom of the wage scale. Immigrants' work ethic worked against them in this regard, and hearings also ensued on the question of sanctions against employers who knowingly employ unregistered migrants or fail to make adequate checks of identification. Each of these premises was asserted at length and refuted at length by competing panels of experts.[17] As readers may have already noticed, some of the premises in favor of stricter border controls against so-called illegals applied just as fully to *legal* immigration. Indeed, some witnesses supported new restrictions or an outright moratorium on *all* immigration, except in rare cases of asylum or family emergency (see, e.g., the Senate testimony of Dan Stein [Federal Document Clearing House eMedia 1995]). As in the welfare hearings, there was little consensus among experts on the definition of the problem, let alone solutions (on "differences within accounts" of immigration law, see Coutin 1996). Consensus emerged less from substantive agreement than from political compromises forged in the course of the legislative process itself.

Chock's analysis of the hearings for one of the main predecessor bills to IIRAIRA (the Immigration in the National Interest Act of 1995, H.R. 1915) focuses on the theme of dependency. Some of the testimony resonated with the discussion in the welfare context, outlined above—but with a critical difference. In the case of unregistered immigrants, children born on United States soil were citizens—and this became a major point of controversy. Chock (1999) details the extent to which migrant status—for some members of Congress—overturned the normal association of birth and citizenship, leading some to propose restrictions on citizenship and naturalization so as to bar the children of unregistered immigrants from access to public services. The controversy over "porous borders" (Chock 1998) opening floodgates to new citizens focused particularly on the exclusion of women—discursively fused with their (unborn) children in a way that men were not (Chock 1999: 50).

Chock's principal conclusion is that legislators most strongly in favor of restricting illegal immigration construct *aliens* and *citizens* as different kinds of persons:

> The contradiction between the rational and the natural in this citizenship framework elides the terms' own work in defining citizens and aliens as different kinds of individuals. In this logic, those aliens who are fit for citizenship are governed by the rationality of the market, they "work hard." Those deemed unfit—largely women and children, I fear—are assumed to be governed by desperate, nearly inhuman need; they "work cheap," depend on welfare, and bear children (or are born) in the wrong place for the wrong reasons. The fit are assumed to be governed by law; they "wait in line" to enter. The unfit are governed by base human nature, the desire to bear a child and to get something for nothing. . . . The contradiction, then, is not only about raced, gendered, and classed individuals, but also about nation and market as they are conceived of in U.S. debates about citizenship. (Chock 1999: 50)

The contradiction between nation and market is not limited to the mythic construction of unregistered migrants, or even foreigners; it also dominated the figurations of personhood in the welfare hearings, and in the civil rights hearings. Taken together, rights were constructed as a form of dependency, and as identity politics came under attack from Congressional conservatives, the new legislation fused identity—whether citizen or alien—to market value on a continuous spectrum.

IIRAIRA broadened the grounds on which immigrants would be subject to detention and removal, and raising bars to admissibility. IIRAIRA also gave the Immigration and Naturalization Service (now part of the Department of Homeland Security) final authority, not subject to review by courts. Critics of the new law challenged the constitutionality of an exclusion from judicial review, as well as the harshness of some of the law's provisions and omissions—such as the absence of any provision for uniting immigrants with family members who were legal residents of the United States (see American Immigration Lawyers Association n.d.)

Controversy over so-called *illegals* focused iconically (and continues to focus) on the U.S. border with Mexico, although the paths to the United States are not only from the south. The immigration debate of the 1990s drew on the same negating discourse surrounding African American urban poor that was aired in the civil rights and welfare debates at the same time—now displaced or extended to the other side of the southern border. In this sense, the "essential cultural difference" ascribed to immigrants in the intensely anti-immigrant mood of the 1990s (Stepick 2006: 393) is labile; it is relevant to citizens, as well. The difference is waiting at the border.

Trouble at Home

In Congressional testimony and debate over antidiscrimination rights in disability and employment, welfare and immigration, key images of raced and gendered subjects were composed in a way that set rights and market principles as trade-offs. In each case, the costing out of rights transferred important elements of citizenship to the private sector—indeed, to the individual him- or herself. As we have seen, IIRAIRA joins this discourse of citizenship fully, even though it ostensibly deals only with unregistered immigrants.

The significance of the Congressional debate sketched here extends well beyond the legislative process. The initiatives themselves were crafted as means to broad ends. Broader still, these legislative outcomes were definitive responses to the civil rights and welfare rights movements that had shaped public debates over the role of government for a generation (Kornbluh 2007). In this context, it is important to resist the temptation to conclude that the relevance of the legislation from an ethnographic standpoint was that Congress "spoke for" its own vision of the new global capitalism, narrow institutional interests, or some triumphalist partisanship. The CRA of 1991 and the Welfare Reform Act restructured politics—dispersing the coalitions of federal, state, and local political parties and activists that together had sustained powerful currents in American politics. Now the mainstream was narrower. Rights movements were by no means gone but held to channels with lower frequencies. The mainstream was also more distant from the community-based arenas where civil rights and welfare movements had flourished—and where anthropologists worked nearby (Goode and Maskovsky 2001; Gregory 1998; Morgen and Maskovsky 2003; Sanjek 2000; Susser 1996, 1998).

In her analysis of the history of social policy in the United States, Theda Skočpol emphasizes the specificity of "the historical formation of each national state" (including national states at different eras) in relation to their effects on "the goals, capacities, and alliances of politically active social groups" (Skočpol 1995: 19). The specificities of neoliberalism's mainstreaming involved the discursive reworking of the meaning of marginality—as we have seen in this chapter. The very meanings of race, gender, and class were reconfigured in highly public and consequential ways in the process of legislative debate. One might say, with accuracy, that neoliberalism's mainstreaming took place through an elision of race, class, and gender—each modality of inequality set up to trump the others according to political purpose. Thus critics used business interests to temper the equality claims of individuals with disabilities. They used class to moot the race discrimination claims in the employment context. They used gender to craft the new welfare law as a defense of marriage and personal responsibility rather than as a measure targeting dependency in African American and Latino communities. But IIRAIRA turned that same discourse the other way, targeting women and children and migrants' work ethic in the name of citizens. We should not imagine that the testimony offers accounts of legislators' motives or reasoning; however, the hearings and floor debate do backfill the language of the legislation with social substance that has weight beyond the chamber.

In turning toward American cities, anthropologists of the 1990s were concerned not with the fate of the old discourse, but with urban communities now excluded from a national conversation, and further disadvantaged by the reformulation of the idea of culture—now either a euphemism for race, or social pathology, or both. The ethnographies took up those pejorative associations and turned them inside out, holding onto the relativity vis-à-vis the national society, and exploring in depth those communities' capacity to act on their own behalf. The choice of subject matter sustained the works' focus on the varied connection between identity and agency, citizenship and constraint, opportunity and illegality, knowledge and legitimacy—in patterned ways, illuminating the political space of U.S. ethnography in the 1990s.

Many anthropologists working in the United States did not address themselves directly to the policy issues involved in these debates, nor directly to issues of race and class. However, most anthropologists engaged in U.S. fieldwork made culture their theme, and in doing so turned to poor ethnic urban neighborhoods where the stereotyped story lines of the new discourse could be tested (if indirectly) through field-based inquiry. These were not direct responses to the legal developments discussed in this chapter (since in many cases the fieldwork preceded the legislation discussed here). Still, as written, the works could be read as substantive critical engagements with the new discourse of responsibility as it channeled the significance of identity in relation to the meanings of nation, state, society, and citizenship. We turn now to the question of what anthropologists did with these same texts and contexts as they reworked their key terms.

CHAPTER 4

Textual Strategy
and the Politics of Form

I n the 1990s, as key elements of New Deal liberalism faded from the federal U.S. legislative arena, they remained objects of interdisciplinary dialogue and academic debate—often indirectly, re-routed as questions of theory and method. As ethnographers called for attention to narrative in their texts, their coding of *voice* as the means and ends of critical agency drew from the politics of representation that the new neoliberal mainstream had made its discursive foil. The new attention to narrative was selective in its tuning to subaltern and marginalized identities—the poor, women, victims of violence, new immigrants, people of color—that is, wherever public policy cancelled commonsense notions of public relief in favor of marketized renderings of the public good.[1] The legislative hearings discussed in the previous chapter make these tunings clear, especially in relation to marriage, family life, employment, and social values as these were coded politically around the work ethic and gender norms. Equal opportunity was open to individuals, but—so it seemed—only to the extent that they might leave their communities behind.

Sociolegal studies, anthropology, and related disciplines were drawn into adjacency by these developments—in particular, in the critical valence they were prepared to find in voice as an expression of subaltern agency, consciousness, and resistance. The critical significance of voice in this sense preceded its interpretive significance within anthropological monographs about the United States, as the *fact* of the speaking subject dominated over the content of the subject's spoken words. To put this another way, voice and agency are more consistent in relation to the structure of the ethnographies than in relation to their substance per se. In this chapter, we examine the structural form that became characteristic of 1990s community studies, reserving questions about their treatment of the liberal subject for later chapters.

In literary terms, anthropologists made the invisible visible—undoing the social conventions of non-recognition, erasure, silencing and negative stereotyping (see Warren 1993). The literary technique was predicated on a recombination and reformulation of distinct notions of the public. One was a construction of the public as *audience*, as readers and spectators (Habermas 1991: 31). The other constituted the public as *critics*—"private people [making] use of their reason . . . [to establish] a sphere of criticism of public authority" (Habermas 1991: 51). As distinct formulations, "applied synchronically to the conditions of a bourgeois society that is industrially advanced and constituted as a social-welfare state, they fuse into a clouded amalgam" (Habermas 1991: 1). Indeed, the ethnographic notions of *society* and *community*—sometimes distinct, sometimes blended, sometimes concrete, sometimes heuristic—are among the amalgamated forms Habermas might have in view. Add to these the very contemporary ambiguity of public and private sectors, their intricate interdependence, and the elusiveness of public judgment relative to actual political communities, and the concept of *the public sphere* becomes all the more necessary (Habermas 1991: 1). The idea of the public sphere might dominate the sensibility of relevance as involving first and foremost a critical relation—for example, constituting the politicization of social space as the corollary of an agentive literary relation between authors and readers.

The community studies of the 1990s are contributions to the public sphere in this sense: localized critiques of the key terms of public authority, presented to the reading public so as to actualize and inform their private lives as critics of government. In this chapter, we relate this diffuse notion of the public to the ethnographies of the 1990s by exploring their highly patterned textual strategies. In particular, I follow the career of the first-person singular in relation to issues of narrative structure and meaning.

The first-person singular—relatively new in ethnographic writing at this time—was well tuned to an emergent neoliberalism's emphasis on the individual as liberal subject. Whereas an older liberal discourse made *neglect* its rallying cry, *neo*liberalism rode the discursive currents of individual choice. Accordingly, the rallying cry of the narrative turn was its resistance to *silencing*—the foil against which *voice* has political significance beyond its linguistic features as communication and self-expression. In the humanities and the humanistic side of the social sciences, then, constructivism emerged as a powerful concept from the fault lines between liberal and conservative approaches to equality and social justice—holding on, as it were, to the sense of alternatives, redirected as interpretive alternatives, long after they disappeared from the mainstream political agenda.

For this very reason, the interpretive risk in the narrative turn is commensurate with its political ambiguity, since the very method emphasizes both resonance and disjunction between narrative content and the frames of significance that make it meaningful as evidence of something beyond itself. Ethnographic narrative is both illustrative and *sui generis*, and the method "belonged" to neither side in the political debates of the day (if one briefly entertains the simplistic binary for the sake of making the point). For liberals, constructivism lent itself to a worldview predicated on identity, cultural diversity, and political pluralism. For conservatives, meanwhile, constructivism lent itself to a worldview based on individualism, cultural standards, and self-regulation.

The differences between these positions were construed as tensions between constructivism and positivism, but both could be accommodated within a broadly constructivist methodology. It was not the methodology that drove debate; rather, it was the oppositional force of *multiculturalism*—a term only very newly in circulation at the time—that called on one to "assess . . . just what it has actually meant in recent history (and what it might mean in the future) to rely upon the U.S. nation-state as a stable container of social antagonisms, and as the necessary horizon of our hopes for justice" (Singh 1998: 472). Multiculturalism was drawn into academic debates among ethnographers mainly as a question of methodology, especially regarding standards of evidence and representation. By this broad path, questions of method were melded into the debates over federal power—means standing in for ends as "the dream of a unified field" (Graham 1995) faded from both.

Constructivism points to the fields of encounter where "identity" is not just a question of demography, but also—more fundamentally—a question of political subjectivity, historically produced. The "unified field" of the nation proffers a classic story line—a "nationalist historicism that assumes that there is a moment when the differential temporalities of cultural histories coalesce in an immediately readable present" (Bhabha 1994: 152). But state, nation, and culture are not unified fields, subject to subdivision as cultural groups, ultimately to unitary citizens. Yet such assumptions are deeply inscribed in liberal and republican thought and their social science extensions (for example, in canons of description and generalization). Scholars who are critical of this vision elaborate the incommensurability of collective identities, the difference between self-identity and identification by others, the effects of law in fragmenting horizons of identification and the mythical status of the nation itself. Scholars who support it celebrate common values underlying difference, and the social mechanisms (primarily capital investment and consumption) that bridge ethnic and racial communities.

These positions should not be reduced to neat antitheses. The constitution of individual and collective identities in the nation cannot be ideologically fixed, nor can theoretical differences be reduced to sheer antagonisms. Urgency and ambiguity thus intensify together. Indeed, the pervasive tension between the sense of theoretical flux around the question of identity amidst high material and political stakes for actual communities is the understory to all of the ethnographic accounts discussed in this book—perhaps all ethnographic accounts, period. The critical positions within and against liberalism function as different narrative registers, with respect both to anthropology and the United States as a diasporic site (see Brah 1996). Accordingly, the narrative structure in these works is fundamentally shaped by the necessity of both sustaining and controlling that interpretive ambiguity.

The narrative structure of the typical 1990s community study tends to take the form of allegory, drawing attention to the first-person singular—and ultimately sustaining a cross-identification of author, reader, and cultural subject. That identification is the kernel of the work's transformative and redemptive potential. Following the first-person narrative allows us to explore more specifically how ethnographers invest their work with democratic implication, and manage that implication as a specifically anthropological analysis. The allegorical "I" in these accounts is a literary figure, in addition to whatever else it might be for the author or others whose testimonies are presented as direct discourse. It is, in a sense, a fictional "I"—fictional in a highly accountable way—that seems to take authors to the limits of what they feel their craft can interpretively sustain.

But beyond the necessarily fictional quality of any interpretation (in Geertz's sense; 1973: 15–16), the ethnographic "I" in these accounts expresses something else at the same time—a scientific observer, the "I" as (eye)witness.[2] The pursuit of science is in this sense also an impulse toward fiction, to the extent that an affirmative embrace of fiction provides a means of expressing knowledge wherever a sense of responsibility exceeds the limits of proof. Interpretive excess, in this sense, does not mean a reckless interpretation, but rather, knowledge that unsettles and overtakes the boundaries established by the author's profession. Anthropology borrows from law, but presses past the rules of evidence. Fiction presses anthropology farther along the lines anthropology has set for itself in relation to law. Fiction, from this standpoint, is not "made up" but represents the breaking through of a discursive impasse to something else, relatable in multiple senses.

To the extent that ethnographers· (in anthropology or adjacent fields) write the relevance of their work in relation to current policy debates, they furnish social description with images, story lines, and purposes already in circulation. Announcing relevance in this way imposes strictures on interpretation, if only because policy relevance entails a priori claims with respect to identity and meaning, deploying identities rather than exploring them—as we saw in the previous chapter. Genre is therefore deeply coded for an author's sensibility as to the limits of actual political and legal institutions. This sense of limits is explicit in some accounts, but it is implicit in any ethnography—to the extent that authors present their work as *giving voice* or providing a record of the otherwise-unsaid. Thus, ethnography draws nigh to fiction at the junctures where the limits of law are most tangible—and where the author therefore asks the most of readers. "To write is . . . both to disclose the world and to offer it as a task to the generosity of the reader" (Sartre 1988: 65).

The patterned choreography of U.S. ethnography around these narrative codes is the theme of this chapter. It is a double theme, involving a question of textual form, and—as a consequence of form—a further question of the performativity of the first-person singular in ethnographic accounts. Along both of these interpretive paths, ethnography's contributions and indebtedness to other genres become clear. The conventional structure of a modern ethnography about the United States divides the text into three clearly demarcated parts: a preface or introduction, the main text, and—generally at the very end of the concluding chapter—a further comment, marked off by a distinctive register or tone. Let us call these sections the prologue, main text, and epilogue or (since they are often very brief) *envoi. Envoi*, in French, means "send-off"—a farewell gesture that contains the implication of an exhortation. These three elements function in quite distinct ways ethnographically, and any single work can be read productively for its strategic management of their disjunctions.

Reading the End First: The Politics of Narrative Structure

The structural pattern of 1990s community studies is striking in its consistency. Evocations of a national society constitute the main register for addressing readers, making *cultural difference* within the nation—minoritarian difference—the principal opening to ethnography. But the substance of the works entails a different register, in which the contingencies of social action are the main theme. These two registers might seem to pull in different directions, the one leaning toward difference and the other away from it (i.e., showing the appearance of difference to be misleading) or resignifying difference (showing difference to be consistent with a national society after all). The gap between these registers itself becomes a focus of narrative—a first-person metanarrative in which the ethnographer relates his or her own process of inquiry, research, and discovery. In important ways, then, the tensions between liberals and conservatives become the field against which ethnographers perform their discipline—reconciling on the page (so to speak) what the society itself cannot reconcile through politics.

"Culture," then, is more than ethnography's object; it is also its method. Constructed as difference, *culture* invites description. But constructed as a problem of knowledge, it invites a narrative of discovery, a conversion of sorts, for the ethnographer. In these works, cultural difference begins as a question about lifeways and worldviews but ends as a question about the future of the nation and the knowledge demands of a society committed to cultural pluralism. Culture thus has multiple functions in the textual choreography of these works, drawing attention simultaneously to the stakes in social description as well as the literariness of policy discourse. The textual functions of difference parallel (albeit tacitly) the widespread critique of identity politics in the federal arena—a root issue for the new liberalism of the 1990s. Writing at the time, Lisa Lowe evokes the intricate critical parameters in this context: "Culture is the terrain through which the individual speaks itself as a member of the contemporary national collectivity, but culture is also a mediation of history, the site through which the past returns and is remembered, however fragmented, imperfect, or disavowed. Through that remembering—that recomposition—new forms of subjectivitiy and community are thought and signified" (Lowe 1998: 19). Once textuality is understood as a dynamic actuality, such a recomposition can be appreciated as the essence of ethnography's "fantastic flourish" (Griswold 2000: 273).

I begin with the envoi, since it is in these brief gestures that the *overall* purpose of the book is announced in terms that spill over from the specifically anthropological aspects of the work, toward a larger democratic project. In the envoi, an author makes a declaration of the *value* of what has come before—characteristically, in terms at once ethnographic and ethical. An envoi is the texts' usual concluding gesture toward a future in which anthropological knowledge will be both valued and practiced. The concluding paragraphs of Ruth Benedict's *Patterns of Culture* (1934) are a classic example, her vision of a new day being neither a prediction nor a program, but an affirmation of anthropology itself as useful knowledge—even if its full potential is still to come, in a world more open to difference. The modern envoi echoes that gesture and its subjunctive mood, a temporality of "not yet" that bridges the distance between the particular and the general, observation and aspiration. Here, again is the germinal disjunction between evidence and interpretation that is essential to ethnography as a "method of hope" (Miyazaki 2004).

Envois point directly to the national arena in which ethnographic knowledge might be relevant as democratic practice, signaling the reader that the book is intended to be read as a commentary on the state of the nation in a newly transnational world. There are sometimes deep disjunctions between envois and the main text in this sense—there is a textual evocation of looking up and away, a shift of tone and concern. Envois—after the fact—situate the main text as a space of tension, suffusing it with double significance as both chronicle and allegory, lending them a prevailing tone of irony. The tensions are not in the text alone; that is the point.

The works are—in classic ethnographic fashion—set in small-scale situations, acutely localized. Yet I say "localized" rather than "local" since the works do not for the most part contextualize the particularities of community in relation to the wider urban nexus of which they are a part. Rather— and this is especially evident from the individual works' bibliographies—they are cast as domestic displacements of foreign worlds. American cities, in this sense, are rewritten as world cities, effectively doubling ethnographic narrative such that it is intimate and "meta" simultaneously. This gives them their allegorical character. As allegories, community studies have something of the form of a morality play in which the reader is confronted with a mounting sense of tragedy, and only at the last minute with the possibility that tragedy might be averted if ethnographic knowledge can be redeemed as democracy. If such images are explicit, they are generally built into the texts as a brief meditation in the book's closing lines.

But whether or not the allegorical element is explicit, the envoi is a general feature of these works, offering a concluding statement that typically evokes redemption or reconciliation in the mythical "time of the nation" still to come (Bhabha 1994: ch. 8). The following examples are drawn from the democratic envois of 1990s ethnographic accounts:

> Thus, immigrants—legal or not—breathe new life into an American dream that has proven elusive to many native-born. . . . Imported rugged individualists and American dreamers, immigrants buttress the foundational ideology, the primal myths of Americana. In sum, though they are often accused of alien beliefs and practices, they fundamentally contribute to the nation's cultural reproduction. (Mahler 1995: 233)

> Having been sojourners, many [Brazilians in New York City] will turn settlers. They will become true transnationals. . . . But like so many immigrants to these shores before them, Brazilians will see their lives and future as intimately tied to the fortunes and future of their adopted home. (Margolis 1994: 275; paragraph break omitted)

> As they experience life in America, Korean Americans create new identities, new cultural forms, and new ideologies. Ultimately, through these acts of creation, they reshape American dreams. (Park 1997: 206)

> Queens is a world town for those people who come from many parts of the world to contribute, like the Chinese, their talents and strengths to make this diverse community more prosperous, more beautiful, and more peaceful. (Chen 1992: 263)

> Nothing is impossible if we believe that people can change. (Sanjek 1998: 393)

> [Cambodian immigrants] have redefined the "American dream" to enable them to live well in America, and to become a productive part of the larger American community while retaining significant elements of their own heritage. (Welaratna 1993: 277)

> As long as there is pride in ancestry and heritage, . . . immigrants can continue to relate to their countries of origin, and the children to

their parents, in meaningful ways. And pride is something the Punjabis and their descendants have in plentiful supply. (Leonard 1992: 219)

Such patterned flourishes signal a break between the localism of ethnography and the future of the transnational community beyond the text, establishing a point of urgent reinterpretation within the text. The democratic envoi projects concern for the future in the sharply drawn juxtaposition between the actuality of the book's contents and the fantasy of its reception and its subjects' futures. In effect, it tells readers what the book is meant to be *for*—beyond its ethnographic content, just before the book ends.

Since the market for ethnographic writing is not, in fact (or not yet), a general market, such narrative stagings would seem to be for the benefit of the anthropological profession, or their students. What does it mean that as anthropologists we address each other as citizens, as if to create for other anthropologists a mirror of our own craft in the convictions of an imaginary general public? The answer depends on what kind of act reading is. The community studies—written to anthropologists as if they were being addressed mainly as fellow citizens—invite readers to experience a break between the "real" world (in which anthropological knowledge is true but arcane) and an imagined world in which anthropological knowledge would be everyday knowledge, alive in the cultural literacy of normal social routines.

Political theorist Rogers Smith concludes his book with a lengthy envoi (in the form of a prescriptive epilogue) in which he looks hopefully to citizenship as a democratic resource. I quote Smith at length since the passage conveys perfectly the implicit message and rationale of most U.S. monographs:

Today the U.S. is the world's sole yet troubled superpower, a startlingly complex, conflicted, still evolving, yet still specific set of territories, institutions, peoples, historical affiliations, and future possibilities. . . . Liberal democrats can forcefully argue, moreover, that the credibility of such a sense of belonging would be enhanced, not diminished, if U.S. citizens constructed their national identity in line with their more consensual traditions and institutions. If political institutions made democratic self-governance as much a reality as possible, and citizenship laws made nationality as much a matter of choice as possible, then Americans could more genuinely regard their Americanism as something they could define as they saw fit. (Smith 1997: 498; paragraph break and note omitted)

As for most of the ethnographers discussed in this book, Smith's notion of citizenship offers a commensuration but not a standardization or assimilation of the different regimes of identity in which individuals might find themselves.

In the 1990s, the distance between anthropologists' understandings of the connections between cultural identity, displacement, impoverishment, and federal policy is audible in a pervasive tone of irony—the classic literary means of simultaneously holding open two knowledges involving different outcomes. The local and the national are both consistently present in the texts—the former as explicit subject matter, the latter implied as the background knowledge of an intended audience. The local and national are held apart by the social distances between citizen and subject—the citizen/audience for whom anthropology is useful as political knowledge, and the subject of both state and anthropological research who are politically marginal except as the symbolic objects of others' power and privilege. At the same time, across these social distances, local and national, subject and citizen are adjoined through the ethical relation of reading. The books—as evinced in their envois—make broad (if only briefly stated) claims on readers' responsibilities. Such responsibilities are for the most part asserted through the language of fellow citizenship. This is part of the significance of the discourse of solutions that pervades these works. The reference to policy—even if only to the identities conjured up by policy debate—is a metonymic reference to a national public, a reading public, a responsible public for whom anthropological knowledge is integral to civility and citizenship.

This indirect address accounts in part for the fact that ethnographies of U.S. communities tend to be intensely local in a *literary* fashion; the main work of evoking "the economy of the whole" is accomplished through something like allegory (Benjamin 1998: 234; see also 186). The author's formal address to other anthropologists and their students *as citizens* commits their pages to a tacit nationalism and transnationalism more than the descriptive contents or argumentation as such. The narrative structure announces the social and political aspirations of the work, and situates the political in relation to the social at the point where the reader is induced to become aware of her or his own silence—that is, beyond the silence of reading in solitude—as a field of new knowledge and moral responsibility. As an allegorical framing, ethnography is a discourse of fundamental unease:

> The immersion of allegory has to clear away the final phantasmagoria of the objective and, left entirely to its own devices, re-discovers

itself, not playfully in the earthly world of things, but seriously under the eyes of heaven. And this is the essence of melancholy immersion: that its ultimate objects . . . turn into allegories, and that these allegories fill out and deny the void in which they are represented, just as, ultimately, the intention does not faithfully rest in the contemplation of bones, but faithlessly leaps forward to the idea of resurrection. (Benjamin 1998: 232–233)

Such ethical and structural assertions are legible, though, only to the extent that one brings to the book some broader knowledge of its times and codings. This brings us to the main text—the ethnography proper, thickly sandwiched by the envoi (its revealed foundation) and, as we shall see, the prologue (its inviting surface).

The cumulative effect of the democratic envoi is a vision of a liberal democratic society freed of social prejudice, in which diverse identities are integral to a flourishing national culture. Such fusions of citizenship and ethnography were not new to the 1990s. They were well rehearsed in an earlier era, when the formulation of citizens as the literal and figurative future of the nation—the embodiment of the "state's interest" in such local affairs as public education—was palpable and powerful as the preeminent legal strategy of rights-making.[3] In this regard, and as we shall discuss in more detail later, the 1990s texts echo the language of *Brown v. Board* and other landmark texts of the civil rights struggles of the 1950s and 1960s. In the 1990s, ethnographers drew on similar figurations of federal subjectivity in their portraits of their subjects—*identities* with a singular face.

Prologues: The Professional Is the Personal

Prologues tend to be written from a highly personalized standpoint, recounting the evolution of the project as a story told in the first person, including the author's personal reactions and involvements, often in terms of an inner conflict between neutrality and engagement. Such prologues have two main functions. First, they orient readers to the subjective demands of the work, preparing them for the alignment (or alliance) that culminates in the democratic envoi. Second, by isolating the most personalized expression of those subjective demands in a separate section, they are providing a staging ground for the journey author and reader will make together into the main text. In other words, one function of the prologues is to establish a performative distinction between subjectivity and objectivity—equipping the reader to self-consciously experience the main text as a disciplined scientific account. The other is to challenge that distinction, drawing science into the registers of personal aspiration.

It might seem inevitable that ethnographers should introduce their texts in their own voice, but that inevitability does not dictate the functions of the first-person singular in relation to the texts as a whole. As already discussed, the primary functions of the ethnographer's first-person testimony are to establish the performative aspects of the work's narrative structure— that is, to draw the reader into experiencing the tone and content shifts between the prologue and main text, and then again between the main text and the epilogue or envoi. This structure (as already indicated) aligns the work's critique with the author's autobiography—literally and figuratively, positioning author, reader, and research subjects on the page. Self-identification as a rights-bearing subject depends in part on one's capacity to identify with other beneficiaries of rights, and ethnography's basic structure of identification and transference appears to be based on just such associations.

In this sense, the basic narrative organization of U.S. ethnography remains rooted to the discursive templates of democratic citizenship and liberal law, even if an author's conclusions range far afield of a legislative agenda or "solutions" altogether. If U.S. ethnography "domesticates" critique it is not by relativizing opposition (cf. Brigham 1996: 153) but by referring it to partisan political debate at the federal level, even if only (for the most part) implicitly.

Within the ambit of ethnographic prologues, the federal implication suffuses conventional rhetorical features. Primary among these is the way the author's first-person singular plays against the foil of nation, culture(s), or law. But it is also inherent in superficially less consequential rhetorical flourishes. For example, one commonplace device—anticipating the democratic envoi—is the evocation of a civic rite (for example, a high school graduation or a holiday celebration) or an everyday routine in a familiar place. These gestures toward a public culture constructed (textually) as mainstream provides a backdrop, a textual foil for identifying the particular difference "hidden in plain sight" (to borrow the title of diLeonardo's [1998] prologue)—the defamiliarizing encounter that yields the subject matter at hand. To offer just a few examples: Freeman's book on Vietnamese refugees in the San José, California, area opens with a vignette of a high school graduation and the sadness of one graduate, a Vietnamese refugee who attends alone (1989: 3). Takezawa opens her book about the Japanese American reparations movement with an evocation of a Thanksgiving celebration (1995: 1). Harding begins her book on the evangelical fundamentalist discourse of Jerry Falwell with an evocation of Halloween (2000: ix). Kasinitz (1992: xi) opens his monograph on "Caribbean New York" with a vignette from a celebration of "West Indian American Day Carnival"—on the day known to most other Americans as Labor Day (1992: 1).

In a different vein, but equally (and more literally) referential to the space of the nation-state, Small (1997: 3) begins her book on Tongan migration to the United States with a multiperspectival evocation of simultaneous points of departure. Margolis (1994: xx–xxiii) begins her account of Brazilians in New York with the story of her cousin's chance remark about having a Brazilian maid. Brown (1991), too, is in New York City, close to home and a world away. Lutz (2001: 3) plays on the trope of home in a different way, opening her account of the civilian community that supports a military base with the observation that "we all inhabit an army camp, mobilized to lend support to the permanent state of war readiness that has been with us since World War II."

Sociological accounts—even when they are similar to anthropological monographs in terms of their subject matter—do not seem to exhibit this rhetorical feature at this time, even if their justice aims are explicit. Sociologists' research questions more fully encompass the socioeconomic characteristics of the research subjects, rather than floating appeals to readers' broad identification with subjects' ambivalent otherness such as structure the ethnographic accounts (see, for example, Balin's monograph on one community's resistance to an AIDS care facility [1999], Duneier's account of ethical discourse among urban African American men [1992, or Lin's study of New York City's Chinatown [1998]). And of course, not all anthropological monographs open in this way—for example, those written prior to the intensification of racism and anti-immigrant xenophobia in the late 1980s (for example, Laguerre 1984; Rose 1989; Shokeid 1988; Williams 1988; and Yanagisako 1989). Monographs more specifically keyed to capital flows or mobility rather than identity (and immobility) seem less likely to make recourse to this device (for example, Chen 1992; Urciuoli 1996; Gregory 1998; Mahler 1995; Park 1997; and Jackson 2001). These authors (along with others) have other means to signal the play of difference in relation to a collective totality—by configuring the collectivity as a rhetorical "we" (in most accounts), or through allusions to policy debate (Gregory 1998; Mahler 1995), or to the United States as a host country (Freeman 1989; Rose 1989). Some authors formulate the totality in textual terms—as the anthropological literature, in relation to which the ethnography of the United States stands apart, the "light-consuming black hole in anthropology" marked for negation (diLeonardo 1998: 16; see also Shokeid 1988: 13; J. L. Jackson 2001: 13; Rose 1989: 63).

The important point is that the interpretive parameters of these works are set in large part by their opening play of the particular against the general, the excluded against the incompleteness of inclusion, difference against democracy. The "I" of the ethnographer's prologue should not be dismissed as the self-evident pronoun of authorship, but as the figuration of the critical difference between the particular identity in question and the nation's broader claims to equality and inclusiveness. Since this critical and theoretical space can be realized only textually (not yet politically) it seems quite pointless to argue over the merits of ethnography's textual and material aspects as if either could exist independently of the other (cf. diLeonardo 1998: 73–78). Prologues (coupled with the envois, discussed earlier) articulate the theoretical frame of the works, by providing a textual space where the author can seize on the modest creative license of the format—outside the main text, signaled by the use of the first-person singular—to establish through personal commentary the terms in which the work should be read.

By answering in advance the question of how the particular ethnographic case might be generalized to the Unites States at large, authors effectively displace their subjects from their particular locale—eliding vast differences of scale (between a neighborhood and the United States as a whole, for example) by compressing them into a single frame, as reflection, motivation, aspiration, critique, and so forth. In this respect, the first-person singular of the prologue is not merely the transparent reference to the author, but the figuration of a certain significance of difference in the contemporary discipline of anthropology, the United States, and the world at large. By writing in the first-person singular, an author signals his or her creative freedom—a freedom taken for the most part to recontextualize the work as a whole beyond the empirical limits of the project itself.

The broader interpretive framings that emerge from such creative warrants are rarely spelled out in programmatic or overtly political terms, or asserted in a discourse of solutions. These would be social portraits in their own right, and the function of the prologue would be lost in that case. The function of the prologue is to prefigure the democratic stake in difference, anticipating the main text, implying from the outset both the necessity and limits of science. It is the prologue that heralds the nature of the textual work on the part of author and reader alike necessary to defending the main text from misreading as escapist exoticism (cf. diLeonardo 1998; Richards 1994). In short, prologues issue their own declarations as to the significance of particularity. Power, race, recognition, and migration loom large in these statements.

Cast as subjective orientation toward the project on the part of the author (rather than methods per se, or findings), these framings serve as screens against which the book's main action becomes visible as a production of the discipline—predicated on the author's making a performance of renouncing his or her subjectivity. Some authors integrate their accounts of the research (with its implicit license to write in the first person) along with their critical prologues; another conventional organization places the description of project goals and methods at the end of the prologue or the beginning of the main text. A more minor convention places the account of the research at the end of the book, in an appendix or epilogue. In any of these textual locations, the story of the ethnography's making can be read as both the extension of the author's announced concerns and a critique of the limits of science.

In this general context, the first-person singular of ethnographic prologues borrows heavily from the autobiographical and testimonial traditions of African American and Latino literature and their critical functions as oppositional discourse. Whether new or only newly available, the literary traditions of opposition were quickly assimilated as discursive templates for the textual breaks crucial to U.S. ethnography's critical self-positioning. The influence of Du Bois, Fanon, Ellison, and Anzaldúa, as well as the more diffuse impact of feminist narrative, is apparent in these textual settings. This is not to say that anthropologists did not write prologues before African American and ethnic studies awakened new readers to the potency of these literary forms and their interpretive demands. But they do appear to have absorbed a critical discourse that effectively resignified the elements of normal ethnographic practice in a way that made plain the works' critical charge.

Like fictional figurations of authorship, contemporary ethnographic authors entice readers to identify with the narrator; however, unlike fictional authors, ethnographers do not have to compete for authority within the text. Fictional author-personae are central to their own stories, but ethnographic author-personae tend to be only marginal participants, exerting their eventual narrative control over or through the textual immobility of their subjects. Quotation and indirect discourse re-animate that stillness, marking speech (and by extension written text) as a form of social action. Thus (for example),

Freeman is careful to stipulate that the Vietnamese refugees' narratives that comprise most of his account are not to be read as merely individual stories, but as a critical historiography of the Vietnam War and corrective to American myths of assimilation and upward mobility (Freeman 1989: ch. 1; also pt. 7).

Sometimes the roles are reversed, and it is the ethnographer who (in the prologue) evokes his or her immobility. For example, Susan Harding writes that she did not convert (in the course of her study of evangelical Protestantism) but "the Holy Spirit dealt with me" (2000: xi): "For years, I stood at the crossroads that [the minister] and others fashioned for me, in between being lost and being saved, listening" (xi). But in either case (to borrow a phrase from the title of Harding's first chapter), "speaking is believing"—and writing is witnessing. In this sense, the revelation of the authorial first person in the prologue is a structural device (not an autobiographical inevitability) to help readers anticipate the interpretive and critical demands of the work (especially to anticipate the significance of first-person testimony quoted in the main text). The play of the ethnographer as first-person singular against the wider collectivity (however this may be framed) in the prologue ushers the reader into the main text through a process of solidarity in Durkheim's sense of the term (1933).

The principal mechanism of such mirroring involves the ethnographer's use of the pronoun "we"—as in, again, Catherine Lutz's prologue: "We all inhabit an army camp, mobilized to lend support to the permanent state of war readiness that has been with us since World War II" (Lutz 2001: 3). This use of the first-person plural is distinctive to U.S. ethnography. Though it may appear to be (again) simply an artifact of the rhetorical demands of writing about the United States for an audience largely "at home," or simply the pedagogical function of the text itself, the pervasive "we" of U.S. ethnographers' prologues can be read in relation to the radically constitutive "we" of high American public rhetoric—originating in the Declaration of Independence (see White 1990 and Ferguson 1984). This is high federal rhetoric, the textual opening for theorizing the United States through (for example) an ethnography of "disillusionment" (Mahler 1995: 3) or of the "fictional worlds" of official discourse—"worlds in which the institutional discourses have only a fictional relationship to the actions taken by those institutions" (Wagner-Pacifici 1994: 7), thereby constituting a space of danger. Indeed, the evocation of the "we" posits federal discourse as the theoretical object for U.S. ethnography, which accordingly takes place in "the small cracks between discourse and violence" (Wagner-Pacifici 1994: x). But the fine grain of those portrayals should not be misread as endorsing detail for its own sake. The function of the prologues critically reworks the representational discourse of anthropology as a critical repertoire of signs in which readers can become fluent once they understand description as ironizing the high federal rhetoric of equality, particularly in its marketized expressions.

If the "we" of ethnographic prologues and epilogues is an intertextual reference to the documentary sources of high federal rhetoric, it also accounts for the presentism of most U.S. ethnographies. To be sure, the ethnographic present (collapsing all description into the present tense) is a pervasive feature of ethnography in general, and the suspension of history and temporality in ethnographic writing is a critical issue of long standing (see esp. Fabian 1983; Comaroff and Comaroff 1992; Moore 1987). But in U.S. ethnography, the ethnographic present has particular functions—literary functions: to heighten the sense of the present by formulating the effects of discourse as a current and concrete reality, and (literally) re-presenting that reality as the makings of a political moment. The present tense performs the discursive disjuncture that is the work's means and ends: "The American present is another country" (diLeonardo 1998: 1). The timespace of U.S. ethnography is achieved through these textual forms even apart from whatever historical specificity unfolds within the work (for example, as intergenerational relationships, or the development of a social movement or the consequences of an event).

The literary presentation of U.S. ethnography is therefore integral both to its ethical demands and its theoretical claims, to the extent that both are conceived as inviting readers to engage critically—and to take active part in transforming—a national discourse. From this standpoint, localized studies such as ethnographies of urban communities are methodologically but not theoretically distinguishable (at least on these grounds) from the discourse-centered studies more commonly associated with postmodernism. In either case, the author's appeal to the reader is for a transformative identification of the reader with the people who are the main focus of the account—but through (that is, with) the author. In this respect, the ethnographer takes up the position created by the diaspora author but without relinquishing the claim to speak both for and to—not a universal audience—but primarily implicitly white Americans (see Sartre on Richard Wright for the historical and critical specificity of this construal of an author's role [1988: 78–80]). This is an ethical tactic of exposing complicity. To paraphrase Sartre, the ethnographer, by means of these textual conventions, "gives society a guilty conscience" (1988: 81; emphasis omitted). But in this context, conscience is a force of history, as Ruth Frankenberg suggests in the dedication of her book: "This work is dedicated to those who struggle for a day beyond racism—to a time when this book will be read as history and not as a study of the present" (Frankenberg 1993).

Ethnographic prologues also constitute anthropology's disciplinary conventions as integral to the discourse in question, although they also participate in it. More accurately, then, prologues announce the nature of the author's ambivalence and the location of his or her critical departures. Significantly, one refrain is the inadequacy of received notions of ethnographic fieldwork. To take just one powerful example, John Jackson's preface to *Harlem World* (2001) includes a trenchant critique of classic methods of social anthropology and sociology in the form of key informant interviewing and standard questionnaires—masked as a self-deprecating personal narrative of his own adaptation to his fieldsite in Harlem. These lines suggest the flavor of the account:

> I wanted to find some special Harlemite whose life would exemplify the entire place. This person would be my "key informant," someone who would show me all that I needed to know about the neighborhood and its inhabitants. Once I hit the pavement, however, I didn't find that person. Instead, I found folks who often wouldn't speak to me, didn't care what I was doing, didn't have the time to think about answering my silly little questions, and didn't necessarily seem to represent Harlem at all—at least not the Harlem I had in my mind or in my research proposal. This fact prompted me to walk Harlem's streets for weeks without a purpose or a clue long before I started my actual fieldwork. (J. L. Jackson 2001: x; paragraph break omitted)

Another refrain is the unexpected demands of authorship. For example:

> This is not the story I set out to record when I first arrived on Long Island to do fieldwork in the summer of 1989. Rather, as happens to many anthropologists, I found that my informants pulled me in directions I had not anticipated pursuing, or at least following, as far as I ultimately did. The principal force that led me to diverge from my original path was the profound, ubiquitous dissatisfaction these immigrants

expressed regarding their experiences in the United States. Though, as I shall argue in detail, they are intensely alienated from mainstream America and its institutions, they focus their resentment on each other, largely exonerating the greater society. (Mahler 1995: 1)

Or this evocation of the limits of the profession within a broader sense of ethnographic possibility: "This chapter exists nowhere in my fieldnotes, or even my letters home to friends and relatives. . . . Most of what is in this chapter is not on tape because it is about things I did not think were anthropology" (Small 1997: 101). Or belatedly, as a reconciliation of professional and personal selves: "This is a tale about Indians and whites living together in a small Iowa community. It is also about an anthropologist returning to his hometown and boyhood memories. The idea for this book came to me during my twenty-fifth high school reunion" (Foley 1995: vii).

Such evocations of the unexpected establish a textual opening for reflection about the nature of anthropology, consistently to link the creative expansion of ethnographic genres to the advancement of the discipline, and even to a better world. These connections are explicit in these further examples: "There is currently considerable debate over what an ethnography study really is. Some still think of ethnographies as objective scientific studies. Others, like me, have lost faith in this grand ideal. I now think of ethnographies more as personal encounters. I make no claims that the tale I am about to spin is absolutely true. I have worked hard to make it more fact than fiction, but as in all so-called factual books, I am characterizing people as I see them" (Foley 1995: ix). And this passage, defending experimentation as an advance on realism:

> Postmodern ethnographers . . . write "messy" texts in which one need not see linear arguments or time sequences. People may contradict one another or interrupt one another in the text, and no one voice holds the premium on the truth. What is real or "true" is socially constructed and culture, like knowledge, is a product of social discourse. As a result, an ethnography will try to represent the range and sources of those different constructions, including the background of the anthropologist which has influenced how he or she constructs the text (reflexivity) and the different voices within a culture that express what is true (multivocality). Marcus has argued directly that new ethnographic forms—such as postmodernism—are really attempts

to grapple with the realities of the postcolonial world, to engage the complexity of twentieth-century relationships. I agree. (Small 1997: 222 ns. 8 and 9; note numbers and references omitted)

Or this critique of the profession and its gatekeeping controls over pedagogy and reward structures:

> Always, as an anthropologist, you go elsewhere, but the voyage is never simply about making a trip. . . . Loss, mourning, the longing for memory, the desire to enter into the world around you and having no idea how to do it, the fear of observing too coldly or too distractedly or too raggedly, the rage of cowardice, the insight that is always arriving late . . . a sense of the utter uselessness of writing anything and yet the burning desire to write something, are the stopping places along the way. . . .
>
> But surely this is not the anthropology being taught in our colleges and universities? . . . And definitely it isn't the anthropology that will win you a grant from the National Science Foundation. Nor, to be perfectly honest, is it the anthropology I usually tell people I do. . . . People, say, like my Aunt Rebeca, who is asking me . . . why I went into anthropology.
>
> No sé decirte cómo fué . . . I was very young. . . . I wanted to write. (Behar 1996: 2–3; ellipses in the last paragraph are in the original text)

In this passage, the profession is a fantasy that has dissolved into reality:

> I have thus ended up writing the ironic obverse of my 1970s fantasy book. Instead of detailing the changing, power-saturated worlds of anthropology's Third World objects . . . I have written a Red Tour of the changing and connected worlds of American anthropological production as they have—and have not—intersected with the histories and popular representations of racial, ethnic, and gendered exotic and domestic Others. These linked histories provide an alternative Archimedean standpoint from which we then can envision American and all other social realities anew. . . . As Dorothy remarked in another context, there's no place like home. (diLeonardo 1998: 15)

Kath Weston plays on this convention, to locate the critical element of surprise within social science, exposing disciplinary strategies of denial: "*Long*

Slow Burn builds upon this legacy by repositioning sexuality at the heart of the social sciences. If sexuality is already deeply embedded in the topics and debates that constitute social science's stock-in-trade, then more explicit attention to those aspects of social life marginalized as 'just sex' has the potential to reconfigure conventional analysis along more productive lines" (Weston 1998: 3). These "I"s—from a spectrum of anthropological prose experiments—establish interpretive toeholds that carry across from prologue to main text. Wherever "I" speaks, such evocations reverberate; "I" speaks again in the epilogue or envoi—but there, verging on "we." Importantly, the ethnographer's narrative "I" in these accounts is not (or not only) the author's self, but the figuration of consciousness. The first-person singular, therefore, is not necessarily or self-evidently reflexive, but rather polysemic—at once citizen and social scientist—and thereby adjoining responsibility, judgment, ethnography, and its ethics to popular sovereignty and the public welfare.

The Method of the Middle: Genre, Means, and Ends

The main text of most 1990s accounts is also narrated in the first person, but here the focus shifts to the professional self, as something different than the authorial self of the prologue. The step from the prologue to the main text is a step into professionalism—a staged entry into a performance of discipline. The prologue will have trained the reader to receive the tone of the main text as a resolution to a problem at once professional, civic, and ethical. In contrast to prologues, the first-person narrator of the main text tends to be reserved, constrained, focused on conditions of knowledge generation (i.e., the data). But the performativity of *that* first-person singular—the social scientist at work—is, perhaps paradoxically, constructed of elements that borrow heavily from the discourse of liberal legalism (the autonomous legal subject) and literary technique. Ethnography, law, and fiction are intricately wound together in these works, each necessary to the other in sustaining the interpretive connection between identities and *American society*—through federal powers and the reading public.

The liberalism in these ethnographic narratives is not announced; rather, it is inherent in the dialogic functioning of the first person. At the same time, these aspects of the text render narrative politically ambiguous, in that it is positionality—not "self-expression" as such—that lends ethnography's braided lines of testimony their democratic allure. To explain: even though the main texts are arranged in such a way that the subject "speaks" for him- or herself, it is exclusively to the ethnographer. In other words, the only evidence of their wider recognition and acceptance is in the presence of the ethnographer in the conversation. Otherwise, the works confirm the pervasiveness of the community's misrecognition or even invisibility—in stark contrast to the very public fluency of the anthropologist (literally his or her publication and the implication of reception in markets of various kinds).

Thus, while the textual forms of ethnography might mimic the testimonial templates of citizenship (as a testifying witness, for example), they function as provocations, calling into question the empirical qualities of citizenship. As already noted, this is the textual context in which the anthropologist as first person is crucial to the ultimate import of the work: the ethnographer prefigures the nation. By the very ordinariness, almost happenstance, of his or her presence in the community, by acquiring knowledge and understanding through ordinary conversation, the anthropologist models attainments of a priori acceptance and attentiveness potentially possible for anyone—that is, a certain democratic practice. Brett Williams makes this possibility explicit in the *envoi* of her study of "stalled gentrification" in Washington, D.C.: "An ethnographic eye may naturally accompany the building of a densely overlapping life. . . . If we are to preserve variety in our cities, I believe that those of us who want to live in such areas have to take on that job, which is first of all the work of culture, and then we must try to link that cultural stand to broader, but also *deeper, dense, more textured, repetitive, and rooted* political action" (Williams 1988: 142–143).

Read in its own terms, then, the anthropological account represents both the means and ends of a more fully inclusive and responsive national society. The ambivalence as to means and ends is evident in the mixed messages of ethnographic realism, and here, too, the narrative "I" is a thread to follow. On the one hand, the salience of anthropologists' use of first-person testimony is less for its mimetic realism (as in the legal textualizations of narrative discussed elsewhere in this book) than as a gesture toward the significance of self-representation. Most prominent in this regard is the extent to which first-person narration inherently resists generalization *by others*. The first-person narration of and in ethnography is in this sense a gesture of resistance and refusal, marking the text as counter-hegemonic, to be read against the liberal conventions of representation by comparison (Fanon 1963: ch. 7). This, too, adds to the political complexity and ambiguity of U.S. ethnography in this critical period.

On the other hand, at the same time, mimetic realism is essential to ethnography's purpose as science. First-person narrative was key to both critical experimentation and scientific authority—eliding science and cultural critique. The necessity of such cover is perhaps unique to the circumstances of U.S. ethnography in this period, when departments fought and fell over so-called postmodernism—even then, a catch-all term for a wide range of experiments with positionality, problem-formation, and prose. For some audiences within the profession, it was the first-person narration of the main text that was key to the mobilization of ethnographic authority—the "I was there" element that makes an account credible as knowledge, and thereby worthy. But for wider audiences, whether within anthropology or beyond, it was the first-person narration of the prologue that was key—establishing a hierarchy of narration that "speaks" in the first person in the prologue and that makes the writtenness of the main text transparent. Authors and readers of such texts would have had ample opportunity to rehearse this canny doubling in their wider practices of reading across genres.

Indeed, this particular move is deeply resonant with the critical cultural studies then emergent as both ethnic and minority literary criticism, and the literatures with which they are engaged. The narration of fiction through a literary persona—that is, through a narrator who is him- or herself an author—anticipates precisely the same sort of agency ethnographers claim for themselves in proffering text as a form of political agency. In fiction, as in ethnography, first-person narration highlights the narrative organization of the work as embedded in the reality of unfolding time. In both genres, too, the first-person narrator provides readers with a counterpart, an interlocutor—perhaps even an object of transference. And in both genres, the "I" highlights the performative production of text (Johnson 2003: 12). These features might involve more poetic license in fiction, but they are more pronounced in ethnography, where, as already noted, the differentiation of first-person narrative registers is key to the works' narrative organization.

If ethnography borrows from fiction—wittingly or not—its proximity to fiction is perhaps most evident in the way first-person testimony constitutes the oppositional character of the works (the term "oppositional" in this context is Ramón Saldívar's [1990: 6]). Oppositionality is a recurring theme in the new criticism of the 1990s (Arredondo et al. 2003: 1–2; Chabram 1991; Krupat 1993: xix; Latina Feminist Group 2001: 2–6; Mitchell 1994; José David Saldívar 1991: 7, 82; Ramón Saldívar 1990: 6 and 1991: 20; Spillers 1991: 2). The referent of opposition is unstable—its very instability being evidence of the contingency of fictional meanings on the political sphere: "Grounded in our understanding of power as relational, we are working toward an explanatory matrix that confronts the shifting boundaries of discourse and captures ties to lived experiences" (Arredondo et al. 2003: 2; see also Chabram 1991: 127). The editors of *Chicana Feminisms* specify Chicana cultural criticism as oppositional relative to Chicanos and a "hegemonic feminist discourse" that singularizes gender, erasing race and class (Arredondo et al. 2003: 1–2; see also Saldívar-Hull 1991). The "structural locations and experiences" of opposition are wide-ranging, including the professoriate in Chicana studies and adjacent fields—Latina/o studies, ethnic studies, gender and feminist studies, and cultural studies (Arredondo et al. 2003: 3, 6, 11).[4] Similarly, and more broadly, Krupat celebrates "ethnocriticism" as an encounter or border with "Western anthropologicality" (Krupat 1993: xix).

Importantly for purposes of our discussion, such claims are themselves cast in relational terms—of indebtedness or alliance with the oppositional critique of new social movements. The refrain of those acknowledgments explicitly and mutually celebrates national and transnational civil rights and feminist movements (Arredondo et al. 2003: 3–4; Giddings 1984; Latina Feminist Group 2001: 3–4; Calderón and Saldívar 1991: 6).[5] These are not merely announcements of intellectual genealogy, but—to borrow from Patrick Johnson again—performances of political alignment. Self-identification as a rights-bearing subject is contingent on an identification with other beneficiaries of rights—specifically historically disadvantaged groups. This compounds the ironies of equating subjectivity with individuality, since the sense of subjectivity—even in the relatively narrow legal sense of the term—is predicated on both identifying with others (see Bhabha 1994: 1) and on particular conventions of literary representation.

Authors of fiction and ethnography are ordinarily on different sides of such gestures of identification—the author of fiction inviting a direct acknowledgment on the part of the reader, and the ethnographic author instead inviting recognition more cautiously through his or her presence in the field (and correspondingly in the text). This puts conflicting pressures on the ethnographic author—particularly in the context of the 1990s, as ethnographic authority became increasingly an issue within the profession. Many anthropologists addressed this dilemma through their prologues—brief evocations of the most pressing motivations, methods, and conundrums (theoretical and existential) of the research process.

Such statements give rise to dilemmas of their own, having to do with the calculated displacement of readers' identifications (whether with the author or "natives"). The gendered figuration of cross-cultural understanding—often cast as same-sex rapport (gender solidarity trumping cultural difference)—heightens the salience of the author's racial, class, and gender identity and makes it integral to his or her claims to effective methodology. The very "art" of ethnographic narrative in this sense leaves an opening for essentializing difference in an idiom of personal responsibility, moral awakening, and intellectual epiphany, as the warrant for "scientific" truth claims. David Richards points to the risks in such a maneuver: "What emerges . . . is a sense of discursive crisis from which the anthropologist's own subjectivity emerges as a guarantor of the truth of his text and the nobility of his intentions but which, in negotiating the pitfalls of representation, effaces the subject of discourse. The apprehension of the anthropologist's crisis of representation substitutes for the apprehension of his/her subject" (Richards 1994: 234).

But such a reading of representation seems to miss what U.S. ethnographers were attempting in the conspicuous scientism of their main texts: showing that it was precisely *representations* that their "subjects" suffered from—that is, not a substitution *in the text*, but a misrecognition *in the society at large*. The question of whether and how these meanings of representation are different necessarily takes into account the inseparability of ethnographers' methods, genres, and commitments—academic and otherwise—beyond the text. For ethnographers writing "at home" such conundrums cannot be avoided, but this is part of the appeal of such research, since (for the very reason of their intractability; Duneier 1992: 139–140) they hold out the prospect of a broad creative license—as broad as the gulf between what is thinkable and actual in the communities around us, viewed through ethnography as we know it and as it might yet become.

Main Texts, Main Points

In these works of the 1990s, the construction of anthropological knowledge as *also* moral and political agency is key to the books' ethical charge (see Benjamin 1998: 230–231). Attending to agency tended to insert a tacit national frame—via a prevailing theory of agency that made it an effect of individuals' participation in political and social structures, but reaching a vanishing point at national borders (for an influential statement, see Giddens 1986: esp. ch. 1). The reading experience in this sense seems designed as a purposive agentive exchange—a division of labor, or partnership, perhaps.[6] Such allusions to a sense of the social that contains author and reader cannot fail to include the ethnographic subject, as well—situating ethnography squarely (if tacitly) within a federal framework. The state framework is explicit in works that are more oriented toward social conflict—for example, Ginsburg on pro- and anti-abortion activists in Fargo, North Dakota (1989), Wagner-Pacifici on police discourse in Philadelphia's campaign against the MOVE organization (1994), Takezawa (1995) on the reparations movement among Japanese Americans in Seattle, Lutz (2001) on the militarization of Fayetteville, North Carolina (civilian host to Fort Bragg), Gregory on neighborhood activism in Queens (1998), Sanjek on neighborhood government in New York City (1998).

Indirectly, the federal state is ethnographically near, too, in anthropologists' work on law—an expanding field in this same period, their ethnographic questions focusing on community identifications with law, the moralization of legal order, and the demand for law (e.g., Engel 1983; Greenhouse 1986; Greenhouse, Yngvesson, and Engel 1994; Merry 1990; Mertz and Bowman 1996; Nader 1980; Yngvesson 1993). A commonality of discourse is apparent in these works with respect to the mutual implication of law use and identity—as evidenced in the expansion of sociolegal studies around identity issues at this time. State agencies are for the most part absent at the level of description, yet still present discursively—as discussed earlier, in the way community is constructed as local cultural difference is against the foil of a national society. Major exceptions to this trend were new studies of community-based social movements (Gregory 1998; Sanjek 1998) and neighborhood development (Jackson 2001).

Most of the new ethnographic works in the 1990s examined the experience of new immigrants, that is, immigrants since 1975, especially from southeast Asia (Freeman 1989), East Asia (Chen 1992; Park 1997), South Asia (Leonard 1992), the Philippines, Oceania (Small 1997), Central and South America (Coutin 2000; Kasinitz 1992; Laguerre 1984; Mahler 1995; Margolis 1994) and the Caribbean (Bourgois 1995; Brown 1991; Urciuoli 1996) (see also Peshkin 1991; Shokeid 1988). There were also new monographs on second-generation or older ethnic communities (e.g., Yanagisako 1985; Takezawa 1995).

Judging from their prefaces and epilogues, these works seemed to have been directly inspired by world developments—new patterns of global capitalism and "cultural flows" (Appadurai 1996)—but the texts for the most part concentrate on the local experiences of singular groups, emphasizing the contingencies and asymmetries of their absorption into the life of city.

In framing their studies around singular ethnic identities, ethnographers conspicuously draw on the dominant national narrative of immigration (analyzed by Chock 1987, 1989, 1991; Urciuoli 1994)—and indeed to the specific categories of the U.S. census form. This is perhaps the most obvious evidence of ethnographers' reliance on federal discourse for key elements of their own lexicons. Individual works tend to treat "groups" as bounded social units (e.g., in presenting a study "of" this or that ethnic group in a particular location). Read cumulatively—which they seem never to be—these same accounts suggest that this is not the case, and that the meanings of race and ethnicity are highly unstable, even for new immigrants. Taken together, the ethnographies suggest what sorts of experiences—both negative and positive—provisionally settle the meanings of "identity": discrimination in public places (e.g., in schools, among hostile neighbors, or at a workplace), competition for jobs, housing and social services, the solidarity of language communities and their rapid dispersal over generations, the search for a spouse and the process of raising a family, and so on. These refrains transcend the singularity of experience, and indeed make evident the nature of the ethnographers' task—to convey experience as simultaneously singular and general, local and national, national and transnational. Understanding both the necessity and the choreography of the ambiguity of these polarities is key to grasping the theoretical and comparative claims of the works.

The localism of U.S. monographs also yields significant evidence of how these works are keyed to federal discourse. Studies of social conflict and law in action are intensely localized, as jurisdiction figures prominently at the level of description and analysis (e.g., as neighborhoods, municipalities, and in the elision of culture and country). Community studies of identity achieve their sense of locale differently—more figuratively, suspending the actuality of legal jurisdiction yet retaining the connection through portraiture that renders identity agonistically as difference relative to the larger public. In this respect, the ethnographic turn to communities in the 1990s echoes a prominent gesture of the civil rights architects of the 1950s and 1960s—turning to sites where agonism and antagonism converge in the demand for federal relief from discrimination. One implication of ethnography's constitution of the author-reader relation through narrative organization is the extent to which anthropology's knowledge work functions as a placeholder for a particular vision of federal agency through law.

The architects of the 1960s civil rights era in a sense remapped the U.S. landscape, placing the federal state above the member states in novel ways that had to be justified in constitutional terms (Gunther 1991: 147–151, esp. 149–150). The crafters of the Civil Rights Act of 1964 answered critics who challenged the constitutionality of federal legislation by invoking the Commerce Clause of the U.S. Constitution. The Commerce Clause requires the federal government to protect interstate commerce, and modern forms of mobility (interstate highways, for example) were the sociological premise behind the proponents' support for a federal implication in local establishments. The new federal landscape was in effect a moral geography as well as a moral order of modernity in which local Southern communities were explicitly constructed (e.g., by the U.S. Supreme Court in *Brown*) as backward (anti-modern) in relation to the inherent modernism of federal civil rights law enforcement.[7] The localizing strategies of modern ethnographers similarly use landscape for its moral significance, the moral authority of the ethnographer him- or herself bound up in his/her ability to cross the very borders that the civic community pretends are unbridgeable.

Even while they tend to dissolve the time and space around the study site, community studies in the United States are cast as direct appeals to general readers. As noted above, the general reader is a citizen—and, in practice, an anthropologist addressed as a citizen. This compaction of expertise with public responsibility and personal ethics is key to the efficacy of these accounts. In a prologue or epilogue or both, the author invites readers to envision this community in some affirmative relation to the society at large. Tolerance, economics, and democracy are the touchstones of such visions. Bracketed by prefaces and endings in these terms, the moves from opening to main text and from main text to closing provide a pair of performances—one from a personal discourse to a discourse of discipline; the other from discipline to personal hope. These are performances of conversion, accomplished through the works' narrative structure. The conversion is to citizenship: the ethnographer's identification with readers (in the prologue or preface), the ethnographer's performance of learning and liberal tolerance (the main text), the ironically hopeful endings envisioning democracy's increase (the conclusion, final paragraph, or epilogue) invite readers, literally and figuratively, to turn the page. The first-person singular thus escapes the text—and this is the object of the exercise.

By methods such as these, the narrative structure of the monographs is organized around desire and disappointment in the American dream (see Ashcroft, Griffiths, and Tiffin 1989). Read cumulatively, their refrain is striking: the elusiveness of equality and opportunity across ethnic and racial groups, as well as the widening income gap *within* racial and ethnic communities. The "refrain" does not announce itself—that is, beyond the fundamental urban condition that makes these projects possible as community studies in the first place. Otherwise, it emerges mainly in an accumulation of sometimes passing references in the course of a cumulative reading, as neighborhood is added to neighborhood, community to community.[8]

It is only in the repetition of passing references in books read seriatim that a window opens onto key developments of the time, that a glance can become a timespace: we are looking at the increasing gap between the rich and the poor; the significant decline in real wages; the resegregation of U.S. cities and suburbs; the feminization of poverty; the criminalization of identity; the expansion of poverty among the full-time employed; the lessened impact of education on personal income prospects; the political imperatives linking welfare to work, and immigration to costs; the shift of employment in the major cities from manufacturing into the service sector, and into the suburbs; the high rates of uninsured or underinsured in the cities, and the crisis of self-care—these are some of the developments that surface in the spaces within the monographs.

It is clear that U.S. ethnographers seek to engage the reading public through their everyday understandings of the new discourse of identity circulating in policy debate, turning these back toward other more positive meanings. But their address was not just *to* the public; it was also *through* the public. The context of the time supports a reading of the work as addressed to the federal powers—in particular, as a counterweight to the discursive framings of neoliberalism around individual choice, and the rewriting of the connections between race and class as an aggregate effect of individual choices. These aims are sometimes explicit, especially in relation to welfare and immigration after the enactment of the 1996 reforms (see, for example, Coutin 2000; Goode and Maskovsky 2001; Morgen and Maskovsky 2003; see also J. L. Jackson 2001). Most of the anthropological community studies of the United States during the late 1980s and 1990s are located in the major cities along the Atlantic and Pacific coasts—and most of these in New York City. Cities have always been prominent in the sociological and ethnographic traditions of the United States as studies of "urban problems," and the performance of continuity was important to the legitimacy claims of this new work. But now cities are also featured in new ways, keyed to current developments. Most prominently, the striking rising trends in migration (affecting North America and Europe similarly) were overwhelmingly to a few urban centers.

Migration is a municipal issue in practice—notwithstanding its politicization in national terms. In 1990, the U.S. Census identified ten cities in which more than half the population was foreign-born; 80 percent of all migrants lived in ten states, with one-third in California and 14 percent in New York State.[9] At the same time, domestic migration was also on the upswing, yielding for the first time a society that was primarily suburban and exurban.

As these peri-urban areas became wealthier and more white, cities became more diverse ethnically and racially, as well as economically—in contrast to the stereotype that made the so-called inner city uniformly poor and African American. The same census data show a wide range of needs more prominent in the urban core as compared to the suburbs and beyond: larger extended families, more generations living together, more residents living at home with disabilities, more chronic illness (U.S. Department of Commerce 1990). Urban employment was down, as the increasingly service-oriented economy shifted investment to suburban and rural areas, and multinational firms specifically selected for rural or small urban populations (see L. Graham 1995: esp. ch. 2).

Meaning and Democracy

For ethnographers of the United States, the self-evident value of the appeal to conscience is anchored to specific assumptions about the contingency of textual meaning on democratic culture: "The art of prose is bound up with the only régime in which prose has meaning, democracy. When one is threatened, the other is too. And it is not enough to defend them with the pen. A day comes when the pen is forced to stop, and the writer must then take up arms. Thus, however, might have come to it, whatever the opinions you might have professed, literature throws you into battle. Writing is a certain way of wanting freedom; once you have begun, you are committed, willy-nilly" (Sartre 1988: 69). Indeed, the fictional persona of the author functions in just this way, to engage the reader with precisely the question of what comes after the text—one thinks of Ellison's nameless protagonist in *Invisible Man* (1952), or Morrison's Claudia in *The Bluest Eye* (1972). The broad emergence of diasporic literary studies as formal academic programs in the 1990s sustained a powerful vision of literature as essential to a progressive public sphere specific to U.S. experience. For example:

> The narratives of Chicano men and women are predominantly critical and ideological. This does not mean that they simply rep-

resent a given set of doctrines or dogmas. Rather, it means that as oppositional ideological forms Chicano narratives signify the imaginary ways in which historical men and women live out their lives in a class society, and how the values, concepts, and ideas purveyed by the mainstream, hegemonic American culture that tie them to their social functions seek to prevent them from attaining a true knowledge of society as a whole. (Ramón Saldívar 1990: 6)

At the same time, the globalization of cultural media sustained transnational cultural studies that both called into question the association of difference and oppression (Chow 1993: 14) and the counter-hegemonic claims of cultural studies (Pollack 1992: esp. intro., ch. 9, and 244–245; Wing 2000).

In anthropology, however indebted the figuration of authorship might be to the textual conventions of fiction in this regard, the question of "what next" (or, for that matter, "what now?") has its own long history in the discourse of solutions, and has been more pressing in sociological terms. The evocation of collectivity that serves as the foil for the author's self-disclosure is the legacy of that discourse—designed to respond to the question, "What is to be done?" The inevitably literary project of social criticism in this sense confronts ethnographers with the question of the limits of liberalism.

The ethnography of the United States illuminates a more general situation in anthropology as discipline and profession—that is, the preeminence of text as both means and ends of ethnographic theorizing. The root metaphor of culture as text was put forward by Clifford Geertz (1973), and notwithstanding the profound influence of his formulation (or perhaps because of it) it was subsequently widely criticized as an aestheticization of power, even escapism. This was already a long critical tradition within anthropology by the 1990s. David Richards's critique captures well its essential terms: "As anthropology has found each of its inventions to be unworkable or unacceptable it has abandoned its claims to science and relocated itself within the refuge of the arts. If it is no longer possible to write 'science,' it is still possible to write 'texts'" (Richards 1994: 226; cf. Moore 1980: intro.).

The manicheism of this formulation—that is, dividing intellectual practice into an art/science binary, and making *power* accessible from science alone—is by no means Richards's alone. It is fundamental to the epistemological debates within anthropology in the 1990s, often under the rubric of debates about relevance—code for postmodernism. DiLeonardo, writing more broadly, turns anthropology's critical literariness back on itself, concluding that "scholarship, like art, cannot stand in for political activism. . . . It is time to speak truth to, to make demands of power" (1998: 367). Not surprisingly, perhaps—even in its bitter intensity—the discipline's debates over postmodernism through the mid-nineties were displaced debates over the limits of liberalism, in a political context in which the old New Deal liberalism had all but disappeared. Indeed, that the term "culture" is presumed always to be coupled to the silent qualifier "other" is crucial to understanding the precarious place of U.S. ethnography in anthropology (Richards 1994: 225). Richards offers the image of "the third eye" for the interpretive anthropologist's (synecdochically Geertz, implicitly masculine) position as "both author and hero of [his] text, father and suitor" (Richards 1994: 223).

For Richards, difference doubles as anthropology's object and its principal trope (1994: ch. 7, esp. 222–223), posing not only an epistemological problem but also a problem of narration: "At a fundamental level, the third eye constructs its narrative upon the foundations of a romantic paradox which states that others are a complete enigma and are transparent to us and that metaphors can be rededicated as metonymies to accomplish the magical acts of science. There would seem to be no clearer indication of the fictional nature of anthropological discourse than the hidden assumptions that the world is an enigma which can be known but which remains an enigma none the less" (Richards 1994: 225; note omitted). The stake in "the fictional nature of anthropological discourse" might at first seem to be equality on a global scale. Richards writes: "However much 'we' as readers may wish to approach the native on equal terms, the textual operations by which 'we' come to know their difference renders 'us' as indelibly dominant" (1994: 222).

But embedded in Richards's formulation is a significant slippage of the arts/science binary, since the hierarchy constituted by (as?) ethnographic narrative is intertextual, not intersubjective. By this I mean that ethnography as text evokes the conventions of narration, location, and agency derived principally from nineteenth- and twentieth-century literary forms—earlier ethnography, to be sure, but also novels, travel writing, and so forth (Richards 1994: 227). That such literary compositions might be implicated in an intersubjective order—politics in the broadest sense of the term—suggests that between art and science, something else intervenes. Indeed, it is only if one ignores or denies the discursivity of power that art and science can be imagined as encompassing all inquiry. The literary realism that pervades anthropology as the narrative basis of its scientific value also circulates as textual and critical conventions in law. Sociolegal studies and legal theory, not surprisingly, have felt their own versions of the developments discussed in this chapter (see Gordon 1982) and in the modern state's "visibility" as a social force (Corrigan and Sayer 1985). To imagine *text* as something other than life—with the power left in—is to essentialize identity and deny the force of law in relation to rights; it is the centrality of race and rights to U.S. experience that makes the United States a particularly appropriate context to examine such questions. Be that as it may, the escapism ascribed to interpretive anthropologists can be turned back on its critics, since it is they who imagine the possibility of art without power, and without "other" knowledges.

Richards is skeptical of anthropological realism in this regard. Quoting M. H. Abrams, he defines realism as a form of "fiction" that "give[s] the reader the illusion of actual and ordinary experience" (Richards 1994: 227). He adds: "The application of the literary conventions of realism to anthropology founders upon the fact that classic realist novels confidently assert that there is nothing within the text which is 'different' from anything outside the text. . . . Anthropology assumes the exact opposite, that the social world described is, above all else, different. Anthropology is anthropology and not realism because what is in the text is predicated upon the fact of its difference" (227–228; emphasis omitted).

But the difference that Richards envisions is not the defining pretext of the ethnography of the United States. As we have seen, attention to difference is an important feature of U.S. ethnography but it is secondary to inequality. That is, U.S. ethnography turns to difference not for its own sake but as a means of demonstrating the incompleteness of American democracy. Whereas American anthropologists whose main concerns are outside the United States might imagine the textual accumulation of anthropology as both sign and symbol of the totality of cultures in global terms, U.S. ethnographers tend to take the nation as their frame. Ethnography (perhaps anywhere) is always predicated toward the future. The narrative distinction between prologue, main text, and epilogue is the temporal break that establishes a parallel between the author's discovery (as awakening or conversion, as evoked in the prologue) and the imagined impact of such knowledge (evoked in the envoi) when—read by an audience of fellow-citizens—the substance of the main text is no longer arcane.

Thus, the critical thrust of Richards's analysis of ethnographic writing must be complicated in relation to the case of U.S. ethnography:

> Speech seems to offer anthropology the opportunity to validate its textualisation of primitive culture. . . . The speaking subject's freedom

of speech is a part of the validation since free speech is implicit in the
ideology of western democracy which gave rise to the myth of origins
as a primitive utopia of speech without tyranny. In this way authority
is approved by the subject's authentic voice of acquiescence. . . . Yet it
is the very idea of the freedom of speech of the speaking subject which
undermines and invalidates the use of written testimonies as a means
of achieving an authentic picture of primitive societies. . . . Speech is
valued not as evidence, but as accent (Richards 1994: 230–231).

The democratic ideology that Richards finds to be reflexively (and implicitly) embedded in anthropologists' deployment of informants' speech is—in
the U.S. case—also explicit in the narrative framing of the work itself and in
the textual construction of the presumed audience. The ethnographic tex-
tualization of spoken narrative mirrors the democratic "meaning" of speech
in national terms. "The world of the text" = the world in the nation—the
very opposite of what Richards regards as the classic ethnographic scenario:
"The timbre of authenticity produces the effect of snatching this voice from
its body, from its world, from the very context the anthropologist's representation of which it is there to underwrite. The primitive speaking subject
inhabits, not the world of living beings, but the world of the text" (Richards
1994: 231).

That said, Richards captures well the sense in which U.S. ethnography in
the 1990s can be read as a postcolonial project: "Dislocated postcolonial identities cannot be constructed outside representation, except as absence. The
space outside representation is an ellipsis, 'silence'. The space inside is filled
with the rejected discourses of 'the philosophical tradition of identity' and 'the
anthropological view of the difference of human identity'" (Richards 1994:
258; unreferenced quotations in original). U.S. ethnography—especially at
its most experimental, critical, or disappointed—features such silences. Even
if (or rather, even *as*) ethnographers ally themselves with diasporic cultural
studies in embracing the ambiguity of "native" and "observer," the persistence
of the national public is inherent in the very notion of *public*—as in *public
sphere*—that animates these works. Still, it is not at all clear that "the end of
the dominance of the nation-state" is "augured" in the flourishing of transnational and postcolonial cultural studies—at least in the United States (quoted
passages are from Chuh 2003: 3).

In this chapter, I have considered the self-identification of ethnographers
as authors as a figuration of citizenship in the public sphere. Deploying such

figurations and establishing their interpretive salience in their prologues, ethnographers open a critical subtext within their work. The function of prologues might be to break away from the "rejected discourses" of identity (to borrow Richards's phrase) —the culture of poverty, social inferiority, welfare dependence, ethnic primordialism, and so forth. In doing so, they resituate identity as a critical evocation of the failures of federal policy and the deceptions of the federal discourse of solutions. The first person of the prologue is not contained there; indeed, it cannot be. The demonstration of that impossibility is part of the prologue's function. How an ethnographer manages that over-spilling of intention into meaning in the main text depends on how he or she chooses to perform the discipline—and this in turn depends on how an author construes its limits (see, for example, Rose 1989; Small 1997; Behar 1996; diLeonardo 1998; among others).

From between the prologue and the main text as these are held apart by the techniques of fiction and the performance of science, liberal law emerges as the missing term—the key to the significance of voice. Law cannot answer questions of equality or mobility by itself, but it defines the working terms of public debate, establishing certain parameters of whatever it is that *relevance* might mean to an anthropologist. The limits are set in part by the author's understanding of the limits of the political sphere. In this connection, writing about "the English-Spanish boundary" among Puerto Ricans in New York, Urciuoli (1996) draws attention to the stakes in anthropology's discursive dependence on terms of relevance borrowed from the officialized language of government: "If the terms of cultural definition are *explicitly* about class immobility and domination, then race cannot be turned into ethnicity, and domination is more readily recognized for what it is. When the terms of cultural definition are explicitly about class mobility as every individual's moral imperative and when race can be recast as ethnic-American identity, then social domination is not easily recognized, and it is much more difficult to resist" (Urciuoli 1996: 174). In this regard, the monographs, read individually and cumulatively, issue a mixed message. They lean toward contestation from the prologue, toward reconciliation from the envoi. In between, they perform their discipline, cleaving to the zone where their descriptive practices and key terms meld ethnographic convention with the discourse of public debate over civil rights, welfare, and immigration. But the story lines differ, ethnography reworking the pejorative construction of *culture* that had been deployed to declare the horizons of opportunity *open,* and telling another story.

CHAPTER 5

The Discourse of Solutions

The community study of the 1990s revived one of anthropology's classic literary forms. As such, it was also part of a broader literary revival featuring anthropology, sociology, and diasporic fiction as publishers reprinted numerous works from the 1960s for new markets in U.S. cultural studies—including several works discussed in this book. Those monographs, novels, and essays lived again in the 1990s but in very changed times. Important distinctions between the older and newer studies include the new works' evidence of the social isolation of individuals and families, the difference between capital insertion and social inclusion, and the strain on the very concept of relevance—as mainstream political discourse spun away from older ideas of relief. In this sense, the revival of the community study in the 1990s can be read as an ironic commentary on the classic community study of the previous generation—borrowing its form, setting, and themes, but conspicuously not the arc of the story line after the book ends.

The community study—in the earlier period or more recently—makes plain the promise and limits of aligning social description with the discourse of federal political debate. I call that project of alignment *the discourse of solutions*. The classic examples of the discourse of solutions are Gunnar Myrdal's *An American Dilemma* (1995 [1945]) or the Moynihan Report (U.S. Department of Labor 1965)—assessments of "the Negro problem" in terms that undertake to inform federal policy as an exercise in social engineering. Closer to the tone, form, and critical implications of the 1990s ethnography, however, were the works strongly critical of Myrdal and Moynihan in their own times. In this chapter, we sample both eras.

We begin with critics—represented here by novelist Ralph Ellison and anthropologist Elliott Liebow—who challenged those mainstream assessments by contesting the root assumption that "the problem" and its potential solutions lay within an African American psyche damaged by a dysfunctional community culture. In related but different ways, Ellison and Liebow insist on the flaws in that analysis, drawing their respective interpretive questions through the intricate interconnections of identity, poverty, and power. For them, the issue—*contra* Myrdal and Moynihan—was disempowerment. Thus they looked for solutions in the political sphere, initially at the community level where individuals are known to themselves and others through linked personal experiences, and their voices can actually be heard.

We then turn to a modern classic, by anthropologist Philippe Bourgois (1995), reading it for signs of more recent times. Like the earlier accounts, this book develops around issues of disempowerment and stigma, but Bourgois also gives explicit attention to the discursive shift of the 1990s from the standpoint of its implications for ethnographic practice. As national politicians moved toward technocratic solutions in a neoliberal mode, the most basic tenets of anthropology acquired a critical valence. Identity as an identification with others, relationships as partnerships, the indeterminacy of norms and values, and the priority on communication (conversation, self-narrative, and self-expression in the broadest sense)—all of these are core elements of ethnographic practice that by the 1990s were missing from the mainstream accountings of communities at the margins.

The Myrdal Problem: Ralph Ellison

In 1994, fifty years after it was written for—and rejected by—the *Antioch Review*, Ralph Ellison published his searing review of Myrdal's *An American Dilemma* (1945) in his own collection of essays, *Shadow and Act*. *An American Dilemma* was a massive study commissioned by the Carnegie Foundation for the purpose of examining the social roots of African American poverty. In his response to Myrdal, Ellison argues the very premise of the study. He counters with a formulation of "the Negro problem" as the figuration of a critical absence, a missed confrontation "between the Left and the Right" (1994: 313): "In our culture the problem of the irrational, that blind spot in our knowledge of society where Marx cries out for Freud and Freud for Marx, but where approaching, both grow wary and shout insults lest they actually meet, has taken the form of the Negro problem" (1994: 311). Ellison's pregnant observation points to the way race figures in the organization of knowledge—indeed, the very legitimacy of knowledge practices—and not just as the symptom (or for some, the cause) of social problems.

In Ellison's rendering, the flaw in Myrdal's thesis is that "the Negro's entire life and, consequently, also his [i.e., Myrdal's] opinions on the Negro problem are, in the main, to be considered as secondary reactions to more primary pressures from the side of the dominant white majority" (315). In the ethnography of the 1990s, the repositioning of culture from the negative to the positive was not altogether a rejection of Myrdal's account, since the effects of discrimination and neglect are everywhere in the works. At the same time, the works are explicitly offered as appreciations of culture understood in terms other than victimage and moral deficit.

Ellison continues: "But can a people . . . live and develop for over three hundred years simply by reacting? Are American Negroes simply the creation of white men, or have they at least helped to create themselves out of what they found around them?" (315; cf. Ellison 1994: 114, on Richard Wright's character, Bigger Thomas). He takes apart Myrdal's thesis of "social pathology" to expose political and cultural tensions left out by that account:

> In the "pragmatic sense" lynching and Hollywood, fadism and radio advertising are products of the "higher" culture, and the Negro might ask, "Why, if my culture is pathological, must I exchange it for these?"
>
> It does not occur to Myrdal that many of the Negro cultural manifestations which he considers merely reflective might also embody a rejection of what he considers "higher values." . . . It will take a deeper science than Myrdal's—deep as that might be—to analyze what is happening among the masses of Negroes. Much of it is inarticulate, and Negro scholars have, for the most part, ignored it through clinging, as does Myrdal, to the sterile concept of "race." (Ellison 1994: 316)

The answer, he suggests, is "not an exchange of pathologies, but a change of the basis of society. This is a job which both Negroes and whites must perform together" (317)—lest "this study . . . be used for less democratic purposes" (317).

The conjuring of absence is central to Ellison's novel *Invisible Man* (1952; see also Ellison 1994: pt. 1, esp. 102–144 and 167–183). The nameless first-person narrator and the pursuit of possibilities to their points of extinction offer a template of sorts for the ethnographic narratives of community life that are our subject in this book. *Invisible Man* unfolds as a series of crises in a young African American man's life as he strives to make a future for himself in New York City—ultimately making a future for others as he is drawn into community organizing and protest leadership. But each of the available platforms fails—cannot but fail, in a sense, by virtue of their fragility or fraudulence. In the course of this experience, the nameless protagonist succeeds in realizing his own identity—literally finding his voice in a moment of deep identification with the community of Harlem and people's struggles for security and dignity (Ellison 1952: 353–354).

The plot unfolds around the narrator's agentive self-discovery through a series of episodes framed around his ideological experiments and aspirations to various forms of leadership. His efforts to find a place for himself in already existing political movements only widen the gap between his emergent self-identity and his prospects for being heard (including hearing himself). These are taken up as a series of scenarios, culminating in a breaking point that drives him underground (in the novel, literally so) as the world above courses toward violence. As the novel closes, though, the narrator crosses another threshold, and he addresses the reader directly, just before he puts down his pen:

> I'm shaking off the old skin and I'll leave it here in the hole. I'm coming out, no less invisible without it, but coming out nevertheless. And I suppose it's damn well time. Even hibernations can be overdone, come to think of it. Perhaps that's my greatest social crime, I've overstayed my hibernation, since there's a possibility that even an invisible man has a socially responsible role to play.
>
> "Ah," I can hear you say, "so it was all a build-up to bore us with his buggy jiving. He only wanted us to listen to him rave!" But only partially true: Being invisible and without substance, a disembodied voice, as it were, what else could I do? What else but try to tell you what was really happening when your eyes were looking through? And it is this which frightens me:
>
> Who knows but that, on the lower frequencies, I speak for you? (Ellison 1952: 581)

Years later, Ellison commented on this passage: "The final act of *Invisible Man* is not that of a concealment in darkness in the Anglo-Saxon connotation of the word, but that of a voice issuing its little wisdom out of the substance of its own inwardness—after having undergone a transformation from ranter to writer" (Ellison 1994: 57). The character's descent underground "is a process of rising to an understanding of his human condition" (1994: 57); the coal cellar to which he retreats is "a source of heat, light, power and, through association with the character's motivation, self-perception" (1994: 57). The break in the protagonist's social field—figured as his invisibility—becomes the space of his art, and by the novel's end, his art is dually the means and ends of his quest. In an interview, Ellison said: "The maximum insight on the hero's part isn't reached until the final section. After all, it's a novel about innocence and human error, a struggle through illusion to reality. . . . Before he could have some voice in his own destiny he had to discard these old identities and illusions; his enlightenment couldn't come until then" (1994: 177).

Ellison explores the condition of "invisibility" as both radically alienating (even fatal) and potentially generative to the extent that personal agency is stirred from inwardness as movement toward the outer world (borrowing "movement" in this context from Bhahba 1998). At the same time, in *Invisible Man* as well as in later writings and interviews (collected in Ellison 1994), Ellison makes explicit the extent to which this central element of the novel is not immediately a comment on a general human condition. Rather, it is an analysis reachable only through a literary exploration of African American experience.

For Ellison, the art of the novel is already an affirmation of the novel's value—value simultaneously aesthetic and social: "The work of art is important in itself, . . . a social action in itself" (Ellison 1994: 137). The aesthetic aspect of fiction is not a vehicle to some social end, but rather, it is the social end. When he insists that his "fiction be judged as art" (Ellison 1994: 136–137), he is affirming aesthetic experience in itself as an experience of freedom for the author: "For the novelist, of any cultural or racial identity," he wrote, "his form is his greatest freedom" (Ellison 1994: 59). And ideally, for the reader, too, this space of freedom is a transformative social space: "As [the American novel] describes our experience, it creates it" (Ellison 1994: 183). In this sense, he says, "the American novel is . . . a conquest of the frontier" (Ellison 1994: 183).

But elsewhere, Ellison's image for what flows between a writer and reader—across the human geography of the writer's subject—evokes a different political register, one more familiar, perhaps, to the "ethnographic imagination" (Comaroff and Comaroff 1992): "American writing . . . is . . . an ethical instrument, and as such it might well exercise some choice in the kind of ethic it prefers to support. The artist is no freer than the society in which he lives, and in the United States the writers who stereotype or ignore the Negro and other minorities in the final analysis stereotype and distort their own humanity" (Ellison 1994: 44). In a 1945 review of Richard Wright's *Black Boy*, Ellison turns to the blues for his critical motif. Concluding, he writes of the "attraction" of the blues: "They at once express both the agony of life and the possibility of conquering it through sheer toughness of spirit. They fall short of tragedy only that they provide no solution, offer no scapegoat but the self. Nowhere in America today is there social or political action based upon the solid realities of Negro life depicted in *Black Boy*; perhaps that is why, with its refusal to offer solutions, it is like the blues" (Ellison 1994: 94).

Art, in Ralph Ellison's formulation, both occupies and molds the space left open by the disjunction between identity and the available terms of recognition. In this sense, art is the critical alternative to the discourse of solutions. Ethnography also, performatively, claims to occupy this space—performing an identification with the minority literature that makes it legible as a political location. Indeed, this is the principal space tacitly claimed by community ethnographies in the United States; however, the discourse of solutions remains evident in the a priori framing of communities around *cultural* identity. Even so, the artfulness of the new ethnographies points to their authors' wider frames of reference: the entwining of direct and indirect discourse that is characteristic of ethnography (speaking as narrator as well as through others' testimony) is fundamentally that of fiction. The narrative form of the new U.S. ethnography in the 1990s is novelistic, predicated on a layering of identifications designed to slip among author, subjects, and readers. Experimentation with ethnography's textual arts—like the art of the novel—is inseparable from its stakes.

This is not to suggest that anthropologists' efforts were all of one kind (they were not) or motivated wholly or only by the issues discussed here. Rather, what is striking about this body of literature is the patterning of the ethnographies themselves—their stated problems, their narrative organization, their constructions of personhood, agency, and social context, and their reflexive accountings of research method and their formulations of ethnography as a genre, together with a sense of its limits. This patterning is the effect of the discourse of solutions, aligning the ethnographic presentation with the lineaments of public policy debate, demonstrating the relevance and utility of ethnographic inquiry, accepting at least to some degree federal policy goals and key terms, but working them toward an alternative (critical) analysis. The discourse of solutions in this sense compresses interpretive ethnography into structural framings borrowed from the discursive charts of partisan politics in the federal policy field. It introduces contradictory impulses—if only because ethnography is opening always outward in time and space, the discourse of solutions always seeking containment. Knowing what an author chooses to make of those round holes and square pegs, and why, is essential to the work's accountability—and in its accountability is its meaning.

An influential and vivid example of making meaning in this sense is Elliott Liebow's *Tally's Corner*. *Tally's Corner* was highly experimental in its own time, and is still widely read (and still fresh) today. My reading focuses on the way the discourse of solutions structures the text—ultimately requiring Liebow, against his stated reservations, to collectivize the men who have been individuals throughout the account in racial terms. This allows Liebow to make policy recommendations in the language of policy debate, and correspondingly, to articulate his most explicit critical response regarding the limits of law in the law's terms. Like others among the books discussed in this volume, Liebow's work was a reissue, its ironies belonging very much to the period we are discussing.[1]

The Myrdal Problem: Tally's Corner

Tally's Corner (Liebow 1967) is based on research during the years of the civil rights era's legislative phase, the early 1960s—also the years of the Johnson administration's "War on Poverty." The book opens with a clear announcement of the project's national policy context: "Problems faced by and generated by low income urban populations in general and low-income urban Negroes in particular have become one of the chief concerns of the nation. We have declared War on Poverty and mobilized public and private resources for a concerted effort to expunge delinquency and dependency from our national life" (3). Liebow proceeds to note the rise of poverty in the United States since 1945. In 1963, 25 percent of the U.S. population was poor, 30 percent of whom were African American (4). Implicit in these opening pages is the extent to which the public debate over poverty programs was shaped by selective attention to African Americans and, beyond this, by particular stereotypes of African American families, especially adult men. Liebow turns this to rhetorical advantage, as an opening for his discussion of life conditions:

> Public interest in poverty tends to focus on Negroes for good
> reasons. A large proportion of the poor are Negroes and, more im-

portant, an even larger proportion of Negroes are poor. Moreover, Negroes in poverty tend to be poorer than their white counterparts and tend more to remain in poverty over generations, so that poverty, like skin color, appears as a hereditary characteristic as well as a circumstance of social and economic life. The transmission of the life style of poverty from generation to generation has logically drawn attention to Negro family life as the context in which this transmission is assumed to occur. To a large extent, the Negro family has become the very model of the dependent, lower-class urban family and a primary target of policy makers and programmers in the war against poverty. (4–5)

Liebow's critical agenda is cast most generally as a thesis linking poverty to racism and policy failure. In this respect, the book is a response to Myrdal's paradigm of "the vicious circle" (see Liebow 1967: 224 n. 8), in which "the Negro problem" was identified in terms of African American men's role in family life, and their presumed lack of motivation to achieve economic self-sufficiency. Liebow is sharply critical of these established views (most explicitly in the book's conclusion [208–231]). The book itself is crafted to demonstrate the realities and complexities effaced by those models, and, more affirmatively, to advocate the necessity of political mobilization on the part of African Americans (230–231). Humanitarian programs designed for African American communities without their initiative and leadership, he writes, amount to "self-deception" (228–229). The book concludes with a call for community empowerment, and community involvement in federal policy making where urban conditions are the issue.

Liebow's specific proposals for a new policy agenda include jobs, skills training, and a minimum wage adequate to guarantee that work will provide a living wage (224–228); in addition, he advocates intervention at "all points in the life cycle" (225) and one-time "reparations" for those beyond the help of such programs (225 n. 9). If the alternative to such initiatives is preserving the status quo, he writes, that is unacceptable: "[The issues arising from African American poverty] are, indeed, fundamental questions, and the maintenance of the lower classes as they are presently ordered is one way of answering them. This solution, however, in which those who are to be at the bottom of our society are selected while they are still in the womb violates every hope and promise this nation has held out to its people" (228). Liebow's book is a project of citizenship and social criticism—aimed specifically at the political and institutional sites where the sociological discourse of the cycle of poverty and the pathology of the African American male had been taken up as federal policy discourse.

Liebow's ethnographic research as a doctoral student was one component of Hylan Lewis's study of "Child Rearing Practices Among Low Income Families in the District of Columbia" funded by the National Institute of Mental Health, a federal agency. Liebow's fieldwork (in 1962 and 1963) concentrated on a small neighborhood in Washington, D.C.'s second precinct—a section of the federal city that was then, as now, primarily African American and disproportionately poor (census figures; cf. Liebow 1967: 19). He describes the purposes and methods of the fieldwork in the book's introduction and epilogue, each an important statement of his interpretive aims and practices.

The introduction opens with a discussion of the theory of the "cycle of poverty"—and its neglect of the real conditions of African American men:

> Much of what we know of Negro families in poverty . . . has been biased by an emphasis on women and children and a corresponding neglect of adult males. Neglect of the lower-class male is a direct reflection of his characteristic "absence" from the household. . . . Neglect of the adult male as a subject of research into lower-class life is also furthered by middle-class concerns with delinquency and dependency, for these are the aspects of poverty which touch most directly on middle-class life. . . . But research on delinquency and dependency usually deals only incidentally with men. Delinquency usually refers to juvenile behavior. . . . Dependency is a status normally reserved for women and children. It typically excludes the able-bodied male adult who is seen as not needing or not deserving societal support. (5–6)

In this passage, as elsewhere in the book, Liebow deftly identifies an alignment of sociological, political, and popular discourses that effectively erase the African American *male* except as a sign (in the hermeneutic sense) marking a location for intervention. He might well have added that by the time he worked on "Tally's" corner, that sign had been specified and elaborated in major works of literature—in the period we are discussing, most importantly (and very differently) in Richard Wright's *Native Son* (1940) and Ralph Ellison's *Invisible Man* (1948). But the image of "the" African American man—a literary trope readily taken up by sociologists and politicians—is, as Liebow insists, not the same as understanding something of the lives of African American *men*.

Liebow lingers over a methodological discussion (11–17), emphasizing the importance of naturalistic inquiry and ethnographic specificity of his ethnography—lest readers miss this performative aspect of Liebow's critique of the generalizations and erasures in the prevailing discourse. For example, he emphasizes the interpretive aspect of his work: "Since the data do not have 'sense' built into them—that is, they were not collected to test specific hypotheses nor with any firm presumptions of relevance—the present analysis is an attempt to make sense of them after the fact" (12). The book is organized into five main ethnographic chapters—titled "men and jobs," "fathers without children," "husbands and wives," "lovers and exploiters," and "friends and networks." These relationships, Liebow asserts, are the principal ties that the men themselves recognize. His claim for the book's narrative organization is that "we look at them in much the same way they look at themselves" (13). Most important to the performed critique of the book is Liebow's emphasis on individual men—not "individuals" as a generic unit of analysis, but people with names and unique backgrounds and concerns, along with common problems and contexts: "There is no attempt here to describe any Negro men other than those with whom I was in direct, immediate association. To what extent this descriptive and interpretive material is applicable to Negro streetcorner men elsewhere in the city or in other cities, or to lower-class men generally in this or any other society, is a matter for further and later study. This is not to suggest, however, that we are here dealing with unique or even distinctive persons and relationships. Indeed, the weight of the evidence is in the other direction" (14). Continuing, Liebow emphasizes his naturalistic approach to social research: the men who feature in the text "were not consciously selected at all; the focus on these particular men at this particular place came about, in large part, through accident" (14–15). There is "nothing distinctive" about them (15).

The methodological discussion has the effect of recalibrating the usual difference of scale between the reader and the subject—now individualized—in a way that emphasizes their equivalence as people, and perhaps all the more, their inequalities as citizens. Against this backdrop, Liebow sets the stage for the action with cinematic flair. He takes us to the "Carry-out shop" and the corner neighborhood where almost everything else in the book will take place. He introduces us to each of the four men whose words and experiences shape most of the account; as we meet "Tally," "Sea Cat," "Richard," and

"Leroy"—the effect is of a voice-over in a documentary—we learn something of their personal backgrounds, their education and employment histories, their physical appearance and style, family and friendships (23–27). Other men whose voices are secondary in the account are listed in a table as a cast of characters under the title "Some of the other men" by first name or nickname, age, and occupation (28). (No women are listed, although we meet some of the men's wives, lovers, and co-workers later.) The first ethnographic chapter also begins in the *sotto voce* of a stage direction: "A pickup truck drives slowly down the street" (29)—opening a description of a day-labor recruiter meeting refusals from the men on the street corner and on the stoops. "What is that we have witnessed here?" Liebow asks (29)—initiating the book's rhetorical first-person plural (marked for white observers), and opening the action of the book itself.

The fabric of the main text interweaves the experiences of the four men. Their very individuality underscores the weight of the common obstacles they face—low wages, low job security, inadequate skills (notwithstanding their military service, in some cases), and confrontations with the low expectations and accusations of their employers (who underpay them on the grounds of an assumption that they steal, for example). Their reputation for low motivation features in employers' reluctance to train them, blocking their mobility further. Less tangible factors are also important—Liebow portrays the men as deeply ashamed of their limits as providers, as well as of the gaps in their education. They protect themselves as best they can by avoiding the people (including their children) who make them feel their deficits, or by striking out against them, literally and figuratively. He draws on the men's accounts to show that trouble at home might make a man refuse work, and vice versa.

In general, Liebow's purpose is to show the "points of articulation" between what he calls the "inside world" of the street corner and the "larger society" (210). The book's central thesis is that the men's situation is not the product of a subculture, but—on the contrary—the result of their *shared* values with the larger society regarding appropriate men's roles, the value of work and education, and participation in a community. Their very belief in the American Dream overexposes them to the negative response of the larger society—white middle-class society—systematically reproducing the conditions in which their fathers failed. The cycle of poverty is not *within* the street-corner society, then, but in the ways the men internalize the rejection and paternalism of the larger society.

In presenting this thesis as the book's conclusion, each of the chapters turns out to have represented a critical point in the process. "The young, lower-class Negro" marries and seeks employment "because this is what it is to be a man in our society, whether one lives in a room near the Carry-out or in an elegant house in the suburbs" (210). But "he hedges on his commitment from the very beginning because he is afraid . . . of his own ability to carry out his responsibilities as husband and father. His own father failed and had to 'cut out,' and . . . he has no evidence that he will fare better. . . . He enters marriage and the job market with the smell of failure all around him" (210–211). The menial job market does not pay a living wage, and so even at best, a man's ability to support a family diminishes quickly once he marries and children are born (211–212). Women, too, are influenced by their fathers' failures, and so, Liebow continues, a wife or lover "keys her demands to her wants, to her hopes, not to her expectations. Her demands mirror the man both as society says he should be and as he really is, enlarging his failure in both their eyes" (212). The humiliation and despair might drive him to violence—by implication another confirmation of his "articulation" with the "larger society's" values: "Sometimes he strikes out at her or the children with his fists, perhaps to lay hollow claim to being man of the house in the one way left open to him" (212). Or alternatively, a man might wish "simply to inflict pain on this woman who bears witness to his failure as a husband and father and therefore as a man" (213). Increasingly, men in this situation are likely to withdraw to the street corner, "permitting them to be men once again provided they do not look too closely at one another's credentials" (213). The ample verbatim testimony richly bespeaks Liebow's conclusion as to the importance of the street corner as a place when men can temporarily renegotiate their positions on the basis of recognition more fully aligned with their self-identities.

Inevitably, though, the sociolegal context of the book demands more than the "attempt . . . to see the man as he sees himself" (208). The same sentence continues Liebow's statement of his ethnographic goals: "to compare what he says with what he does, and *to explain his behavior as a direct response to the conditions of lower-class Negro life rather than as mute compliance with historical or cultural imperatives*" (208; emphasis added). Indeed, a response to the discourse of the vicious circle or the cycle of poverty demands an alternative *explanation of behaviors*—and this requirement draws Liebow's analysis into another frame. At the very juncture where the inside and outside meet—the rhetorical border in the book mirroring lines of exclusion in the city—the need to account for men's *behaviors* shifts the burden of argument back to the inside world. This move pulls the issue of poverty back into the question of individual identities and psyches. But the discourse of solutions—while individualistic in the abstract—resists personal accounts. The demand for explanation compels Liebow to generalize.

Liebow is clearly aware of this contradiction. He structures the book along the horizon of tension between these two framings, and addresses it in his methodological discussion. His ethnographic frame is intensely naturalistic, highly interpretive, and specifically personalized. The policy frame is programmatic, behavioristic, and generalized. Each of these frames relies on the presentation of individual cases as well as personal testimony; however, they do so in different ways. The ethnography takes up the individual cases as embodied speaking subject; the presentation is (as already noted) literary in its contextualization, characterization, and evocation of speech. The policy frame takes up individual cases as *examples*, speech taking on the aura of testimony in the more legal sense—as subject to judgment. The organization of the book retains its coherence notwithstanding this tension precisely *because* individuals and first-person narrative are vital elements of *both* literary and legal processes. Indeed, their convergence in ethnography underscores the extent to which the social science concept of identity itself is a legal/literary fusion.

In the context of *Tally's Corner*, Liebow's figuration of himself as "the anthropologist" (209) completes the joinery between these two framings, as he portrays himself moving in and out of the street corner, and ultimately, in and out of the roles of friend and scientific analyst. The inside and outside are not just two worlds at street level, in other words. They represent the edges of an epistemological break between knowledges and purposes—on the one hand, as these are emergent from conversation and identification, an exchange of self-expression (us) and on the other, from a field of policy objectives and authoritative explanation (them). It is Liebow's first-person testimony—his constant low-key reference to his own role in the conversation—that ultimately sustains the book's coherence across that epistemological divide, since "the anthropologist" in this context is not just interlocutor and/or analyst, but also the very figure of a reconciliation of these perspectives so far impossible in the actually existing public sphere.

Liebow's book provides a vivid example of how ethnography is situated—and that is with difficulty—between literature and social policy. *Tally's Corner* challenges the discourse of "solutions" to the extent that individual agency, narrative, action, subjectivity, and social position are inherently unstable and socially contingent. The discourse of solutions—in the specific milieu we are discussing—cuts across or compresses those contingencies, resulting in a construction of behaviors as motivated, and narrative as literal or transparent as to intention. Moreover, while the literary aspects of *Tally's Corner* resist generalization, the commitment to solutions demands it. These crosscurrents underscore the different methodological aspects of the book. The specificity of the men's situations and personal testimony is more naturalistic and (in his own word) interpreted. The generalizations by definition take us past *these* men to African Americans in poverty as a class. By definition, then, the generalizing move means shifting from an *interpreted* account to one that moves past their words, to their behaviors.

In the heart of the book, Liebow treats disparities between the men's words and their actions (e.g., in relation to reasons for avoiding or quitting work, leaving their families, or hitting their wives) as deep-seated tensions—not always conscious—between the men's aspirations and their situations, expressed as fantasy, violence, or just talk (among other things). In the conclusion, where the ethnography is more programmatic, those disparities become conscious: disappointments, losses of self-esteem, rationalization, fear of failure (e.g., 222)—that is, they become theoretical objects *for science* and policy targets *for politicians*. The commitment to solutions in effect creates an analytical shortcut, bypassing the book's central interpretive question about self-identity and—by compressing identity into the rubric of choice—revises the focus, shifting it from the men's words to their behavior. In other words, the interpretive side of the book involves one formulation of agency (as self-identity); the more explicitly programmatic side of the book involves another (as behavior).

This slippage also involves quite different demands on the reader. In the main text, the focus is on the broad relationships that Liebow encourages us to identify with the individual street-corner men by thinking of them in terms of core relationships that they probably *share* with most middle-class Americans (Liebow 1967: 13). In the conclusion, this shared reality takes on a different significance, as Liebow asks readers to disregard the men's statements when they disavow middle-class goals: "If, in the course of *concealing his failure*, or of *concealing his fear of even trying*, he pretends—*through the device of public fictions*—that he did not want these things in the first place and *claims* that he has all along been responding to a different set of rules and prizes, we do not do him or ourselves any good by accepting this claim at face value" (222; emphasis added). As the book moves from its ethnographic chapters to its programmatic solutions, *Tally's Corner* shifts subtly from one "we" to another. The first "we" is a first-person plural that includes Tally and the others with whom he is in conversation. The second is one that excludes them. As I have already suggested, it is Liebow himself, in the anthropologist's role, who commutes back and forth between these two discursive positions across an epistemological divide. But the gap between the book's two dimensions corresponds to another gap in a field of action that is more concretely political, as Liebow himself emphasizes in calling for recognition of African American leadership in the war on poverty at the book's close (Liebow 1967: 229–231).

One might reasonably ask whether there might be an alternative to the discourse of solutions and its distorting effects (collectivizing identities, pathologizing behavior). Liebow's concluding point suggests one, given that the war on poverty was a federal program with state and local involvement. The epistemological shift is accentuated by the fact that the geography of the study remains local, even when the subject has turned from *these* men to African American men in poverty in cities across the nation. While the book's analysis does not altogether leave the street corner, its implications travel widely on the association of the men's behaviors with those documented and commented upon by social scientists closer to the policy-making process. Perhaps one alternative might have been to look away from the street corner, to those wider spheres. But that would have been a very different book—and that is precisely my point. The street corner in the main text is an actual location; the street corner in the conclusion is figurative—an object of social and political judgment.

Liebow's ethnography is shaped by a liberal political space in which an interpretive project is possible but not assimilable to the prevailing policy discourse. Some readers might imagine that this shift of discourse is essential if social problems are to be addressed on a meaningful scale. But it is not the case that interpretive or discourse-centered ethnography is necessarily small gauge or that it operates outside the political arena. Liebow's main proposal—that African Americans should mobilize to develop their own political leadership and substantive initiatives—is entirely consistent with his ethnographic approach. The contradictions I have mentioned arise in relation to his other proposals (appealing or intuitively persuasive though they might seem to some readers even now) in that they presuppose the reality of an "inside world" enclosing African Americans and within which their "behaviors" can be "explained." That such a mobilization was and perhaps still is inconceivable at the federal level is evidenced by Liebow's distinction between the inner and outer worlds of the Washington, D.C., ghetto—and, indeed, by the fact that he circumscribes the study around the location and assembled identities of the street corner. The very fact that identity falls away as the project's theoretical object betrays the depth of the neighborhood's exclusion from even the local arenas of political life. Liebow's ethnographic approach is keenly interpretive, until he reaches the edge of the neighborhood—where the ethnographic conversations do not carry to other geographies. I am tempted to say: "to travel to the centers of power." But this is precisely the discourse of citizenship—with its federalist fictions of a central location of power, accessible via a network of more local channels—that pervades the ethnography of the United States. The book itself is what carries—literally and figuratively, as an idea of another United States.

Readers may feel I am reading far too literally; however, that is precisely my purpose—to find the specific textual locations where ethnography surfaces in the crosscurrents between the social knowledge that circulates as federal social policy and the other formulations (other knowledges) that circulate in other spheres. The purpose of such an exercise is not to turn politics or ethnography into art, but to cultivate an eye for the places where hegemony makes the life story and personal narrative into ambiguous resources for public use. The discourse of solutions elides the difference between specificity and generalization in its usage of culture, and compresses personal self-identities into rubrics that remake them into individual representations of social types. The discourse of solutions prevails when providing solutions for social problems is the precondition for anyone's interest in the experiences of men and women who live at the margins of recognition as neighbors, citizens, and human beings.

The disjunction between the conversations that supply the evidence for interpretive ethnography and those other conversations that result in policy points to a deep divide in the geography of power and knowledge in the United States. Anthropologists identify this gap as having significant implications for their professional knowledge practices—in particular, their attention to discourse, to the truth claims of policymakers, and to the unintended consequences of policy in practice (Coutin 1994; Morgen 2001: 748; Morgen and Maskovsky 2003: 317, 323–326; Susser 1996: 412; Traube 1996). This is a paradox, since critics of so-called postmodernism tended to construct discourse analysis, the analysis of texts, and symbolic anthropology as diversions from the materiality of power. Such criticisms misname their object: it is not attention to texts and talk that fails to grapple with the realities of power, but rather, political institutions that immure themselves from the realities of social life. The question of textual integrity, then, leads quickly to other issues: the connections between identity, politics, and the limits of social policy in the United States.

In Search of Respect

Philippe Bourgois's *In Search of Respect: Selling Crack in El Barrio* (1995) may be the most widely read ethnography of the United States in the 1990s In some ways, Bourgois's book parallels that of Elliott Liebow, published almost thirty years earlier—and this makes the differences between them all the more trenchant. Here, again, is the American Dream, punishing new arrivals, confronting them with the toxins of their own failures. And here, again, is the discourse of solutions, punctuating the interpretive analysis of social experience with the required language of diagnosis and cure. But this time, there is no wider public dialogue—no Moynihan or Myrdal to correct, no national commitment to take up as a call for community participation. Bourgois writes in the language of liberalism, into the void of neoliberal silence— which he features in vivid imagery.

The book opens with an epigraph from Bourgois's key informant, a man he calls "Primo": "Man, I don't blame where I'm at right now on nobody else but myself" (Bourgois 1995: 1). Bourgois narrates the main text in the first person; from the outset, it is both memoir and monograph. Its opening lines, in Bourgois's voice, account for the book's dual register, evoking theory and politics as different perspectives—politics being "personal," theory presumably something else:

> I was forced into crack against my will. When I first moved to East Harlem . . . as a newlywed in the spring of 1985, I was looking for an inexpensive New York City apartment from which I could write a book on the experience of poverty and ethnic segregation in the heart of one of the most expensive cities in the world. *On the level of theory,* I was interested in the political economy of inner-city street culture. *From a personal, political perspective,* I wanted to probe the Achilles heel of the richest industrialized nation in the world by documenting how it imposes racial segregation and economic marginalization on so many of its Latino/a and African-American citizens. (Bourgois 1995: 1; emphasis added)

From the beginning, then, Bourgois as ethnographer fuses his personal role to national politics, undertaking local ethnography as an ethnography of global capitalism and its social effects. This is the modern situation of the community study—localist before it is local, national before it is theoretical, personal before it is political. By the book's close, Bourgois unsettles these dichotomies—as he himself becomes local, his informants become his friends, and interviews become conversations of another kind. But the theoretical frame he gives the project also demands cultural difference, and ultimately the dichotomies reemerge through his formulation of *culture*. Bourgois alerts us to this possibility at the very beginning, in observing that "substance abuse in the inner city is merely a symptom—and *a vivid symbol*—of deeper dynamics of social marginalization and alienation" (Bourgois 1995: 2; emphasis added).

Theorizing the consumption, trade, and talk of crack as symbolic equips Bourgois—or any of us, as readers—with the agility to move between the two "levels" of his study; the symbol occupies the space of the gap between the inner and outer worlds of the project, to borrow Liebow's earlier formulation. Crack-as-symbol opens its "sensuous husk" (Marx 1975a: 277) to yield its relational and subjective content: "The two dozen street dealers and their families that I befriended were not interested in talking primarily about drugs. On the contrary, they wanted me to learn all about their daily struggles for subsistence and dignity at the poverty line" (Bourgois 1995: 2).

The ethnographic project accordingly widens to explore the "explosive cultural creativity" that Bourgois calls "inner-city street culture" or a "street culture of resistance"—"a complex and conflictual web of beliefs, symbols, modes of interaction, values and ideologies *that have emerged in opposition to exclusion from mainstream society*. Street culture offers *an alternative forum for autonomous personal dignity*" (Bourgois 1995: 2; emphasis added). The parallels between this formulation and Liebow's are evident in this passage, and throughout the book, which presents finely textured observations and extensive transcripts of conversation that Bourgois taped over the course of the five years of his research. But there are also differences: Bourgois notes the extent to which street culture is taken up and restyled by the "mainstream" as "pop culture" (Bourgois 1995: 8). The illegal economy, then, is a channel between the study's inner and outer worlds. But—and here is another difference—it is also dangerous, "embroil[ing] most of its participants in lifestyles of violence, substance abuse, and internalized rage" (8). Bourgois presents the book's central thesis in similar terms: "The street culture of resistance is predicated on the destruction of its participants and the community harboring them. . . . . Although street culture emerges out of a personal search for dignity and a rejection of racism and subjugation, it ultimately becomes an active agent in personal degradation and community ruin" (8).

He quickly generalizes this statement about identity, pairing it with an assessment of the situation of immigrants living in poverty in the United States and, beyond immigrants, "major sectors of any vulnerable population experiencing rapid structural change in the context of political and ideological oppression" (11). In relation to these larger populations, Bourgois adds, "there is nothing exceptional about the Puerto Rican experience in New York, except that the human costs of immigration and poverty have been rendered more clearly visible by the extent and rapidity with which the United States colonized and disarticulated Puerto Rico's economy and polity" (11). But having established crack as a symbol of exclusion and alienation in that local context, a generalization in precisely those terms makes it difficult to accommodate some elements of local street culture in the broader formulation of the thesis—in particular, the men's violence against women.

Bourgois presents his own rationales for ethnography in oppositional terms such as these. He positions himself against both the "positivis[m]" (13) of "traditional social science research techniques that rely on . . . statistics or random sample neighborhood surveys" (12) on the one hand and "the profoundly elitist tendencies of many postmodernist approaches" (14) on the other—associating "deconstructionist 'politics'" with "hermetically sealed academic discourses on the 'poetics' of social interaction, or on clichés devoted to exploring the relationships between self and other" (14). At the same time, he details his debts to postmodernism in terms of his attention to ethnographic authority and reflexivity, and comments at length on the tensions inherent in taking an ethnographic approach to violence and "self-destruction"—tensions arising from a functionalist legacy that "imposes order and community" and an ethical (as well as strategic) emphasis on empathy, reciprocity, and rapport with one's research subjects. The situation of conducting participant-observation research in "extreme settings full of human tragedy" is cast as an ethnographic frontier of sorts—novel and dangerous, posing a range of personal, ethical, and *textual* difficulties (14–15). The textual problems he refers to involve the risks of exoticism and voyeurism, and even more so, of reinforcing elements of "popular racist stereotypes" from which the community already suffers (15). As a result of this combination of factors:

ethnographic presentations of social marginalization are almost guaranteed to be misread by the general public through a conservative, unforgiving lens. This has seriously limited the ability of intellectuals to debate issues of poverty, ethnic discrimination, and immigration. They are traumatized by the general public's obsession with personal worth and racial determinism. . . . Intellectuals have retreated from the fray and have unreflexively latched on to positive representations of the oppressed that those who have been poor, or lived among the poor, know to be completely unrealistic. (Bourgois 1995: 15)

This evocation of the narrow arenas of policy discourse open to ethnographic research appear to be narrower still for "progressives" and "cultural nationalists" who are "terrified of the potential for 'negative connotations'" (15). The passage quoted above continues: "Indeed, I have noticed this when presenting the main arguments of this book in academic settings. Progressive and often cultural nationalist colleagues—who are almost always middle class—often seem to be incapable of hearing the arguments I am making" (Bourgois 1995: 15).

Bourgois's response to these issues is to commit himself to a highly personalized portraiture. The *literary* specificity of Bourgois's book combines the memoir of identification with ethnographic reportage, drawing especially on the individual testimony of the men (and one woman) who represent (for readers) and reproduce (for themselves) the street culture. The *sociological* specificity is in his treatment of identity as an intersection of personal, psychological, and contextual factors. As in the original templates for those forms, the specificity of attention to individuals' lives and words must ultimately remain a literary device, since that specificity offers no discursive access to any institutional arena available at the *federal* level—which (as we have seen) is the counterpart Bourgois assigns to the "theoretical level" of his book. Across the break in the federal/local field, then, "identity" beckons from the federal side as the destination, so to speak, of the individual accounts.

The generalizability of the book inevitably depends on readers' identification with both the author and the people whose testimony we "hear." But occasionally, Bourgois's own identification with individuals falters. Sometimes he registers shock, disgust, or offense within the transcript, so to speak—for example, when he listens to Caesar's boasting about the way he and his childhood friends used to torture a boy with cerebral palsy. Caesar changes narrative course when he sees Bourgois's reaction, a strong emotional reaction that he explains as an identification of that boy with his son (188–189). His reaction to those moments is personal ("I never forgave Caesar for his cruel brutality" [189]) and becomes part of the narrative.

In other instances, his response is structural; he temporarily sets aside the men's testimony in favor of a metanarrative of sociological explanation or psychological assessment. To be sure, such recourse is not wholly a departure from the canons of local talk; Primo, Caesar, Candy, and others have also internalized a certain repertoire of metadiscourses (some of them therapeutic) from their encounters with social workers, welfare offices, hospitals, police, employers, teachers, and the media. When they want to justify themselves (or add authority to their bravado) to "Philippe" or "Felipe" (Bourgois's doubles in the transcripts), they draw on these terms.[2] Bourgois, too, draws on such idioms to maintain the coherence of his text, especially when dealing with developments he says he found impossible to assimilate personally at the time. The register of explanation releases him momentarily from the conversational obligation of reciprocity that otherwise sustains the text so effectively as a performance. It is as if an explanatory metanarrative allows him and perhaps his readers a short break from identifying with the men.

The first occasion that prompts the need for distance in this more structural sense arises in a discussion of adolescent gang rape (189 and 205–212). At first, Bourgois tries to hear the men's stories about violent sexual disciplining as "metaphor" or "exaggeration" in a conversational context that is already highly marked by "macho bonding" (189). But later, as he absorbs the reality of gang rape, he constructs it carefully for his readers in highly specific terms as a "brutal dimension of the school-age, childhood socialization of *the members of Ray's crack-dealing network*" (205; emphasis added). But Bourgois also makes it clear that the rape narratives represented a crisis for him. The stories "spun me into a personal depression and research crisis. . . . Caesar's voyeuristic bonding and sexual celebration of Primo's brutal account made me even more disgusted with my 'friends.' Although I might have expected such behavior from Caesar, I felt betrayed by Primo, whom I had grown to like and genuinely respect" (Bourgois 1995: 205). The transcript of Primo's story then follows, followed by Bourgois's extended recollection of his personal and professional doubts as he was preparing his own narrative in the form of the book, debating whether to include the rape: "With notable individual exceptions, I had grown to like most of these veteran rapists. I was living with the enemy; it had become my social network. They had engulfed me in the common sense of street culture until their rape accounts *forced me to draw the line*" (207; emphasis added). What was that line? The project (and the book) continue well past this point, so readers already know that "the line" did not finish those friendships. Rather, it emerges as a shift of register, as Bourgois stops to reflect on his own textual practice:

> From an analytical and a humanistic perspective, it was too late for me to avoid the issue or to dismiss their sociopathology as aberrant. I had to face the prevalence and normalcy of rape in street culture and adolescent socialization. . . . I was tempted to omit this discussion, fearing that readers would become too disgusted and angry with the crack dealers and deny them a human face. As a man, I also worry about the politics of representation. . . . I am also worried about creating a forum for a public humiliation of the poor and powerless. . . . There is obviously nothing specifically Puerto Rican about rape. (207–208)

Ultimately, he decides to include the material on the grounds that "rape runs rampant around us, and it is as if society maintains a terrifying conspiracy of silence that enforces this painful dimension of the oppression of women in everyday life" (208)—an assessment that broadly parallels his earlier discussion of the need for ethnographic research on poor and marginalized populations in the United States, quoted above.

In that other register, then, Bourgois tells us that the men themselves "develop a logic for justifying their actions" (209) involving the women's moral reputations as well as what they presume to be their own lack of appeal. That logic appears to be deliberately misleading, however, since "when specifically confronted with the issue, Primo admitted that ultimately violent force and physical terror were the organizing mediums" (209). Indeed, later, Bourgois—momentarily outside the role of memoirist and friend—situates the men's rape narratives in more generalized terms as providing "an insider's perspective on the misogyny of street culture and *the violence of everyday life*" (213; emphasis added). The effect is to accommodate the rapes textually through a process of generalization—not along the lines of Puerto Rican or even masculine identity—but rather as symbolic of the social reproduction of brutality in the fundamental condition of marginality.

Importantly, for the men, too, violence has symbolic dimensions (how else could Bourgois have imagined the first rape account as "metaphorical"? [189]). Many of the conversations are either violent talk or concern the theme of violence; this appears to be another side (I will not say "*the* other side") of the search for respect. But it is not just talk. The transcripts are sometimes punctuated by gunshots. Everyone, including Bourgois, is motivated to learn the variations of "the personal logic of violence in the street's overarching culture of terror" (88). That the culture of terror should extend to men's power over women is not surprising. This by itself does not exclude women from the study; rather, it is the drawn line—a register of explanation that displaces women in favor of a generalizing semiotics of violence—that marks the identity of street culture as essentially male.

The second textual break is related to this one, and is more sustained in that the book as a whole is shaped by the relative absence of women, at least from the published interviews—an unavoidable omission, as Bourgois explains, given the constraints of decorum and risk in male-female relationships in the street culture. Bourgois accounts for these constraints in a discussion of gender norms and etiquette that develops directly out of his discussion of gang rape in the preceding chapter. The opening section of the chapter titled "redrawing the gender line" begins an extended discussion of "the crisis of patriarchy" (213–217) inherent in the widespread local recognition of the "anachronism" of a family modeled on the "traditional 'Spanish ideal'" and the problems this transition poses "in the worst case scenario" for men (215): "As men on the street lose their former authoritarian power in the household, they lash out against the women and children they can no longer control. . . . Worse yet, the stabilizing community institutions that might have been able to mediate the trauma do not exist in the U.S. inner city. Instead, men struggle violently in a hostile vacuum to hold on to their grandfathers' atavistic power. The crisis of patriarchy in El Barrio expresses itself concretely in the polarization of domestic violence and sexual abuse" (214–215).

But women, too, hold onto a self-image (as desirable, passionate, nurturing, and maternal) that Bourgois associates with "*jíbaro*"—defined as the values of the old Puerto Rican countryside. The absence of women is thus constituted as the sign of the study's overall *temporal* and *spatial* limits. In a sense, women were hidden in the divisions men and women faced (and posed for each other) in this New York City neighborhood (215–216). The absence of women from the text, then, is more than a comment on their lack of availability for the research project; it is a comment on their absence from a public identity as Bourgois develops the concept. Men, too, suffer from dislocation, but the identity repertoires of street culture are available to them, of their own making—as the book's title and transcripts indicate (see 143).

The final break in the text emerges in the discussion of women who use crack while pregnant, and whose addiction ruins their children's lives (276–286). While sharply critical of the demonization of crack-addicted mothers, his longest metanarrative unfolds from their devastation. Bourgois adumbrates an explanation:

> The causes of [infant death] are substance abuse, racism, public sector institutional breakdown, and a restructuring of the economy away from factory jobs. . . . Perhaps the addicted mothers I met in crackhouses were simply those who had given up fighting the odds that history has structured against them. Abandoning their children, or poisoning their fetuses in a frantic search for personal ecstasy, accelerates the destruction of already doomed progeny. By destroying the so-called mother-nurture instinct, and by disabling their children during their tenderest ages, vulnerable mothers escape the long-term agony of having to watch their children grow up into healthy, energetic adolescents, only to become victims and protagonists of violence and substance abuse. (285)

In sum, it is in relation to men's violence toward women and women's drug-induced violence against their fetuses and infants that the book's widest cultural and political critique is articulated—in terms of racism, poor employment prospects, inadequate wages, "structural maladjustment" (221), and a variety of "state-imposed contexts that mediate daily survival among the inner-city poor" (242). Throughout the book, the men's (and Candy's) agency is constituted against the foil of factors such as these.

Bourgois's registers of explanation combine love and violence as braided contingencies—love referring back to Puerto Rico, and violence referring outward, too, but to U.S. policy failures. This outward turning marks a horizon where the form of the book must struggle against itself, just as Liebow made his book struggle against itself at precisely the same juncture. It is at the locations where Bourgois must confront gender violence—as rape and battery, sanctioned absence, and as crack addiction among pregnant women—that the narrative of identity emerges, made to turn outward toward explanation, suspending the men within their own circle and women without it. The discourse of solutions narrows identity to the figuration of social problems and explanations of behavior. Where Liebow wrote of empowerment in the terms of his time, Bourgois captures his own times by writing about stigma and its distorting prisms for the men and women of the neighborhood and for American society at large. To return to Bourgois's main thesis: "Although street culture emerges out of a personal search for dignity and a rejection of racism and subjugation, it ultimately becomes an active agent in personal degradation and community ruin" (9).

While the book is primarily focused on men's lives, the life story Bourgois tells at greatest length—almost a full chapter—is Candy's. Candy is the only woman Bourgois can interview at length. Her life story is set against the discussion of patriarchy and jíbaro; she stands in for those other women as well embodying a noteworthy exception to their norm. Candy is distinctive among women in her own readiness to use violence to manage her sexual and illegal business relationships; she is also successful in the legal economy. A survivor of a lifetime of physical abuse and several suicide attempts, she is in the process of actively renegotiating her public gender role by the time Bourgois meets her. Bourgois's first-hand description of Candy details what her efforts to defend her business interests and her hard-won personal independence with her personal power (including but not limited to her capacity to verbally intimidate others, her sexual aggressiveness, and her willingness to use violence). Other elements of her story come from interviews with Candy and Primo.

Candy was born in Puerto Rico, eloped as an adolescent to escape her father's beatings, and as a young teenaged mother, found herself in New York City, fending for herself against her husband's abuse and the city's attempts to remove their child from her custody. At one point in Primo's account of gang rape, Caesar interjects: "They just was training her, Felipe" (206). Candy uses the same word—training—to describe the way her husband treated her during their nineteen years of marriage, frequently beating her, and restricting her mobility to the point of forbidding her to look out of their apartment window (223). Her teens and twenties were punctuated by the births of her five children, repeated beatings by her husband, several miscarriages, suicide attempts, drug addiction, and encounters with city and state social service agencies and employers. A month after Bourgois first interviewed her, her life changed dramatically. She shot her husband in a dispute over his affair with her sister, and gained control of his business—the club where Bourgois was hanging out with Primo, Caesar, and the other men who feature in the book.

Bourgois characterizes Candy as smart, energetic, self-dramatizing, colorful, charismatic, an astute businesswoman, and a caring mother—an appealing portrait of a complex and difficult person facing complex and difficult circumstances. Readers are acquainted with elements of the men's personal histories by the time they reach this section of the book, but no other individual story is given so much space. Indeed, Candy's story is more than her own, in several respects. The account of Candy's story blends several voices; it is Primo's portion of the account that is the longest—longer than Candy's own. Further, it is clear from the outset that Candy's life is a subject of commentary—not just for Bourgois, but also for others. For example, Primo and Caesar offer their own (different) interpretations of Candy's life at age thirteen (before they knew her) when she eloped with Felix (219). Other fragments of her life story surface from Candy's experiences with social services, psychotherapists, and other public and private agencies—providing her with some of her own language of self-description (220). But perhaps most fundamentally, Candy's story is intended to speak for the experiences of other women, and, through them, to the fundamental schism in personal experience hewn by the divide between Puerto Rico (represented as "jíbaro culture") and the United States.

Candy's story is a vehicle for Bourgois's strongest claims as to the persistent hold of jíbaro culture in "inner city street culture" (see 221–222). In this sense, Candy is central to both the temporal and spatial infrastructure of the book—that is, the hold of tradition and the rendering of diaspora and displacement as cultural crisis felt in a personal way. In his portrait of Candy, the crisis is manifest in her sexuality and violence—specifically, in both contexts, in a marked ambivalence between aggression and victimage. In his analysis, these are signs of other contradictions—between past and present, Puerto Rico and New York. The "more traditional" (219) elements of Candy's story include her insistence on telling the story of her marriage as a love story (219), her attachment to her role as a mother (222), her protection of Felix from the police (even after the shooting; 224–226), her lack of expressed solidarity with other women (230), and her continued flirtation with Primo even after they ended their formal relationship.

At the chapter's close, Bourgois's evocation of a "jíbaro time warp" (258)—a window onto the rural pleasures of an earlier generation at home in Puerto Rico, viewed through Candy's story—seals the presentation of Candy as a bridge to another place, even to another time as an anachronism. Candy's difference (her craziness, in Primo's narrative) is re-rendered as their common difference, arising from the persistent pull of jíbaro culture from an irretrievable past. Her femininity and Puerto Rican traditions become one and the same. This interpretive move is essential to the way Candy represents the other women behind the book's pages, as well as other men—perhaps the men even more so, since she makes their displacement visible, literally embodying it—and most keenly as an object of her husband's abuse.

Candy's story is essential to the ethnographic and political efficacy Bourgois claims for personal narrative at the outset. It is her story that permits the men's stories (which dominate the book) to be read as Puerto Rican in a cultural sense and at the same time as modern American dreams. Candy, then, is doing considerable work in the account in terms of how her situation (literarily and culturally speaking) positions readers to identify with the men, that is, reading the book as citizens and as social theorists.

Reading and the Ethics of Narrative Form

Bourgois's conclusion articulates a clear association of street culture with a national society:

> I hope to contribute to our understanding of the fundamental processes and dynamics of oppression in the United States. . . . Highly motivated, ambitious inner-city youths have been attracted to the rapidly expanding, multibillion-dollar drug economy during the 1980s and 1990s precisely because they believe in Horatio Alger's version of the American Dream. . . .
>
> "Mainstream America" should be able to see itself in the characters presented on these pages and recognize the linkages. The inner city represents the United States' greatest domestic failing, hanging like a Damocles sword over the larger society. . . . From a comparative perspective, and in a historical context, the painful and prolonged self-destruction of people like Primo, Caesar, Candy, and their children is cruel and unnecessary. There is no technocratic solution. Any long-term paths out of the quagmire will have to address the structural and political economic roots, as well as the ideological and cultural roots of social marginalization. The first step out of the impasse, however, requires a fundamental ethical and political reevaluation of basic socioeconomic models and human values. (1995: 326–327)

This prescription demands that the book break free of its formal alignment with the discourse of citizenship so as to transfer its ethical burden to the readers. Bourgois's epilogue, written after a visit back to the neighborhood as the book went to press, seems to explore this possibility. These last few pages take a cinematic form, listing each character and place, with accompanying notes to bring the action up to date. They are the notes of a nightmare. In closing, there is no metanarrative. He writes:

> Witnessing [people's situations] during the few weeks that I spent back in the El Barrio in the spring and early summer of 1994 made me realize I had lost the defense mechanisms that allow people on the street to "normalize" personal suffering and violence. For example, I still cannot forget the expression of the terrified, helpless eyes of the five-year-old boy who was watching his mother argue with a cocaine dealer at 2:00 a.m. in the stairway of a tenement where Primo and I had taken shelter from a thunder shower on my second night back in the neighborhood. Primo shrugged when I tried to discuss the plight of the child with him. "Yeah, Felipe, I know, I hate seeing that shit too. It's wack." (337)

In the book's double closure, Bourgois specifies two moments of loss. The first is the public one in the conclusion to the monograph: "*There is no technocratic solution.*" The second is the private one in the personal epilogue: "*I had lost the defense mechanisms that allow people on the street to 'normalize' violence.*" And then at the last instant, in a powerful moment of identification with the child, he aligns these as a problem of knowledge that remains his (and possibly Primo's)—and certainly now, ours. His text positions the reader—or rather, he makes use of what is inevitably the reader's position, physically holding the book, and (figuratively) reading over Bourgois's shoulder. The lines yield a strong impression of this terrified child, staring back from the page into the reader's eyes. The book's conclusion also has a performative aspect, in that the conclusion is not just in words, but also in the arrayed distinctions among silences from which the reader cannot avoid choosing: indifference, numbness, terror, or excessive knowledge.

Bourgois's conclusion and epilogue lend the book the structural form of allegory—the allegorical form doing some of the work of evoking "the economy of the whole" (see, again, Benjamin 1998: 234; see also 186). The book ends by encompassing the reader's very presence—through this ambiguous silence and the inescapability of choosing—into the scene itself. To ask, "What does this book mean?" becomes the same as asking, "What kind of person am I?" Here, we might consider Bourgois's and Liebow's books together, once again. Both works are committed to finding solutions to the problems represented by their research communities—and, at a minimum, to challenging the casual presumption that the people they write about *are* the problem. In both works, as we have seen, anthropology and apologia are powerfully joined. The discourse of solutions effaces individual identity and agency, leaving "culture" as a surrogate subjectivity without an individual referent. As Elizabeth Abel writes in a related context, "position has come to stand for race" (Abel 1993: 482).[3] Gender difference—in both works most intensely expressed as gender violence—bears the weight of culture in this sense, as its most visible index.

In these and other ways, the works are similar. But in other respects, they are strikingly different. The earlier work envisions a solution in terms of democratic organization: local governance—and government—that would include this community and others like it. The later work conjures no such hope—emphasizing instead the personal and community effects of structural displacement within the social formations of post-Fordist global neoliberal capitalism. In other words, where Liebow looks to the prospects for local democratic mobilization as a means of linking personal and national futures at the height of American liberalism, Bourgois leads readers to expect this move through his own use of genre—but, at the last instant, he withdraws it. Indeed, he inverts it—leaving the reader alone with the reformulation of this community and everyone in it as the localization of a crisis of hegemony that encompasses "the whole of imperialism" (Poulantzas 1975: 87).

Neoliberal Tensions

The illumination of responsibility that is central to the "anthropology of credibility" (de Certeau 1997: viii) involves more than the analytical demands of the evidence at hand. As we have seen, it is also a literary problem. For U.S. anthropologists in the 1990s, the literary problem was to assert the relevance of their work in a volatile and divided public sphere while also sustaining its viability in a fractured intellectual marketplace within the academy. In that situation, the discourse of solutions was a major literary response—and so, too, its ironies. Irony prevails in the ethnography of U.S. community studies in this period of their revival. Indeed, the revival itself should be viewed as an ironic statement about the redirection of the nation's political will in comparison with the civil rights era. And this irony, in turn, calls on readers to take stock of their own accounts in the democracy deficit from their relatively advantaged position. The irony is the message: through irony, anthropologists rework the key terms of the discourse of solutions against their dominant prescriptions, marking the era of solutions as past. Irony announces ethnography as counter-hegemonic, in particular in its rendering of personal identity and subjectivity:

> What makes the hegemonic process effective is less its "taken for grantedness" or coherence as a belief system than its capacity as an ensemble of political relations and practices to command the social processes through which meanings are publicly articulated, communicated, and invested with contextual authority and social legitimacy. Hegemony works less on the hearts and minds of the disempowered than on their ability to articulate and exercise a political identity able to realize the social force necessary to change the order of power relations. *Hegemony is the power to make and remake political subjects.* (Gregory 1998: 246)

The discourse of solutions is *federal*—embedded in the long association of federal power and social science that accounts for law's realist traditions— and its critical reworkings by anthropologists at this period are also heavily structured around signs of federal power, as we shall see. This is what lends them their counter-hegemonic element, in the sense that Gregory's formulation suggests.

The discourse of solutions pulls toward generalization, while ethnography pulls toward specificity—a fundamental tension that contributes to the prevailing tone of irony in the ethnography of the United States, encoding it with counter-hegemonic implication. The problem of generalization—or even of cumulative reading—is unavoidable for an author of ethnography, since ethnography (not only in the United States) was from its very inception a medium of critical engagement with the determinisms that failed to take account of the human imagination and sociability in their specificity. Ethnography—anywhere—writes *against* such erasure by means of its conspicuous absorption in a methodology of sustained attentiveness (classically involving an immersion in the field, a year or more of fieldwork, fluency in local language[s], involvement in local ties of kinship, friendship, and clientage, and detailed attention to individuals' circumstances and points of view— among other things). Early ethnography wrote itself, so to speak, against material determinism, racism, and the "just so" story line of savagery-to-civilization evolutionism. In that effort, the central task was to demonstrate that the contingencies of social life were not determined by nature (or genes) but were produced by creative imaginations engaged with the human prospects surrounding them both near and far. In our own times, the need to renew those demonstrations continues; it is apparently never fulfilled. In the United States, the history of ethnographic endeavor pre-codes specificity as yielding questions of exclusion, assimilation, and judgment in national terms, and lends hope the character of dramatic irony (Miyazaki 2004).

Irony is by definition a gesture toward a gap in knowledge between subjects and spectators (who see beyond those actors' limits), and it proved to be an abundant ethnographic resource in this regard as policy fields distanced themselves from local social fields. A pattern emerged in ethnographers' accounts of community life that played on the critical gap between public stereotype and anthropological knowledge—the classic pretext for ethnography. Such doubling of knowledge needed little explicit attention since generalized stereotypes of foreign cultures, and generic stereotypes of U.S. ethnic and racial communities, were abundantly available through the media. The ethnographers who responded to the negative renderings with irony did so by turning back that negation as error, and by relocating culture *between* the individual and the group, rather than as determining individual behavior. Irony, in this sense, points more directly to issues of stigma than to empowerment—unless one imagines readers, armed with new knowledge, entering the ballot box to effect change. We have seen these dynamics at work in different ways—and with different skepticisms—in the work of Ellison, Liebow, and Bourgois. All three authors are explicit in addressing themselves to the challenges of *re*-personalizing social description—*person*, here, meaning not just the self, but the social surround that sustains one's sense of identity as real.

Reading the 1990s revival of the community study as a critique of neoliberal globalization helps account for several of its most salient textual features—a series of interrelated tensions over issues of community, identity, and political agency. As already noted, the "community" in a community study must play a double role—as both an actuality—alive amidst local causes and effects, and an arrangement of signs—displaced and localized elements of a global condition. This much might be said of any ethnography, since ethnography by its very nature posits a wider significance in relation to the particular. However, in the United States in the 1980s and 1990s, "community" was also the keyword of new communitarian movements on the right and left—as conservatives invoked community as a counterweight, or alternative, to the demands of identity politics on the federal social agenda, liberals looked for a revival of deliberative democracy, and progressives promoted direct democratic participation, all at the local level. The romance of "community" was central to the community study revival, providing the methodological and empirical parameters of the works, their subtext regarding democracy, and their predominantly ironic tone—but importantly, not an endorsement. Community remains ambivalent at the end of each of these works—in effect justifying the projects and allowing the books to be written, but not providing the basis for solutions to problems encountered on the ground. It is that specific vanishing point that leads to the horizon where the community study can be read as global critique.

The double casting of community involves a number of challenges. The elision of community and globality creates textual strains in the literary sense, to which ethnography's modern literariness is (consciously or not) well adapted. But that elision involves more than blurred categories. It is also crucial to how narratives of identity convey meaning in the ethnography of the United States in this period, as references to sources at once legal, political, and literary. For anthropologists writing about the United States in the 1990s, cultural identity on the page conjured a figure of displacement both ethnic and civic. This rendering of personhood as the figuration of America's incompleteness—of equality still to come—was iconic of the civil rights advocacy in the 1950s. In this new context of the 1990s, it sustained anthropologists' discursive attachment to citizenship as a way of making their readers feel their own responsibilities with respect to the marginalization of their subjects—even as rights discourse was edged out of national politics in favor of the market. As we have seen, the discourse of solutions ventures its own limitations uneasily, and anthropology's literary experiments in this regard were theorized as inherently performative and agentive, particularly in relation to the emerging politics of consumer privilege. The discourse of solutions brings ethnography, law, and fiction together in a particular way— making ethnography into fiction's double, in mutual seriousness, through the figure of the citizen.

CHAPTER 6

Democracy in the First Person

The discourse of solutions was a significant form of interdisciplinarity, drawing ethnography into fields well beyond anthropology. Anthropologists and sociolegal scholars alike—though not always known to each other—turned to the novelistic tropes of identity and narrative voice to articulate new means and ends for their professional visions of equality as a function of mutual understanding and acceptance. In this chapter, we juxtapose examples drawn from anthropology, sociolegal scholarship, and fiction to explore their varied formulations of self-identity before the law through the discourse of solutions. In those formulations, ambivalence is strategically key. First-person narration in these texts is oppositional, refusing encompassment. At the same time, the first-person singular—with whatever ironies—is iconic of the liberal subject: the responsible individual, making choices and taking ownership of his or her successes and failures. The tensions between these two positions is crucial to the play of genres in these works, as they entail different intertextualities and fundamentally different futures. First-person testimony bridges social science, fiction, and law—the suspension of disciplinary and genre difference in these instances being no mere signs of an eclectic age or one in tatters, but evidence of the effort needed to make new language out of old.

In the ethnographies of the 1990s, first-person testimony became iconic of progressive ethnography—answering the "crisis of representation" with self-representation in a register at once novelistic and legalistic. It also evokes *pro se* representation in a prosecutorial setting, in which the accused refuses the spokesmanship of another. In the community studies, significantly, the first-person singular borrows its "I" from the registers of both radical opposition and liberal association—the difference between them predicated on implied questions of citizenship and the efficacy of law as a means of inclusion. Indeed, the rhetorical conventions of legal citizenship are indebted to the novel form—"a narrative spun by and around a notion of a coherent and unified subject, posed by the European Enlightenment" (Azim 1993: 4; see also 215).

In ethnography—and not just in U.S. community studies—first-person testimony repositioned authorship as well, drawing it into a dialogic, collaborative frame (see Tsing 1993). In this, ethnography was not alone. Across the humanities and humanistic social sciences, *stories, voice,* and *narrative* situated identity in a collaborative frame of recognition. This implication linking dialogue to agency through self-representation indicates the broad influence of feminist practice on disciplines' knowledge practices and on the constitution of disciplines themselves (Heinzelman and Wiseman 1994: viii). The "call for stories" (Coles 1989) gained broad appeal as moral pedagogy and as apologia for the relevance of the humanities in relation to democracy (see Nussbaum 1995). Nussbaum's image of "poetic justice" (1995) captures the sense that stories do not merely make accounts more interesting (French 1996) but also more ethically compelling by "loosening the imagination" for difference (the phrase is borrowed from Davis 1997: 25; see also Coutin 1996; French 1996: 421; Abrams 1994).

For ethnographers and advocates alike, stories were keenly relevant as means of demonstrating the law's incompleteness with respect to its guarantees of equal rights. This demonstration had strategic value in relation to activists' efforts to protect and extend the application of already-existing rights in courts, as Congress signaled its reluctance to renew a legislative expansion of rights.[1] For example, in her essay on "telling stories" as a litigation strategy in Title VII (employment discrimination) cases, legal theorist Vicki Schultz argues that women's stories are a corrective answer to the question of women's underrepresentation in certain job categories—putting to rest the "lack of interest" argument that was used against women in their discrimination claims (Schultz 1990: 1751). Presenting plaintiffs as authors of their own stories is effective, she suggests, because it reminds judges that they, too, "are the authors of women's work aspirations" (Schultz 1990: 1843). In her essay on "the narrative and the normative," Kathryn Abrams, also a legal theorist, notes the extent to which "the valuation of experiential knowledge, the conviction that the exclusion of women's perspectives has distorted the development of legal rules, and a growing frustration with the abstraction and distance conventionally required of legal decisionmakers have produced a wave of women's storytelling" (Abrams 1994: 44). Improving the "correspondence between method and message" through stories can "help legal decisionmakers develop less partial, more broadly responsive legal solutions" (Abrams 1994: 44).

The relevance of stories in ethnography is related to the prospects of reform in a sense parallel to the advocacy claims of Abrams, Schultz, and other feminist legal scholars—importing into ethnography an implication of federal remedies. That implication constitutes personhood in a particular way that I call *federal subjectivity*—a discourse of personhood constructed in the registers of high federal power in relation to which self-narrative compels recognition and opens a space for relief. The discussion follows from the previous chapter on the constitution of identity—and fictions inherent in its legalism—in the discourse of solutions. In this chapter, I trace federal subjectivity as it circulates across sociolegal studies, fiction, and ethnography. While these genres converge in an assertive endorsement of self-narrative as social knowledge, they differ in terms of what they make of citizenship. For sociolegal scholars, stories express an individual's legal consciousness—one's ideas about law being an element of one's self-identity. For authors of fiction, self-representation is outside of the law, revealing its limits. For ethnographers—and this is the point of the chapter—self-narrative is in between, combining the "I" of legal claims-making with the "we" of fiction.

Lives do not make their own stories. How identity is wrestled into narrative is never a simple question, calling not only on subjective understandings of experience but also conventions of expression keyed to the particularities of time, place, and audience. The break into self-representation that takes Ellison's narrator into the light at the end of *Invisible Man* is not simply a choice; the whole novel tells the story, materializing the narrator's agency in (and as) the story's continuation. In a similar spirit, the authors of these works present them as necessary and complete in the same sense—as integral to the situation, their interiority presented as a challenge, and an immediate and irreversible compact among author, reader and subjects.

Afterlives of *Brown*

In her analysis of the interpretive aspects of the litigation in *Brown v. Board of Education*, legal scholar Peggy Davis observes that a crucial element of the plaintiffs' strategy was their evocation of the United States as a "multicultural political community": "The lawyers for the African American plaintiffs who brought *Brown* to the Supreme Court simultaneously played upon and subverted the image of the United States as a white polity. In some respects, they manifested a strategic, albeit culturally ingrained, deference to social, judicial, and doctrinal authority. At the same time, however, they commanded unprecedented authority in the interpretation of constitutional doctrine" (Davis 1997: 25). Continuing, she suggests that the effect of their strategy was to "open" constitutional interpretation to new participants and perspectives: "In the end, their efforts transformed our Constitution, establishing it as an open text—a text to be (real)ized in interpretive deliberation informed by previously neglected perspectives. Moreover, as they brought neglected American perspectives to constitutional deliberation, the *Brown* lawyers loosened the national imagination from its inability to conceptualize African American participation in the processes of political self-definition" (Davis 1997: 25).

The loosening of imagination through a performance of ambivalence involved more than issues of constitutional doctrine. As Davis implies, achieving critical ambivalence meant re-imagining social life—indeed, the very constitution (so to speak) of personhood. Anthropologists' figurations of minority personhood resonated with the imagery that was central to the social science brief in *Brown* (itself an interdisciplinary composition). With that figuration of subjectivity, they absorbed *Brown*'s critical positioning of the individual relative to the nation, constructing the subject as both a potential object of federal relief but also as an object of political anxiety. I refer to this amalgam of agencies as *federal subjectivity*.

The association between progressive critique and direct discourse in ethnography in the 1990s was shaped in part by meanings imported from the federal arena—which, at a critical juncture, had relied on social science to substantiate the national interest in racial equality (J. P. Jackson 2001). Among the many afterlives of the alliance between social scientists and the plaintiffs' team in *Brown v. Board* was an enduring template for the legitimacy of social science in relation to legal controversy involving social policy. That template can be seen in Congressional hearing rooms; however, legislative action is by definition general, whereas courtroom action—even if it has broad implications—is personal. Plaintiffs' (and other proponents') idioms in the federal arenas associated with the expansion of civil rights in the 1950s and 1960s—along with their literary resources and extensions—circulated through the hermeneutic fields of federal law-making and law enforcement. It is perhaps these idioms in this context that lends first-person testimony its contemporary democratic allure. Third-world feminism and postcolonial literary criticism internationalized and complicated these associations in ways that thickened their political resonances as commentary on the domestic fronts of global power, compacting these with ethnographic resonance as well (Moraga and Anzaldúa 1983; Ashcroft, Griffith, and Tiffin 1989).

In ethnography, readers are addressed as members of the public more than as fellow anthropologists—that public missing in the mainstream, the political gap reconfigured as a knowledge gap. We have explored this positioning of the reader in relation to Elliot Liebow's *Tally's Corner* and Philippe Bourgois's *In Search of Respect*. In those works, among others in this book, narrative form absorbs important elements from the testimonial templates of citizenship—as the research subject becomes a testifying witness, for example, presented by the advocate-anthropologist to the reader-judge. It is the substantive benefits of citizenship that are most explicitly in question in these works.

The scope for such questions was experientially near in the first half of the 1990s—as a contentious national debate over rights touched on an extraordinary range of social life. "Political correctness" was invoked to rebuke what some saw as the informal regulation of speech around the very identity categories the rights debate had made into icons of federal powers. Affirmative action and antidiscrimination laws were felt by some to be federal regulation of personal association. The abortion debate was a major political issue. Debates over the criminalization of homosexuality and the rights of gay partners (like the abortion debate, tied strategically to debates over federalism) also carried questions of federal powers into the intimate spaces of private living. In this sense, federal subjectivity was pervasive in its varieties, making *the individual* an ambiguous sign of both personal uniqueness and an expression of a national society somehow constituted in law.[2] Its polyvalence made it available to the full political spectrum, having been assembled there episodically in the course of oppositional struggles over civil rights.

The liberal construction of society presupposes both the nature of the nation as a totality of identities and the nature of the individual as a self-knowing subject. The politicization of discourse around the meanings of individualism with respect to its implications about federal power and its limits was—and remains—a crucial feature of the public political sphere in the United States. In the 1990s, as we have seen, the individualism in liberalism was actively promoted as the central feature of the conservative and neoliberal coalition campaign against the expansion of civil rights around racial equality and continuation of welfare entitlements as the core of social security. Liberals in the older mode—evoking the New Deal—instead emphasized the collective side of this formulation, in their evocations of the nation, with *the public* as its social dimension. In the 1990s, the politics of discourse was sharply focused on the individual, constructed as a tension between competing values—rights and responsibility—especially with respect to minority individuals and, in the context of the abortion debate, women. Iconically African American, the minority individual's autobiography acquired profound public significance as the nation's affirmation or challenge, depending on which version of liberalism was in play. As a consequence, a minority subject's life story was always at least dual—twice-told around the linked chronicles of the private individual and the national society. In the rest of this chapter, we consider how federal subjectivity—through the workings of first-person narration—sustains the connection between personhood and federal power, and, for ethnography, ambivalence over the efficacy of law.

The Federal Subject

In 2002, when the U.S. Supreme Court upheld the University of Michigan Law School's approach to admissions in a long-awaited case, *Grutter v. Bollinger*, the Court's opinion brought to a provisional close a long political and legal struggle over affirmative action. In a sharp dissent, Justice Clarence Thomas wrote a rueful assessment of affirmative action as a source of stigma:

> It is uncontested that each year, the Law School admits a handful of blacks who would be admitted in the absence of racial discrimination. . . . Who can differentiate between those who belong and those who do not? The majority of blacks are admitted to the Law School because of discrimination, and because of this policy all are tarred as undeserving. This problem of stigma does not depend on determinacy as to whether those stigmatized are actually the "beneficiaries" of racial discrimination. When blacks take positions in the highest places of government, industry, or academia, it is an open question today whether their skin color played a part in their advancement. The question itself is the stigma—because either racial discrimination did play a role, in which case the person may be deemed "otherwise unqualified," or it did not, in which case asking the question itself unfairly marks those blacks who would succeed without discrimination.[3]

It is difficult not to read this passage in personal terms (for one thing, it is wholly unfootnoted). It seems to comment on his own experience, including the Senate confirmation process in fall 1991, which—until the second hearings over his conduct as an employer—had rhetorically unfolded around the symmetry that this child of *Brown* would succeed Thurgood Marshall, *Brown*'s legal architect (see Greenhouse 1996; Trix and Sankar 1998). Old liberals could celebrate "firsts." But for the new conservative movement, *seconds* were even better, as they seemed to validate their position that the need for new civil rights lawmaking was now past. The George H. W. Bush administration consistently took this position, and, like other critics of affirmative action—including the new majority of the current U.S. Supreme Court—argued that legal protections on the basis of race are themselves discriminatory. In 1991, Justice Thomas had participated actively in telling and retelling his life story as an integral part of his qualification for the court. Now, eleven years later, he seemed to be reworking the key terms of that very narrative—race, equality, discrimination, stigma—and in the process, pushing the prospect of equality to an ever-receding horizon of misrecognition.

Over the course of the Thomas hearings, the dominance of his life story—as it was told and retold in context—structured the hearings around the stereotypical identity of an African American man. In context, this stereotype blended with the rhetorical figure of the future citizen evoked in *Brown*. In other words, the relevance of Thomas's life story was established as the life story of an African American man who had overcome the negative aspects of his identity and kept the positive ones. Those positive features were rhetorically reduced to his "memory," his "sensitivity," and his availability as a "role model" to others, presumably younger African American men (see Greenhouse 1996). Whether or not the Thomas dissent in *Grutter* reaches the merits of affirmative action in the legal sense, it makes clear the extent to which the federal subjectivity that dominated the repeated performance of his life story in the confirmation hearings was dated—rendered so by the conservative critique of rights.

The concept of *identity* can never stray very far from the histories, solidarities, and ambivalences that are the essence of its counter-hegemonic implication, nor from the federal legalities that have sustained that implication as an actual choice for the social movements of the mid- and late twentieth century. This means that that identity is not a neutral term for something everyone has, but a political relation across transnational fields of knowledge production that are highly asymmetrical, the durability of which cannot be guaranteed.[4] If identity before the law can only be negative—as in the Thomas dissent—this would signal a major transformation in the field of power/knowledge, including the conditions that sustained *identity* as an answerable question at the core of anthropology's methods and ethics since the turn of the last century.

The advocates of the legislation that eventually became the Civil Rights Act of 1991 and the Welfare Reform Act of 1996 put forward their proposals as explicit correctives to what they deemed to be the anachronism of liberalism—its excesses, in other words, relative to the challenges of the new global economy. For the most part, neoliberalism came packaged as a rhetoric of *endorsement* and *reform*—not a rejection of earlier programs. Thus, both sides of the debate over civil rights could express liberal endorsements of the values of *Brown* and the Civil Rights Act of 1964, and all sides of the welfare debate could endorse New Deal and Great Society programs in their acknowledgments of public responsibility for the most vulnerable citizens. But such universalistic expressions of values crumbled against questions of pragmatics. The Civil Rights Act of 1964 had opened access to legal remedies to race discrimination that the Reagan and Bush administrations strove openly to curtail. The Congressional hearings over the Americans with Disabilities Act and the Civil Rights Acts of 1990 and 1991 tested the limits of those curtailments against the new realities of neoliberal economics. In the end, liberals were able to renew the affirmation of equality only to the extent that its implementation did not impose financial burdens on the private sector or "the taxpayers"—in this context, a proxy term that evokes the state through a condensation of a national public to a contributive fiscal identity.

These issues dominated the public sphere, and put key images, logics, and prescriptions of value into wide circulation—with heavy material effects. The debate over the new civil rights legislation showed that there was no liberal consensus over equality when it was set up as a trade-off against profitability. The debate over welfare officialized a highly pejorative view of the urban poor—stereotypically African American—as illegitimate consumers in a universe of limited goods. This is not merely a point about the hermeneutics of political persuasion. Through the Congressional testimony and debate over these measures, specific constructions of race became hegemonic, and, written into law, worked their effects on actual communities. Their hegemonic effect is less a question of the direct power of law, but rather of the highly public spectacle by which discourse is selectively consolidated from a diverse communicative field, and made a condition of access to the public arena (see Greenhouse 2005).[5]

In this regard, two striking elements of Justice Thomas's dissent are his tacit refusal to identify himself either *as* a beneficiary of civil rights law or *with* beneficiaries of civil rights law. Justice Thomas the nominee came to his hearings in the midst of a partisan program to rework civil rights law around notions of responsibility that made race an individual attribute without any compelling rights implication. By the end of the 1990s, that uncoupling was more insistent, and more negative. Reading Justice Thomas's dissent in this context suggests that if the positive valence of the old liberal version of the federal life story is depleted, this does not mean that the rationales for affirmative action are exhausted—only that the life story is no longer their most compelling expression in the contemporary milieu.

Legal Consciousness—Patricia Ewick and Susan Silbey

The Thomas dissent reflects one mainstream view that affirmative action is stigmatizing, and I have suggested that this position reflects a lapse in an identification with beneficiaries of the law. Perhaps the representational value of the life story as a call for state action has been trumped by its functions—that is, conjuring powers rather than persons. Anthropologist Marilyn Strathern calls this sort of slippage "transactability" (1987: 7), noting that one element in "the building of relationships requires that things/persons also be conceptualized as standing for things/persons they are not. . . . Contrasts between men and women [the theme of her book] become a vehicle for the creation of value: *for evaluating one set of powers by reference to another*" (1987: 7; original emphasis). The transactability of the life story shifts the fundamental question in inequality from the status differential of groups to the content of the differential itself in reference to federal power—constituting identities as entailing relationships through federal power, in other words. This is a potent suggestion that introduces the question of how "powers" themselves are constituted and differentiated in relation to identity. Attending to how such representations function politically (and not just descriptively) points to their implication in the constitution of state powers, and (accordingly) to the historic specificity of the politics of genre. The literariness of identity does not suspend its material stakes—on the contrary, identity in a sense becomes those stakes (as we see in the Thomas dissent).

Sociolegal scholars Patricia Ewick and Susan Silbey (1998) develop this connection from below, as a question of legal consciousness made accessible through stories. In their analysis, legal consciousness—ideas about law—constitutes a diffuse and pervasive legality. Legality, in their usage, is broader than law in the strict sense. Their premise is that law is both "a constituent of social life" (17) and social life itself: "The law—or what we will call legality—embodies the diversity of the situations out of which it emerges and that it helps structure. Because legality is embedded in and emerges out of daily activities, its meanings and uses echo and resonate with other common phenomena, specifically bureaucracies, games, or 'just making do'" (17). Law, for Ewick and Silbey, is produced as a natural and normal effect of everyday social action: "The commonplace operation of law in daily life makes us all legal agents insofar as we actively make law, even when no formal legal agent is involved" (20).[6]

For Ewick and Silbey, the main question is not whether law can accommodate diversity (that it already does so is stipulated from the beginning) but rather whether and how ordinary people understand their own roles in the everyday production of law. Accordingly, their research involves gathering evidence of legal consciousness in the form of "stories":

> People tell three stories. In one story, legality is imagined and treated as an objective realm of disinterested action, removed and distant from the personal lives of ordinary people. In this story, law is majestic, operating by known and fixed rules in carefully delimited spheres. . . . But people also tell a second story where legality is depicted as a game, a terrain for tactical encounters through which people marshal a variety of social resources to achieve strategic goals. . . . People also told us a third story of legality. In this account, the law is a product of power . . . legality is understood to be arbitrary and capricious. . . . In this third story, people talk about the ruses, tricks, and subterfuges they use to appropriate part of law's power. (28)

The Common Place of Law is composed as a series of stories, interleaved with interpretive commentary (for details of their research objectives and methods, see Ewick and Silbey 1998: xi–xiii and appendix A; Silbey 2005). "We adopted the concept of narrative [for their scholarly presentation] because people tend to explain their actions to themselves and to others through stories" (29). For Ewick and Silbey, it is the dialogic aspect of stories that lends them their extraordinary flexibility as simultaneously sociological rationale, means and ends. Stories are vehicles for self-revelation as well as a "form of social action" (29) and vernacular sociological analysis: "Stories . . . reflect and sustain institutional and cultural arrangements, bridging the gap between daily social interaction and large-scale social structures. In other words, stories people tell about themselves and their lives both constitute and interpret those lives; the stories describe the world as it is lived and is understood by the storyteller" (29; note and paragraph break omitted). Therefore, they continue, "narratives can enter scholarly research as either the object, the method, or the product of inquiry" (29). They explain their own use of stories as both "a lens to study law in everyday life" and "a metaphor to represent what we have discovered" (29). Their "note on story-telling" (258 ff.) details the methodological and editorial issues they faced in their effort to "preserve the voice of our respondents" (258).

Importantly, Ewick and Silbey look to law stories not merely as a genre of narrative, but as evidence of "types of legal consciousness" that influence individuals' uses of law (223–224). They group their collected narratives according to whether a respondent positions him- or herself "before," "with," or "against" the law (reflecting the three types of stories mentioned above). These might or might not constitute stable or consistent subject positions; in fact, they most likely do not, as Ewick and Silbey emphasize themselves, observing that a single individual might tell all three types of stories, and that all three types entail internal variation and contradiction (227). One conclusion to be drawn from the study is that encounters with law—quite apart from the outcomes of those encounters—provide individuals with a highly flexible idiom for narratively reworking their own status positions relative to whatever they regard as "society" and its structures of power. This leaves open the question as to whether that idiom is a means of transforming those power relations—or yielding to them.

Ewick and Silbey acknowledge this question regarding the indeterminacy of law's hegemony—and this revives the conundrum of legality posited at the outset. They evoke their own opening depiction of legality as both constitutive of and constituted by narrative: "Here then is the mystery. How can legality be what it is and at the same time what it is not? How can legality be autonomous from and simultaneously constitutive of everyday life? How can legality be both sacred and profane, God and gimmick, interested and disinterested, here and not here? . . . Now it is time, as in any good mystery, for resolution" (223). Their "resolution" to this "mystery" unfolds in steps, toward a thesis regarding the power effects of legal consciousness. They begin this part of the book by expanding their association of stories with legal consciousness so as to encompass social structure. "Consciousness . . . must be construed as a type of social practice, in the sense that it reflects and forms structure" (225). *Structure* also includes nonnarrative elements and effects, "encompass[ing] ideas as well as resources . . . emerging out of, even as it impinges upon, social interactions" (225). "To what extent do structures embed power?" they ask (225). Here, power becomes external, part of the material world: "How does the distribution of resources and relative access to legitimating cultural schemas produce and preserve social inequality and relative powerlessness?" (225). Structures are hegemonic, they add—defining hegemony as a state of affairs in which "the operation of power in and through structures is obscured, remaining unquestioned and unrecognized" (225; cf. Lazarus-Black and Hirsch 1994; Comaroff and Comaroff 1991: 19–23).

At this juncture, *consciousness* refers to "participation in the production of structures" (225)—that is, in the production of "specific pattern[s] in social structure"(226). Ideology always "embodies a particular arrangement of power and affects life chances in a manner different from that of some other ideology or arrangement of power" (226). Importantly, Ewick and Silbey argue that ideologies cannot be totalized sociologically—that is, they do not add up to "culture or structure in general" (226). Rather, "ideology has to be lived, worked out, and worked on. . . . People have to use it to make sense of their lives. It is only through that sense making that people produce . . . the specific structures and contests for power within which they live" (226). Hegemony "works," they say, by maintaining an "illusory opposition between the particular and general"—and this leads them to listen for "counterhegemonic" consciousness in the midst of whatever "circumstances . . . encourage people to recognize the relationships among personal experience, local practices, institutions, and authority" (226).

In sum, for Ewick and Silbey, stories are expressions of legal consciousness, revealing the ideological framings of social structure. Social structure, in their formulation, is the source, object, and effect of agency—hegemonic in directing individual agency away from the generality of power; therefore, law stories are by definition counter-hegemonic in that they reestablish the relationship between the specific and the general. However, the mystery remains—since the same reasoning could lead to the conclusion that law stories are the very essence of law's hegemony, as individuals fit their personal experiences into those large structures. Ewick and Silbey address this issue in a broader discussion of consciousness. They identify three interrelated conditions for counter-hegemonic consciousness—"social marginality, recognizing the world as socially constructed, and storytelling" (226 ff.). "The marginal" are a large group: "the poor and working class, the racially and ethnically stigmatized, physically and mentally disabled persons, women, children and the elderly" (234–235)—the majority of the population. "To state the obvious," Ewick and Silbey write, "those who are most subject to power are most likely to be acutely aware of its operation" (235). But here is a paradox: Their definition of hegemony stipulates that those most subject to law's power would be precisely those who are *not* aware of its operation. Hegemonic legality at its extremes would presumably preclude narration. To borrow the playfulness of their concluding chapter's opening paragraph, how can one be socially marginal and yet not?

One can be marginal while not being marginal, so to speak, by identifying with others.[7] The stories are performances of identification and alliances with others through the language of law, as the findings reported in the book's appendix suggest. However, the individuality and interpretive qualities of those accounts are held to one side of the question of consciousness. In this regard, the book's focus is consistent with the discourse of solutions that was prevalent in the 1990s. The context of the times put legality into question relative to diversity (as discussed in Chapter 2). Accordingly, the stories in Ewick and Silbey's account are analytically pre-coded with structural significance—law and social structure (in a sense) speaking for each other through the storytellers. In other words, the fact of first-person narration carries a structural implication more or less independently of the content of the narrative or the relationships in question. Read in retrospect, the authors' theoretical concern to broaden the concept of law to encompass the sum of such narratives is interesting as evidence of both the indebtedness of empirical social science to the canons of liberal subjectivity and the relevance of law in the significance of narrative as genre.

Anthropologists writing about American cities in the 1990s for the most part left state institutions and law out of the picture altogether, but their assumptions about stories appear to be similar to those set out by Ewick and Silbey. Informants' narratives—that is, stories within the text—are tacitly mobilized to tell the larger story (the ethnographic narrative as a whole) about social marginality in relation to the nation and a generalized concept of power. As in *The Common Place of Law,* the researcher as narrative persona performs an identification with his/her research subjects as a particular sort of counter-hegemonic performance addressed to state power and the selectivity of social justice. The figuration of the conscious subject as standing before the law is the essence of federal subjectivity and its functions in the discourse of solutions.

Rights, Narrative, and Personhood

Lawyers David Engel and Frank Munger turn the question of legal consciousness the other way around. Their interest is in how a specific law—the Americans with Disabilities Act of 1990—figures in the life stories of individuals presumed to be its beneficiaries. As we have seen, the ADA was proposed to Congress so as to consolidate separate state laws at the federal level, as well as to make a political test of further rights advances. That larger context is beyond the scope of the study, but not beyond the concerns of some of the authors' interviewees. The study is based on extensive interviews with individuals with a variety of disabilities covered by the ADA (for an account of their research goals and methods, see Engel and Munger (2003: xi–xii).

The book is presented as a series of life stories, interspersed with the authors' commentary as well as subsequent commentary by some of their respondents. Their goal is not an evaluation of the efficacy of the law—there is no discourse of solutions here. Rather, they are interested in how law affects the lives of people it is created to help: "Few studies have attempted to trace the interconnections between a new law and the everyday lives of ordinary people who are its potential beneficiaries. In our research, we try to understand the life stories and 'legal consciousness' of a group of individuals during the time when a major civil rights law is being implemented, a law that might potentially transform their lives and their very identity within American society" (Engel and Munger 2003: 4). Their research method required few advance definitions beyond the parameters of the study itself:

> The interviews themselves were designed to reveal the presence or absence of rights consciousness and the influence of law at various moments in the interviewees' employment experience and career planning. We did not ask directly about the law, or even mention its existence, until the conclusion of the interview. Rather, we invited the interviewees to use their own language to describe their life histories. . . . We tried to discern whether and how the interviewees themselves incorporated legal concepts in their narratives and whether the law in some obvious or subtle way had shaped their experiences. We

> encouraged the interviewees to explain their perceptions of situations they themselves identified as problematic or unfair and to describe the framework they used to analyze such situations and respond to them. . . . Near the end of each interview, we asked more explicitly about the interviewee's awareness of legal rights and his or her readiness to invoke them. (8–9)

Thus, keywords such as law, rights, and identity emerged—often quite differently—from interviewees' responses.

Engel and Munger draw on narrative to understand something of individuals' repertoires of participation in social relationships across a variety of personal and institutional settings. In other words, their concerns are not with representation. Narrative, for them, does not reveal some underlying matrix of (self-)representation, nor are they delimited by issues of health status. Rather, their respondents' stories are about their social experiences: "People tell and retell their personal histories in different ways under different circumstances. These narrative variations enable individuals to go out and meet the world, to engage with different kinds of people and experiences, to present themselves to others and to return with a sense of who they themselves are" (10). The efficacy of a new law, they argue, should be assessed over the course of beneficiaries' lifetimes since life stories reveal different experiences and different engagements with law over time. This is the first of two theses developed across the book as a whole (10).

Their second thesis, based on the first, is that "rights become active in many other ways beyond the relatively rare situations in which they are explicitly invoked. . . . Thus, in our research we do not assume as a starting point that the normal or proper response to unfair treatment is the assertion of rights, or that the lives of our interviewees would invariably improve if they were to invoke the ADA. . . . The ADA represents one resource among many that could play a part in their lives" (10–11). Indeed, the stories differ widely in the extent to which individuals say their lives have been affected by disability, and their sense of options shaped by the availability—at least in theory—of new remedies. Engel and Munger's major finding is that rights and identity are mutually entwined—in different ways for different people, as well as according to circumstance and over time.

Engel and Munger turn to contemporary sociolegal scholarship (including Ewick and Silbey's book) to discuss "legal consciousness," but their own usage is original and distinctive. For them, legal consciousness is but one aspect of someone's sense of self, "distributed" over one's social circles, and part of the dynamic of a person's self-awareness over time (12). One set of issues involves people's sense of identity in relation to their disability—that is, whether they see their disabilities as who they are, or as something more or less separate from the question of their self-identity. The latter tends to coincide with a sense that rights are personally relevant; the former tends to lead people "to question their right to participate fully in mainstream settings" (69). Another set of issues has to do with the way rights affect a person's sense of possibility, as well as (more concretely) their options, the prevailing social discourse, and incentives for third parties to take the initiative in acknowledging an individual's rights (94–98). The combination of "risks and rewards" (97) inherent in the active mobilization of rights differs in everyone's personal calculus.

Engel and Munger examine how people invoke rights discourse in discussing their attitudes and experiences, finding that a person's sense of rights in the disability context flows to and from rights contexts well beyond the ADA. For example, in telling their own stories, respondents sometimes volunteer accounts of the benchmarks in the development of their own rights consciousness in the course of their experiences as consumers, employees, and citizens, or as members of a religious faith or unions, or as women (see esp. pp. 133, 139, 149–151, 175). Their main conclusion is that "a recursive theory of rights must consider identity as a precursor as well as a consequence of rights, and rights as a result as well as a cause of change" (253). It seems that the extent to which people identify with others whom they perceive as potential beneficiaries of civil rights is integral to their legal consciousness, as well as to their readiness to participate in society on that basis. In other words, in Engel and Munger's account, legality is not all-encompassing, nor is it claimed as a reflection of identity. Rather, more radically, their exploration of law and identity prompts questions about the locations, purposes, pleasures, and pain of their respondents' social participation, and of the extent to which rights feature in their self-recognition and their repertoires of identification with others (whether positively, negatively, or something in between). Their methodological emphasis on stories, and the prominence of stories in their account, underscore the transformative potential in engaging with its interpretive demands. Primary among these—in this account—is the enlargement of the capacity for some individuals to identify with others who are rights beneficiaries in other ways, and (therefore) to think of oneself as a citizen among fellow citizens. The discourse of solutions is unsettled as individuals formulate their relationship to the law the other way around, as a question of the law's relationship to them—and as related a question of their social connections and distances.

Law's Limits

The discourse of federal subjectivity circulates as a standardizing conflation of personhood with the rights-bearing citizen—and indeed, of law and society more generally. It also circulates as a critical discourse targeting law's limits in relation to subjectivity. These limits of law are evident in Toni Morrison's *The Bluest Eye* (1972), which we reread here as a work of the 1990s since it was republished in 1993. In the novel, the issue is not just whether one can identify with others, but with the stakes in one's identification with and by others.

I choose Morrison's novel because it draws some of its key images from *Brown*. Indeed, if read too quickly, it might even seem to promise a corroboration of a key element of the plaintiffs' brief. In preparing for *Brown* before the Supreme Court, the plaintiffs' team drew on the findings of social psychologists Kenneth and Mamie Clark, claiming to show that even very young African American children were aware of and had internalized a standard of beauty restricted to whiteness.[8] The Supreme Court accepted the doll test as evidence of the extent to which even very young children were fluent in the signs of stigma—that is, as evidence of segregation's deep yet intangible harm. This element was pivotal in the plaintiffs' argument, since it meant that the harm of segregation could not be averted by making black and white schools "separate but equal"—equality as envisioned in *Plessy v. Ferguson* in 1896.

The book's title is a reference to the central character's yearning for the blue eyes of those white dolls. That this is a sign of vulnerability is clear from the beginning, as the narrator, Claudia, recounts her own reaction to a "Shirley Temple" doll as a child: "It had begun with Christmas and the gift of dolls. The big, the special, the loving gift was always a big, blue-eyed Baby Doll. . . . What was I supposed to do with it? . . . I had only one desire: to dismember it. To see of what it was made, to discover the dearness, to find the beauty, the desirability that had escaped me, but apparently only me" (Morrison 1972 19–20). Like most of the northern children tested by the Clarks, the main character, Pecola, prefers the white doll. But in the passage just quoted, the narrator has already let us know to read Pecola's desire as a symptom of dis-ease.

The narrator is Claudia MacTeer, now an adult, remembering the winter of 1940–1941 in Lorain, Ohio—remembering what she and her elder sister witnessed, heard, imagined, and later understood of Pecola's life and losses. Claudia's perspective is anchored to her own family and childhood home, the safe center of the novel's geography of risk. But for Pecola there is no safety; the novel is the story of her destruction. It is not (or not just) that Pecola is fragile; it is that the sources of her injuries are everywhere.

In her own small frame, Pecola has absorbed an overdose of this toxic air, such that—with the exception of the MacTeer sisters and their mother—she experiences no encounter in the space of the novel that does not injure her. Even at the candy shop (even the owner has blue eyes) she pays for her Mary Janes twice over: "He hesitates, not wanting to touch her hand. . . . Finally, he reaches over and takes the pennies from her hand. His nails graze her damp palm" (41–43). Pecola's mother, too, would like to enter the world of style and stylish things, but that way is barred to her; she enters instead a world of fantasy—at the movies and in her work as a maid in a white household.

For Cholly, Pecola's father, there is no such escape. His story—told in the third person, like Sethe's in *Beloved*—unfolds around his losses: abandoned by his mother, left alone by the death of his Aunt Jimmy, and brutally rejected by his father. But it was something else that made these injuries irreparable. In the woods with Darlene after Aunt Jimmy's funeral, Darlene gives him his first experience of lovemaking. They are interrupted by two white hunters. At gunpoint, and shining their flashlight on Cholly and Darlene, they force them back to the act; Cholly goes through the motions. Claudia narrates the episode with great empathy. Cholly never recovers, in the sense that after this rape—their rape by light and gunpoint—he can no longer distinguish love from hate. Claudia writes of Cholly that he was "dangerously free": "He was alone with his own perceptions and appetites, and they alone interested him" (125). Later, in this "godlike state" (126) Cholly—drunk on alcohol and briefly inhabiting a memory of tenderness he once felt for Pauline—reaches for Pecola. The touch becomes a rape. Pecola is helpless, cannot even scream. Later, pregnant, mad, and alone, she drifts around the town, and it is this image that haunts the book.

But the novel does not stop with Cholly, or Pauline. The novel is not an explanation of a crime, nor a sociology of causes—it withholds excuses from perpetrators and witnesses alike. If the novel explains anything, it is the need to write, the possibility of speaking. While the novel poses its central questions through the account of Pecola's and Claudia's childhoods, their different fates confirm the limits of explanation, the limits of life stories, the ethical—rather than descriptive—content of identity: Pecola's tragedy was not inevitable, and yet she could not avoid it. Ethical responsibility vastly surpasses explanation; at the end of the story, the sisters resolve to save Pecola's baby: "We decided to change the course of events and alter a human life" (149). Their techniques include a talismanic planting of marigolds in their own backyard—"and when they come up, we'll know everything is all right" (149). But the seeds do not grow.

Timeliness is central to the book's narrative organization and ethical challenge. While Morrison makes everyone in the novel—and the readers—in some way responsible for Pecola (as in *Brown's* figuration of the person in the nation), she also challenges *Brown*. In establishing the grounds for overturning *Plessy v. Ferguson* in *Brown*, the Supreme Court distinguished the United States of the late nineteenth century from modern American society of the 1950s. In that modern milieu, education is concomitant with citizenship, and there is no returning to *Plessy's* world—"we cannot turn back the clock." But Morrison's temporality explodes the notion of the passage of time since nothing is ever over. Pecola bears the injuries inflicted on Cholly, as he was made to bear injuries not of his own making, yet there is no redemptive symmetry in the narrative—their injuries compound. In a searing riposte to *Brown's* phrase, "all deliberate speed," the book opens with the sound-image, a taped reading of a child's primer ("Here is the house. It is green and white" [3])—stuck on fast-forward.

In *Brown*, time passes lineally into the history of the nation. The timeliness of *The Bluest Eye* is entirely different. It is radically personal, resonant with Fanon's temporality in *Black Skin, White Masks*: "The architecture of this work is rooted in the temporal. Every human problem must be considered from the standpoint of time. Ideally, the present will always contribute to the building of the future. And this future is not the future of the cosmos but rather the future of my century, my country, my existence" (Fanon 1967: 12).

Implicitly, Morrison's narrative, through Claudia, moves across Fanon's imagery, and back again. With Fanon, she explores the particular way in which the white gaze marks what he calls "a definitive structuring of the self and of the world—definitive because it creates a real dialectic between my body and the world" (Fanon 1967: 111). In a crucial episode, she relates an unexpected encounter between the young white girl who is Pauline's charge and Pauline's daughter, Pecola. The white child is terrified—a reenactment of Fanon's narrative of his experience in a French train ("Look, mother . . .

a Negro . . . I'm frightened" [Fanon 1967: 109–115]). Pecola's quest for blue eyes reveals the depths of her inability to survive her alienation, as she can see herself only through others' eyes. Between the uninhabitable gaze of others and one's consciousness of personhood, Fanon writes, is a zone of revolutionary self-making: "The explosion will not happen today. It is too soon . . . or too late" (Fanon 1967: 7). He locates the scene of that explosion within self-recognition as both subject and object of history: "There is a zone of nonbeing, an extraordinarily sterile and arid region, an utterly naked declivity where an authentic upheaval can be born" (Fanon 1967: 8).[9] Claudia ends her narrative with this same imagery:

> And now when I see [Pecola] searching the garbage—for what? The thing we assassinated? I talk about how I did not plant the seeds too deeply, how it was the fault of the earth, the land, of our town. I even think now that the land of the entire country was hostile to marigolds that year. This soil is bad for certain kinds of flowers. Certain seeds it will not nurture, certain fruit it will not bear, and when the land kills of its own volition, we acquiesce and say the victim had no right to live. We are wrong, of course, but it doesn't matter. It's too late. At least on the edge of my town, among the garbage and the sunflowers of my town, it's much, much, much too late. (Morrison 1970: 160)

As the novel's tension mounts around Pecola's crisis, the issue of remedies becomes more pressing—and the absence of law more complex. What will come next, after Claudia puts down her pen, is not clear. What is certain in Claudia's narrative of Pecola's story is that it cannot be limited to the skin-bound individual. It is not the individual who "has" race, but the society as a whole. If there is a vision of justice in the novel, it is a justice that will not come from legal remedies, yet cannot come without them.

High Cotton

In fiction, the ground from which law's absence is perceptible is not always represented as jurisdiction or place; sometimes it is temporal. Darryl Pinckney's *High Cotton* (1992) is a fictional memoir, narrated by an unnamed African American man—like the narrator of *Invisible Man*—reflecting on his life up to the fictional present in mid-1980s, when he is about forty-five. He chronicles his coming of age as heir to his grandfather's generation, but divided from it by their faith (and his loss of faith) in law. At the climax of the novel, the narrator refers to the Supreme Court as having once been his "Lourdes" (the past tense is crucial; Pinckney 1992: 309). Of the examples considered in this chapter, the representation of law as an absence is most explicit here, ultimately becoming an absence neces-sary to the narrator's sense of both obligation and freedom to rebuild his life, and to write it.

The story begins in the narrator's middle-class household in Indianapo-lis, in the early 1950s. Pinckney's narrator acquires his racial education in the course of the novel. Some of the novel's power is in the way Pinckney uses narrative to evoke—rather than describe—thresholds of understand-ing. The book begins this way:

> No one sat me down and told me I was a Negro. That was some-thing I figured out on the sly, late in my childhood career as a snoop, like discovering that babies didn't come from an exchange of spinach during a kiss. . . . There was nothing to be afraid of as long as we were polite and made good grades. After all, the future, back then, as-sembled as we were on the glossy edge of the New Frontier, belonged to us, the Also Chosen. The future was something my parents were either earning or keeping for my two sisters and me, like the token checks that came on birthdays from grandparents, great-uncles, great-aunts. (3)

Pinckney develops the theme of difference with a series of plays alter-nating high national (federal) rhetoric and popular culture icons: "All men were created equal, but even so, lots of mixed messages with sharp teeth waited under my Roy Rogers pillow. . . . You had nothing to fear, though every time you left the house for a Spelling Bee or a Music Memory Contest the future of the future hung in the balance. . . . Those who dwelled in the great beyond out there could not stop His truth from marching on, but until His truth made it as far as restricted Broadripple Park, you did not go swimming" (4).

The narrator seeks some meaning of difference that he can actually live—ironizing the immigrant myth (Chock 1991) as the duty to "act as though you belonged": "You were not an immigrant, there were no foreign accents, weird holidays, or funny food to live down, but still you did not belong to the great beyond out there; yet though you did not belong it was your duty as the Also Chosen to get up and act as though you belonged, especially when no one wanted you to" (4).

The central relationship in the book is the one between the narrator and his grandfather. Throughout the book, his grandfather is present from another time: "Grandfather Eustace was the emperor of out-of-it" (6). Early in the book, Pinckney indexes the generations of grandfather and grandson with references to legal decisions that identify the narrator's lifespan with the *Brown* generation: "Grandfather looked at me, a severe expression. . . . 'Come here, . . . if you please,' Plessy vs. Ferguson contemplated Brown vs. Board of Education" (26–27). Pinckney develops the intergenerational theme. The "old country" in the following passage is Alabama, where the narrator's aunts live, a place of special knowledge, piled up with federal referents:

> The Old Country . . . was a place of secrets, of what black people knew and what white people didn't. No old-timer said openly that Rosa Parks had been secretary of her NAACP branch and a student of interstate commerce rulings and the Equal Accommodations Law of 1948 before she decided she was too tired to move.
>
> The old-timers fell silent whenever I entered the room . . . and then went back to the possibility that Roy Wilkins of the NAACP hated Martin Luther King of the SCLC because there was not enough real estate in the social-studies textbooks to house them both. Meanwhile, television passed on its pictures. . . . The representations survived the subject and eventually overtook my own images, which were less durable than waxwork figures in an exhibition of Black life at the Smithsonian. (49)

The "representations" divide black from white, and the narrator from his "black classmates": "My fellow black classmates pulled such faces I was asked to interpret the anger. Nothing about me could make whites feel bad, as if I had been inculcated against carrying terror" (107). As a "slave in heaven" (107)—a black teenager in a white high school—the narrator refers to himself as the "uninhabited me" (123–124).

Years later, the "uninhabited me" is uncomfortably tenanted: "The ledger of how to be simultaneously yourself and everyone else who might observe you, the captain's log of travel in the dual consciousness, the white world as the deceptive sea and black world as the armed galley, gave me the comic feeling that I was living alongside myself, that there was a me and a

ventriloquist's replica of me on my lap, and that both of us awaited the intervention of third me, the disembodied me, before we could begin the charade
of dialogue" (220). And as his world widens, the narrator's crisis develops
around his growing certainty that others see him as an individual example
of a generic type: "I bumped against television images and wet newsprint,
against people in the street" (291).

The novel's refrain is the narrator's relationship with his grandfather—
ultimately (and explicitly) embodying his relationship to the past and future
(and of the past *to* the future): "Perhaps the old-timers were right to insist
that we, the Also Chosen, live wholly in the future. . . . I used to wonder how
they managed to be all-inclusive. It never occurred to me that they might
be making it up as they went along and sometimes backing down" (304).
Near the end of the book, his grandfather dies. Grieving, he finds that grief
had become the object of his quest. Finally, he imagines himself in his own
old age, looking back on his generation: "One day—if it comes— . . . I may
elect myself a witness and undertake to remember when something more
important than black, white, and other was lost. Even now I grieve for what
has been betrayed. I see the splendor of the mornings and hear how glad the
songs were, back in the days when the Supreme Court was my Lourdes, and
am beyond consolation. The spirit didn't lie down and die, but it's been here
and gone, been here and gone" (309).

To miss the ironizing of law in these stories is to miss the stories themselves. As readers, we are clearly expected to bring our understanding of law's
failures to *The Bluest Eye*, and the politics of rights for the narrator's generation in *High Cotton*. We are expected to understand why Dorcas died (in
Morrison's *Jazz*)—why the ambulance would not come—and why the killer
lived. We are expected to understand the irreversibility of the Chinese immigrations in the works of Tan and Jen, the ready reversibility of immigration
in Cisneros's *Woman Hollering Creek*, and the dreamtime reunions in Garcia's
Dreaming in Cuban. We are expected to know that the law permitted slavery,
required segregation, and created reservations and internment camps. This
knowledge—diversely, constructs of race—must be in place before the books
can begin; the authors meet their readers on that ground, without explanation. U.S. community studies, too, play on background knowledge of a similar order. One must understand something of the struggles for racial equality
in the United States to appreciate how the figure of the minority subject that
emerged from those movements features critically.

In the ethnographies, the expectation of that background knowledge is—significantly—general, even global. By this I mean that authors do not presuppose knowledge of a specific neighborhood, but of urban conditions generally; nor the status of a particular community, but politics of difference in general; not poverty, but global capitalism in general. The transactability of ethnography is in this sense like that of fiction. However, in ethnography more than fiction, the generality of condition reinforces a federal subjectivity attuned to the promise of citizenship—even if the benefits of citizenship are, for some, stalled somewhere. In fiction, the transit from home to street, home to the world, is the hyphen of ethnic U.S. citizenship, a bridge across the "crack in the world" (Morrison 1992: 22–23; Walker 1992: 281)—an epiphanic moment of rending that liberates the self from the public script of identity.

E Pluribus Plurum

In the chapter on domination at the end of her magnum opus, *The Gender of the Gift*, anthropologist Marilyn Strathern sums up some of the key points in her discussion of Melanesian concepts of male and female: "One body is . . . conceptually unitary, whether in a singular or a plural form, and encompasses future relations within itself. But the conceptual equation between one and many hides a crucial sociological difference. The factor that is hidden is one of its terms, namely plurality itself" (1988: 327). At first this observation might seem to be specific to the ethnographic material she has in view but it is also suggestive for our purposes, as an indication of the contingent relation between identity and legal discourse across institutional fields.

In the hearings described in Chapter 3, the references to Americans were either singular (*this* person of color, *this* welfare client) or plural (all of them), but the difference between singular and plural dissolves in the fact that the individual—the person with rights—is never more than a figuration of a statistic. Even the witnesses—sometimes as many as seventy in one day—were limited to just enough speech to make their representational claims performative, and their appearance convincing as democratic participation. Thus it is not just that the individual in these instances is limited to the figuration of the many. The hearings constructed individuality only with respect to figurations of broader categories that are themselves plural.

The statistical layerings of officialized identity do not recognize a person's multiple commitments to communities of different kinds, but are sedimentations of the prerequisites of federal power. Thus, those senators who sought to curtail the power of the courts over business practices claimed that taking race into account rendered the equal *un*equal—while claiming to defend the equality rights won by a previous generation. Those who sought to disembed the state from the social sector by ending welfare as we knew it similarly suspended racial difference in favor of its reference—hidden in plain sight—to gender difference, while claiming to support the values of the New Deal. In the United States, culture's protean omnipresence in this sense is the other side of a neoliberal consensus whose zone of compromise is narrowly fixed to the question of the limits of federal obligation. The emphasis on marriage—explicitly in the welfare context and implicitly in the CRA context—points to the underlying importance of the question of the value of labor and the gift within competing visions of capitalism; the insistence on an economy of the gift within marriage corresponds directly to the political value of supporting the state's withdrawal from social programs. This correspondence is obviously gendered, but it must also be racialized, too, since it is only via the legal history of racial equality claims that federal powers may come so close to private life in the name of liberalism.

In the contexts discussed here, the category *race* is predicated on the political limits of the federal government's constitutional powers, a context in which it never functions alone—even if those functions can be reworked as elements of individualized description. Actual persons become vulnerable to recomposition and erasure even from the middle of the field of citizenship, even at the moment of their recognition. That citizenship itself is categorically available for recomposition in this way is a reminder of Marx's implication regarding citizenship as artificial personhood (Marx 1975b: 97–98).

The life stories discussed in this chapter are not based on continuous direct discourse on the part of their subjects. Rather, they are fragmentary accounts—fragmentation made evident in the ways the works are structured around the necessity (construed differently in each case) of interpretation. In each case, that necessity adjoins interpretation to responsibility, in the process attaching—again, differently in each case—ethical conditions to representation and to the transactability of federal subjectivity. Ewick and Silbey's analysis is the broadest in these terms, as legality itself (so to speak) is rendered as the promise of people's mutual relevance in relation to law. Engel and Munger question the security of that mutuality, as they register the different positions of individuals before the law, and the practical difficulties individuals face in fitting their circumstances to its templates. In different ways, Pinckney and Morrison also interrogate the conditions—whether of right, circumstance, or art—that enable (or disable) the telling of one's own story, and unequal means people have in relation to fulfilling the formal requirements of autobiography. Justice Thomas's dissent in *Grutter* registers something of that same dilemma, though in his case turning it back on the law as its own defect.

The assumptions linking individual narrative to collective forms of law and society verge on fiction at these junctures—where the individual presumes him- or herself to reflect something in the society as a whole. The sites where such assumptions are taught and learned make fruitful ethnographic terrain. On that ground, one can examine the rhetorical conventions of legal citizenship and their indebtedness to the novel form. In their midst, ethnography plays its part in circulating the federal implication across everyday landscapes. I am not suggesting that anthropologists borrowed consciously from *Brown*, but rather that the federal subjectivity that was *Brown*'s accomplishment was available to them as a template for the depiction of life chances in relation to the fulfillments of citizenship. To the extent that ethnographers found themselves resisting the pejorative elision of race and culture that featured in the new mainstream discourse, they took up the template of federal subjectivity that *Brown*'s plaintiffs crafted out of law, social science and fiction, and made it over into a generalized rendering of subaltern identities and minority citizenship. The relevance of this observation for our purposes is not as a point-to-point connection between texts, but as path—along the trail of discourse—to the wider national and transnational political and social movements of which *Brown* was a part, and their legacies in other domains.

CHAPTER 7

Gendering Difference
and the Impulse to Fiction

The "distaff voices" (in Marcus's pregnant metaphor; 1991a: 127) of the new ethnography of the 1980s and 1990s self-consciously conjured the possibility of an anthropology reconfigured around new ethnographic relations—relations reframed around new meanings of difference. The negative elision of race and culture in the national political discourse coincided with anthropology's internal critique of these same terms on essentialist grounds. For ethnographers (not just those whose fieldwork was in the United States), this conundrum was implicit in the demand for fresh thinking about the nature of difference, and accordingly, new textual practices. Community studies were novelistic in some respects, and even where their self-presentation was more standard, authors drew increasingly on elements of literary strategy associated with fiction, particularly from diasporic, post-colonial and subaltern literatures—even as they continued to work a discourse of solutions borrowed from the policy domain. In these community studies, the enfolding of postcolonial subjectivity within federal policy discourse constituted the most visible horizon between locality and globality.

In this chapter, I turn to the broader implications of ethnography's dual indebtedness to national policy and subaltern literatures, since the textual knot tying these literary practices together also bound local ethnographies to their global context. Calibrating the local and global dimensions of community studies was an editorial problem as well as an analytic one—and in some ways even more of a problem editorially, given the conventions of localism in ethnography. Strategic shifts of genre discharged some of these burdens, as genres retain associations acquired in use.

In this context, the discourse of feminism was evidently a resource—for some scholars, by direct reference; for others, by osmosis. Feminist anthropology and women's studies were still new as institutional programs in the 1990s; however, the trope of gender as a generalized discourse of difference and cultural critique would have been all around them at the time. At that time, particularly for mainstream American feminism, the categories *women* and *men* were universal references to subjectivities and structures of inequality. Feminist theory was (is) not a monolith, however, and the category *women* hovered ambiguously between the singular and plural, the universal and the relative, the essential and the contingent. These ambiguities appear to have made feminist discourse more useful, rather than less, as an idiom with which ethnographers could align their textual practices with the situation of their local interlocutors as both local and global subjects. Marilyn Strathern's magnum opus, *The Gender of the Gift* (1988), is framed as a dialogue between anthropology and feminism as it was at this time, in these terms.

In the community studies of the 1990s, women's experiences are very much in the foreground, as if representing the essence of minority or subaltern experience. This is not to say that women are misrepresented as being culturally different (or more different) than men, but that the ethnographies seem to draw on women's recognizability as figurations of inequality (within their own communities, or within the national community, or both) made familiar by women's movements. The gendering of difference in these ethnographies extends the referents of federal subjectivity while also retaining the discursive connection—reworked positively—between race and culture as discussed in the previous chapter. This connection would have been all around them, explicitly so. The Equal Rights Amendment had failed (in 1993) but the category *woman* was newly relatively secure alongside race in federal guarantees of non-discrimination (see Chapter 6, note 1).

We have already noted (in Chapters 3 and 4) the extent to which the discourse of solutions channels politically framed identities into position for mutual displacement—each covering for each other, so to speak. In the 1990s, *race* was popularly marked as African American, *gender* marked as female—a dual schema of binary differences. As referents for *cultural difference*, these binaries implied another—between "cultures" construed as Self and Other. All three binaries could be worked simultaneously, and our examples offer different combinations of their elements—in doing so, taking up (more or less critically) the arrangement of these key terms in the new political discourse.

In the new liberal discourse of the time, *gender difference* was to some extent idealized as a model of diversity, given the implication of durable heterosexual partnership (that is, a relationship across difference) and mutual personal choice. One influential formulation of multiculturalism rested prominently on this unidirectional analogy. In his seminal essay on the "politics of recognition" Charles Taylor introduces the parallel this way:

> Some feminists have argued that women in patriarchal societies have been induced to adopt a depreciatory image of themselves. They have internalized a picture of their own inferiority, so that even when some of the objective obstacles to their advancement fall away, they may be incapable of taking advantage of the new opportunities. . . . An analogous point has been made in relation to blacks: that white society has for generations projected a demeaning image of them, which some of them have been unable to resist adopting. (Taylor 1994: 25–26)

Such associations were legible in their broad availability, but the freedom to float the significance of gender in this way—as a series of controlled displacements (Chow 1993:57–59)—was sharply contested as a political privilege by "'native' scholars" with critical vantage points in feminisms "of color" and ethnic social movements (Arredondo et al. 2003: 6; see also Latina Feminist Group 2001: 3–4; Krupat 1993: xix). Critical race feminists were also sharply critical (Grillo and Wildman 1997; Harris 1997).

In the mainstream political discourse we have been considering in this book, the occlusion of race and culture is prominent. In the terms of that discourse, gender is mainly an identity category (marked for *women*), functioning primarily—as we see especially in relation to welfare and immigration—as the embodiment of a state's interest (to borrow a legal phrase) in regulating labor markets from the border (by checking entry) and among the urban poor (by terminating entitlements). The young mothers who figure in the Congressional testimony on welfare and unregistered immigration are a literary trope, pivotal to the conservatives' position—as we have already seen. In a sense, their discourse erased women, to the extent that they were relevant mainly as means to ends involving men's legal status and their place in the labor force. In the literary context of the hearing rooms, women were constructed from the negative aspects ascribed to *men's* cultural difference—and then rejoined to men in stereotyped images of male-female relationships as a programmatic rationale. It is through such portrayals that the discourse of policy debate suspended the category of *race* and brought to the fore the agonism of personal responsibility, choice, and constraint. That agonism is equally available to the right and the left, as we saw in the previous chapter—but this proximity puts an analytic premium on how the social reality of women and men is accounted for in the text.

For ethnographers, navigating difference meant managing these competing interpretive claims on women's identities—as actual women, cultural icons, or as theoretical displacements (or articulations) of race. The proximity of ethnography, fiction and policy made fiction available to ethnography, especially where the author's interpretive narrative is most strained by the discourse of solutions. The impulse to fiction is self-conscious in the ethnographic experiments discussed in this chapter—experiments that are inseparable from the discursive pressures on race and gender that imbued the public sphere at the time. When U.S. ethnographers began to experiment self-consciously with other genres in the 1980s and 1990s, it was consistently with the stated purpose of overcoming the limitations of their own discipline with respect to commonly accepted values such as realism, understanding, authenticity, and authority—the synergy of genres intensifying the power of the works' analytical claims. But so, too, was feminism a claim to knowledge—insight, body knowledge, intuition—inherently critical of academic convention. This was also the case in fiction, where fictional anthropologists, it seems, constituted a minor convention wherever a critique of relativism or value-neutral social science suited the story line.[1]

In our examples in this chapter—drawn from ethnographies, novels, and feminist jurisprudence—we consider how authors work cultural identity as gender identity (and their own interpretive authority in gendered terms). The examples vary in patterned ways, leaning either toward fiction or law. Where the gendering of the difference is more methodological, ethnographers' literary practices draw more heavily on fictional genres. Where it is more substantive, it tends toward legal discourse. Legalisms are also at work in fiction, to the same effect—drawing attention to questions of interpretive authority. Meanwhile, feminist jurisprudence draws on a diffuse notion of community to lend social substance to comprehensive equality claims. Taken together, these examples from ethnography, fiction and law evince a complex discourse of differencing and equivalencing that was a sign of the times.

One dominant motif in the ethnographic accounts of identity discussed in this chapter is the fieldwork story itself—the narration of the author's transit across this dynamic space of disorientation and ambivalence. By a combination of planning and accident, trial and error, intrusion and invitation, conversion (a word I choose deliberately) from outsider to insider, novice to initiate to expert, stranger to friend, the anthropologist finds his or her way and gives an account of the process of understanding.[2] The narrated transit to friendship between ethnographer and informant tends to be both an authorizing claim to empirical validity *and* an emplotment device that enables the ethnographer to frame otherwise incommensurate knowledges within a single narrative frame. In the community studies of the 1990s, the authoritative and subjective "I" of the prologue and envoi, and the ethnographic and transferential "I" of the main text, is unfailingly a gendered self. The gendering of the ethnographic relation conjures the character of fiction even when fiction is not the genre at hand. It is as if the social relations of fiction are necessary to the experience of reading ethnography. (Do your beginning students, too, refer to ethnographies as *novels*?) When an ethnographic author deliberately steps over into fiction, the step can be but a small one, easily missed if a text is read too quickly (as I learned—to my interest—in the classroom with some of the examples in this book).

Fiction in this sense offers anthropology an ally against indifference. Indeed, for anthropologists, and perhaps not for anthropologists alone, the other of difference is not sameness, but indifference. It is indifference that is antisocial, uninhabitable. Accordingly, then, the formal presence of fiction does not destabilize the truth value of ethnography so much as it insists on the truth value of experience, extending fiction's "essential gesture" (Gordimer 1988) into ethnography. The seamlessness of that horizon temporarily suspends the difference between "fact and fiction"—as invoked in the conventional phrase. Doing so significantly heightens the truth-claims of the main text, by intensifying the reading experience around a more transparently authored account, and in a more transparently emotional register. Fictional ethnography borrows the reading conventions of fiction at the specific junctures where the alignment of envoi, prologue, and main text is (from the author's perspective) most critical to ethnographic understanding. And ethnographic understanding itself takes shape as the transformative potential of an explosive release of creative energy born out of the identification across author, subject, and reader that fiction classically encourages and demands.

The convergence among the illustrative examples in this chapter is in their varied ways of gendering difference, and the functions of that compression in terms of signaling the works' wider message and stakes in political fields. The anthropological works incorporate fiction explicitly to heighten the truth claims of the ethnography. In Louise Krasniewicz's *Nuclear Summer*, fiction fills in where the conventional limits of "thick description" would bar attributions of motive, intent, and emotional response. In Karen McCarthy Brown's *Mama Lola*, fiction plays a larger role, establishing the credibility of a knowledge system alien to the conventions of western rationality and accounting for the narrative structure of the work as a whole. In both cases, the fictional horizon emerges from a gender solidarity that allows the author to contextualize the condensation of identifications in the form of sociability—at once professional and personal—that point in yet further directions. In the novels, too, gender difference is constructed as knowledge, open to discovery and reformulation, though within limits made clear by the story lines and narrative organization. There, gender difference is more explicitly sexual difference—sexuality explicitly set beyond individual choice, and implicitly put to work as critical commentary on the conventions of multiculturalism in the public sphere. In Alice Walker's *Possessing the Secret of Joy*, the fictional anthropologist's figuration as biracial and bisexual is crucial to the fate of his knowledge. In Paule Marshall's *The Chosen Place, the Timeless People*, the public sphere involves both ends of an international development project. In David Guterson's *Snow Falling on Cedars*, it is the aftermath of internment on a small island community off the coast of Washington just after the Second World War. Finally, Robin West's *Narrative, Authority, and Law* envisions the public sphere as jurisprudence itself, or rather as it might become—if fully opened to the stories of women, and through them, of others.

In various ways, the examples show how the discourse of solutions makes gender a figuration of the immanence of state power in relation to identity. They also show that that figuration does not work in just one way. It can be an image of resistance as well as domination, but it is never neutral. Anthropology, feminist jurisprudence, and fiction work those images and implications in common—differently.

Nuclear Summer

Louise Krasniewicz's (1992) ethnographic study of the Seneca Women's Peace Encampment (in Seneca Falls, New York) engages women's efforts to articulate a lesbian identity and an antinuclear politics, as integral registers of identity and resistance. The core of the book details the events of one summer, as members of the encampment negotiated the terms of their community at their farmhouse on the outskirts of town, and outside—with townspeople and in relation to the arms depot at the nearby U.S. Army base. Their negotiations culminated in a protest march through the town of Seneca Falls. This was likely to be dangerous; they faced physical threats and intense pressures from townspeople. Krasniewicz evokes the situation as a multiple crisis of representation, arguing that the extremity of near-violence—"the unthinkable almost became real" (158)—in the political sphere in turn demands ethnographic extremity. Krasniewicz borrows her prose experiments from the protesters, turning to fiction—here, in the form of collage and dramatization—as narrative strategies for producing "a moment of awareness, to admit other possible voices, styles, common senses, and interpretive strategies" (Krasniewicz 1992: 158). Significantly, her identification with the women is political—anchored to their respective efforts to "rewrite . . . discourse with their protests" (158).

Her hoped-for "disorientation" (Krasniewicz's play on Edward Said's "orientalism") of normal ethnographic discourse "forbids a search for the 'truth' of the events and encourages uncertainty about who was right or wrong and who was effective, powerless, oppressed, fetishistic, or simply boring. It is in some ways a duplication of the fieldwork experience as much as the ethnographic event" (158). Although she reserves her genre experiments for the moment of crisis in the summer of protest, her rationale for them would appear to be generalizable to the political realities of conducting research in the United States: "An anthropologist working in the United States . . . has not only the traditional problem of juggling participation and observation but also the problem of switching sympathies among the many communities and factions that try to claim her as a logical member of their group" (24). Continuing the same passage, Krasniewicz imagines this complexity as a function of doing fieldwork in one's own country: "In a foreign place, an anthropologist is a clear and definite outsider, but in her own country, she discovers little comfort in trying to fall back on her professional status as an excuse for distancing herself from the communities she studies" (24).

An alternative reading would suggest that—no matter what the "identity" of the anthropologist—social description is inherently political in the United States. As we have seen, identity cannot but implicate the discourse of nationness on which it is an ambiguous comment. Identity is imagined on the one hand as relative difference (i.e., inherently uncivil), and on the other as a function of socially regulated bodies (i.e., inherently civil). This ambiguity is closer to surface in the book's concluding lines, as Krasniewicz celebrates it as the confirming sign of the women's effectiveness:

> In Seneca County the dangerous women of the encampment undermined the local community's certain discourses on man and woman, on nuclear war and weapons, on community loyalty, on political action and power, on the sexuality of adults and children, and on peace, safety, and security in a nuclear world. The women ruined the summer of 1983 for the people in and around Seneca County, and they also ruined, perhaps only for a moment, perhaps forever, patriarchal modes of representation and the easy, comfortable power structures that keep them in place. (240)

Importantly, Krasniewicz turns to fiction at the junctures where the ethnographer's identification with her research subjects (as individuals or as a community) escapes the usual conventions of containment she associates with professional anthropology. We turn next to Karen McCarthy Brown's *Mama Lola*. Their constructions of ethnographic convention are rhetorically parallel—especially their common emphasis on (and resistance to) the normativity of social distance, disengagement, information-gathering, and the fixity of cultural difference. This said, their responses are different. Brown, as we shall see, identifies with vodou, ultimately making vodou a materialization of women's knowledge. Krasniewicz—perhaps because she feels she was not accepted in the women's community (as she states herself)—does not claim authority in gendered terms in the fieldwork story. However, she does so in theoretical terms in her identification with the women as political activists—writing the streets of Seneca Falls and the pages of her monograph as congruent arenas of protest. By holding onto gender within the ethnographic frame, and (instead) fictionalizing politics, Krasniewicz disrupts the hermeneutics inherent in federal discourse, exposing the whiteness and heterosexual premise in the canon of citizenship.

Mama Lola

Karen McCarthy Brown's *Mama Lola: A Vodou Priestess in Brooklyn* (1991) is explicitly structured in terms of the stages of the ethnographer's acquisition of knowledge, conversion, and friendship. Indeed, Brown's transition to knowledge gives the book its form and contents, since it is both "an intimate spiritual biography of a Vodou priestess and her family" (ix) and an ethnographic fieldwork story that becomes Brown's spiritual autobiography, punctuated by her own marriage to a fetish husband (Ogou) and her initiation in Haiti. In effect, Brown's literary device for presenting Alourdes as "Vodou priestess" and healer is Brown herself, vis-à-vis her own entry into Alourdes's world—a displaced fragment of Haiti in Brooklyn (1).

The literariness of this device (i.e., deploying herself as anthropologist = figuration of difference) is highlighted by her alternation between the genres of ethnography and fiction. Every other chapter is fictional, but in the service of the ethnography. Brown refers to the fictional chapters as "true stories" that confirm her own authority to speak for (as?) Alourdes and Alourdes's fetish "husband" Gede (20) among others in Alourdes's family over the course of several generations. But she is careful to stipulate that she is qualified to speak as Alourdes only because she is herself an adept, and only relative to her readers:

> I soon realized that my personal involvement in Vodou repre-sented both gains and risks in relation to my work. The potential gains were in depth of understanding. One of the major risks involved los-ing the important distinction between Vodou interacting with the life of a Haitian and Vodou interacting with my own very different blend of experience, memory, dream, and fantasy. My experiences with Vodou both are and are not like those of Haitians. The stories I tell about these experiences have authority only in the territory between cultures. I have attempted to stay clear on this point and even to use these stories quite self-consciously as bridges for my readers, most of whom will be more like me than Alourdes. (20)

In the same context, she mentions that as she was drawn increasingly into "the casual rhythms" of her "growing friendship" with Alourdes, the technol-ogy of the tape recorder was no longer appropriate, and had to be abandoned. She describes a process between transcription and invention—a midpoint, perhaps, between the different processes and accountabilities of research and friendship—the latter marked (for Brown) by the fuller engagement of memory, mimesis, and imagination: "I began to work in another way. . . . It seemed important to capture not only what she said but also how she said it. I found I could use her mnemonic devices, the repeated refrains of her stories, and some of my own memory tools. . . . Beginning with these condensation points and working myself into the rhythm of her speech, I could construct a record . . . of conversations that had taken place hours earlier" (20–21). Importantly, then, Brown's claim is not that she knows Alourdes from insider knowledge or as Alourdes knows herself, but rather, that her ethnography was (literally and literarily) produced out of the way she experienced their friendship.

But crucially, that opening came as the result of an ethnographic insight: "I realized that if I brought less to this Vodou world, I would come away with less. If I persisted in studying Vodou objectively, the heart of the system, its ability to heal, would remain closed to me. The only way I could hope to understand the psychodrama of Vodou was to open my own life to the ministrations of Alourdes" (10). Continuing, Brown summarizes her own engagement: "I entered gradually. I accepted Alourdes's invitations to salute the spirits and pour libations for them. On occasion I brought her dreams and asked for interpretation. Sometimes I requested card readings. At one difficult point in my life, she suggested that I undergo a ritual "marriage" to two of the Vodou spirits, Ogou and Danbala. I did that. And in 1981 [three years after meeting Alourdes] I went through the rituals of initiation" (10). Her claim to authority, specifically, arises from the juncture where the ethnography and the friendship became inseparable as openings to knowledge: "As Alourdes and I became friends, I found it increasingly difficult to maintain an uncluttered image of myself as scholar and researcher in her presence. . . . As I got closer to Alourdes, I got closer to Vodou" (9). Alourdes, she says, treats her "like family" (9, 120).

She is critical of "academics [who] have overemphasized those things that separate individuals and cultures from one another" (12–13). Nonetheless, Brown retains the imagery of "cultural lines" to evoke "the reality of diversity" (13)—as she must, since her claim to "authority" for her stories is valid "only in the territory between cultures . . . as bridges for my readers" (13). At the same time, she does not avoid the word "truth" as a reference to what ethnography, fiction, or vodou can produce.

In this way, Brown configures the story of Alourdes and Karen (as she calls herself in the book's final fictionalized chapter) as not just parallel to, but one and the same as, a story of Haitian vodou as encountered by (for want of a better term) Western rationality (cf. Brown 1991: 20). For example, her description of a Vodou card reading sounds very much like the way an ethnographer might conduct an interview:

> The question-and-answer part of a Vodou card reading can be a
> delicate diagnostic tool. Little specific information is exchanged be-
> fore readings begin. Taking his or her inspiration from the cards, the
> reader asks various questions that lead to a description of the situation
> under review. . . . The one for whom the reading is being done accepts
> some descriptions and rejects others. The card reader then follows the
> path indicated by the responses and, working on the issue at deeper
> and deeper levels, poses new diagnoses, and so on. Working in this
> manner, both parties can discover surprising truths. (187)

But more fundamentally, Brown places ethnography, fiction, and vodou
along one continuum of understanding. Each is a means of entering the
space between worlds—cultural and spiritual. Continuing the passage cited
earlier (regarding her techniques in the field), Brown refers to her growing
"acknowledgment that ethnographic research, whatever else it is, is a form
of human relationship. When the lines long drawn in anthropology between
participant-observer and informant break down, then the only truth is the
one in between; and anthropology becomes something closer to a social art
form, open to both aesthetic and moral judgment. This situation is riskier,
but it does bring intellectual labor and life into closer relation" (12). Importantly, throughout Brown's account, her evocations of friendship (and kinship) do not amount to a claim to having crossed from one side of a line to
another, but of approaching the line with another who comes to it from the
other side. Thus, friendship does not supplant one kind of understanding (or
motivations, for that matter) for another, but rather, multiplies the repertoires
of understanding and motivation.

For this reason, perhaps, Brown evokes friendship as an issue of knowledge, not (except initially) as one of openness or good will. Drawing on feminist theory and her ethnographic experience (including her experience of
vodou), Brown argues that fiction is more suited to the special knowledge
that comes with friendship—the need for fiction (like friendship) arises from
a space of betweenness (12) and is truer to that space (16–20, 106–107). The
ability to write fiction, then, is not merely an aesthetic choice; one is pushed
to it by a certain quality of knowledge. Brown's references to knowledge
that is transformative in this sense are not to any particular worldview or
culture—to the contrary, she emphasizes the extent to which vodou arrived
comfortably alongside her prior knowledge and beliefs (11). Rather, she refers to her vodou knowledge as a form of excess—as if knowing about vodou

pulls you toward it. It is her excess knowledge in this sense that becomes a challenge to her identity, as Alourdes's daughter Maggie makes clear: "Maggie suddenly shouted: 'You know too much, Karen!' Seeing my startled response, she laughed and continued in an ordinary conversational tone, 'You my friend and you around a lot, and sometimes I just tell you things. You see thing, you hear thing. I think those spirit say, "Karen know too much." It is like the Mafia—once you know too much, then they got to Christian [baptize] you. I think you going to have to go to Haiti like me, get your head washed . . . you know.' She grinned mischievously" (124). "Priestly power" is also a form of excess knowledge—called *konesans* in Creole (356): "Konesans is the ability to read people, with or without cards; to diagnose and name their suffering, suffering that Haitians know comes not from God and usually not from chance but from others—the living, the dead, and the spirits. Finally, konesans is the ability to heal" (356). For Brown, then, ethnography (the desire to know), fiction (breaking down barriers between knowledges), and vodou (ability to know and heal suffering) are three open-ended segments along a continuum of knowledge; for this reason, her own narrative is inseparable from what she can say to readers about Alourdes. For the same reason, perhaps, she turns to fictionalized narrative at the junctures where her presentation opens out from the here and now toward Haiti, history, and individual circumstance—including the narrative of "Karen's" initiation. The accounts of Brown's marriages to Ogou and Danbala, however, are presented in the ethnographic register (136–139, 306–308).

Speaking as another is essential to vodou (and ultimately for the credibility of Brown's book), but in Brown's analysis it is neither an appropriation of agency nor its relinquishment. The special gift of trance enables a healer (in Brooklyn, usually a woman) to vacate her own body so that the fetish spirit (always a named individual, usually male) can "mount" or "ride" her—that is, borrow her physical body and voice. Importantly, then, a vodou healer is not a spokesperson for the fetish, but neither is she the fetish. Rather, by virtue of her combination of inherited gift and willingness to learn through apprenticeship, the healer becomes the spirit's agent, and the fetish speaks his wit, encomiums, and commands through her. The adept's facility is in not a relinquishment of agency, however, but rather a form of agency in its own right. One can recognize the signs of one's own power or not, choose to serve the spirits or not, choose to make oneself available to the fetish at any particular moment or not. Brown highlights these agentive possibilities in both the ethnographic and fictional registers of her narrative; her own agency—and ultimately Gede's (the fetish of death)—undergirds the ethnographic narration; the agency of others (and other fetishes) comes through the fictional chapters. The ethnographic chapters are named for fetishes; the fictional accounts are named for individuals or social situations.

Beyond the personal stories, or rather, between them—to re-invoke her own imagery—Brown grounds her analysis in issues of women's power. The space between, in other words, is not a void; it is profoundly gendered, even sexual. Brown acknowledges the book's debts to feminism (16) and the broader context for her project in studies of immigration, "Third World women," "even micro-economics" and vodou elsewhere (15)—explaining her preference for leaving these issues largely implicit in favor of the finer-grained account described above. Still, her willing identification with Alourdes—their relationship is specified several times as that of mother and daughter—opens up these other questions as gendered associations on a larger scale. Vodou itself is for the most part passed across generational lines among women (the fictional accounts explore three generations of women on the maternal side of Alourdes's family). In practical terms (it is expensive), vodou also corresponds to women's relative dominance in local markets—especially in Haiti. For Brown, this complex of powers leads her to associate vodou with a "gender politics" (157) and the maternal side of history—history's other side, so to speak. In Haiti, she describes the land itself as a female body (171), perhaps picking up on the local euphemism for sex work as "selling my land" (164). The book's last chapter (titled "Gede") concludes with the observation that Gede—a male fetish—seems now to be rivaled by a new member of the pantheon in the female Gedelia. She is not just Gede's counterpart, Brown insists: "Surely a full-blown Gedelia will be more than a Gede who happens to be female. Women's energy, their sexuality, and their humor have sources different from men's and are manifested in different ways. . . . I anxiously await Gedelia's emergence from the cocoon of Haitian history and religion" (381). The inherent literariness of identity invites and is reinforced by the conflation of understanding and sexuality—the trope for understanding that surpasses and yet does not cancel difference, at least insofar as sexuality is theorized as simultaneously interior and exterior, private and public, personal and universal.

Fictional Ethnographers

Significantly, ethnographers' literary gestures in this regard are reciprocated by some authors of fiction. When novelists turn their characters into anthropologists, it is to map a path across extremes of misunderstanding explicitly marked out as *cultural* misunderstandings. Fictional anthropologists are figurations of a particular type of crisis—a crisis of knowledge occasioned by cultural confrontation. But while the fictional anthropologist's transit to understanding is part of the story line, the character is designed to confront the limitations of expertise divorced from personal commitment and commonality of stakes. Dreams of cross-cultural understanding, relativized knowledge, and development projects of various kinds become foils for these protagonists' journeys to engagement through self-knowledge. Fictional anthropologists, too, are figures "in between."

Fictional anthropologists are made to grapple with the alienating effects of expertise without intimacy. The agility of the fictional anthropologists in achieving cultural mediations (if that is what they are ultimately able to do) is predicated on the way they work through a crisis of self-identity around the issue of commitment—or fail to do so. Overcoming neutrality is crucial in the fictional accounts, and in the works I consider here, that inner work takes the form of a sexual crisis. Fiction's paradox is that self-knowledge and personal commitment are necessary but insufficient conditions of anthropological knowledge. True anthropological insight depends (fictionally) on changing one's identity—taking sides. In fiction, this is both a political dilemma and, simultaneously, a dilemma of sexual identity. Sexual self-recognition is one trope; another involves the recognition of others—that is, breaking social taboos to embrace (literally) the partnership of another. Recognition must work through sameness—same-sex or same-race, same-culture collaborations, as in the extended examples to follow. Productive recognition of others is expressed in the *r*eproductive potential of heterosexual partnership.

An example of self-recognition emerges through the character of a fictional anthropologist in Alice Walker's *Possessing the Secret of Joy* (1992). Walker makes the character Pierre—the son of (African American) Adam and (white French) Lisette—into an anthropologist. Lisette was Adam's lover; Adam's wife was Tashi—the book's central character. Pierre plays a minor but crucial role in the novel in undertaking to decipher the imagery of Tashi's tortured dreams and paintings—imagery arising from deeply buried memories of her "circumcision" (Walker's term) and her sister's death in the course of her cutting. Tashi has suffered horrific psychological and physical trauma as the consequence of these experiences, and struggles to connect her suffering to conscious memories. Pierre explains Tashi's unconscious knowledge to her—knowledge that refers to ancient customs and folkloric meanings. "We think it was told to you in code somehow," another character says. Tashi kills the ritual specialist who killed her sister. She is tried and convicted of murder, and is ultimately executed. But before that ending, Tashi undergoes intensive innovative psychotherapies, and the psychoanalysis eventually extends into Pierre's cultural analysis of the main image that haunts her. After Tashi's execution, Pierre "will rededicate himself to his life's work: destroying for other women—and their men—the terrors of the dark tower" (278).

The book is composed as a set of memoirs, interleaved in chronological order. Tashi writes that Pierre "wants to be the first anthropologist to empower and not further endanger his subjects" (230). At one point, Tashi gazes at Pierre, unseen by him—as she melds his psychoanalytic understanding with his parents' multiple cultural and racial origins, and his own biracial origins with his bisexuality:

> As Pierre reads I study his face seeking signs of Adam, signs of Lisette. He seems a completely blended person and, as such, new. In him "black" has disappeared; so has "white." His eyes are a dark, lightfilled brown; his forehead is high and tan; his nose broad, a little flat. He has told me he likes men as well as he likes women, which seems only natural, he says, since he is the offspring of two sexes as well as of two races. No one is surprised he is biracial; why should they be surprised he is bisexual? This is an explanation I have never heard and cannot entirely grasp; it seems too logical for my brain. (174)

Walker makes Pierre biracial, transnational, bisexual; his world is his work. But in the novel, anthropological knowledge is marked as incomplete, insights true but unproductive—in a sense *unrealistic*. The allure of anthropology, and the dubious relevance of cultural understanding as an end in itself, is only a secondary note in Walker's novel. In Paule Marshall's *The Chosen Place, the Timeless People* (1992), this same trope is reworked as a central theme. There, the main protagonist is an anthropologist who discovers himself in the course of a professional crisis that engulfs and transforms his life.

Making Choices

The Chosen Place, the Timeless People, originally published in 1969, was reissued in 1992—made current once again by the new context of globalization and development-oriented NGOs in poor countries at the margins of the

U.S. sphere. The novel tells the story of an American anthropologist about to begin a development project on the fictional Caribbean island of Bourne. The main action involves three white Americans undertaking a bold development project on Bourne, and three black islanders from the destitute village of "Bournehills." The Americans are Harriet (Main Line Philadelphian), Saul (celebrated anthropologist), and Allen (Saul's assistant). The islanders are Merle, an outspoken activist/advocate; Lyle, a barrister from the capital; and Vere, a young man just returned from a labor scheme in Florida. Well funded by the Philadelphia Research Institute (thanks in part to behind-the-scenes intervention by Harriet, whose family fortune endowed the institute), Saul is determined to succeed where other development projects have failed (these are recounted in detail, 55–59). Eventually, he does succeed.

At the core of each character's development is a problem of identity—cultural, class, racial, and sexual—but in the novel, identity is not left as a question of attributes and orientations. It is about recognition of others as well as the "others" in one's own past. It is also about the capacity for acknowledging one's failings and potential, as well as one's sense of responsibility for one's own acts and the acts of others. Moreover, identity is transnational for Marshall's characters: except for Harriet, each has spent substantial portions of their adult lives abroad (Saul in Europe and Latin America as an anthropologist, Allen on Bourne as a researcher, Merle as a student in England, Vere as a worker in Florida). Their histories are also adjoined: Harriet's family profited from the slave trade and the very sugar plantations that now dominate Bournehills; Merle is descended from a white owner of the sugar refinery. Difference is not black and white in the novel, nor is race ever relevant alone (except to Harriet)—whiteness is also diverse, and gender, sexuality, and class are always specified.

For Saul, success in Bourne will be tantamount to lifting the sense of curse that has haunted him since his first wife's death, a reawakening of his own capacity for engagement. For Harriet, success will mean managing Saul's success—to her, the project is the gateway to the rest of his career. Merle wants freedom for Bournehills. Allen wants a different life. Vere wants to win the local road race with his fire-red Opel. Only Saul and Merle are dreaming dreams they can actually achieve. Harriet and Vere are destroyed by theirs.

It is the *process* of self-identity—of becoming comfortable in one's own skin, literally and figuratively—that Marshall explores through the figuration of gender identity. Getting identity right will mean recognizing the connections between conditions in Bourne and the oppression in their own lives, as both oppressed and oppressors. As they become more involved with island life, each of the Americans voices a sense of foreboding unease, a sense of unexpectedly confronting a mystery within themselves (21, 216–218, 113). Harriet is ultimately overwhelmed by the phantoms of her past (406, 408). But those who can identify the past in the present—understand their own identifications with the oppressed and the oppressors—can break free. It is Saul and Merle who, finally, make this discovery and voice the parallel between persons and nations (359). And it is Saul and Merle who eventually can enjoy each other, no longer as Others, but as individuals—as lovers, partners, and friends. For them, categories of black and white, superpower and island nation, cease to matter as their partnership deepens around the fact of their individuality as man and woman (360–361, 376, 427).

In the novel, getting comfortable in one's own skin also means coming to terms with the skin of others, literally and figuratively. Marshall provides detailed descriptions of each of the main characters' physical presence—the color of their skin, the nature of their gestures, their gaze, and their way of touching others. These sensual portraits are crucial to the novel, since seeing, hearing, and touching form a hierarchy in the novel's sense repertoire of confirming signs of recognition and acceptance. On her first evening in Bourne, Harriet's host takes her arm as a gesture of hospitality. She withdraws without attracting attention to her own gesture—but her distaste for Lyle's black skin on hers lingers (78, 79). Over the course of the novel, Lyle's touch becomes a recurring motif (297, 425, 458). Marshall deploys Lyle (in scenes that echo Fanon) to clarify Harriet's blindness—evident in various ways through the book—as racism (421–422). Her gaze is drawn to his blackness (168, 371)—and where Lyle touches her, she imagines a black stain erupting on her own skin (425).[3] In her fantasy, that touch merges with a memory of her first husband (who was white). The gendered intimacy of the fantasy touch of Andrew/Lyle explodes racial difference, and suddenly she can see herself in the stain—a "dark splotch like an ugly bruise or one of those Rorschach inkblots that would reveal her, surging to the surface. Only this time it did not confine itself to the one spot. . . . It spread, and in the spreading stain which soon covered her entire body, she saw . . . all the things she had denied" (458). Ultimately, Harriet drowns herself in a sea that has already been described as hungry for vengeance: "It was Atlantic this side of the island, a wild-eyed, marauding sea the color of slate, deep, full of dangerous currents, lined with row upon row of barrier reefs, and with a sound like that of the combined voices of the drowned raised in a loud unceasing lament—all those, the nine million and more it is said, who in their enforced exile, their Diaspora, had gone down between this point and the homeland lying out of sight to the east. This sea mourned them" (106).[4] The day after her death, it is a "new sea, slaked and limpid" (461).

Meanwhile, Saul represents the possibility of another kind of knowledge, another vision of the relationship between the United States and Bourne and of Bourne itself. He knows that his assignment will mean convincing his sponsors and the islanders that his project is not hopeless. Early in their visit to Bourne, Saul is clearly marked out by the locals as a well-meaning person with good ideas—including the novel idea of actually working in the fields alongside the cane workers (e.g., 142). Still, conventional wisdom is that his project is doomed, like all the previous improvement schemes. Saul's project would have failed, too, except that at a crucial moment he intuitively abandons his researcher's neutral role and lends crucial help at a potentially devastating moment of crisis (see Merle's critique of neutrality in social science research, 389–391).

But that comes later. Saul's project in Bourne is funded through the "Center for Applied Social Research," an agency of the Philadelphia Research Institute (36–38) in turn funded by the conglomerate that has made Harriet's family wealthy. Fighting poverty in Bourne, in other words, will mean fighting the project's sponsors and his own wife's inherited birthright. This eventually becomes a crisis for Harriet and Saul—a test that she fails. Marshall develops Harriet as a person who cannot function when she is not in control—a characterization she introduces with the scene of their first sexual encounter—Saul "lying beneath her on the bed" (44). Marshall specifies this as a position of subordination that Saul prefers to revise: "'All right, Harriet,' he had said, . . . 'All right. We'll do. Only it'll have to be the other way around—' and reaching up again he had slowly drawn her down so that she lay beside rather than on top of him" (44). Later, when Saul is with Merle, Marshall has their faces touch on the pillow (361)—a position that this earlier scene has already marked as mutual.

Indirectly at first, but with increasing force, the project comes between Harriet and Saul; figuratively, it is their difference. For Harriet, difference invites social distance and control (43–44, 46–47). For Saul, difference is pleasure. His relationships with Harriet and Merle highlight his appetite for difference. Harriet attracts him with her intensity, and for a while he enjoys losing himself in her. Merle is the opposite: scarred by her previous relationships, she now avoids intimacy. But she likes Saul, and trusts him, and so is willing to play along when he invites her to reverse roles and play the anthropologist, interviewing him (320). Their conversation becomes serious, leading to a candid exchange of life stories and secrets (320–339). As Saul tells Harriet later, "What followed was simply part of that feeling of closeness" (427). The narrative of his sexual relationship with Merle makes no reference to physical acts; their encounters are occasions for Marshall to hone her double portraiture of their mutual recognition (338–339, 360–361, 427).

As Saul takes an active part in rescuing Bournehills, the readers do not need to know any more than Saul himself whether he is acting for love of Merle, Bournehills in general, or (more crassly) to save his pilot project. It is only important to know that it is a spontaneous *human* act, another "part of that feeling of closeness". Within the terms of the novel, Saul's special knowledge as an anthropologist is confirmed and valorized by his masculinity, and ultimately redeemed by it. By contrast, Allen—also grasping the novel's connection between sexuality and social knowledge—is shown realizing that his sexual isolation is analogous to the impersonal nature of his chosen field (statistical demographics) (301–312, 378). Marshall constructs anthropological knowledge as a masculine domain (most explicitly at 40–41), heterosexuality paralleling interculturality. Her figuration of the anthropologist does not call for a suspension of difference but—on the contrary—pleasure in cultural and racial differences from within the ambit of heterosexual difference. This is the exclusive domain of mutual sexual pleasure in the novel. Within the terms of the novel, masculine-feminine difference informs and governs the prospects for cultural reconciliation and social transformation.

The heterosexual norm in a sense channels difference in Marshall's novel—as it does in Walker's, too, except that Pierre lives outside the norm and Saul within it. For Saul, sexual pleasure with Merle is of a piece with the authenticity of his commitment to Bournehills—a commitment even beyond his anthropological calling, but also (therefore) confirming it as calling, as the novel also makes plain. Professionalism, self-knowledge, and personal commitment also rise and fall together in David Guterson's *Snow Falling on Cedars*. There, too, the sexual pairings authenticate cultural identity and dictate the terms of cross-cultural relations. But in Guterson's book they are contained, realigned in the scenario of a criminal trial.

Culture on Trial

Snow Falling on Cedars is the story of one man's awakening to his personal identity as a moral and social actor. Ishmael Chambers is a reporter, his profession serving unambiguously as a figuration of his ambivalence—present but not as a participant (30). Ishmael identifies himself with that other Ishmael, the narrator of Moby Dick (31); in the same context, he mentions his taste for Twain's *Huckleberry Finn* and Hawthorne's *Scarlet Letter*—going so far as to specify his reaction to the injustice done to Hester Prynne (32). This presentation of Ishmael's taste for American classics seems calculated to prefigure something of the book's action, in which he will be called upon (if he acknowledges the call) to take the side of a man of another race, and to right something of the wrong done to a woman. Indeed, race and gender are the principal lines of difference and calibration in the novel as a whole.

The setting is the fictional island of "San Piedro," placed (and carefully mapped before the main text begins) in the San Juan Islands, offshore from Seattle, in the fall and winter of 1954–55. As the book opens, we are in the ironically named "Amity Harbor," in the local courthouse where a murder trial is just getting under way. Those proceedings structure the novel. But the trial is not the story; it is a device for bringing together characters whose lives are entwined in other ways. The trial will provide closure not only to the legal question of guilt, in other words, but also to Ishmael's unresolved personal relationships. At the end, it turns out that the defendant has been falsely accused, and by taking part in the revelation of this injustice, Ishmael, too, is set free. But first he must overcome his paralyzing ambivalence and *decide* to act. The genesis and resolution of his personal crisis are the main story—set within the criminal trial scenario by means of flashbacks and contemporaneous outtakes. The trial framework and Ishmael's profession as a journalist provide a double framework in which Ishmael's quest can be set up as a search for truth.

Ishmael's search for self is configured as a question of whether he can escape from his social and moral paralysis—and so rescue the defendant, Kabuo Miyamoto, from a miscarriage of justice. Kabuo is on trial for his life, for the murder of Carl Heine, a local fisherman and former high school classmate of Kabuo's and Ishmael's. Kabuo had both motive and means, and he has already been condemned by local public opinion—an explicit parallel to the cultural paranoia that led up to internment in 1942 (424). The motive would have been land. Heine's father had rented seven acres of strawberry fields to Kabuo's father, in a "lease-to-own" arrangement (121) that technically violated Washington state law at the time (122). Mr. Miyamoto had made a substantial investment in the property by the time the war intervened. By the time Kabuo returned to complete the sale of the property, the elder Heine had

died, and earlier that same day, Heine's mother had sold the land to a neigh-
bor. Carl—who had inadvertently witnessed the original agreement between
the two older men—clearly regrets the indifferent injustice done to his old
friend by his mother, but we do not learn until much later what he plans to
do to correct it (403–405). Meanwhile, when Carl is found dead on his fishing boat, Kabuo is immediately the prime suspect, since everyone is aware
of his resentment over the loss of the land. Guterson makes Kabuo an expert
in Japanese martial art (the result of careful tutelage in Japanese culture by
his father). This becomes relevant to the trial through the testimony of his
former commanding officer in the army, whom Kabuo had tutored in turn.

The war experience changed Kabuo, and he struggles in silence to rebuild
his life. On the stand, he is stoic and silent: "Kabuo showed nothing—not
even a flicker of the eyes" (3). He will not speak in his own defense. Later, the
description shifts to the gallery's perspective:

> Kabuo Miyamoto rose in the witness box so that the citizens in
> the gallery saw him fully—a Japanese man standing proudly before
> them, thick and strong through the torso. They noted his bearing and
> the strength in his chest; they saw the sinews in his throat. While they
> watched he turned his dark eyes to the snowfall and gazed at it for a
> long moment. The citizens in the gallery were reminded of photo-
> graphs they had seen of Japanese soldiers. The man before them was
> noble in appearance, and the shadows played across the planes of his
> face in a way that made their angles harden; his aspect connoted dig-
> nity. And there was nothing akin to softness in him anywhere, no part
> of him that was vulnerable. *He was, they decided, not like them at all,*
> and the detached and aloof manner in which he watched the snowfall
> made this palpable and self-evident. (412; emphasis added)

This turns out to be a misreading of Kabuo's appearance of detachment.

The novel entertains a parallel between the trial of Kabuo Miyamoto and
the trials of Ishmael Chambers—whose life is at stake only metaphorically,
but (within the terms of the novel) in some way equivalently. The connection between these two sides of the story is accomplished as a question of the
meaning of "truth." On the legal side, at a crucial stage in the proceedings,
Kabuo and his attorney have a conversation about the nature of truth. Kabuo's
attorney tells him: "Tell the truth. . . . Decide to tell the truth before it's too
late." Kabuo replies: "The truth isn't easy." His lawyer responds in turn: "Just

the same . . . I understand how you feel. There are the things that happened, though, and the things that did not happen. That's all we're talking about" (391–392). (In a secondary equilvalencing, the attorney's fatherly counsel to Kabuo plays on an earlier conversation between Ishmael and his father, at the height of post–Pearl Harbor paranoia on the island, when Arthur responds to Ishmael's challenge to stick to the facts by saying, "Not every fact is just a fact" [188].)

Ishmael discovers evidence that will exonerate Kabuo, but he keeps it to himself for a full day, imagining that he might use it to elicit a renewal of his relationship with Kabuo's wife Hatsue—who rejected Ishmael long ago but (as she seems to understand) remains his love object. Ishmael's conflicting impulses bring his crisis to a head: "The truth now lay in Ishmael's own pocket and he did not know what to do with it. He did not know how to conduct himself and the recklessness he felt about everything was as foreign to him as the sea foam breaking over the snowy boats and over the pilings of the Amity Harbor docks" (428). He must navigate that inner storm produced by knowing and not knowing, and his first response—through intellect—leads down a false road. In a long conversation with his mother, the evidence in his pocket (figuratively *inside* him, awaiting revelation), he tells his mother he believes Kabuo is guilty—to which she responds in terms much like his father (345).

But first, Guterson has Ishmael remember an earlier conversation with his mother, about faith in God. Ishmael voices skepticism, to which his mother responds by saying that knowledge of God is a "feeling" of belief: "Nobody *knows*," she tells him. "What do you believe?" (342). But he is unpersuaded. Now, in the trial context, too, he argues on the side of facts: "Everything else is emotions and hunches. At least the facts you can cling to; the emotions just float away." His mother responds: "Float away with them. . . . If you can remember how, Ishmael. If you can find them again. If you haven't gone cold forever" (346). Later, in a moment of intense identification with his late father, literally sitting in his father's chair, he grasps her meaning (439)—finding a way to fuse his mother's faith and his father's professional calling. This epiphany finally enables him to act—and, after a brief detour to the old hollow cedar tree where he long ago courted Hatsue, he walks to her family's farm to present her with the evidence that will lead to the dismissal of the charges against her husband.

Truth is constructed by Guterson as knowledge for which an individual might be unprepared—or (as we see elsewhere in the novel) of which she or he might be consciously unaware. The situation of knowing yet not knowing, knowing the truth only at the moment of its revelation, finding the truth within oneself, comprises a refrain across the book. Truth is consciousness, insight—not consistently expressible in language. Ishmael must go home—literally, return to the scenes of his childhood and the trauma of his separation from Hatsue—in order to find the truth for and of himself. The interiority of truth in this sense is given a metaphorical register of sexuality. Indeed, a second level of equivalences important to the novel involves the main characters' sexuality, revealed to them—and to readers—in terms that fuse self-knowledge to truth through a basic symbolic formula that ties adult heterosexuality to racial and cultural sameness. The permutations of heterosexual acceptance, refusal, appetite, and renunciation are neatly squared off around the novel's four couples: Ishmael and Hatsue, Hatsue and Kabuo, Carl Heine and his wife Susan, and—from the vantage point of widowhood—Ishmael's mother, who has transcended grief and "coldness," and now lives "in grace," free of appetite (346). Ishmael cannot (or rather, does not) resolve his crisis until the couples align racially and generationally, at which point he can—belatedly—become his father's son (439).

Ishmael's crisis is revealed in a series of flashbacks. The young Ishmael was deeply in love with Hatsue Imada, the American daughter of Japanese immigrants, now married to Kabuo Miyamoto (also an American born to Japanese immigrants). Ishmael and Hatsue first encountered each other as young children. By the time we reach the main flashback narrative, set in 1941–42, they are eighteen—about to be interrupted in different ways by the war. Their friendship, always affectionate, has intensified; they are now physically intimate but still virginal. Their favorite meeting place is a hollow cedar tree halfway between their families' properties. They retreat there for the last time on the eve of the Imada family's departure from the island in compliance with Executive Order 9066. The attack on Pearl Harbor and the mounting political pressures to intern everyone legally designated Japanese (i.e., including their American-born children and grandchildren) have already been part of the story, in part as a canvas to portray Ishmael's father's moral courage as a reporter and editorialist—and in part to add dramatic irony to the narrative of the young couple's relationship (chapters 13 and 14).

When that last evening comes, Ishmael takes the occasion to declare his love (not for the first time), begging Hatsue—who is distraught—to "marry" him. Guterson describes their lovemaking in detail, including the moment when Ishmael enters Hatsue—at which point she suddenly realizes "with clarity that nothing about it was right" (214); "in his arms she felt unwhole" (215). This "knowledge," as Guterson refers to it (214), retrospectively illuminates the earlier account of Hatsue's wedding night—also vividly described, culminating in her whispered "It's right. . . . It feels so right" (92). Although Guterson has Hatsue tell herself that she never loved Ishmael and that their cultural difference was not the cause of her break (206), the novel as a whole leaves no doubt that the "rightness" Hatsue feels with Kabuo is both sexual and cultural, and that these are—in this novel—one and the same. Marrying Kabuo, she becomes her mother's daughter by choice—just as Ishmael must eventually choose to be his father's son. The truth Ishmael ultimately comes to share with Hatsue is the understanding that authentic desire is a compact with cultural generations as well as between two individuals.

By the time we witness Ishmael and Hatsue in each other's arms in the tree, we know already that she will find her life with Kabuo, and that she loves him deeply. As portrayed in the novel, Manzanar was, for them, a place of hardship and privation but also romance.[5] But Ishmael's body knowledge is otherwise. Their "less than three seconds" made him "love her even more" (354): "Wasn't that the strangest part? That by entering her he'd granted her the means to understand the truth? He'd wanted to be inside of her again . . . and on the next day she'd gone away" (354–355). This *gone away* makes Manzanar vanish for him. Indeed, for Ishmael, Manzanar does not exist at all—it is the name of a space within his own life marked by her absence.[6] Before that crucial last encounter, he and Hatsue have already traded addresses and devised a means of exchanging letters without risk of parental discovery (this attempt fails on Hatsue's side). It is as if she is leaving for college, or for some other destination on a journey of her own choosing. "Goodbye," she says to him as she leaves that evening, "I'll write" (215). We read her letter over Ishmael's shoulder twelve years later (353–354). She writes: "I loved you and I didn't love you at the very same moment" (354).[7]

While Guterson has Hatsue finding her identity in Manzanar, Ishmael was in the process of losing his in war. The narrative of the conditions at Manzanar is immediately followed by the chapter detailing Ishmael's experiences at boot camp and on the front (chapter 16). We learn in an extended flashback about the circumstances of his emotional and physical wounds, including the botched amputation of his lower left arm. Under the morphine, Ishmael curses "the fucking Japs" but cannot frame his thought except as "that fucking goddamn Jap bitch" (251). Elsewhere, the narrative moves quickly over his college years, his sense of being at sea, his search for partnership and meaning—all to no avail. His missing arm prefigures these other losses, and is itself prefigured in Hatsue's last glimpse of him "standing at the edge of the strawberry fields beneath the cover of the silent cedars, a handsome boy with one arm outstretched, beckoning her to come back" (215). After his father's death he returns home to settle his affairs at the newspaper, and ends up staying. As the book opens, we learn that he cannot bring himself to sit with the other reporters; he moves upstairs to the gallery with the locals. It is there that he encounters Hatsue in the corridor—a painful reunion for both. Eventually it becomes clear that the outcome for both of them will hinge on their ability to encounter each other with an acceptance of what their relationship once was and now is. They achieve this, opening the path by which Ishmael can free himself, and in the process, Hatsue's husband.

The symbolic resolution of Ishmael's crisis comes in the form of a kiss from Hatsue— "like a whisper against his cheekbone" (446). It is a Sleeping Beauty sort of kiss, a repetition of their first kiss (when he "put his lips on hers for no more than a second") years before, when they were still children (87). Released from the spell that descended on him then, Ishmael completes his awakening. As a literally returned kiss, it is also a symbolic cancellation of Hatsue's lie. It is that kiss that distracts Hatsue on her wedding day, and that specific kiss she has in mind when her husband asks if she has ever kissed anyone before (87); perhaps she lies again on their wedding night, when he asks if she is a virgin (91). And in turn, if these were lies, they are symmetrical with Ishmael's lie, in effect, when he continues to speak of Kabuo's guilt while concealing evidence of his innocence. With this returned kiss, the spell is broken, and Hatsue unwittingly repeats the advice his mother gave him the day before: "Find someone to marry," she tells him. "Have children, Ishmael. Live" (446).

Ishmael must pass three tests before he can resolve his crisis and begin to "live" in Hatsue/Helen Chambers's sense of entering into the adult world as a man, husband and father. The first test requires that he accept the challenge of seeking the truth, literally and figuratively. The second requires him to go to Hatsue, so as to confirm his ability to resist the temptation to avenge himself of her rejection by failing to prevent the condemnation of her husband. The third requires him to free himself from his childish belief in happiness, so as to enter into a deeper type of faith. These tests correspond to the three registers of Ishmael's emergent identity. First, he must become his mother's son (faith over facts). Second, he must become his father's son (capable of moral action through his profession). Third, he must relinquish Hatsue and become like Kabuo—that is, a sexually adult man who accepts the terms life offers him, including the terms of his own cultural traditions.

These identifications correspond to the layered equivalences that structure the novel: the equation of legality with life, of authentic identity with sexual self-knowledge; and reconciliation as the acceptance of cultural difference. Underlying these metaphorical and symbolic equivalences is the novel's fundamental balancing of Hatsue's internment with Ishmael's war injury as equivalent sacrifices on the part of citizens. In *Snow Falling on Cedars*, cultural identity is sexual integrity, aligning desire and racial identity; together, these support the book's tacit motif regarding the limits of cultural integration as the foundation for social reproduction. The conclusion articulates a particular vision of multiculturalism—as the restoration of a normative (culturally homogeneous) family as both the means and ends of a multicultural society. While it is the cultural encounter that genders the story, it is the framework of the trial that makes gender and cultural difference equivalent, key to the symmetry by which Ishmael eventually finds himself.

Gender and the Unified Horizon of Difference in Jurisprudence

Expanding law as the container for difference through jurisprudence is explicit in the theoretical account of feminist legal scholar Robin West. Drawing on feminist jurisprudence, West coined the term *narrative jurisprudence* to capture the means and ends of self-representation in the context of demands for recognition and relief before the law. In *Narrative Jurisprudence* (1993) West influentially advocates for the prospects for a progressive renewal of jurisprudence by means of acknowledging the normative implications of ordinary people's stories.

For West, law's promise in this regard is most vivid in relation to women's stories. West opens her book with an assertion of "the law's" moral authority: "It is a shared premise of many, perhaps most, American legal scholars that the authority of law in liberal societies—the law's power to influence our behavior and lives—consists not only of the obvious 'powers of the sword' but also of the more subtle powers of the moralist as well" (West 1993: 1). She continues, introducing a universal "we": "The law's authority over our lives is thus doubly enhanced: we are inclined to obey the law's commands not only for fear of the sanction if we do otherwise, but also because we tend to find its precepts, institutions, and structures morally salutary" (1). This gives rise to the book's main concerns with the problem of assessing "the content of our moral beliefs—the ordinary beliefs of most citizens regarding what is right and wrong, just and unjust, or good and evil" (1–2).

In particular, West is interested in the theoretical and methodological conundrums arising from this problem of "content," given the likelihood that moral beliefs are themselves "heavily influenced by the particular legal system under which we live" (2). In other words, "we" obey the law because it appears to be not law at all, but common moral sense; however, what we know as common morality is actually specific to the particular force and content of "our" law. This is a "critical dilemma" for West (2), because she is interested in rescuing legal critique and civil disobedience from what would otherwise appear (to her) to be an infinite regress of cultural and moral relativism.

Her path to rescue unfolds initially as a critical engagement with legal positivists, firmly separating law and morality (3–4); and then, with critical legal scholars, subjecting the law's moral claims to "radical critique" (5). But these steps lead to a further dilemma: "How might we develop a moral sensibility with which to criticize law that is itself independent of the influence of law?" (6). Her answer to this question involves "the humanities" as a resource for developing "a description of our shared human nature" (6)—that description being crucial to her purposes. In her view, "universal descriptions of human nature" would provide reliable "grounds for criticism of law, as well as for social and cultural criticism" (7).

West takes her raw material from three sorts of texts: modern fiction containing "depictions of human experience" (9), storytelling, or everyday "narrative practices" that "facilitate" the "empathic knowledge of others" (10), and legal texts. It is the second category—"telling, listening to, and responding to stories" (10)—that she identifies as the political centerpiece of her project.

West aligns "narrative jurisprudence" with feminist and critical race theory, and endorses "the larger project of changing law so as to make a more just and humane social world for liberalism's traditional outsiders: women, poor people, and racial, sexual, or ethnic minorities" (10). Social science can be omitted from this resource base, apparently, since West rejects the view that subjectivity and experience are socially constructed (19–20)—associating that view with a "postmodernism" denying "the meaningfulness of subjective experience" (20). She counters what she sees as that "denial" in an extended passage that launches her argument in favor of according legal recognition to people's exchanges of subjective experience through empathy:

One would think that progressive theorists and activists would claim that a world in which we are subjectively and intersubjectively enriched by the pleasures of safe intimacy, education, and culture; challenged and engaged by meaningful and compensated work; nurtured by caring, compassionate community; and mutually respected through the lens of a strong and autonomous regard for individuality and individual differences, is a *good* world. . . . And surely, if the quality of our lives . . . is the measure of our moral progress, then our subjective experiences must be not just relevant but central to our critical appraisal of the degree to which we have created a society—through law and otherwise—that respects and nurtures those lives. If we want to create a better world, we must be able to communicate the quality of those lives and to empathically respond to others who attempt to do so. (20)

In this same context, she evokes family—in this case, a parental bond—to punctuate her appeal: "We must be able to say, to quote my two-year-old, 'Don't do that—you're hurting me,' and we must be able to hear that utterance as an ethical mandate to change course. The coherence of just such a statement and mandate is denied by the postmodern attack on the subjective self" (20–21; paragraph break omitted).

West's goal is to broaden the inclusivity of law with respect to difference but without relinquishing the idea of a unifiable sociolegal field. She stipulates women's experience as constitutive of their collective identity, and turns to "narrative jurisprudence"—based on women's stories—as a means of representing women more fully in law. In her formulation, individuals are members of collective identity groups before they speak, and also through their speech; thus, when they complain or testify before a court of law they do so (in West's view) both as members of a group (i.e., for their group) and as individuals (speaking for themselves). This is a significant tacit claim about the nature of identity and its relevance to law as experience.

West's recommendation for law reform turns on what she calls "hedonistic criticism"—"a critical method that aims directly for women's subjective well-being" based on women's narrative accounts (and body-knowledge) of pleasure and pain (246). At the core of West's critique is her rejection of formal *equality*—or rather, the "equality discourse" (246) that she maintains precludes true equality by virtue of forging "proxies for subjective well-being" (246). Misled by equality discourse, West argues, women are alienated from their own nature, encouraged to believe that they can and should "assimilate" (246). She advocates a strategic discursive emphasis on "the pain in women's lives" rather than "oppression and subordination" (246). Pain becomes the basis of her identification of women with African Americans—a crucial gendering of difference:

> To draw an analogy, Martin Luther King argued again and again that the essence, the dominant fact, of the Negro's life is *pain*, that that fact would not change until the white liberal would come to *share* it, that he would not share it until he *felt* it, that he would not be able to feel it until he understood it, and that he would not understand it until the *Negro* succeeded in bringing the pain to the surface—until he could make its content palpable . . . I believe that the same is true of women: the fundamental fact of women's lives is pain, that fact will not change until men share it, which will not in turn occur until its meaning and content are communicated. (247)

The prospect of men's "sharing" women's experience appears to be driven more by the parallelism in her rhetoric rather than expectations of change. Her analysis rests on the premise that one must *be* a woman to be able to hear or read "women's subjective, internal pain"—since women's pain is "so silent and invisible" and "so different" from anything a man might know (247). "To state the obvious," she writes, "men do not understand, have not shared, have not heard, and have not felt the pain, the numbing terror of an unwanted pregnancy. They have not heard, shared, or felt the tortuous violence of a stranger rape or the debilitating, disintegrating, and destructive self-alienation of marital rape." For this part of her argument, West inserts a new "we" (= women) to cover "our differences from men" (246)—differences at once biological and sexual, distinctive and collective, and accessible through narrative. "Women must start speaking the truth," she writes (248), since "it is only by starting with our own experiences that we will be able to develop a description of human nature that is faithful to our lived reality" (248).

West is concerned to widen the space (literal and figurative) for the moral critique of law, and pursues this project by mining fiction, narrative, and legal texts for previously untapped depictions of human nature that might expand the law's representational repertoires. By consolidating and selectively displacing difference onto the sexual differences between women and men, she navigates around the constructivist critique of universals and primordial identities (i.e., older formulations of race and culture). Importantly, the field of difference she envisions is unifiable (if not yet unified) first and foremost as a *textual* field—a textual field she associates with law. Narrative—while signifying radical alterity—is for West ultimately assimilable to the law's comprehensiveness. West's project, like that of some ethnographers, is to reverse the negative association of identity and difference, affirming a necessary place for cultural difference in liberal jurisprudence. The categories of alterity in question are already the law's own; this is part of what accounts for the substitutability of gender for other forms of difference. The oppositional character of women's stories as envisioned by West strives for a vanishing point—a federal subjectivity cured of a history that hurt.[8] Well away from the scenes of law, ethnographers' stories of difference lean toward a similar imaginary vanishing point, where difference may belong wholly to the domain of pleasure.

CHAPTER 8

Markets for Citizenship

M y concerns so far have been with literary practices drawn into ethnography from circuits of wider circulation with the mainstreaming of neoliberalism, particularly with respect to the mutual implications of identity and federal power. The discourse of solutions and federal subjectivity name key junctures where the mutual contingencies of identity and the scope of federal power are especially visible as textual practices. Those practices also link institutional fields and literary genres. I have concentrated on the convergence of policy fields, ethnography, and fiction around discursive zones shaped by contemporary debates over rights, since that was the context in which neoliberalism's bipartisan advocates valorized markets as a corrective to the effects of policies framed around racial equality. It is the specifics of those claims that account for my focus on the uncoupling of race and class, the elision of race and culture, the iconicity of the individual, the salience of voice, the gendering of the field of difference, and most broadly, perhaps, the nature of explanation. The connections between explanation, power, and risk were palpable in the policy debates of the time, but that in no way implies that they originated there. In this book, we are led to Congressional hearing rooms along the path charted by the internal debates within anthropology. Registering zones of convergence means appreciating the way key terms are turned over again and again as critical objects, in support of different conclusions—that is, as lines of opposition in the process of emergence. Reading ethnography across policy debates and fiction from the 1990s allows us to reconstruct a political moment when the question of rights versus markets had not yet been settled, and to appreciate the stakes in that contest for social knowledge—that is, not just as means or ends. The interpretive possibility linking knowledge to power as I pursue it in this book is thus ethnographically and historically specific; it arises from the field of discursive opposition, as it emerged in that critical period.

In this chapter, I consider how ethnographers addressed themselves to the neoliberalization of identity as marketization gained hold, monetizing identity. Faced with the question of how diversity might survive democracy on these terms, especially following the reforms of 1996, U.S. ethnographers found a voice in the otherwise unclaimed space between rights- and market-based movements. In what follows here, the discussion again draws on zones of convergence across law, fiction, and ethnography, as these fields worked with the new proximity of identity and markets in national political discourse. The fundamental issue connecting the works of this period—judging from their patterned points of contact—is the shift in the significance of citizenship from an affirmation of membership to an indeterminate register of market value. As we saw in the immigration context, market value could sink below zero, into the negative range. Anthropologists and authors of fiction recognized that the negation of market value was not limited discursively to unregistered immigrants, even if it was so limited legally; conversely, they also noticed that market value was no guarantee of inclusion. They drew on these insights primarily in relation to minority identities.

The principal motifs through which ethnography, sociolegal studies, and fiction drew nigh to each other in this context involved formal associations of minority identity and marketization that were still novel in the 1990s: reparations, fees, entrepreneurship, and free trade. We may think of these four motifs as arranged along two intersecting axes, discursively centered on a generalized notion of equality. Equality in this new context should be understood in market terms as the dual promise of a fair valuation of property and a fair return on investment, balanced against the premium on maximizing the circulation of value.

On the first axis, *reparations* and *fees* lead in opposite directions. Reparations look back to lost value; fees look ahead to future value. Reparations constitute a motif of historical closure through compensation for past harms. The Reagan administration passed a reparations act, mainly for survivors of the wartime internment camps for Japanese residents in the United States and U.S. citizens of Japanese descent (Civil Liberties Act of 1988, H.R. 442). Early in the first Clinton administration, Congress appropriated the funds for these reparations and delivered checks with letters of acknowledgment and apology to about fifty thousand individuals over the course of several fiscal years in the 1990s (Takezawa 1995: 58).

At the other end of the same spectrum, fees look forward, to the renewable value of cultural property in an open-ended market exchange. Fees provide renewable return on the market value of a territory's productivity in exchange for title. The fee arrangements devised by Congress for indigenous lands were designed to preclude future land claims. The major case in point involved the Alaska Native Land Claim Settlement Act ("ANSCA") (PL 100-241 1988). ANCSA was first passed by the Congress in 1977, giving native Alaskan communities an opportunity (and a deadline) for entering into agreements that would extinguish their title to land in return for fees for third-party development. The deadline was moved several times, as native communities faced local ballots on the question of whether to incorporate and enter the fee system. Communities divided—sometimes generationally—ahead of the vote. ANCSA established native communities as corporations in 1988, and marketization of indigenous identity gained favor among policymakers as a pragmatic approach to recognition consistent with the principles of neoliberal reform.[1]

Between these two motifs—holding them apart, in a sense—was (is) another axis. Here, too, we find two motifs—*entrepreneurship* and *dependency*. These are related to the discourse of identity as two cultural paths through poverty. Entrepreneurship is consistently discursively positive—representing the joint investment of a local entrepreneur and the widest possible circulation of capital (through institutions of credit, investment, consumption, community development, and so forth). Dependency is negative—discursively cast as a form of private taxation by the poor on those who are wealthier. In the public policy domain of the 1990s, these motifs frequently arose in relation to African American and Latino/a urban poor as well as to immigrants. The stereotypes were essentially the same in their common imagery of dependency as a cash-based form of urbanism with little or no return on value. We have already considered the welfare reform act, targeting the urban poor. Also in 1996, Congress passed the Immigration Reform and Immigrant Responsibility Act (IIRAIRA), drawing on a similar discourse in relation to immigrants—particularly unregistered immigrants arriving from Mexico. IIRAIRA set up elaborate administrative barriers to admission and broad grounds for detention and removal on the grounds of unfair labor competition and illegitimate demands on public coffers by immigrants. Immigration reform was important among legal developments at the federal level, contributing to a general situation in which cultural minorities were transparently objects of federal restructuring of rights through markets.

Each of these motifs was highly consequential in policy terms; however, their relevance to this study is in the way their literary elements make the federal visible through identity. Location, crisis, testimonial narrative, competing registers of the meaning of membership, as well as competing currencies of market value—all of these are prominent in the policy debates, *as well as* in the ethnography and the fiction of this period. It may seem obvious that studies of ethnic groups should be associated with their place in a national history of justice movements; however, this should not be taken for granted, nor does it account for there being (judging from the texts) no other story to tell.[2] For example, in the monographs, we do not find Japanese Americans in monographs *except* in relation to the experience of exclusion and generation-making. We do not find monographs about African Americans *except* in relation to the barriers to inclusion. We do not find monographs about Latinos *except* in relation to the proximity and permeability of borders. Perhaps the strongest textual segregation remains that of American Indians (Cattelino 2010b: 282–286).

It is not only ethnography that works these motifs as the connection between context and content, subject and story line, identity and its market value. In fiction, too, dealing with these same communities in this period, the federal implication and the ironies of neoliberalism are also prominent points of reference—legible through signs of crisis and resolution, subjectivity, narration, and textual organization. The literary trial—a well-known literary device of containment, as in Guterson's novel discussed earlier—is but one strategy for positioning readers in a way that puts them in the position of the judge or jury on the question of whether difference is compatible with union. Here, we may take note of the ways market motifs offer further registers of solidarity and judgment to readers who find themselves invited to enter the text as debtor, partner, investor, or creditor.

Motif 1: Reparations, Literal and Figurative

Let me begin by referring once more to *Snow Falling on Cedars*. As in other classic trial novels, the author positions the reader as witness to the narratives in the courtroom itself, as a fellow citizen and ultimately as a peer—that is, in a juror's role. Without the trial setting (if Carl's death had been recognized as an accident right away, for example) there would have been no relationship among the characters: nothing of the crisis and resolution between Ishmael and Hatsue, no equivalencing of Kabuo and Ishmael in their war experiences and injuries, no story at all, unless Ishmael covered the accident for the local newspaper, and something else happened to enable him to find a way forward for himself. But even as an extended reminiscence, such a story would not *necessarily* involve (as this one does) the issue of cultural difference. Cultural difference comes into Guterson's novel only as the jury's judgment of Kabuo stands in for Ishmael's judgment of Hatsue. The constitution of cultural difference as necessitating a judgment (particularly in the criminal trial motif) is the essence of Ishmael's problem. He must rise above it, learn once more to think of Hatsue as herself, not as *a Japanese*, in order to go on with his life. The choice is evident in the work even if it is not explicit in those precise terms. Hatsue's mother insists on Hatsue's Japanese-ness; Ishmael's recovery is inseparable from his rediscovery of his own parents, as he listens to his mother, and steps up to his father's calling as a journalist.

In her ethnography about the Japanese American redress movement, Yasuko Takezawa structures her account around legal proceedings—combining informants' responses in her own interviews with those culled from transcripts of witnesses' testimony in Congressional hearings and other documentary sources. These are distinguished mainly by the citation in each instance; otherwise, there is a strong continuity of voice. Takezawa explains her purpose as that of showing ethnic identity to be constituted in historical experience (1995: xvi)—that is, against primordialism. Rejecting assimilationist, pluralist, and symbolic approaches to ethnicity, Takezawa presents her question as dual: first, how and why it is that Japanese ethnicity deepened over time in the United States, and second, why "the rest of America" (3), initially so nonresponsive to the survivors of the internment camps, ultimately supported a formal federal apology and reparations.[3] In this second element, the symbolic conflation of the nation ("America") with the Congress and White House is clear, accounting for the work's staging as a series of testimonies on the part of former internees, reflecting on events from personal and generational standpoints. It also serves to anchor the question of identity to the workings of federal law—in both the original order that compelled internment and the act of reparations.

The book opens with a chapter on the redress movement and two chapters of testimonies, one each for the first- and second-generation American descendants of Japanese migrants (*Nisei, Sansei*). The concluding two chapters emphasize the redefinition of the past and present, and accordingly, the resignification of ethnicity for these Americans. Significantly for our purposes, the testimonies—drawn from a variety of sources, including Takezawa's interviews with fifty-five Japanese Americans—include the unpublished transcripts of the Commission on Wartime Relocation and Internment of Civilians, from their hearings in Seattle (the study location) in 1981 (21). The seamless interweaving of field interviews and commission testimony underscores the extent to which the textual practices of ethnography and law—under some circumstances—lend themselves to each other. It is composed, too, to align the ethnographer with federal authority, as respondents' testimonial "I"—addressed to these different interlocutors—become one (see, for just one example among many, the series of testimonies on pages 78–79).[4]

At the level of description, the testimony from the hearings is particularly vivid in highlighting the extent to which camp experience revolved around tensions over compliance with regulations, regimentation, traumatic losses of privacy, and other humiliations. These accounts are deeply moving—challenging the more arithmetic approach to injury that structures Guterson's novel. Through these passages, the question of ethnic identity by which her book is framed morphs into a question of inmate identity—critically engaging the conflation of identity and military status that gave the War Relocation Act its key terms, as well as those central to Takezawa's theory of ethnicity (as critical objects).

Importantly, though, the redress movement, in Takezawa's analysis, was not merely a legal "undoing" of the harms of marking, relocation and internment. Participation in the movement was, she argues, an education in—among other things—"the American system" (191). "Redress is, after all, an American issue," she writes, "supported in Congress and by many other Americans" (191). Demanding redress as a right was, she claims in a concluding chapter that functions as an envoi, essentially Americanizing for Japanese Americans. Thus the intensification of ethnic self-identity—the book's explicit theme—uncovers an underlying thesis as to critical discontinuities in that process. At the end of the book, it becomes clear that her respondents' accounts of having internalized a sense of being Japanese American as an *ethnic* identity was (at least for some) ultimately *attained* through the process of identifying with other minority groups (specifically African Americans) and their rights struggles before the law (Takezawa 1995: 148–149).

In this respect, Takezawa's account of the reparations movement remakes ethnic identity from questions of origins and reception to one of political subjectivity in relation to the federal government. Conflating the federal government with the nation, Takezawa refers to this effect as Americanizing (Takezawa 1995: 148–149)—as individuals and communities claim their own identity as Japanese Americans, so as to hail the state in their own names to claim federal remediation. However, it is only the rights claim in its contemporary formulation (i.e., the winning claim after decades of legal and political setbacks) that, in her account, makes the crucial difference. Takezawa's account, albeit tacitly, critically extends earlier anthropological accounts of cultural self-identity among Japanese Americans through generational experiences periodized by internment. Sylvia Yanagisako's ethnographic study in Seattle in the 1970s, for example, insists on the specificities of local experience and accordingly rejects the then-standard hyphen so as to mark the absence of a general ethnic category (Yanagisako 1985: v).

Writing about her own wartime experiences as a Berkeley graduate student in an account republished in 1986, Rosalie Wax (1971) also emphasizes the inadequacy of a generalized concept of *difference* in relation to what happened to Americans of Japanese descent—in notable contrast to the identity technology of the exclusion order, based crudely on national origins, parentage, language, and religion. Wax conducted ethnographic fieldwork in the camps as a graduate student, seconded to a multi-university and foundation research team through her adviser. Although she does not say so outright, she makes absolutely clear that from the standpoint of their self-identity, there was no unified horizon marking out "Japanese" among Americans either prior to internment or even during the loyalty trials within the camps (to which she gives extensive attention in her account). Instead, she emphasizes the asymmetries of power and knowledge that illuminate the nonreciprocity of the federal government's distinction between nationality and race (a distinction crucial to the U.S. Supreme Court's majority opinion in *Korematsu v. United States* [1944]) and internees' prewar experiences as Americans. Accordingly, her account exposes the fallacy in any conventional narrative that would remake the camp fences into cultural boundaries marking a horizon of known oppositional difference. The loyalty tests during the war years generated opposition among internees but—as the Supreme Court acknowledged even in defending the legality of the exclusion order—no Japanese resident in the United States or American of Japanese descent was ever charged with an offense related to security before or during the war. Wax's account—narrated as a chronicle of first fieldwork—details the everyday routines that treated Americans as hostile foreigners—ultimately, upon release, turning them into immigrants destitute of place and property. It is the children of that generation, and their children, whose voices dominate Takezawa's account and the struggle for reparations.

Federal reparations in the case of Japanese and American internees were calculated as a flat sum of twenty thousand dollars. This was not a market calculation of the value of seized property, lost earnings, unmet financial needs, or other grounds for personal compensation, but the arithmetic outcome of the Congressional appropriation divided by the number of eligible individuals. Devising reparations in this way reserves value outside of a market calculus. As advocates of neoliberal reform pushed market-based policies into the mainstream as ways to reconcile equality with liberty, such questions of the limits of the market became not only politically fraught, but also (in the process) made issues such as reparations, antidiscrimination rights, and welfare—all of which involve fairness and equality checks on marketization—volatile zones of discursive opposition. We have already seen how the winning positions in 1990s debates over employment discrimination and welfare partitioned race and class with culture—disarming by dividing into separate discursive domains the principal terms of opposition to the majority consensus. That this was possible points to the spurious materiality of *race* as an individual attribute as well as the equally illusory *im*materiality of *class*.

Motif 2: Cultural Property and the Timespace of Ownership

The second motif drawing cultural identity into a market relation—converting indigenous land title into fee arrangements, as in the case of ANCSA—formulates these complexities differently. The tangible finiteness of land makes the simultaneous force of opposed discourses contradictory in a way that is not necessarily the case when their object is abstract or generalized. The ANCSA solution, so to speak, is to separate land title from beneficiary status—that is, extinguishing title and shifting the restricted good to a corporation as successor to community ownership. ANCSA represents a compromise, in a sense, relative to earlier approaches to the alienation of indigenous lands through the marketplace. From the beginning of the federal reservation system, federal Indian law has been inconsistent in its approach to the alienability of Indian title.

In the 1970s and 1980s, numerous land claims and boundary disputes were waged in federal courts—an increasingly conservative federal judiciary as the Reagan administration's appointments took effect in the 1980s. The U.S. Supreme Court took a "strict constructionist" approach—reversing earlier gains by some tribes—in ruling against Indians claiming jurisdiction over portions of original reservation land grants now held by non-Indians. This reversal was significant. In some parts of Indian country, checkerboard jurisdictions—discontinuous reservation land punctuated by individual non-Indian holdings—had been the result of selective terminations of federal trustee arrangements, allowing individual Indian property owners to sell their land. Indian and non-Indian holdings may be adjacent lots under these circumstances. But indigenous land is subject to contradictory legalities, as the federal politics affecting Indian country shift back and forth over time between alienation and reservation—sedimenting the land with multiple bases for assigning title and asserting ownership (Biolsi 2001: 29–35). Biolsi dates the beginnings of the modern politics of race on Rosebud to *Rosebud Sioux Tribe v. Kneip*—five years of federal litigation, ultimately decided against the tribe by the U.S. Supreme Court in 1977 (439 U.S. 584 [1977]).

The theme of Thomas Biolsi's *Deadliest Enemies* (2001) is the direct effects of the politics of land on Indian self-identity and Indian-white "race relations" as worked through the legalities of land title "on and off the Rosebud Reservation" (to borrow phrases from the book's subtitle). More accurately, his ethnography examines the racialization of the politics of land, since the consolidation of the racial categories "Indian" and "non-Indian" were, in his analysis, the consequence of an antagonism sustained by the existence of contradictory legal foundations under the competing rights claims, and consequently, the impossibility of a resolution (except in law) that would bring definitive closure to the conflict: "The conflicting regimes of rights-claims, enabled by conflicting law, underwrite this 'racial' struggle. It might be going too far to say that there would be no racial tension in South Dakota without the contradictions of Indian law, but the discourse of Indian law crystallized an opposition in Indian and non-Indian political interests and called forth a bitter, zero-sum rights-game played against one's neighbors" (Biolsi 2001: 74).

Biolsi's analysis clarifies the lines of opposition, a series of triggering events (e.g., a protracted and bitter dispute over a liquor store license) and openings for new relations. While the *Kneip* litigation was in its early phases, the American Indian Movement (AIM) pressed demands for tribal sovereignty, occupying Wounded Knee in 1973 and staging subsequent protest actions. Representing the AIM actions as a threat to civilian security, the governor supported the non-Indians' ownership claims on the grounds that continued Indian jurisdiction would constitute a threat to civil order. In Biolsi's account, these events contributed to the consolidation of collective self-identity among Indians in racial terms (2001: 57–58). The suppression of the protest criminalized Indian identity—becoming iconic of Indian-federal relations, and for some, federal race relations in general:

> To many "outsiders"—and to many Indian people who live in South Dakota—the state has come to stand for racial injustice toward Indian people in America at large, and even American racism in general. In a 1971 journal article, for example, a New Zealand historian asked, "Why are race relations in New Zealand better than in South Africa, South Australia or South Dakota?" Here, South Dakota clearly stands for American racism on the global stage; it was, in the clever alliteration of the article's title, even more "southern" than the American South, and *racism toward American Indians was depicted as even more paradigmatic than racism toward African-Americans.* (Biolsi 2001: 199; emphasis added, notes omitted)

Most of Biolsi's account details the events of the 1970s and 1980s, as *Kniep* worked its way through the courts and back again, this time in the form of sharp racial conflict. He details the local sovereignty movements in the region, and voices skepticism that such highly "regulated" (his terms) forms of rights struggle can be effective in delivering what Lakota people need to flourish, physically and culturally—since they are "technical" and "partial" in relation to those needs (185–187). Demands for sovereignty, however, are the opening created by the very confrontation over land under Federal Indian law, constituted and, for many, experienced as racial confrontation. Citing an article in *Indian Country Today* ("widely read on Rosebud Reservation" [188]) Biolsi draws a connection between the discourse of Indian demands for sovereignty and the movement to terminate welfare entitlements: "In [the author's] reasoning, sovereign nations should expect to address their 'own' problems with their 'own' resources, just as an individual should take 'personal responsibility' for his welfare" (188; cf. chapter 3). But—like critics of the winning consensus in the welfare debate in the 1990s—he is skeptical of the logic that would make fiscal self-sufficiency *follow* from independence. The welfare connection draws Biolsi into broader reflection. He continues, vividly evoking the so-called race-blind *equality* that had become mainstream in the 1990s, the same equality affirmed in the debates that produced the Civil Rights Act of 1991 and the Welfare Reform Act of 1996:

It is now widely recognized by scholars interested in class, race, and gender that although the constitutional rights of equal protection and private property provide certain protections for the subaltern, they also make it next to impossible to allow concrete injuries rooted in class, racial, or gender experience in the United States to be *admitted* into court or mainstream politics. "Equality before the law" deradicalizes the law by excluding class, race, and gender inequalities from its cognizance and from the practical political struggles it underwrites. . . . *The more tribal sovereignty is formally realized under existing federal Indian law, the more difficult it is for Lakota people to make credible legal and political claims regarding the full range of daily forms of oppression they are subjected to . . . [and] to articulate local problems as connected to larger—ultimately continental and global—* colonial *problems* (188–189; emphasis added, notes omitted)

"Law," he concludes at the end of the book, where the envoi should be, "—especially Indian law—is a 'racial politics machine' with powerful— hegemonic—ideological and political effects. We must always remain alert to the critical fact that there is no will to racial justice that stands behind the discourse of Indian law and guarantees its humane unfolding" (210).

Though critical of law as the answer to the problems Lakota people face, Biolsi is careful throughout to explain their turn to federal law as a strategic choice in the interest of taking advantage of an available opening. He is also careful to specify the racialization of land disputes as among the consequences of that strategy, not an irresolvable antagonism. That sense of discursive entrapment—the hegemony of law being precisely the corollary of its availability without alternative—is also a powerful theme of fiction. Leslie Marmon Silko's *Ceremony*, (1996, originally 1977—the height of the indigenous land litigation in the federal courts) begins where Biolsi's book ends—at the point where self-identity is foreclosed in any relation to the world of whites. For Tayo, the young Navajo veteran of the Pacific front during the Second World War, suffering from—but that is the question: post-traumatic stress disorder? or a rending of his spirit that predates even his own birth, stretching back centuries? He is home from the war, sickened and grieving, above all, for his cousin Rocky, whose death he witnessed at the front. As Rocky lay dying or already dead on a stretcher, being carried in a soaking jungle rain to a Japanese prison camp, a Japanese soldier smashes his skull with the butt of a bayonet. Rocky and Tayo had been raised as brothers. As the novel opens, Tayo is leaving the psychiatric hospital for home, where he is eventually shown a path to healing—in the process healing more than himself. Guided first by his family, then by a healer, he completes a ceremony begun three generations before—partly by accident, partly through faith and insight. The rains return, ending a long drought that began when Tayo cursed the rain in the jungle. The rains signal a reversal of the "witchery" that did not begin in the war, or before that, in the lessons at the Indian School run by whites, or even before that. To search for its origin in some judgment is not the point. Rather, witchery enters as a question of identity—since those caught in its snares are sealed off from themselves and the knowledge that was their birthright. The end of the story metes out different fates, not by blood (Tayo is half white) but according to individuals' openness to the knowledge that fulfills the ceremony, knowledge that is life itself.

A powerful motif in the narrative of Tayo's wartime memories is his nightmare fantasy that among the Japanese soldiers who faced his platoon's firing squad—he did not pull the trigger—he saw his own uncle's face. He is haunted by this identification with the dead soldier, felt as kin (7–8, 195). As the veteran returning home, he knows about internment—"I thought they locked them up" (18)—but his return coincides with the release of internees, and his eye catches the gaze of a little boy at the train station. Once again he feels the stirring of a sense of kinship—and once again, he experiences this as trauma (17–18). Much later, a healer explains his reaction as body knowledge, the trace of an eons-old kinship dating to a time before the separation of one people long since divided by an ancient transit across the Pacific, or perhaps the Bering Strait, to the Americas (124). Tayo's healing enables him to realize that time flows in all directions, and that "he is not crazy; he had never been crazy. He had only seen and heard the world as it always was: no boundaries, only transitions through all distances and times" (246).

Tayo's healing does not come all at once. Episodes with his aunt and grandmother, the local medicine man, a stronger healer named Betonie, and a woman/life force named T'seh who (as is eventually revealed) has appeared to Betonie, Tayo's uncle, and others in all the generations comprising the story. The reader learns to recognize T'seh only as Tayo does. The generational accounts that lead to his revelation are contrapuntally arranged against increasingly menacing encounters with his boyhood friends. Caught up in the self-contempt learned in the Indian School and eager for the highs of competition in sports and, in the war, of killing, these young men are broken—poisoned by their addictions to alcohol, violence, death. The turning points in Tayo's recovery are marked by passages of poetry. (Behind the story is a storyteller who never appears.) As his own insight deepens it becomes clear to him that his friends have been consumed by the witchery that made the war, plundered the land, and turned Indians against themselves within themselves (203–204). Thus the novel moves, not along a line dividing tradition and change, or white and Indian, but between change and death. Betonie explains that "after the white people came, elements in this world began to shift; and it became necessary to create new ceremonies. . . . Things which don't shift and grow are dead things. They are things the witchery people want. . . . That's what the witchery is counting on: that we will cling to the ceremonies the way they were, and then their people will triumph, and the people will be no more" (126).

Tayo's quest is to find his uncle's cattle and reclaim them. The narrative of that journey occupies the last section of the book—as Tayo finds revelation upon revelation along the way. He learns to accept knowledge he does not understand, to read his path in the stars, to embrace memory as presence. He learns to choose life when he is at the verge of dying, to trust himself, to love, to recover his sense of connection to the earth, and through the earth, to life that accumulates but does not pass away. Betonie teaches him to think of land outside of the question of ownership. At one point, he admonishes him that he can break the cycle of theft and counter-theft between Indians and whites by realizing that no one owns the land: "it is the people who belong to the mountain" (128). In search of the cattle, Tayo enters the ceremony, completes it by continuing it. He finds the cattle, and breeds them to flourish in the drought and hardness of Navajo country. At the end, he is healed, and his friends—consumed by their own witchery—are dead or gone. Tayo returns to his family, to begin his life anew.

Ceremony, like Biolsi's *Deadliest Enemies*, pulls against a discourse of solutions, in the process unscrolling the federal implication from the idea of *identity*. Tayo succeeds in his quest when—in pursuit of his cattle, alone on the mesa—he loses the sense of himself as Indian = not-white. In part, this is a conscious historical analysis, narrated as his inner speech as he looks out over the land (Silko 1996: 204–205); however, the consciousness that saves him comes not in words, but as a revelation. Silko, who narrates Tayo's inner life in part through descriptions of his physical state (tense, relaxed, nauseated, aroused), consistently situates his consciousness first as body-knowledge—a physical state the source of which must be respected even before it is known or named. Ultimately, he is healed by his own body as he allows himself to become realigned with the timespace of the world.

For Biolsi, too, the critical burden of his deconstruction of the federal in relation to Lakota identity is not to rework "Indian identity" as a social construction or as invented tradition. Rather, it is to open the discursive terrain beyond the limits of federal recognition, to open a space for another discourse (or discourses) of kinship (literal and figurative) and well-being. The exploration of those potential counter-discourses necessarily falls beyond the scope of the ethnography, since those counter-discourses are not emergent in the field situation; Biolsi makes this absence clear, throughout. Here, I am not about to suggest that Biolsi or other anthropologists take their sense of problem from novels, but I have drawn on *Ceremony* to show where and how fiction might be necessary to anthropological work committed to the problem of hegemony such as Biolsi's. Fiction makes thinkable a discourse of identity outside the domain of the discourse of solutions. This in itself is not a solution, but another story.

Motif 3: Aligning Culture, Class, and Capital

The sharp tensions over Indian sovereignty and land claims make explicit—in bold relief—the federal implication in minority identity. The creation of federal boundaries in the U.S. interior is of a piece with the federal politics of border control, although these issues are ordinarily treated wholly apart. Viewing them as configurations of identity, land, markets, and legal jurisdiction illuminates their connections. The third and fourth motifs begin in immigration, as anthropologists work these same connections from different directions. Internment and sovereignty involve U.S. citizens; so does immigration, in bridging the foreign and the domestic. Anthropologists encompass both under the rubric of *ethnicity*, converting national borders into lines between generations (first generation, and so forth). The third motif, in the context of the times (e.g., as portrayed by Peshkin 1991, discussed above), could be read as a success story—as business success pushes ethnicity into the background as significant to private life but not the primary organizing feature of public life. The fourth motif (discussed in the next section) begins in the anti-immigrant politics of the time, as anthropologists rework the border from periphery to center in various ways. Anthropologists in either of these veins argue explicitly against ethnicity as rendered by the conservative right (as primordial, conflictual, menacing, outside of "our culture" [Buchanan 1992]). Both lines of analysis involve double negatives—refuting the automatic (negative) associations of ethnicity with resistance and rebellion (in the third motif) and with subordination (in the fourth). Either way, the conservative right's misrecognition of ethnicity—the constant object of anthropologists' critique—is just below the surface of these texts.

Illustrative of the third motif is Hsiang-shui Chen's *Chinatown No More* (1992). Chen takes his readers to New York City, where immigration from Taiwan has recently led to the expansion of the Chinese community from Manhattan's Chinatown to the outer borough of Queens. Chen's book opens with his central argument, a double negative challenging political and academic stereotypes of Chinese immigration and settlement in the United States: "Most Americans have the impression that the Chinese in the United States live in Chinatowns, isolated from the broader community. Indeed, this stereotype was fairly accurate during the first hundred years of Chinese immigration, between 1850 and 1950, when most Chinese immigrants were single men who lived in Chinatowns under a hierarchical structure. With Queens as its area of focus, this book aims to introduce a new type of Chinese community" (3). Chen reviews the literature on Chinese migration and situates his findings against recent social and economic developments in New York City; his attention to the municipal context makes his work distinctive. His main thesis going into the study was that class functions more prominently than ethnicity (i.e., national origin) among new immigrants, given the different means and ends of migration for individuals and households situated differently prior to their emigration (41). His findings confirm this thesis, leading him to the conclusion that "the Chinese" are not a single ethnic group (41): "The more contact I had with the Queens Chinese population, the less it seemed that 'ethnic group' was a suitable concept for one study of these new immigrants. Although many cannot speak English, as they go about the business of survival in this country they shop at various ethnic stores. I have also found that Chinese of different classes do not often interact with one another" (41).

Anticipating the relevance of class associations, Chen approaches his study by dividing the community of new immigrants into four groups—capitalists (owners of large factories, companies, hotels, restaurants), small-business owners (knitting factories, small shops, restaurants), the "new middle class" professionals (including professors, civil servants, and medical doctors), and workers (in knitting factories, garment factories, restaurants, and stores) (categories and terms drawn from his chart on page 43). There are important points of contact among these groups. For example, patterns of upward and downward mobility connect the upper three groups and the lower three; only capitalists and workers appear to be outliers. (He did not interview capitalists, for lack of access [44].) Highly educated individuals are situated in all four groups. Traditionalism and modernism—as cultural preferences—are also distributed across all groups.

At the same time, personal networks and associations are circumscribed by class—particularly among workers, who are more isolated than the business and professional households, and whose employment is almost entirely within the enclave of the community. Chen draws on this observation to refute the assumption that new immigration takes jobs away from the native born (102–103). Professionals have been the main "agents of struggle for the welfare of the Chinese community" (143) but Chen emphasizes that the welfare associations are distinct from the clan and district organizations of older Chinese immigrations (183); the new associations are "bridges" linking the community to other ethnic associations and New York City services (183 ff.). Indeed, Chen concludes that the existence of "a" Chinese community should be regarded with skepticism. It was only in the context of the Queens Festival in 1985 and its "Asian village" initiative that Chinese organizations in Queens first worked together to create an "inclusive arena" for the community as a whole—a tent called "the China Pavilion" (245). Queens, he concludes, is "a *world town*" (263; original emphasis).

The situation of one tent for "China" points to a wider discourse of multiculturalism—a sort of post-ethnic amalgam through which public-private partnerships (in this case the borough and community organizations) promote the circulation of capital across ethnic lines. Capitalism, from this angle, is conjured as a conversion of ethnicity's negativity to utility as an asset available for re-investment and growth. At the same time, the story of the tent—coming at the very end of Chen's book—also highlights the ironies of that motif. The new immigrants might be professionals and small-business owners—model members of the middle class—but, for the most part, they brought their education and capital with them to the United States; this is what qualified them for entry. For these new immigrants, capital accumulation within the United States comes at the expense of even the most modest personal comforts (126–127). Chen's interviews suggest that isolation, discrimination, glass ceilings, burglary, extortion, fines, and long hours are routine problems for workers, small-business owners, and professionals in Queens (pt. 2: esp. 102–103, 126–127, 142–143). Thus, the motif turns back on itself, as alienation ironizes capital value.

That irony is a powerful theme in fictional works of this same period—

central, for example, to the "winning ironies" of *Typical American* (*People Magazine,* quoted on the back cover of Jen 1992). Jen's novel chronicles a Chinese family as circumstances take them from pre-Mao Shanghai to New York City—where upward and downward mobility become indistinguishable, except as a series of assaults on their dreams and expectations. And central, too, to *The Kitchen God's Wife* (Tan 1991), sequel to the best-selling *The Joy Luck Club* (1989), where alienation and value cross borders, generations, and figurative currencies many times over before the story reaches its resting point. The novel form makes a disjunction between internal and external worlds—the precondition of irony—accessible, and this theme is by no means reserved for fictionalized accounts of Chinese migration. However, the iconic association of Chinese migration in relation to the global capitalism emergent in the late twentieth century lends those ironies a particular currency and legibility.

Motif 4: Alienation as the Predicate of Value

The second motif makes the alienation of property (including land) the predicate of its market value, and the third motif reworks alienation as investment. The fourth motif formulates alienation as *dis*investment, reflecting the pervasive anti-immigrant politics of the 1990s. As reformers attempted to close the border by law, it opened as a subject of study in anthropology and fiction, contesting the ironies of inadmissibility in narratives of memory and attachment. Susan Coutin's *Legalizing Moves* (2000) is based on fieldwork and analysis from this period, as the Salvadoran asylum seekers with whom she worked navigated the crosscurrents of immigration and refugee law. For asylum seekers, the border appears again and again, in the form of papers—lines on the page to be filled in so as to tell a certain kind of story.

Coutin studies the contexts and content of Salvadoran immigrants' efforts to legalize their residency (for details of her fieldwork project, see Coutin 2000: ch. 1; see also Coutin 1993, 2007). "I viewed my research as an ethnography of a legal process rather than of a particular group of people," she writes (23). Indeed, the question of how a discourse of "identity" is constructed (or precluded) by law is central to the book. The legal process Coutin studied spans wide geographical distances and national borders. Immigration law is radically changeable, variously understood, unpredictably complex, inconsistently practiced and unevenly enforced. Thus, social relationships in two countries (and in between) are subject to a host of dangers and vexed promises. The legal process also extends—through political processes and legal practices—well beyond the situation of Salvadorans or other immigrants. "The book demonstrates that far from being marginal or segregated social processes, the practices that define individuals' legal statuses are central to determining and contesting what it means to be American" (25).

Coutin begins her exploration of the legal process at the wide gulf between personhood and legal recognition—"enforcing immigration law makes it appear that *status inheres in papers, not persons*" (55). The bureaucratic requirements for proper documentation are as important to the process as the less tangible notion of eligibility. In other words, eligibility is not just the outcome of a certain chain of experiences for people in migration, but also—as if independently—a process of preparing and producing paper forms. The lack of correspondence between the realities of people's experiences and the steep selectivity of the bureaucratic process creates serious problems of nonrecognition, confusion, exploitation, and personal risk.

Coutin connects these problems to the "spaces of nonexistence" inherent in a terror state, as victims are "simultaneously defined and erased": "Victims were defined in that they were named as subversives, guerrillas, the unwanted, illegals. . . . They were erased in that they were defaced, killed, or forced into exile. As they were defined and erased, pulled in and out of existence, victims were torn apart" (Coutin 2000: 38). The legal process of immigration is in significant respects an extension of those spaces, since the person who enters the United States without registering, who lives and works without legal status, who cannot provide the appropriate answers to questions at the hearings, or who lacks proper papers, passes out of existence from a legal standpoint—sometimes briefly, sometimes permanently. The legal process reconstructs the personhood of the migrant through a process of documentation, substituting the paper reality for the living person (24, 116).

The bureaucratic demands for documents and forms are an important part of a petitioner's legal experience, and Coutin examines these from the human side of the process. Petitioners for work permits, for example, "imbue immigration criteria with . . . morality"—but "a morality that differs from the notions of merit and meeting requirements that are used to decide immigration cases" (61). Asylum seekers, for example, must provide accounts of their personal history in terms that immigration authorities are prepared—that is, legally mandated by statute—to hear. Coutin details numerous instances in which a petitioner is interrupted, deflected, or silenced as the administrator (or sometimes the petitioner's advocate) combs through the mesh of circumstances in his or her account, to isolate specific bits of information, so as to align them—now as "evidence"—into a linear account that can be checked against the legal requirements of eligibility (97) and the discursive norms of official discourse. "Only rarely did a client's response take the form of an immediately coherent and logical narrative," Coutin writes. "Rather clients recounted one bad experience after another, seemingly connecting these experiences by the suffering they entailed more than through temporal cause and effect" (97). The gaps between a petitioner's narrative form and the available terms of recognition sometimes lend the exchanges between petitioners and their advocates or Immigration and Naturalization Service (INS) officials an air of surreality. For example:

> To differentiate what ASOSAL [an community advocacy group] staff termed a "real" asylum case from asylum applications that were filed as a means of obtaining a work permit, advocates asked clients the following sorts of questions: Why did you leave your country? Are you afraid to go back? What do you think would happen to you if you had to return? Like INS officials, advocates sought to distinguish victims of generalized violence (who were ineligible for asylum) from individuals who had been singled out by their persecutors. This distinction was implied by an ASOSAL staff member's question of a Salvadoran man who had been wounded by the Salvadoran National Guard: "Were they shooting at you in particular; or did you just happen to get shot?" (90)

Or this example from Coutin's experience as a volunteer in one of the community organizations: "I resented the legal system's emphasis on details and consistency as measures of credibility. The woman with whom I was working remembered events but not dates. After she described the brutal assassination of a family member or another equally tragic event, I often had to ask what I thought she would consider an extremely irrelevant and insensitive question: 'And on what *date* was your brother killed?'" (4; original emphasis).

The petitioners' textual reconstructions were thus retooled for their hearings. Coutin reports that judges tended to emphasize personal character, and she examines at length the extent to which this meant eliding or omitting altogether structural issues (such as collective danger) and interpersonal connections (such as feeling threatened when family members were killed) (chapter 5). Officials also tended to focus on a petitioner's interest in "U.S.

popular culture"—recent films, for example—and other experiences outside of El Salvador as measures of the moral credibility of their professed interest in obtaining legal status. Coutin summarizes these discursive manipulations as yet further contingencies of legal personhood, by which individuals are discursively assimilated to the nation in an idiom that is both legal and (in the constructions of the official personnel) cultural: "Officials' attention to acculturation (and deculturation) suggests that . . . applicants' narratives of deservingness are simultaneously individual and national stories" (127).

In her analysis of the process of legalization, Coutin emphasizes such contexts as these, in which personal identity, legality, and nation are substantively reworked in—or rather, as—the process itself. Importantly, such constructions (and deconstructions) do not simply create a mask (to borrow Richards's metaphor; Richards 1994). Sometimes, of course, they do create situations in which one or another actor might be conscious of playing a role. But the more important issue from Coutin's perspective is the extent to which the state's practices retool identity—indeed, *insist* on a coherent, self-contained individual subject—as the precondition (literally, the *pretext*) for hearings in the various administrative arenas of the legal process. Her ethnography in this sense challenges the convention of theorizing "legal consciousness"—or "society," for that matter—as composed of individuals, since the very idea of a person's "having" an individual, stable, and uncontingent identity is itself a legalism. That ethnography borrows this legalism so easily and extensively is easily overlooked as a sign of anthropology's intertextuality with the discursivity of citizenship.

Anthropologist Ruth Behar, too, draws attention to the precariousness of membership and identity—weaving her professional identity as an anthropologist through the fabric of her personal story. She situates *The Vulnerable Observer* (1996) intertextually—alongside Gloria Anzaldúa's autobiographical *Borderlands* (1987) (Behar 1996: 161–162) and Sandra Cisneros's fiction. She cites Cisneros's *The House on Mango Street* (1989) as a "model of how to construct a narrative that respects the fluidity of the border between the girl and the woman" (Behar 1996: 131–133; passage quoted is from 131). Indeed, Cisneros's novel—presented as a series of short stories, some very brief—presages some elements of Behar's tone and positionality, as Behar, like the novel's narrator/persona "Esperanza," chronicles her rising consciousness as a constant work of passage. Her border is within herself; and Behar—again, like Cisneros—relies on us to know that it is also elsewhere, and for some people, impassable.

The Vulnerable Observer is an experimental autobiography/ethnography. Behar embraces the border as a central location—at the figurative "heart" (to borrow from her subtitle) of the matter. Her narrative persona is American, Cuban, Spanish, Jewish, professional, familial, child, adult, girl, woman, reader, writer, student, teacher. Rewritten in this way, as a feature of a personal interiority, *the border* loses its unity in time and space, and becomes a problem of knowledge, self-expression, and recognition: "Loss, mourning, the longing for memory, the desire to enter into the world around you and having no idea how to do it, the fear of observing too coldly or too distractedly or too raggedly, the rage of cowardice, the insight that is always arriving late, as defiant hindsight, a sense of the utter uselessness of writing anything and yet the burning desire to write something, are the stopping places along the way. At the end of the voyage, if you are lucky, you catch a glimpse of a lighthouse, and you are grateful. Life, after all, is bountiful" (1996: 3). In the process, Behar shifts the question of hegemony from the law's force to the question of how individuals internalize the conditions of their own alienation. In the paragraph immediately following the one just cited, she multiplies and displaces *borders* to the disciplinary practices of anthropology—as the lines between the story as lived and the one that cannot be told, the permissible and the punishable: "But surely this is not the anthropology being taught in our colleges and universities? It doesn't sound like the stuff of which Ph.D.'s are made. And definitely it isn't the anthropology that will win you a grant from the National Science Foundation. Nor, to be perfectly honest, is it the anthropology I usually tell people I do" (3). Some of the people she cannot tell are people close to her—her example is "Aunt Rebeca"—but she returns to an indictment of what she deems to be anthropology's beginnings. The passage begins as a reply to Aunt Rebeca's identification of anthropology as "'The study of people? And their customs, right?'" (4): "Right. People and their customs. Exactly. *Asi de facil.* Can't refute that. Somehow, out of that legacy, born of the European colonial impulse to know others in order to lambast them, better manage them, or exalt them, anthropologists have made a vast intellectual cornucopia. . . . Anthropology . . . is the most fascinating, bizarre, disturbing, and necessary form of witnessing left to us at the end of the twentieth century" (4–5). Her meditations turn to problems of method, and ultimately, to the question of genre:

> As a mode of knowing that depends on the particular relationship
> formed by a particular anthropologist with a particular set of people

in a particular time and place, anthropology has always been vexed about the question of vulnerability. . . . Our intellectual mission is deeply paradoxical: get the "native point of view," *pero por favor* without actually "going native." Our methodology, defined by the oxymoron "participant observation," is split at the root: act as a participant, but don't forget to keep your eyes open. . . . When the grant money runs out, or the summer vacation is over, please stand up, dust yourself off, go to your desk, and write down what you saw and heard. Relate it to something you've read by Marx, Weber, Gramsci, or Geertz and you're on your way to doing anthropology. . . . We are definitely in the theater of farce as our uncertainly and dependency on our subjects in the field is shifted into a position of authority back home when we stand at the podium, reading our ethnographic writing aloud to other stressed-out ethnographers at academic conferences held in Hiltons where the chandeliers dangle by a thread and the air-conditioning chills us to the bone. Even Geertz recognizes there is a problem: "We lack the language to articulate what takes place when we are in fact at work. There seems to be a genre missing."

Consider this book a quest for that genre. (5, 9)

Behar's genre is autobiographical ethnography—not autobiography as such, but a reflexive accounting of the fieldwork process (i.e., one in which anthropologist is present—not some distant observer) (6–7). For Behar (drawing on Devereux), this is necessitated by the nature of the inquiry itself—the "relentless subjectivity of all social observation" (6). Here, too, she claims a departure from the discipline's norms, which she frames as the norms of science (12): "No one objects to autobiography, as such, as a genre in its own right. What bothers critics is the insertion of personal stories into what we have been taught to think of as the analysis of impersonal social facts. Throughout most of the twentieth century, in scholarly fields ranging from literary criticism to anthropology to law, the reigning paradigms have traditionally called for distance, objectivity, and abstraction. The worst sin was to be 'too personal'" (12–13). But for Behar, there is no accountability without "vulnerability" (to borrow from the book's title and theme, throughout)—as there must be, if there is (as she implies) no interpretation without risk. She offers an example: "To assert that one is a 'white middle-class woman' or a 'black gay man' or a 'working-class Latina' within one's study of Shakespeare or Santeria is only interesting if one is able to draw deeper connections between one's personal experience and the subject under study. That doesn't require a full-length autobiography, but it does require a keen understanding of what aspects of the self are the most important filters through which one perceives the world and, more particularly, the topic being studied. . . . Vulnerability doesn't mean that anything personal goes" (13–14). She continues, recounting the tangled intellectual and identity politics of her tenure case at Michigan, a series of breakthrough moments as she experiments with *vulnerability*, and her experiences of vulnerability in professional settings. After the title essay—the source for the passages quoted above—she presents a series of ethnographic essays in the first person.

She returns to the issue of academic norms and sanctions more forcefully at the end of the book, where the epistemological and critical strands of her book come together—in the most intimate autobiographical register of the collection, and the one most explicitly situated in a wider politics of knowledge around the issue of identity. The concluding chapter—titled "Anthropology That Breaks Your Heart"—is set at a meeting of the American Ethnological Society (AES), as she awaits her turn as discussant at a session honoring Renato Rosaldo for his newly published *Grief and the Headhunter's Rage*, and his upcoming presidency of the AES. She looks around, at the audience, the room, and finds herself thinking, "'Is this why my parents left Cuba?'" (161). The paper she plans to give was a late-night revision, rewritten so as to bring her remarks closer to her feelings for the late Michelle Rosaldo as well as her appreciation for Renato Rosaldo's book. But giving the paper taxes her own courage. The chapter is set up almost in real time, as, awaiting her turn at the podium, she reflects on the state of the discipline as she sees it then—at that very moment. Ultimately, the essay takes the form of quoted speech (her own) interspersed with her remembered inner dialogue. Her reflections on the discipline set the stage:

> I say I am here to "defend" the kind of anthropology that matters to me, which suggests that it is under attack. That may be too strong a way to put it, but lately there is tremendous anxiety that anthropology is becoming "activist art" overrun by "interpretive virtuosos." And it is no exaggeration to say that anthropology is going through another terrible identity crisis. There have been crises before, about anthropology's complicity with conquest, with colonialism, with functionalism, with realist forms of representation, with racism, with male domination. But the discipline has always managed to weather the storms and

come out stronger, more inclusive, at once more vexed and more sure of itself. (162–163; notes omitted)

She continues, gesturing toward the public sphere where representation is ethnography or nothing, site of competition over anthropology's formerly proprietary space, especially for scholars working on or in the United States:

> This time, however, it may not recover so easily. There are serious problems. Many of them. For one thing, anthropology has lost exclusive rights over the culture concept, which was its birthright. . . . In our time, in this special period, this *periodo especial*, where bearing testimony and witnessing offer the only, and still slippery, hold on truth, every form of representation must pay homage to its roots in the ethnographic experience of talking, listening, transcribing, translating, and interpreting. . . . And now that . . . too many of us are doing research at home, is there anything left that makes us unique? Has anthropology finally become dispensable? (163)

Prevarication cast aside, she situates the politics of method in that wider struggle over identity and representation that anthropology shares with other disciplines, other institutions: "The critics of the kind of anthropology that matters to me claim that the price anthropology must pay to survive into the next century is to become science, or risk becoming nothing. . . . Anthropology, what a vulnerable observer you are! You may well have to jump into the arms of the scientists if you are going to try to keep your grass hut in the academy" (164). Then it is her turn to speak. But it turns out it is not scientists who are her antagonists in this "bullfight" (165), but "humanists" who have delivered "ruthless criticisms" of Rosaldo's book. When she looks at them they do not look back. It is one of several moments in the book when the narrative of professional exchange must pause, to register the nonverbal and the visceral.

Realism in Question

These motifs bring together issues of identity and value through markets. It would not be accurate to say that the research projects cited in this chapter were intended as studies of neoliberalism. That said, the textual framings of the works are deeply imbued with the varied positionings of minority subjects (as victims, natives, aliens, and immigrants) entailed in the federal government's neoliberal turn toward privatization and marketization. The marketized nation provides a broad foil for anthropologists' assertions of the relevance of anthropological knowledge.

My examples in this chapter and throughout the book are illustrative—selected for the thoroughness of their reflexive accountings—and no doubt readers will have other sources in view that would modify the discussion in one way or another. I realize I cannot do justice to the literatures in question or the critical repertoires associated with them. The point is to show how ethnography is bound up in its times through its literariness and subject matter, and these, in turn, are related in a politics of genre that is not anthropology's alone. *Culture* loomed large in the new discourse as the politics of law shifted from rights to markets—the terms of recognition and misrecognition having become one and the same. David Wong Louie captures this conundrum in his haunting short story, "The Movers" (1992), in which a Chinese American man and a Caucasian woman—strangers to each other—make a spontaneous and silent compact around their intricate invisibilities. For ethnographers, too, the pressures of the time placed increasing demands on their literary arts—fiction, irony, autobiography, reflexivity filling in to mark the zones where convention would have foreclosed ethnographic engagement altogether.

Advocates from any point on the political spectrum could acknowledge the individual as federal subject, but in different ways that underscore the pitch of their differences. Where old-style liberals presented individual identity as the effect of membership in a historical community of experience, new liberals seemed to see individual identity mainly as the effect of self-making—essentially a form of alienation (as we see in Motif 4). Such a construal of identity quickly reaches a horizon where aspects of identity beyond one's control—parentage, affinities outside of the state, benefiting from rights, and so forth—become potential sources of stigma. It is important to note that in the formulation of 1990s rights critics discussed in this book, stigma does not derive directly from race or any other identifier per se, but from a construction of antidiscrimination rights as *special* rights or reverse racism. This construction was explicit in the Senate debate over the measure that would have overridden the president's veto of the Civil Rights Act of 1990, but it was not new then—and it remains a commonplace today. Thus did the major social legislation of the 1990s divide government from certain elements of the rights-bearing aspect of citizenship while retaining taxation as the fundamental social compact.

In this contentious milieu, ethnography found a theme—the social compact understood otherwise—and affirmed its relevance in a voice borrowed in part from current antiracist fiction and rights jurisprudence. Thus did ethnographers both honor and offset the limitations of the empirical method in their pursuit of relevance. And so, too, did they honor and offset the limits of law. New Deal liberalism had been integral to the methods, history, and ethics of their discipline in the United States, and its ending occasioned a period of productive disciplinary self-scrutiny as the story changed. Consciously or not, anthropologists borrowed elements of their discourse from law and fiction, through depictions of actual conditions that doubled as figurations of cultural situations: race, ethnicity, and gender being primary among these double figures. Policy was a template of relevance but meanwhile, policymakers borrowed crucial elements of their legitimacy discourse from fiction and social science. From fiction, they borrowed the expressive authority of the first-person singular and the redemptive significance of the life story; from social science, they borrowed a certain fantasy of collective interests and their expression as demonstrable outside of the political sphere. Meanwhile, fiction derived a critical register from the immediacies of injustice under law—or, conversely, the power of law to make justice. From social science, it drew a performed accountability to historical and cultural complexity in which identity is at once arbitrary and essential, symbolic and material. We have noted just some of the textual practices that sustained these elisions and exchanges until the times changed and anthropologists moved on to other necessary things. But by then, the literariness of ethnography had become inseparable from its claims to relevance as science and as democratic implication. And so forth—there is more than one way around.

Empirical Citizenship

Before scholars talked about "identity," there was not one word but many other words: race, class, sex (gender came later), ethnicity, culture, subculture, custom, colonialism, independence movements, new nations, developing countries, inequality, legal pluralism—among others. Identity came belatedly to refer to all of these at once, encompassing (and refusing) the older, separate frames of reference, and evoking their common stakes.[1] As a term in usage in the United States, identity is specific to an era when rights discourse came under attack and scholars sought to broaden the discourse of liberal pluralism past singular minority experience, and past the nation-state, toward the critical exposure of contradictions in the sphere of recognition. As modernity was increasingly theorized as contingent on the disavowal of such contradictions (as we have seen in relation to elements of the legislative debates discussed in previous chapters), anthropologists and others made a new critical venture in the contexts and institutionalizations of such disavowals, focusing on contradictions posed by transnationalism for classic theories of citizenship (see, for example, Coutin 1999; Ong 1999). Identity, in other words, is a form of agency in its tacit acknowledgment of both personal association and the social movements that are its history and potentiality (Bhabha 1998; von Eschen 1997).

The transformation in the fields of identity, then, poses questions of the historical specificity of state citizenship in relation to the "global rise of neoliberal capitalism": "The geographically localized, nationally bounded conception of society and culture, of a homogeneous imagined community, is at once compromised, pluralized, problematized. So, concomitantly, is the nature of identity: no longer contained neatly within citizenship, in the modernist subject, it is 'free' to redefine itself along any number of axes of being in the world" (Comaroff and Comaroff 1999: 15). Lisa Lowe evokes the mutual relativity of states and subjectivities as ambivalence:

> Cultural forms are not inherently "political," indeed in the modern nation-state, culture has been traditionally burdened to resolve what the political forms of the state cannot. Alternative cultural forms and practices do not offer havens of resolution but are rather often eloquent descriptions of the ways in which the law, labor exploitation, racialization, and gendering work to prohibit alternatives. Some cultural forms succeed in making it possible to live and inhabit alternatives in the encounter with those prohibitions; some permit us to imagine what we have still yet to live. (1998: 19)

Lowe's doubling of time and identity around the political conditions adjoining alternative futures evokes W. E. B. Du Bois's "double-consciousness."

For Du Bois, time, space, and consciousness meet at the horizon of the "color-line": "The problem of the twentieth century is the problem of the color-line—the relation of the darker to the lighter races of men in Asia and Africa, in America and the islands of the sea" (Du Bois 1990 [1903]: 16). Coming early in the book, this passage offers a concise depiction of a temporal axis (Middle Passage, enslavement, emancipation, struggle for justice—and identity) in relation to a spatial axis ("Asia, Africa, America and the islands of the sea"). The "color-line" is the intersection of these two planes, and together, they form the matrix of "double-consciousness"—the "gifted . . . second-sight" that permits self-consciousness through "the eyes of others" (Du Bois 1990: 8–9).

Importantly, Du Bois makes double consciousness not an *attribute* of the people to whom he refers as "the Negro" but a *relation* formed in what Nahum Chandler later calls the "vortex" of "the double articulation since the 16th century of the history of slavery . . . in the Americas and the Caribbean and the emergence of a global practice of racial distinction" (Chandler 1996: 78–79). Conceived this way, identity is always implicitly a reference to the nation-state in a global context. As Chandler explains, what is at stake in Du Bois's concept of double consciousness is not the identity of "the Negro" but the "schema of [a] discourse" that precludes the production of "a non-essentialist discourse" of identity in relation to the nation:

> There is not now nor has there ever been a free zone or quiet place
> from which the discourse of Africanist scholars [including Du Bois,
> among others] would issue. . . .. It emerges in a cacophony of enuncia-
> tions that marks the inception of discourses of the "African" and the
> "Negro" in the modern period. . . . At the core of this cacophony was
> a question about identity. On the surface, its proclaimed face, it was a
> discourse about the status of the Negro (political, legal, moral, philo-
> sophical, literary, theological, etc.) subject. On its other and hidden
> face, the presumptive answer to which served as a ground, organiz-
> ing in a hierarchy the schema of this discourse, and determining the
> elaboration of this general question, was a question about the status
> of the European (and subsequently "White") subject. (Chandler 1996:
> 79–80; note omitted)

The keyword *identity* names this temporal/spatial juncture within social relationships, including—as for Du Bois—the relationship of social scientists to
the people whose circumstances are their subject matter. This is something of
the context in which Chandler calls for a continual "desedimentation" (1996:
80) of the discourse of double consciousness as a means of ongoing reflexive
cultural critique.

Neither History nor Nature

"In the situation of radical world-alienation, neither history nor nature is at
all conceivable," Hannah Arendt writes in "The Concept of History" (1968:
89). Meaning, she observes, is never decided by action; it is settled afterwards,
post hoc; agency is inevitably a retroactive assessment of causality—an artifact of the requirements of narrating causality (1968: 75–82, esp. 77; see also
Bhabha 1994: 190). In *The Human Condition*, Arendt (1998: 175–247) specifies a variety of conditions under which agency and history might be either
connected or disjoined. Agency is contingent on the political sphere, and she
enumerates specific conditions of access, audience, and acknowledgment.
Agency is no synonym for individuality or action in the conventional sense
of deeds, then, but rather rests on the fact of what she consistently calls "plurality" (see Arendt 1998: 176). Arendt evokes these conditions as the essence
of freedom—a freedom so available, and so valuable, that she compares it to
"a second birth": "With word and deed we insert ourselves into the human
world, and this insertion is like a second birth, in which we confirm and

take upon ourselves the naked fact of our original physical appearance. . . . Its impulse springs from the beginning which came into the world when we were born and to which we respond by beginning something new on our own initiative" (Arendt 1998: 176–177). But when the conditions of agency—self-disclosure in one's public speech and acts—are not met, when the agent has no name, Arendt sees instead the makings of a second death:

> Without the disclosure of the agent in the act, action loses its specific character and becomes one form of achievement among others. It is then indeed no less a means to an end than making is a means to produce an object. This happens whenever human togetherness is lost, that is, when people are only for or against other people, as for instance in modern warfare. . . . Action without a name, a "who" attached to it, is meaningless, whereas an art work retains its relevance whether or not we know the master's name. The monuments to the "Unknown Soldier" after World War I bear testimony to the then still existing need for glorification, for finding a "who," an identifiable somebody whom four years of mass slaughter should have revealed. The frustration of this wish and the unwillingness to resign oneself to the brutal fact that the agent of the war was actually nobody inspired the erection of the monuments to the "unknown," to all those whom the war had failed to make known and had robbed thereby, not of their achievement, but of their human dignity. (Arendt 1998: 180–181)

Perhaps it is because Arendt herself uses a single lifetime as synecdoche in her argument that Bhabha refers to her "temporal break in representation" (1994: 191). One cannot "make history" nor can one make oneself, she argues, but under some circumstances one can reveal oneself (to oneself and others)—or under other circumstances be subject to violent erasure from collective memory. There is an enduring dignity for an artist in an unsigned work of art because it remains art, she asserts, in a way that the nameless war dead are lost utterly, more than dead (Arendt 1998: 180). In context, through this assertion she performs a calculated reversal of the conventional weighting of actions over words, weapons over flesh.

There is temporality in agency in this sense, to the extent that agency originates in the bond between speaker and listeners, in the attention of audiences, in the durability of beauty, in personal and collective memory, and in the meaning post-hoc narrative accords to an individual. Temporality emerges from the generative split between action and agency, that is, between an act and its meaning, but not because these are in some sense sequential. Rather, they constitute the experiential dimensions of relevance. Everywhere, officializations of time bridge and conceal the temporalities inherent in agency and its varieties (Greenhouse 1996). And temporality can be extinguished by violence (Arendt 1998: 180–181; see also 50–51).

For Arendt, the temporality in agency begins in speech and acts recognizably one's own, but it does not end there. Arendt makes time from the conjunction of personal expression and public acknowledgment in narrative—but the name she gives this conjuncture is identity: "The unchangeable identity of the person, though disclosing itself intangibly in act and speech, becomes tangible only in the story of the actor's and speaker's life; but as such it can be known, that is, grasped as a palpable entity only after it has come to its end" (Arendt 1998: 193). Identity is contingent on the assessments and acknowledgments of others; in this sense, identity is the active principle of agency. One does not "make" the meaning of one's own life (Arendt 1998: 193–194), except in the individualist's delusions.[2]

Arendt's discussion dwells on ideals she associates with classical Greece, but it is not a study of Greece. Her classical references serve primarily as tropes with which to substantiate her evocation of modern disenchantments, to mark them as modern. Thus, when she states that the space of the *polis* was defined by laws, she is asserting the failure of modern law to provide safety: "To them, the laws, like the wall around the city, were not results of action [agency in the sense just described] but products of making. Before men began to act, a definite space had to be secured and a structure built where all subsequent actions could take place, the space being the public realm of the *polis* and its structure the law; legislator and architect belonged in the same category" (Arendt 1998: 194–195). Within the space of the law, agency, identity, and politics form a single constellation of possibilities; they are—for Arendt—different modalities of a potentiating and always plural humanity, confirming them as the essence and empirical reality of *time*. Arendt's time is a particular dream of citizenship.

For Arendt, humanity's "plurality" is the precondition of political life within the nation. Citizenship is at the core of her reflections on identity and agency, in that the polis was restricted to citizens. Reflecting on a related question, Homi Bhabha suggests that "nationness" is to be found in the emergence and negotiation of "interstices—the overlap and displacement of domains of difference" (Bhabha 1994: 2). What interests me in these formulations is the concreteness, or sitedness, of citizenship—as being not first or immediately a location of the individual in the symbolic order of the nation-state, but a potentially unbounded nexus of partnership and communication.

Narration and the Nation

Historian Mary Ryan draws on Arendt's writing on citizenship to specify the public life of cities as "the empirical center of the history of democracy peculiar to the United States" (Ryan 1997: 8)—a discovery for which she gives credit to Alexis de Tocqueville. For Tocqueville, the fact of an empirical federal center within the abstraction of the federal system made very tangible a set of contradictions and risks in U.S. democracy, and today those remain relevant to contemporary struggles for justice. Arendt turns often to Tocqueville, largely for his analysis of the American Revolution and the character of U.S. democracy. *Democracy in America* is both specific and concrete in terms quite parallel to Arendt's sketches of the polis—but it is also different in ways that are relevant for our purposes. Tocqueville portrays Americans as individualists. Their sphere of meaning-making is not the political sphere alone, but also the market—to which the political sphere is thereby fused. And Tocqueville is concerned with the limits of U.S. democracy, specifically as revealed by the condition of Indians and slaves—complementary exclusions from without and from within, in his formulation.

Individualism arises in Tocqueville's analysis as an attitude, orientation, or identification with society predicated on state citizenship. It is an identification with the state—not membership as such.[3] Thus, citizenship is much more than a legal status—and more than eligibility to participate in the polis as an equal. But the association of self and state brings into proximity two incomparable subjects, representing them as if they were two elements of a single entity distinguishable mainly by their obvious differences of scale. Importantly, this representation of scale can be misleading. Further, the association of incommensurate subjects obviates a demography of the empirical nation; the personal association of self and state and the symbolic and material work required to sustain it as an identity relation *are* "the nation." In other words, if one follows the arc of this thought, "the nation" is not hyphenated to the state, but—from an empirical standpoint—to the self and its social surround.

Individualism gives citizenship a person's face and form, and perhaps it seems obvious that citizenship should be figured in this way. But this is a figuration, an image—not demography. Citizenship becomes empirical—if it does become empirical—through the claims of actual persons from within their self-identity as citizens: what they ask the state's agents to do for them, or what they demand from the state so that they can act on their own or others' behalf. This empirical dimension of citizenship makes citizenship crucial to survival under some circumstances, or to mobility, or simply satisfaction, even pleasure. Legal citizenship (the symbolic order of the citizen from the state's side) does not account for the significance of citizenship as a crucial dimension of personal experience. Those realms of significance import the state into spheres of activity far beyond its own jurisdictions, technically speaking, in the lives of individuals and collective purposes of groups.

As a topic for social theory, discussion of citizenship in the 1990s tended to focus on the state's according of rights to citizens as a matter of law (e.g., Kymlicka 1995; Toniatti 1995; Turner 1993; Yeates 1996) and acknowledgments, through citizenship, of particularities within national identity conceptualized in collective terms (van Steenbergen 1994; Shapiro and Kymlicka 1997: and Habermas 1995). Tocqueville's discussion of individualism is relevant in that context (and today) because he begins the question of citizenship on the *other side* of that legal relation, that is, at the point where an actual person embraces the "artificial person" (Marx 1975b: 98, cf. 234) created by the state as his or her personal warrant. Not everyone has the knowledge or standing do this. Citizenship is (at least) two-sided, and its two sides do not necessarily mirror each other, making it all the more important to understand how individuals' needs for citizenship stem from their desires (tangible and intangible) and their personal sense of responsibility and dignity in their relations with other people, as well as how these are (or are not) recognized by the state through citizenship.

Furthermore, viewed from that "other side" citizenship turns out to be a different relation altogether. In theory, citizenship confirms an individual's relevance in (and to) the state through rights and duties; however, in practice, it is first and foremost a form of charisma. The paradox of relevance begins here—that is, in the fact that the pursuit of relevance leads to issues of interpretation, since the connection between state and citizen is not one of a whole and its parts, but signs, their referents, their necessary fictions, and their ambiguous afterlives.

Concretely, the state's legal regulation of society derives from something other than the individualist's identification with the state through his or her personal actions; the one involves effective bureaucratic measures (including persuasion and coercion), while the other involves private needs and wants, and subjective worlds of meaning.[4] This means that there is an ethnographic question to be asked about citizenship, regarding whether and how people incorporate the state into their own self-understandings and agency. As the decade of the 1990s ended, ethnographic studies in the United States offer numerous examples of people's needs for and uses of citizenship to forge bonds *through* the state, but not necessarily *to* the state. These studies confirm the multisitedness and fluidity of empirical citizenship, as the following examples illustrate.

In *Black Corona*, Steven Gregory (1998) considers grassroots activism in a neighborhood of New York City that borders LaGuardia Airport. Part of the book details a property dispute between local residents and a variety of public and private entities associated with the development of LaGuardia Airport. The neighbors—mostly African Americans—organize to oppose the airport's expansion into their community. Under local "sunshine laws" that guarantee the public access to certain government proceedings, they have the right to receive information about, observe, and participate in the decision-making processes that affect their property; however, they also face procedural obstacles at various points, in part because the agencies involved are not exclusively public—they also include corporations. The residents' effort borrows something of its organization and rights discourse from the civil rights movements of the 1950s and 1960s—which focused on legal rights precisely because constitutional doctrines of citizenship provided a basis for remedies where the private sector would not. Their mobilization highlights the extent to which the expansion of the private sector displaces some of the arenas, but not the substance, of citizen action.

Aihwa Ong's (1999) study of "flexible citizenship" includes many examples of contemporary reworkings of citizenship as a modality of transnationalism. One vignette involves a woman from Hong Kong who has made a large fortune as a transnational developer, and who purchased a home in an elite neighborhood of San Francisco. When she began architectural modifications that would have added a third story to her house, her neighbors objected, addressing their objections—as is their right as citizens—to the city zoning board. At first, their objections were on the grounds that the higher elevation of the modified roof line would block the scenic vista from their own properties. But tensions flared when one of her neighbors said publicly: "We don't want another Chinatown here." Eventually, city officials apologized to the homeowner, but—enraged—she donated her house to the homeless of San Francisco with the stipulation that no Chinese should be sheltered there—a double insult to her neighbors since there are no Chinese among San Francisco's homeless population (Ong 1999: 102–103).

Barbara Yngvesson (1997) writes about adoption, including a moving account of her personal experience, which she presents among other testimonies gathered in interviews. She describes how she and her husband, living in Massachusetts, learned of a woman in California who was anxious to place her baby with an adoptive family. Thus begins a relationship that brings Finn into the Yngvesson family as their younger son. Among the details of the adoption process, Finn's birth mother wants to bring the baby to the couple personally. This poses legal problems since adoption requires state action; it cannot be private. Accordingly, Massachusetts law prohibits the direct transfer of a child from birth parents to adoptive parents. The plan for the process in this case involved separate rooms, in which each family would be represented by a lawyer who would pass the baby between them, taking him from his birth parents and placing him in the arms of his adoptive parents. But when the time comes, they arrange to be together in a "complex ceremony of severance and of joining" (1997: 35) that they improvise to respond to the legalities but also to suit their own sense of the occasion. Thus, "the legal moment that was to separate Finn irrevocably from his mother and join him . . . to us . . . became inseparable from an illegal moment, an outlaw time in which we violated Massachusetts adoption law, agreeing that this was not only a transaction between a birthmother and the state, and between potential adoptive parents and the state, but that it was also, in Finn's birthfather's words, a parent-to-parent matter" (1997: 35). In the event, the bonds of citizenship are appropriated—as the substance of ceremony—by the parents and the others present, and reformulated as enduring connections between the Yngvessons and Finn's birth parents.

These are just moments from much longer stories, and there are many more such stories—of collective action, individual survival, "transnational belonging" (Susan Coutin's phrase), and family life. I choose these because they give some sense of the way "citizenship" juxtaposes domains of life that are ordinarily imagined as separate, differentiated by scale, location, or interest. My main point is that citizenship is not merely the architecture of the state or an abstract sense of belonging to a nation, but a medium—more accurately, a range of media—of social action and active social connection. I make this point cautiously and provisionally with the United States in mind—since law has long doubled as an everyday language among the American middle class (see Bowman and Mertz 1996; Engel and Munger 1996; Ewick and Silbey 1998; Greenhouse 1986; Greenhouse, Yngvesson, and Engel 1994; Kourilsky-Augeven et al. 1997; Merry 1990: Yngvesson 1993). But it would seem that citizenship is as much a matter of the "loci of the heart" as it is of law.[5]

While the public discourse of citizenship emphasizes membership and belonging to a nation, empirical citizenship is about belonging or not belonging in one's own life. Empirical citizenship reveals the centrality of citizenship to living one's chosen ties to others. Perhaps the most striking ethnographic finding in this area is the extent to which people call on citizenship for more collective purposes. Referring once again to the examples cited earlier: Modern immigrants want citizenship precisely so that they can have the freedom to visit home. Reuniting families, or nurturing adoptive families, often means adjustments to citizenship. Ethnographic studies of citizenship suggest that in practice citizenship is deeply important to people. Its importance is less in its exclusivity than in securing the autonomy necessary for maintaining multiple commitments, sometimes in multiple locations—as if the world were without borders and citizenship were the key to mobility.

These examples (and others we might consider) suggest that while the state treats citizens as units in an administrative arithmetic, subject to addition and subtraction (see Peutz 2006), the person's embrace of citizenship as his or her own involves an entirely different set of issues—potentially not referring to administration and by no means necessarily limited to or contained by the nation-state. The citizen looks not so much up to the state, as inward, and outward, to other people. The image of the self as citizen makes the state integral to the constitution of the person and draws the idea of legality directly into the personal subjective realm—as desire, pleasure, pride, pragmatism, fear, shame, and terror (among other possibilities) in a host of public and private settings. As William Maurer writes: "We cannot view the kinds of individual persons constructed in modern worlds as separate from the kinds of states they inhabit and construct, and which at the same time inhabit and construct their personhood" (1998: 6).

Individualism, as drawn by Tocqueville, encompasses the contradictory gap at the center of citizenship; perhaps this is why Tocqueville refers to individualism as a defect of reason.[6] An individualist is always simultaneously inside and outside the community, simultaneously performing for it and judging the performances as part of the audience.[7]

Conditions and Contradictions

In the state's mythic space of contradiction, law and life of necessity include some element of fantasy with respect to each other (Žižek 1996a: 112–118). In citizenship's "space of symbolization" (borrowing Žižek's phrase again) desire—which I mean here as a broad reference to conscious needs and wants—maintains a vital and revitalizing link between the symbolic form of the citizen and the empirical reality of the person, and locates that connection centrally within the empirical individual (Dolar 1996: 27). I draw on the language of psychoanalysis here, since it lends itself to the task of exploring how the incommensurabilities within citizenship yield problems of narrative; however, this is not a psychoanalytic argument about individuals. It is an argument about the capacity of a powerful public discourse to obscure its own contradictions, limits, and alternatives—with consequent challenges to personal and collective experience. Arendt, more concerned with equality of members of the polis than with its criteria of membership, seems not to have considered that the desire for membership is also a potent form of desire—or that desire (for equality, for example) is a form of agency not necessarily enabled by the law's sheltering walls. In the aftermath of enforced school integration in Little Rock, Arkansas, for example, she wrote critically of the Supreme Court's intervention in what she regarded as a private area of concern (a child's education).[8] Tocqueville understood the contradictions and concreteness of desire within the frameworks of citizenship: the production and consumption of wealth, as literal investments of physical energy, are important themes of his study. In *Democracy in America*, it is not the analysis of individualism that carries the burden of his analysis, but his chapter linking the subjects of racism, commerce, and federalism. Indeed, if there is a fulcrum to *Democracy in America*, where it might be said that all preceding is introduction and all following is development, it is the final chapter of the first volume, at the literal middle of the work. The chapter, entitled "The present and probable future condition of the three races that inhabit the territory of the United States," contains more than 25 percent of the pages of the first volume. Structurally, too, it links the two halves of the work—the first volume on institutions, the second volume on democratic myths and experiences—with an analysis of the relationship among the themes of race, commerce, and federalism as mutual contingencies.

Importantly, in Tocqueville's analysis, individualism (as a social structure built around self-interest within a national space) endows commodities and material desires with nationalist meaning, making these into elements of the experiential machinery of federal power and providing federal power with some of its extraordinary flexibility and concreteness. In experiential terms, as Tocqueville goes on to suggest, the federal movement takes capital as its engine, the body as its vehicle, "community reason" as its cargo (409). Its sites of exchange encode the country's celebrated surfaces (Baudrillard 1988) with hidden presences and lines of jurisdiction. The mobility of capital and the individual body answer to the fundamental ambiguity of federalism—that is, the ambiguity of sovereignty (as between the federal government and states).

It is interesting to register Tocqueville's absorption in the fact that the constitutional ambiguities of federalism define a subjective problem for individuals—and a subjective problem that demands personal resolution. Specifically, Tocqueville sees the subjective crisis of federalism as a split in every citizen's identity, making moot the ordinary distinction between here and there. Commerce restores the dimensions of time and space to the nation where federalism complicates them or seems to cancel them outright (by trumping state power with federal power). Indeed, commerce, from Tocqueville's point of view, seems to provide the means for a resolution to the subjective crisis of federalism. Importantly, he regards commerce not just as a means of accumulating capital, but also as means of concretizing the self— that is, the mobility and energy of the empirical person—within the state. The nation has empirical meaning within the framework Tocqueville maps out only to the extent that commerce—like a royal progress—traverses its territory on the legs and backs of its citizens. By their expenditures of energy, they fill in that territory, making it and its boundaries real.

"The condition of the three races" is Tocqueville's description of U.S. democracy's most telling contradiction and an object lesson in its most profound risks. Then (and now), federalism was in a state of dynamic tension as between states' rights and a strong federal government. Tocqueville rues what he regards as Andrew Jackson's tactics for strengthening the central government at the expense of federalism, by offering special privileges to the strong states-rights states (431–432). He is not explicit, but we might imagine that the privileges Tocqueville had in mind included the expulsion of the Creeks and Cherokees from Georgia and concessions to slave-holding states. The stronger the central government, the greater the resistance, pressing not inward toward the center but outward against these margins; thus, there was a practical politics that extended the precariousness of the federal government to the situation of Indians and people living in slavery. Crucially, Tocqueville's discussion does not focus on the sole fact these people are outside the democracy, but that they were pushed out and kept out by democratic means. Tocqueville presents the reality of enslavement and the illusory freedom of Indians living outside the American democracy as social realities arising from the specific political conflicts over federalism in the United States.

Importantly, these margins are not just at the nation's borders, though as 1990s ethnography in the United States made clear, the national borders figure importantly in the symbolic orders of citizenship (Chock 1998; Coutin 2000; Urciuoli 1998). Then as now, well inside those borders, the practical realities of federalism remain integrally tied to the social judgments and allocations of resources that make inner cities frontiers, as well (Davis 1992: ch. 5; Greenhouse 1998; Herbert 1997). No less than in Tocqueville's times, perhaps, the modern crosscurrents of federalism and globalization are integral to social status and social judgment. The tensions between states and the federal government continue to be integral to the pragmatics of citizenship today, and similarly occasion deep emotion—for example, in public debates over immigration and welfare, over abortion, or in an earlier period, over integration, or (even earlier) over abolition and "Indian removal." "The nation" of the United States is not any one model of federalism, but all such possibilities together with whatever is at stake in the differences among them.

From an empirical standpoint, therefore, the nation cannot contain difference (as prevailing public discourse claims), but only confirm its own incompleteness. This is the context in which the idea of empirical citizenship is a reminder that any categorical distinction between relevance and irrelevance—from the standpoint of cultural inquiry—can only be radically ambiguous. This must suffice as a happy ending.

NOTES

Prologue

1. Lukács draws a distinction between the epic and novel from their respective formulations of the hero's situation—as interior to the "organic" community (as in the epic; 67) or in relation to a formal problematic (as in the novel; 1971: 56–69). Lukács does not refer to ethnography, but his discussion suggests continuities with an ethnographer's textual relationship with his or her subjects: "The epic gives form to a totality of life that is rounded from within; the novel seeks, by giving form, to uncover and construct the concealed totality of life. . . . All the fissures and rents which are inherent in the historical situation must be drawn into the form-giving process and cannot nor should be disguised by compositional means. Thus the fundamental form-determining intention of the novel is objectivised as the psychology of the novel's heroes: they are seekers" (Lukács 1971: 60). The literary features of U.S. ethnography at this period are in effect those of an epic hero writing a novel in the form of ethnography—the anthropological significance of any description is ultimately global and without beginning or end; however, the subject matter is delimited by time, place, and the actions of individuals "seeking" partnership, sustenance, and meaning.

2. On the mutual convertability of race and culture in the neoliberal policy discourse in the United States, see Stepick 2006: 393.

3. For reviews of that emergent literature, see Low 1996 and Susser 1996; see also Newman 1999.

4. And even if, at the same time, those contradictions open discursive spaces for opposition, as Gregory shows (1992, 1993, 1998).

5. On narrative politics in feminism, see Smith and Watson 1992 and Heinzelman and Wiseman 1994. On *testimonios* and the politics of truth, see Beverley 2004 and Moreiras 2001: 208–238. The essays by Beverley and Moreiras respond to the controversy surrounding the verifiability of Rigoberta Menchú's *I, Rigoberta Menchú: An Indian Woman in Guatemala* (Menchú and Burgos-Debray 1984)—a controversy waged extensively among anthropologists (see, for example, Gelles 1998).

6. David Schneider both parodies and parries the contending positions in these terms in a fantasy interview—written entirely by Schneider as if in dialogue with one "RH," Richard Handler (Handler 1995: 8–10).

7. In general, see Haney 2008 and Calhoun 2007 for in-depth historical accounts of the development of modern sociology in the United States.

8. On 1990s conservatives' appropriation of the language of the left in the United States, see Dean 2009: 7, 18.

Chapter 1. Relevance in Question

1. The reference is to Clifford Geertz's "thick description" (1973), that is, ethnography aimed at questions of meaning through interpretive frames of reference.

2. By "opposing discourses" I mean opposition on other principles, as a challenge to neoliberal ideology, for example. Opposition is not necessarily discursive opposition.

3. On the fate of canons in relation to particular understandings of the nation, see Marcus 1991b: 404; Fischer 1999: 456.

4. The phrase borrowed from *Feminism Beside Itself* (Elam and Wegman 1995) evokes the integral place of reflexive analysis within the theoretical field.

5. I say "mediation" since the appeal is always cast in terms of anthropology's already-existing repertoires of concepts and practices, as sufficient for resolving debates and healing divisions. This is usually implicit, but it is explicit in Murphy's effort to "call anthropology back to its center" from "within the chaos" (1990: 331).

6. For example, in the United States: Biolsi 2001; Coutin 2000; Dávila 2004; Domínguez 1986; Engel and Munger 2003; Frankenberg 1993; Ginsburg 1989; Gregory 1998; Heyman 1999; Loewen 1988; Lutz 2001; Holland et al. 2007; Wagner-Pacifici 1994; and elsewhere, particularly in colonial and postcolonial contexts: Baumann 1996; Comaroff and Comaroff 1991, 1997.

7. See Mascia-Lees et al. 1989 for earlier accountings.

8. Cf. Lukács 1971:preface; consciousness as the sense of being both subject and object of history.

9. The counterhegemonic efficacy of that field was necessarily linked to global markets for print (Marcus 1991a: 121; cf. Anderson 1993)—the literary field in the more material sense.

10. For "brackets" in this context, I am indebted to Riles 1998.

11. For a related observation with respect to ethnographic writing on poverty (but not in the community-study genre), see Susser 1996: 415–416.

12. The ease of intelligibility is not explained, since it would have been a commonplace view among anthropologists—and characteristic of a mainstream view that cultural practices in the U.S. are transparent to its natives.

13. Baker 1993; Handler 1998; Lieberman 1997; Liss 1998; Visweswaran 1998: 79.

14. Schneider 1968; Domínguez 1986; Frankenberg 1993.

15. Hopper 2003; Santiago-Irizarry 1996; Sullivan 1989; Wells 1996.

16. Dávila 1999; Gable et al. 1992; Gregory 1993; Lugo 1990; Maira 1999; Sanjek 1998.

17. Alvarez 1995; LiPuma and Meltzoff 1997; Martinez 1996; Schneider 1998.

18. Bright 1998; Chin 1999; Coombe 1996; Hermann 1997.

19. Gregory 1992: esp. 255; Hartigan 1997: 495; Page 1997: 99; Rouse 1995: 380–388; Schneider 1999: 777.

Chapter 2. Templates of Relevance

1. The phrase "global city" and the sense of globalization as a rescrolling of the lines of U.S. investment abroad originate with Saskia Sassen (1985, 1991). Early ethnographic studies of the social and cultural effects of global economic restructuring reworked the terms of ethnography itself. Influential examples include anthropologists' work on China (Anagnost 1997), Eastern Europe (Verdery 1996), Great Britain (Darian-Smith 1999), European Union (Zabusky 1995), Africa (Comaroff and Comaroff 1993; Ferguson 1994), Latin America (Coronil 1997), India (Gupta 1998), and the United States (Sanjek 1998); more generally, see Appadurai 1996 and Ong 1999.

2. Drawing on Adam Yarmolinsky's *The Military Establishment* (1971), Lowi cites 179 call-ups of the National Guard and other military forces between August 1965 and December 1968, involving 184,000 troops and, over the course of the decade of the 1960s, "at least 100,000 civilians" under surveillance by the army (Lowi 1979: 276–277).

3. For examples of such neutrality claims, see Sollors 1986, 1989 and Fischer 1986; cf. Hall 1985.

4. Dworkin's defense of liberalism, originally published in 1978, is in terms that suggest the extent to which social anthropology is a liberal discipline, quite apart from any practitioner's political commitments, given the proximity of political organization to social organization, and the broad tolerance for difference built into the idea of equality as he describes it: "[Liberalism's] constitutive morality provides that human beings must be treated as equals by their government, not because there is no right and wrong in political morality, but because that is what is right. Liberalism does not rest on any special theory of personality, nor does it deny that most human beings will think that what is good for them is that they be active in society . . . The liberal conception of equality is a principle of political organization that is required by justice, not a way of life for individuals, and liberals, as such, are indifferent as to whether people choose to speak out on political matters, or lead eccentric lives, or otherwise to behave as liberals are supposed to prefer" (Dworkin 1984: 77–78).

5. Varenne's thesis made its way into Robert Bellah's *Habits of the Heart*—a best-selling critique of American individualism (Bellah et al. 1985).

6. For further discussion of the impact of neoliberalism and globalization on New York City, see Abu-Lughod 1999; Gregory 1992, 1998; Sanjek 1998; Sassen 1991. More generally, see Lash and Urry 1994 (esp. pt. 3)—but see also Abu-Lughod (1999: 399) for a cautionary note regarding the risks of overgeneralization, given the extent to which globalization affects cities in ways that appear to be specific to their situations.

7. Peshkin's main thesis is that "social interactions that normally, elsewhere, occur within an ethnic group, can and routinely do take place across ethnic groups at RHS" (1). Peshkin seems to see his thesis as requiring some special accountability on his part—perhaps a sign of how deeply he was concerned that his audience would be skep-

tical of so optimistic an account, given the tensions of the time. Be that as it may, the book's prologue and epilogue frame the work around the subjective demands of studying ethnicity as a Jewish anthropologist—and with the awareness of the historic specificity of the project's very possibility in light of a near past where racial and ethnic conflict would have been insurmountable (4 n. 2, 285–295). Indeed, almost two decades later, the testimony that made him optimistic seems in some instances stunningly raw to the ear, and part of the book's value must be the listening post it offers to the tenor of everyday speech at the time, through his many interviews with administrators, teachers, and students and their parents.

Chapter 3. Texts and Contexts

1. The ADA of 1990 (Public Law 101-336) passed the House 377-28 (with 27 not voting), and passed the Senate 91-6 (with 3 not voting). Congressional Record—House: July 12, 1990, page 17296; Congressional Record—Senate: July 13, 1990, p. 17376.

2. Congressional documents regarding testimony on the Americans with Disabilities Act are reproduced and compiled in Reams, McGovern, and Schultz 1992, a six-volume documentary history of the act. I cite them as separate government documents, since the pagination in Reams et al. is not consecutive (instead reproducing the pagination of the originals).

3. Unless otherwise noted, all references in this section are to the published hearings on the bill (S. 2104) (U.S. Senate 1990).

4. In *Griggs v. Duke Power Company* (401 U.S. 424 [1971]), the U.S. Supreme Court ruled that tests of employment qualifications must be relevant to the substantive responsibilities of the position in question; otherwise, their disparate impact is evidence of discrimination.

5. The reference to turning back the clock is an echo of *Brown*'s prologue to overturning *Plessy v. Ferguson* (163 U.S. 537 [1896]).

6. In the same context, Loury observes that "Americans seem to be trying to balance our cultural budget on the backs of our poorest, most vulnerable citizens" (Loury 2001: 451). For an assessment of the impact of the 1996 welfare law on children (among other issues), see Sawhill et al. 2002.

7. Hardening on key points discussed here is evident in the exchange between Senator Kennedy and the Deputy Attorney General Donald B. Ayer (pp. 114–117); see also Kennedy's statement in response to the president's veto message, implying that the administration had broken faith with a longstanding compromise.

8. 104 H.R. 3734, enacted as P.L. 104-193. See U.S. Congress 1996. If passage of the legislation fixed the terms of consensus within the Congress, they should not be assumed to be the terms of a national consensus, even granting widespread electoral support for welfare reform. In her ethnographic study of attitudes regarding welfare among working people in poverty, J. Schneider (1999) finds that her respondents supported broader inclusiveness as the key to welfare reform.

9. For a timeline of the development of the 1996 law, see American Public Human

Services Association 1998. For analysis comparing the 1996 with the old law, see Find-Law n.d.; U.S. Department of Health and Human Services 1997; Urban Institute 1998.

10. For legislative history see Lexis-Nexis n.d.

11. See, for example, U.S. House 1996, part 1: 238.

12. See, for example, the testimonies of Kate Michelman and Clifford Johnson (U.S. House 1996: part 2).

13. The Personal Responsibility and Work Opportunity Reconciliation Act of 1996 (Public Law 104-193) passed the House on July 31, 1996, by a vote of 328 to 99 (5 not voting). Democrats split 98 yea to 97 nay, with 2 not voting; all but two Republicans voted for the bill. In the Senate the following day, the measure passed by 78 to 21. Democrats split 25 yea to 21 nay, with 1 not voting; all 53 Republicans voted for the measure. U.S. Social Security Administration n.d.

14. Chock was the first anthropologist to read Congressional transcripts as ethnographic texts, and to analyze the literariness of political debate on immigration in relation to what she finds to be myths of ethnic subjectivity that (literally and figuratively) govern the legislative process (Chock 1987, 1989, 1991, 1994, 1996, 1998, 1999).

15. Like the welfare bill, IIRAIRA divided the Democrats and united Republicans, especially in the Senate. It passed the House 273-126, with 30 not voting (88 Democrats and 190 Republicans voting aye; 92 Democrats and 33 Republicans voting nay). In the Senate, it passed 72-27 (with one not voting) (22 Democrats and 49 Republicans aye, and 24 Democrats and 3 Republicans nay). Library of Congress n.d.; U.S. Senate n.d.b.

16. See Chavez (1991: 259–260) for a discussion of the politics of naming in relation to immigration across the southern border of the United States.

17. I rely on Chock 1999 and my own reading of the hearing transcripts for the Immigration in the National Interest Act of 1995 (H.R. 1915) (U.S. House 1996). H.R. 1915 did not become law, but in the next Congressional session was subsumed into H.R. 2202—one of the principal legislative parents of IIRAIRA (Govtrack.us n.d.).

Chapter 4. Textual Strategy and the Politics of Form

1. For a brief history of the discourse of common good in U.S. social policy, see Grossberg 1997.

2. My thanks to the anonymous reader who suggested the relevance of the first person in relation to the conventions of objectivism. Science (including anthropology, in this context) and legal rules of evidence share the convention that ascribes special priority to the eyewitness.

3. On the performative aspects of rights, see Brigham 1996.

4. The anthology includes contributions from anthropologists, and anthropologists feature among the editors, but anthropology is not among the disciplines listed. On the identification of scholars with identitarian social movements, compare the affirmative accounts of Alvarez, Holguín Cuádraz, Latina Anónima, and Behar in Latina Feminist Group 2001 with the negative critique by Chow 1993.

5. Specifically, the debt to Giddings is in the analysis of racism and sexism as mutu-

ally imbricated, as well as the implications of feminism for racial justice (see Giddings 1984: esp. preface).

6. Division of labor in Durkheim's sense of the phrase (1933), as a partnership among specialists; see also Mauss 1967.

7. The constitutive effect of federal law on establishing the space of the nation as a moral geography does not begin with modern civil rights legislation; it is inherent in the structure of federalism itself—the powers of states and federal government devised in part as a compromise over the legality of slavery (Stone et al. 1991: 471–472).

8. On the ethnic partitioning of the U.S. labor market and the economic immobility of new immigrants (sometimes relative to their own children, or other U.S.-born ethnic groups, or both), see Gibson 1988: 63; Lamphere, Stepick, and Grenier 1994: 19; Stepick 1994; Goode 1994: 217; Leonard 1992: 19–24; Margolis 1994: 18; Park 1997: ch. 3; Chen 1992; Kasinitz 1992: 93–110; Mahler 1995: 225; Stoller 2002; Urciuoli 1996: esp. ch. 1—as well as other works discussed at length in this volume. A significant proportion of the works considered in this volume are based on fieldwork in New York City. For a comprehensive account of the political and social economy of New York in the 1990s, see Sanjek 1998: esp. ch. 6; see also Abu-Lughod 1999.

9. The ten cities were New York, Los Angeles, Chicago, Houston, San Francisco, San Diego, Miami, San Jose, Santa Ana, and Hialeah. These urban and state data can be found in the Census Bureau's report, "We the American . . . Foreign Born" (U.S. Department of Commerce 1993).

Chapter 5. The Discourse of Solutions

1. Toni Morrison's *The Bluest Eye* (1972 [1970], republished in 1993) and Paule Marshall's *The Chosen Place, the Timeless People* (1992 [1969])—discussed below—are similarly relevant afresh as contemporary texts by virtue of republication and new critical reception.

2. Bourgois makes a similar assessment of Candy (220); however, the men also use therapeutic discourse. For example, see Caesar on 179 and 190–191 or Primo on 209.

3. The context of Abel's remark is her critique of Barbara Johnson's reading of Zora Neale Hurston. I am indebted to Nicola Evans for this source.

Chapter 6. Democracy in the First Person

1. On the gradual expansion of equality rights from race to other identity categories—notably women—see Gunther 1985: 621, 642–643, 684–685.

2. Ginsburg 1989 notes the centrality of individualism to the main groups of activists, whether they are for or against abortion rights.

3. *Grutter v. Bollinger*, No. 02-241, June 23, 2003. Electronic document: Http://laws.findlaw.com/US/000/02-241.html (accessed March 28, 2007).

4. On the intricacies of identity in relation to globalization (of movement, finance, and adoption), see Coutin, Maurer, and Yngvesson 2002. The spread of neoliberal re-

form movements expands the conditions of trade-off and uncertainty but in ways that remain grounded in particular national and community histories.

5. In this sense the displacement from center to periphery noted by Kearney (1995: 551) as a condition of postcoloniality was here strategically inverted in the process of establishing the hegemony of neoliberal reform: displacing identity- and rights-based social movements to the center, as costs.

6. Susan Silbey reviews and reaffirms the original aims of *The Common Place of Law* in Silbey 2005.

7. The demographics of Ewick and Silbey's study are detailed in the tables of appendix A (pp. 258–260). The frequency of legal problems does not vary significantly across racial/ethnic categories or by income; however, frequencies do vary significantly by gender—women reporting more legal problems than men. Of all the problem areas reported by respondents for which there was a statistically significant gender difference, women were in the predominant group except in three categories (injury on the job, back pay, and problems with the Department of Motor Vehicles). At the top of the women's legal problems were noisy neighbors, kids playing/fighting, mail-order purchases, and credit-card errors—all except mail order also being at the top of the list of problems reported on separate tables dividing respondents by socioeconomic status and race/ethnicity. In other words, stories about certain problem areas appear to be common stories among women across the social spectrum, providing a basis for identifying with women superficially unlike themselves.

8. For an alternative reading of African American girls and their white dolls, see Chin 1999.

9. The formulation of consciousness as the realization of being simultaneously the subject and object of history belongs to Lukács (1971: 2–3), paraphrasing Marx.

Chapter 7. Gendering Difference and the Impulse to Fiction

1. Fictional anthropologists were not new at this time, however; see J. P. Marquand's *Point of No Return* (1949), featuring an anthropologist in a New England town—and whose project looks very much like that of Lloyd Warner in "Yankee City."

2. The formulation of "stranger and friend" is Hortense Powdermaker's (1966). It must be added that the emphasis on the transformation of the anthropologist's status is not only a narrative device, of course, but also central to the daily preoccupations of field research—an activity that often involves intricately gendered complications. The collection edited by Bell, Caplan, and Karim (1993) was the first to explore ethnographic knowledge production from standpoints in postmodernism and feminist theory: "The gendered nature of our fields has been left to the women anthropologists to ponder and feminist scholars to critique" (Bell 1993: 1).

3. At a critical moment of emotional and physical collapse, Harriet is taken in by Lyle's wife, Enid, whom she dislikes. Harriet is troubled by an identification she sees between Enid and her own mother: "For a frightening moment it was almost as if her mother had assumed the guise of Enid and come to sit beside her on the high-roofed

veranda" (300). Later, this transference extends to a terror of blackness in herself—that is, of finding herself to be Enid's daughter.

4. The waves, too, are full of signs. The narrator describes "a huge white-crested breaker which looked as if it had been gathering force and power and speed across the entire breadth of the Middle Passage broke with the sound as of some massive depth charge on the most distant of reefs" (106). To Harriet, the sound of those waves reminds her of her nightmares of nuclear explosions. To Saul, they trigger memories of the war, bombs making "the earth shudder and recoil under him" (107).

5. Guterson's description of the conditions at Manzanar concentrates on the embarrassments of limited privacy (see especially chapter 15)—in the wedding night scene, for example, Kabuo asks Hatsue's family (listening from the other side of an improvised curtain) to turn up the radio (90).

6. The snow of the novel's title is explained by Kabuo, whose absorption in the snowfall, seen through the courthouse windows from the witness stand, prompts a powerful memory of Manzanar. "Do you remember that snow at Manzanar?" he asks Hatsue later. She replies: "That was jail, too. . . . There were good things, but that was jail." But Kabuo rejects this equivalence, correcting her: "It wasn't jail. . . . We thought it was back then because we didn't know any better. But it wasn't jail." Hatsue "knew, as he spoke, that this was true" (87–88)—her own thoughts returning to their wedding night, yielding the scene already described.

7. He remembers his late father's ambivalence toward San Piedro islanders in almost exactly the same terms: "Arthur confessed to not liking them and at the same time loving them deeply" (439).

8. The image of history as what hurts is Jameson's—as well as the formulation of historical contextualization as the recovery of emergent discursive opposition (1981: ch. 1).

Chapter 8. Markets for Citizenship

1. In this sense fees may be contrasted with *damages*—compensation for loss at the hands of a third party—such as in two Oneida cases, in which the Court of Appeals for the Second Circuit recognized the Oneida Nation's federal common law right to damages in a case of trespass (414 U.S. 661 (1974) and 470 U.S. 226 (1985). I am grateful to an anonymous reader for referring me to the Oneida cases. Indigenous communities' rights to damages remain legally relevant throughout the period of this study—see, for example, *Cayuga Indian Nation of New York v. Pataki* (413 F. 3rd 266 [2005]); however, it is the more marketized forms of recognition that feature in the motifs ethnography shared with sociolegal studies and fictional accounts in the 1990s, as discussed in the text. For current discussion of the relationship between marketing and sovereignty among Florida Seminoles, see Cattelino 2008, 2010.

2. See Sollors 1986 for an analysis of the relationship between ethnicity and literature (especially literary form) in the United States just prior to this book's periodization—the main difference being the association of ethnic writing with individualized subjectivities in his analysis, and, in the works of the 1990s, with counter-hegemonic expressive communities.

3. Takezawa acknowledges the role of African American rights movements in creating a discourse through which the demand for apology and redress could be articulated (147–148; see also 210).

4. It was my students who insisted this was not a continuity to take for granted; I am indebted to them. The context was our discussion of Takezawa's book in the course of our seminar on "Ethnography and Democracy" at Princeton.

Envoi

1. Roger Rouse dates social scientists' contemporary usage to the 1950s, noting its acceleration as a "generalizing" element of social science and popular discourse over the decade of the 1980s— "the most vivid idiomatic symptom of the anxieties and opportunities that the recent challenges to the old topographies of difference have brought about" (Rouse 1995: 381; see also 381 n. 28).

2. Arendt's conditions are stringent ones, especially in contrast to the more usual social science formulation of agency, influenced by Anthony Giddens, for whom agency is purposive action as well as the intended or unintended effects of people's acts (Giddens 1979: ch. 2). Perhaps because of its universalism, Giddens's formulation of agency is the more familiar one in the human sciences today (see, e.g., Castells 1997: 6–12). Arendt's usage is more demanding in terms of its preconditions; it is strikingly narrow in its specific reference to a concrete political sphere (1998: ch. 2, esp. 22–28)—to emphasize that the conditions for agency are met only where (she might say "when"—it is a temporal issue) there is a public commitment to making political institutions available and responsive to the self-disclosing expressions of individuals (see also Arendt 1965: 32; Williams 1997).

3. The implication of individualism as Tocqueville defines it (and as contemporary ethnographers have rediscovered it; see especially Varenne 1977, 1986) is that American citizenship redistributes a charismatic identification of self and state borrowed from kingship. Individualism rests on the presumption of citizenship (i.e., kingship) by birth, thereby providing the symbolic tools for fashioning state authority as if it were natural and unmediated (see Marx 1975a: 99). As Iris Marion Young observes, a distinction between the individual and the universal is itself universalizing (Young 1995; see also Laclau 1996). This absent mediation (of the already-universal) is the object of Tocqueville's evident fascination with the American view that political authority should be based on public opinion (1945, 1: 409–410). Both of these symbolic messages—reallocating sovereignty to individuals, and making state authority real (in a symbolic sense) by deriving it without mediation from *the people*—remain important to any plausible reading of the contemporary political landscape of the United States.

4. On the inevitability that political identities involve a symbolic "gap," see Laclau and Zac 1994. Laclau and Zac view the problem of incommensurability as arising from "the originary split constitutive of all representation" (1994: 15). See also Laclau's discussion (1996: esp. 46–52) of the universal and the particular.

5. I borrow this phrase from Elizabeth Mertz's "Legal Loci and Places in the Heart" (1994).

6. Bhabha (1994: 163) also notes the transgressive aspect of a concept of difference that cannot "add up," but only "add to."

7. The tensions arising from this hyper-substitutability of citizenship's subject and object can expand to any scale without altering its basic form: in the Midwestern town he called Appleton, Varenne found that individualism works (so to speak) among friends, within households, voluntary associations, civic organizations, churches and municipal government (Varenne 1977, 1984).

8. Of the situation in Little Rock, she deploys a racialized discourse of solutions that allows her to refer to "the Negro population alone": "The American Republic is based on the equality of all citizens, and while equality before the law has become an inalienable principle of all modern constitutional government, equality as such is of greater importance in the political life of a republic than in any other form of government. The point at stake, therefore, is not the well-being of the Negro population alone, but, at least in the long run, the survival of the Republic" (Arendt 1959: 47). In this same passage, she reflects on Tocqueville's assessment of the discursive centrality of equality in the American politics he knew, and confirms her own skepticism: "Tocqueville saw over a century ago that equality of opportunity and condition, as well as equality of rights, constituted the basic 'law' of American democracy, and he predicted that the dilemmas and perplexities inherent in the principle of equality might one day become the most dangerous challenge to the American way of life. In its all-comprehensive, typically American form, equality possesses an enormous power to equalize what by nature and origin is different—and it is only due to this power that the country has been able to retain its fundamental identity against the waves of immigrants who have always flooded its shores. But the principle of equality, even in its American form, is not omnipotent" (Arendt 1959: 47–48).

REFERENCES

Abel, Elizabeth. 1993. Black Writing, White Reading: Race and the Politics of Feminist Interpretation. *Critical Inquiry* 19: 470–498

Abélès, Marc. 1999. How the Anthropology of France Has Changed Anthropology in France: Assessing New Directions in the Field. *Cultural Anthropology* 14(3): 404–408.

Abrams, Kathryn. 1994. The Narrative and the Normative in Legal Scholarship. In Susan Heinzelman and Zipporah Wiseman, eds., *Representing Women: Law, Literature and Feminism*, pp. 44–56. Durham, N.C.: Duke University Press.

Abu-Lughod, Janet L. 1999. *New York, Chicago, Los Angeles: America's Global Cities*. Minneapolis: University of Minnesota Press.

Abu-Lughod, Lila. 1991. Writing Against Culture. In Richard G. Fox, ed., *Recapturing Anthropology: Working in the Present*, pp. 137–162. Santa Fe, N.M.: School of American Research Press.

Alvarez, Celia. 2001. Snapshots from My Daze in School. In *Latina Feminist Group, Telling to Live: Latina Feminist Testimonios*, pp. 177–184. Durham, N.C.: Duke University Press.

Alvarez, R. R., Jr. 1995. The Mexican-U.S. Border: The Making of Borderlands. *Annual Review of Anthropology* 24: 447–470.

Aman, Alfred C., Jr. 2004. *Democracy Deficit: Taming Globalization Through Law Reform*. New York: New York University Press.

American Immigration Lawyers Association (AILA). n.d. AILA InfoNet: IIRAIRA Reform. Electronic document: http://www.aila.org/content/default.aspx?bc=6714|6729|11769|3545 (accessed January 6, 2009).

American Public Human Services Association. 1998. A Recent History of Welfare Reform. Electronic document: http://www.aphsa.org/reform/timeline.htm (accessed July 30, 2001).

Amsterdam, Anthony G. 1994. Telling Stories and Stories About Them. *Clinical Law Review* 1: 9–40.

Amsterdam, Anthony G., and Jerome Bruner. 2000. *Minding the Law*. Cambridge, Mass.: Harvard University Press.

Anagnost, Ann. 1997. *National Past-Times: Narrative, Representation, and Power in Modern China*. Durham, N.C.: Duke University Press.

Anderson, Benedict. 1983. *Imagined Communities*. London: Verso.

Anzaldúa, Gloria. 1987. *Borderlands: The New Mestiza = La Frontera*. San Francisco: Spinsters/Aunt Lute.

Appadurai, Arjun. 1990. Disjuncture and Difference in the Global Cultural Economy. *Public Culture* 2(2): 1–24.

———. 1996. *Modernity at Large: Cultural Dimensions of Globalization*. Minneapolis: University of Minnesota Press.

Appadurai, Arjun, ed. 1986. *The Social Life of Things*. Cambridge: Cambridge University Press.

Apter, Andrew. 1999. Africa, Empire, and Anthropology: A Philological Exploration of Anthropology's Heart of Darkness. *Annual Review of Anthropology* 28: 577–598.

Arendt, Hannah. 1959. Reflections on Little Rock. *Dissent* 6(1): 45–56.

———. 1965. *On Revolution*. New York: Viking Press.

———. 1968. *Men in Dark Times*. New York: Harcourt, Brace and World.

———. 1977. *Between Past and Future*, enlarged ed. Harmondsworth, UK: Penguin.

———. 1998. *The Human Condition*, 2nd ed. Chicago: University of Chicago Press.

Aretxaga, Begoña. 2003. Maddening States. *Annual Review of Anthropology* 32: 393–410.

Arredondo, Gabriela F., Aída Hurtado, Norma Klahn, Olga Nájera-Ramírez, Patricia Zavella, eds. 2003. *Chicana Feminisms: A Critical Reader*. Durham, N.C.: Duke University Press.

Asad, Talal, ed. 1973. *Anthropology and the Colonial Encounter*. New York: Humanities Press.

Ashcroft, Bill, Gareth Griffiths, and Helen Tiffin. 1989. *The Empire Writes Back: Theory and Practice in Post-Colonial Literatures*. London: Routledge.

Attinasi, John. 1996. Review of *Between Melting Pot and Mosaic: African Americans and Puerto Ricans in the New York Political Economy*. Andres Torres. *American Ethnologist* 23(1): 171–172.

Azim, Firdous. 1994. *The Colonial Rise of the Novel*. London: Routledge.

Baker, Houston. 1993. *Rap, Black Studies and the Academy*. Chicago: University of Chicago Press.

Baker, Lee D. 1998. *From Savage to Negro: Anthropology and the Construction of Race, 1896–1954*. Berkeley: University of California Press.

Bakhtin, M. M. 1981. *The Dialogic Imagination*. Michael Holquist, ed. Austin: University of Texas Press.

Balin, Jane. 1999. *A Neighborhood Divided: Community Resistance to an AIDS Care Facility*. Ithaca, N.Y.: Cornell University Press.

Battaglia, Debbora. 1995. Fear of Selfing in the American Cultural Imaginary or "You Are Never Alone with a Clone." American Anthropologist 97(4): 672–678.

Baudrillard, Jean. 1988. *America*. Trans. Chris Turner. London: Verso.

Baumann, Gerd. 1996. *Contesting Culture: Discourses of Identity in Multi-ethnic London*. Cambridge: Cambridge University Press.

Behar, Ruth. 1996. *The Vulnerable Observer: Anthropology That Breaks Your Heart*. Boston: Beacon Press.

———. 2001. Temporary Latina. In Latina Feminist Group, *Telling to Live: Latina Feminist Testimonios*, pp. 231–237. Durham, N.C.: Duke University Press.

Beiner, Ronald. 1992. *What's the Matter with Liberalism?* Berkeley: University of California Press.

Bell, Diane. 1993. Introduction 1: The Context. In Diane Bell, Pat Caplan, and Wazir Karim, eds., *Gendered Fields: Women, Men and Ethnography*, pp. 1–18. London: Routledge.

Bell, Diane, Pat Caplan, and Wazir Karim, eds. 1993. *Gendered Fields: Women, Men and Ethnography.* London: Routledge.

Bellah, Robert, Richard Madsen, William M. Sullivan, Ann Swidler, and Steven M. Tipton. 1985. *Habits of the Heart: Individualism and Commitment in American Life.* Berkeley: University of California Press.

Bender, Thomas. 2002. *The Unfinished City: New York and the Metropolitan Idea.* New York: New Press.

Benedict, Ruth. 1934. *Patterns of Culture.* Boston: Houghton Mifflin.

Benjamin, Walter. 1986 [1968]. *Illuminations: Essays and Reflections.* Hannah Arendt, ed. Harry Zohn, trans. New York: Schocken.

Berlant, Lauren 1991. National Brands/National Body: Imitation of Life. In H. Spillers, ed., *Comparative American Identities: Race, Sex and Nationality in the Modern Text*, pp. 110–140. New York: Routledge.

Berman, Daniel. 1966. *It Is So Ordered: The Supreme Court Rules on Segregation* New York: W. W. Norton.

Beverley, John. 2004 [1989]. *The Margin at the Center. In Beverley, Testimonio: On the Politics of Truth*, pp. 29–44. Minneapolis: University of Minnesota Press.

Bhabha, Homi. 1994. *The Location of Culture.* London: Routledge.

———. 1998. Anxiety in the Midst of Difference. *Political and Legal Anthropology Review* 21(1): 123–137.

Biolsi, Thomas. 2001. *Deadliest Enemies: Law and the Making of Race Relations on and Off the Rosebud Reservation.* Berkeley: University of California Press.

Bloom, Allan. 1987. *The Closing of the American Mind: How Higher Education Has Failed Democracy and Impoverished the Souls of Today's Students.* New York: Simon and Schuster.

Bloomington United. 1999. A Community Gathering to Heal and Unite (Program). July 12, 1999. Bloomington, Indiana (on file with author).

Borneman, John. 1995. American Anthropology as Foreign Policy. *American Anthropologist* 97(4): 663-672.

Bourdieu, Pierre. 1990. The Scholastic Point of View. *Cultural Anthropology* 5(4): 380–391.

Bourgois, Philippe. 1995. *In Search of Respect: Selling Crack in the Barrio.* Cambridge: Cambridge University Press.

———. 1996. Forum: Confronting Anthropology, Education, and Inner-City Apartheid. *American Anthropologist* 98(2): 249–265.

Bowman, Cynthia Grant, and Elizabeth Mertz. 1996. A Dangerous Direction: Legal Intervention in Sexual Abuse Survivor Therapy. *Harvard Law Review* 109(3): 551–639.

Boyarin, Jonathan, ed. 1993. *The Ethnography of Reading.* Berkeley: University of California Press.

Brady, Ivan, ed. 1991. *Anthropological Poetics.* Savage, Md.: Rowman and Littlefield.

Brah, Avtar. 1996. *Cartographies of Diaspora: Contesting Identities.* London: Routledge.

Brenneis, Donald. 1994. Discourse and Discipline at the National Research Council: A Bureaucratic Bildungsroman. *Cultural Anthropology* 9(1): 23–36.

Briggs, Charles. 2004. Theorizing Modernity Conspiratorially: Science, Scale, and the Political Economy of Public Discourse on Experiencesof a Cholera Epidemic. *American Ethnologist* 31(2): 164-187.

Brigham, John. 1996. *The Constitution of Interests: Beyond the Politics of Rights.* New York: New York University Press.

Bright, Brenda. 1998. "Heart Like a Car": Hispano/chicano Culture in Northern New Mexico. *American Ethnologist* 25(4): 583–609.

Brightman, Robert. 1995. Forget Culture: Replacement, Transcendence, Relexification. *Cultural Anthropology* 10(4): 509-546.

Brinkley, Alan. 1998. *Liberalism and Its Discontents.* Cambridge, Mass.: Harvard University Press.

Brown, Karen McCarthy. 1991. *Mama Lola: A Vodou Priestess in Brooklyn.* Berkeley: University of California Press.

Brown, Wendy. 1995. *States of Injury: Power and Freedom in Late Modernity.* Princeton, N.J.: Princeton University Press.

Buchanan, Patrick J. 1992. Address to the Republican National Convention, August 17. American Rhetoric: Online Speech Bank. Electronic document: http://www .americanrhetoric.com/speeches/patrickbuchanan1992rnc.htm (accessed January 10, 2009).

Calderón, Héctor, and José David Saldívar. 1991. Editors' introduction: Criticism in the Borderlands. In Calderón and Saldívar, eds., *Criticism in the Borderlands: Studies in Chicano Literature, Culture, and Ideology,* pp. 1–7. Durham, N.C.: Duke University Press.

Calhoun, Craig. 2007. *Sociology in America: A History.* Chicago: University of Chicago Press.

Canclini, Nestor Garcia. 1995. Mexico: Cultural Globalization in a Disintegrating City. *American Ethnologist* 22(4): 743–755.

Canovan, Margaret 1998. Introduction. In Hannah Arendt, *The Human Condition,* 2nd ed., pp. vii–xx. Chicago: University of Chicago Press.

Carrier, James. 1991. Occidentalism: The World Turned Upside-Down. *American Ethnologist* 19(2): 195–212.

Castells, Manuel. 1997. *The Power of Identity. The Information Age: Economy, Society and Culture,* vol. 2. Oxford: Blackwell.

Cattelino, Jessica R. 2008. *High Stakes: Florida Seminole Gaming and Sovereignty.* Durham, N.C.: Duke University Press.

———. 2010a. The Double Bind of American Indian Need-Based Sovereignty. *Cultural Anthropology* 25(2): 235–262.

———. 2010b. Anthropologies of the United States. *Annual Review of Anthropology* 39:273–292.

Chabram, Angie. 1991. Conceptualizing Chicano Critical Discourse. In Héctor Calderón and José David Saldívar, eds., *Criticism in the Borderlands: Studies in Chicano Literature, Culture, and Ideology,* pp. 127–148. Durham, N.C.: Duke University Press.

Chandler, Nahum. 1996. The Economy of Desedimentation: W. E. B. DuBois and the Discourses of the Negro. *Callaloo* 19 (1): 78–93.

Chavez, Leo R. 1991. Outside the Imagined Community: Undocumented Settlers and the Experiences of Incorporation. *American Ethnologist* 18(2): 257–278.

Chen, Hsiang-shui. 1992. *Chinatown No More: Taiwan Immigrants in Contemporary New York.* Ithaca, N.Y.: Cornell University Press.

Chin, Elizabeth. 1999. Ethnically Correct Dolls: Toying with the Race Industry. *American Anthropologist* 101(2): 305–321.

Chock, Phyllis. 1987. The Irony of Stereotypes: Toward an Anthropology of Ethnicity. *Cultural Anthropology* 2: 347–368.

———. 1989. The Landscape of Enchantment: Redaction in a Theory of Ethnicity. *Cultural Anthropology* 4: 163–181.

———. 1991. "Illegal Aliens" and "Opportunity": Myth-Making in Congressional Testimony. *American Ethnologist* 18(2): 279–294.

———. 1994. Remaking and Unmaking "Citizen" in Policy-Making Talk About Immigration. *Political and Legal Anthropology Review* 17(2): 45–56.

———. 1996. No New Women: Gender, "Alien," and "Citizen" in the Congressional Debate on Immigration. *Political and Legal Anthropology Review* 19(1): 1–10.

———. 1998. Porous Borders: Discourses of Difference in Congressional Hearings on Immigration. In *Democracy and Ethnography: Constructing Identities in Multicultural Liberal States,* ed. C. Greenhouse, pp. 143–162. Albany: SUNY Press.

———. 1999. "A Very Bright Line:" Kinship and Nationality in U.S. Congressional Hearings on Immigration. *Political and Legal Anthropology Review* 22(2): 42–52.

Chow, Rey. 1993. *Writing Diaspora: Tactics of Intervention in Contemporary Cultural Studies.* Bloomington: Indiana University Press.

Chuh, Kandice. 2003. *Imagine Otherwise: On Asian Americanist Critique.* Durham, N.C.: Duke University Press.

Cisneros, Sandra. 1989. *The House on Mango Street.* New York: Vintage.

———. 1992. *Woman Hollering Creek: and Other Stories.* New York: Vintage.

Clifford, James. 1988. *The Predicament of Culture: Twentieth-Century Ethnography, Literature, and Art.* Cambridge: Harvard University Press.

———. 1994. Diasporas. *Cultural Anthropology* 9(3): 302–338.

Clifford, James, and George Marcus. 1986. *Writing Culture: The Poetics and Politics of Ethnography.* Berkeley: University of California Press.

Coles, Robert. 1989. *The Call of Stories: Teaching and the Moral Imagination.* Boston: Houghton Mifflin.

Comaroff, Jean, and John L. Comaroff. 1991. *Of Revelation and Revolution: Christianity, Colonialism, and Consciousness in South Africa,* vol. 1. Chicago: University of Chicago Press.

———. 1997. *Of Revelation and Revolution: The Dialectics of Modernity on a South African Frontier,* vol. 2, Chicago: University of Chicago Press.

Comaroff, Jean, and John Comaroff, eds. 1993. *Modernity and Its Malcontents: Ritual and Power in Postcolonial Africa.* Chicago: University of Chicago Press.

Comaroff, John L. 1996. Ethnicity, Nationalism, and the Politics of Difference in an Age of Revolution. In E. Wilmsen and P. McAllister, eds., *The Politics of Difference: Ethnic Premises in a World of Power,* pp. 162–183. Chicago: University of Chicago Press.

Comaroff, John L., and Jean Comaroff. 1992. *Ethnography and the Historical Imagination.* Boulder, Colo.: Westview Press.

———. 1999. Introduction. In Comaroff and Comaroff, eds., *Civil Society and the Political Imagination in Africa,* pp. 1–43. Chicago: University of Chicago Press.

Congressional Record—Senate. 1990. Civil Rights Act of 1990—Veto. Wednesday, October 14, 1990. 101st Congress, 2nd session. 136 Con Rec S 16562 (90 CIS S5401).

Coombe, Rosemary. 1996. Embodied Trademarks: Mimesis and Alterity on American Commercial Frontiers. *Cultural Anthropology* 11(2): 202–224.

Coronil, Fernando. 1996. Beyond Occidentalism: Towards Nonimperial Geohistorical Categories. *Cultural Anthropology* 11(1): 51-87.har

———. 1997. *The Magical State: Nature, Money and Modernity in Venezuela.* Chicago: University of Chicago Press.

Corrigan, Philip, and Derek Sayer. 1985. *The Great Arch: English State Formation as Cultural Revolution.* Oxford: Basil Blackwell.

Coutin, Susan. 1993. *The Culture of Protest: Religious Activism and the United States Sanctuary Movement.* Boulder, Colo.: Westview Press.

———. 1996. Differences Within Accounts of US Immigration Law. *Political and Legal Anthropology* Review 19(1): 11–20.

———. 1999. Citizenship and Clandestinity Among Salvadoran Immigrants. *Political and Legal Anthropology Review* 22(2): 53–63.

———. 2000. *Legalizing Moves: Salvadoran Immigrants' Struggle for U.S. Residency.* Ann Arbor: University of Michigan Press.

———. 2001. The Oppressed, the Suspect, and the Citizen: Subjectivity in Competing Accounts of Political Violence. *Law and Social Inquiry* 26(1): 63–94.

———. 2007. *Nations of Emigrants: Shifting Borders of Citizenship in El Salvador and the United States.* Ithaca, N.Y.: Cornell University Press.

Coutin, Susan, William Maurer, and Barbara Yngvesson. 2002. In the Mirror: The Legitimation Work of Globalization. *Law and Social Inquiry* 27(4): 801–843.

Cover, Robert. 1986. Violence and the Word. *Yale Law Journal* 95: 1601–1629.

DaMatta, Roberto. 1991. Review of Jocks and Burnouts: Social Categories and Identity in the High School, by Penelope Eckert. *American Anthropologist* 93(4): 1005–1006.

Darian-Smith, Eve. 1999. *Bridging Divides: The Channel Tunnel and English Legal Identity in the New Europe.* Berkeley: University of California Press.

Das, Veena. 1998. Wittgenstein and Anthropology. *Annual Review of Anthropology* 27: 171–195.

Dávila, Arlene. 1999. Latinoizing Culture: Art, Museums, and the Politics of U.S. Multicultural Encompassment. *Cultural Anthropology* 14(2): 180–202.

———. 2004. *Barrio Dreams: Puerto Ricans, Latinos, and the Neoliberal City.* Berkeley: University of California Press.

Davis, Allison, and John Dollard. 1940. *Children of Bondage: The Personality Development of Negro Youth in the Urban South.* Washington, D.C.: American Council on Education.

Davis, Mike. 1992. *City of Quartz.* New York: Vintage Books.

Davis, Peggy Cooper. 1997. Performing Interpretation: A Legacy of Civil Rights Lawyering in Brown v. Board of Education. In Austin Sarat, ed., *Race, Law, and Culture: Reflections on Brown v. Board of Education,* pp. 23–48. New York: Oxford University Press.

Dean, Jodi. 2009. *Democracy and Other Neoliberal Fantasies: Communicative Capitalism and Left Politics.* Durham, N.C.: Duke University Press.

De Certeau, Michel. 1997 [1974]. *Culture in the Plural.* Tom Conley, trans. Minneapolis: University of Minnesota Press.

diLeonardo, Michaela. 1998. *Exotics at Home.* New Haven, Conn.: Yale University Press.

Dirks, Nicholas. 1998. In Near Ruins: Cultural Theory at the End of the Century. In Nicholas Dirks, ed., In *Near Ruins: Cultural Theory at the End of the Century,* pp. 1–18. Minneapolis: University of Minnesota Press.

Dolar, Mladen. 1996.. The Object Voice. In R. Salecl and S. Žižek, eds., *Gaze and Voice as Love Objects,* pp. 7–31. Durham, N.C.: Duke University Press.

Domínguez, Virginia. 1986. *White by Definition: Social Classification in Creole Louisiana.* New Brunswick, N.J.: Rutgers University Press.

Dominy, Michele. 1993. Photojournalism, Anthropology, and Ethnographic Authority. *Cultural Anthropology* 8(3): 317–337.

Donald, James. 1996. The Citizen and the Man About Town. In Stuart Hall and Paul Du Gay, eds., *Questions of Cultural Identity,* pp. 170–190. London: Sage Publications.

Drake, St. Clair, and Horace Cayton. 1993 [1945]. *Black Metropolis: A Study of Negro Life in a Northern City.* Chicago: University of Chicago Press.

Du Bois, W. E. B. 1990 [1903]. *The Souls of Black Folk.* New York: Vintage Books.

Duneier, Mitchell. 1992. *Slim's Table: Race, Respectability, and Masculinity.* Chicago: University of Chicago Press.

Durkheim, Emile. 1933 [1893]. *Division of Labor in Society.* George Simpson, trans. New York: Free Press.

Dworkin, Ronald. 1984. Liberalism. In Michael Sandel, ed., *Liberalism and Its Critics,* pp. 60–79. New York: New York University Press.

Elam, Diane, and Robyn Wegman, eds. 1995. *Feminism Beside Itself.* New York: Routledge.

Eller, Jack David. 1997. Anti-anti-multiculturalism. *American Anthropologist* 99(2): 249–256.

Ellison, Ralph. 1952. *Invisible Man.* New York: Random House.

———. 1995. *Shadow and Act.* New York: Vintage.

Engel, David M. 1984. The Oven Bird's Song: Insiders, Outsiders, and Personal Injuries. *Law and Society Review* 18(4): 551-582.

Engel, David M., and Frank W. Munger. 1996. Rights, Remembrance, and the Reconciliation of Difference. *Law & Society Review* 30(1): 7–53.

———. 2003. *Rights of Inclusion: Law and Identity in the Life Stories of Americans with Disabilities.* Chicago: University of Chicago Press.

Enslin, Elizabeth. 1994. Beyond Writing: Feminist Practice and the Limitations of Ethnography. *Cultural Anthropology* 9(4): 537–568.

Ewick, Patricia, and Susan S. Silbey. 1998. *The Common Place of Law: Stories from Everyday Life.* Chicago: University of Chicago Press.

Fabian, Johannes. 1983. *Time and the Other: How Anthropology Makes Its Object.* New York: Columbia University Press.

———. 1992. Keep Listening: Ethnography and Reading. In Jonathan Boyarin, ed., *The Ethnography of Reading,* pp. 80–97. Berkeley: University of California Press.

Fanon, Frantz. 1963. *Wretched of the Earth.* Trans. Constance Farrington. New York: Grove Press.

———. 1967. *Black Skin, White Masks.* Trans. Charles Lam Markmann. New York: Grove Press..

Fardon, Richard, ed. 1990. *Localizing Strategies: Regional Traditions of Ethnographic Writing.* Edinburgh: Scottish Academic Press and Washington, D.C.: Smithsonian Institution Press.

Federal Document Clearing House (FDCH) eMedia. 1995. Congressional Testimony— Capitol Hearing Testimony. March 14, 1995. Dan Stein, Executive Director, Federation for American Immigration Reform, Senate Judiciary Immigration Issues. Before the United States Senate, Committee on the Judiciary, Subcommittee on Immigration, 104th Cong., 1st sess. Electronic document: http://web .lexis-nexis.com/congcomp/document?_m=536b42317c77a78f771186fe24cf 75e8&_docnum=2&wchp=dGLbVtz-zSkSA&_md5=9483480b1cc11702ab2436b 4cc310804 (accessed May 20, 2010).

Feldman, Allen. 1994. On Cultural Anesthesia: From Desert Storm to Rodney King. *American Ethnologist* 21(2): 404–418.

Ferguson, James. 1994. *The Anti-Politics Machine: "Development," Depoliticization and Bureaucratic Power in Lesotho.* Minneapolis: University of Minnesota Press.

Ferguson, James and Akhil Gupta. 2002. Spatializing States: Toward an Ethnography of Neoliberal Governmentality. *American Ethnologist* 29(4): 981-1002.

Ferguson, Robert A. 1984. Law and Letters in American Culture. Cambridge, Mass.: Harvard University Press.

FindLaw. n.d. Comparison of Prior Law and the Persona Responsibility and Work Opportunity Reconciliation Act of 1996 (P. L. 104-193). Electronic document: http://www.library.lp. Findlaw...le.pl?file=federal/dhhs/dhhs000075 (accessed July 30, 2001).

Fischer, Michael M. J. 1986. Ethnicity and the Post-modern Arts of Memory. In James Clifford and George Marcus, eds., *Writing Culture: The Poetics and Politics of Ethnography*, pp. 194–233. Berkeley: University of California Press.

———. 1991. Anthropology as Cultural Critique: Inserts for the 1990s Cultural Studies of Science, Visual-Virtual Realities, and Post-Trauma Politics. *Cultural Anthropology* 6(4): 525–537.

———. 1999. Emergent Forms of Life: Anthropologies of Late or Postmodernities. *Annual Review of Anthropology* 28: 455–478.

Foley, Douglas E. 1990. *Learning Capitalist Culture: Deep in the Heart of Tejas*. Philadelphia: University of Pennsylvania Press.

———. 1995. *The Heartland Chronicles*. Philadelphia: University of Pennsylvania Press.

Foucault, Michel. 1978. *History of Sexuality*, vol. 1: *An Introduction*. Trans. Robert Hurley. New York: Pantheon.

Frankenberg, Ruth. 1993. *White Women, Race Matters: The Social Construction of Whiteness*. Minneapolis: University of Minnesota Press.

Fraser, Nancy. 2009. *Scales of Justice: Reimagining Political Space in a Globalizing World*. New York: Columbia University Press.

Freeman, James M. 1989. *Hearts of Sorrow: Vietnamese-American Lives*. Stanford: Stanford University Press.

French, Rebecca. 1996. Of Narrative in Law and Anthropology. *Law & Society Review* 30(2): 417–436.

Friedman, Leon, ed. 1983. *Argument: The Oral Argument Before the Supreme Court in Brown v. Board of Education of Topeka, 1952–55*. New York: Chelsea House.

Gable, Eric, Richard Handler, and Anna Lawson. 1992. On the Uses of Relativism: Fact, Conjecture and Black and White Histories at Colonial Williamsburg. *American Ethnologist* 19(4): 791–805.

Garcia, Christina. 1993. *Dreaming in Cuban*. New York: Ballantine Books.

Garland, David. 2001. *The Culture of Control: Crime and Social Order in Contemporary Society*. Chicago: University of Chicago Press.

Gates, Henry Louis, Jr. 1989. *Figures in Black: Words, Signs, and the "Racial" Self*. New York: Oxford University Press.

Geertz, Clifford. 1973. *The Interpretation of Cultures*. New York: Basic Books.

———. 1983. *Local Knowledge: Further Essays in Interpretive Anthropology*. New York: Basic Books.

Gelles, Paul H. 1998. Ethical Dilemmas—Testimonio, Ethnography and Processes of Authorship. *Anthropology News* 39(3): 16–17.

Gewertz, Deborah. 1991. Review of Gone Primitive: Savage Intellects, Modern Lives, by Marianna Torgovnick. *American Anthropologist* 93(4): 977.

Gibson, Margaret. 1988. *Accommodation without Assimilation: Sikh Immigrants in an American High School.* Ithaca: Cornell University Press.

Giddens, Anthony. 1979. *Central Problems in Social Theory: Action, Structure and Contradiction in Social Analysis.* Berkeley: University of California Press.

———. 1986. *The Constitution of Society: Outline of the Theory of Structuration.* Berkeley: University of California Press.

Giddings, Paula. 1984. *When and Where I Enter: The Impact of Black Women on Race and Sex in America.* New York: Bantam Books.

Ginsburg, Faye. 1989. *Contested Lives: The Abortion Debate in an American Community.* Berkeley: University of California Press.

Glick Schiller, Nina, Linda Basch, and Cristina Szanton-Blanc. 1995. From Immigrant to Transmigrant: Theorizing Transnational Migration. *Anthropological Quarterly* 68(1): 48–63.

Glissant, Édouard. 1997 [1990]. *Poetics of Relation.* Trans. Betsy Wing. Ann Arbor: University of Michigan Press.

Goode, Judith. 1993 Polishing the Rustbelt: Immigrants Enter a Restructuring Economy. In Lamphere, Louise, Alex Stepick, and Guillermo J. Grenier, eds. *Newcomers in the Workplace: Immigrants and the Restructuring of the U.S. Economy,* pp. 199-230. Philadelphia: Temple University Press.

———. 2001. Let's Get Our Act Together: How Racial Discourses Disrupt Neighborhood Activism. In Judith Goode and Jeff Maskovsky, eds., *The Ethnography of Power, Politics, and Impoverished People in the United States,* pp. 364–398. New York: New York University Press.

Goode, Judith, and Jeff Maskovsky, eds. 2001. *The New Poverty Studies: The Ethnography of Power, Politics, and Impoverished People in the United States.* New York: New York University Press.

Gooding-Williams, Robert, ed. 1993. *Reading Rodney King/Reading Urban Uprising.* New York: Routledge.

Gordimer, Nadine. 1988. *The Essential Gesture: Writing, Politics and Places.* Ed. Stephen Clingman. New York: Knopf.

Gordon, Robert. 1982. New Developments in Legal Theory. In David Kairys, ed., *The Politics of Law,* pp. 281–293. New York: Pantheon Books.

Govtrack.us. n.d. H.R. 1915: Immigration in the National Interest Act of 1995. Electronic document: http://www.govtrack.us/congress/bill.xpd?bill=h104-1915 (accessed May 21, 2010).

Graham, Jorie. 1995. *The Dream of the Unified Field: Selected Poems 1974–1994.* Hopewell, N.J.: Ecco Press.

Graham, Laurie. 1995. *On the Line at Subaru-Isuzu: The Japanese Model and the American Worker.* Ithaca, N.Y.: ILR Press.

Greenhouse, Carol J. 1985. Anthropology at Home: Whose Home? *Human Organiza-tion* 44(3): 261-264.

——. 1986. *Praying for Justice: Faith, Order and Community in an American Town.* Ithaca, N.Y.: Cornell University Press.

——. 1996. *A Moment's Notice: Time Politics Across Cultures.* Ithaca, N.Y.: Cornell University Press.

——. 1998. Figuring the Future: Temporality and Agency in Ethnographic Problems of Scale. In A. Sarat and B. Garth, eds., *Justice and Power in Sociolegal Studies,* pp. 108–135. Evanston, Ill.: Northwestern University Press and American Bar Foundation.

——. 2005. Hegemony and Hidden Transcripts: The Discursive Arts of Neoliberal Legitimation. *American Anthropologist* 107(3): 356–368.

——. 2009a. Fractured Discourse: Rethinking the Discursivity of States. In Julia Paley, ed., *Democracy: Anthropological Approaches,* pp. 193–218. Santa Fe, N.M.: School for Advanced Research Press.

——. 2009b. Introduction. In *Ethnographies of Neoliberalism,* Carol Greenhouse, ed., pp. 1-10. Philadelphia: University of Pennsylvania Press.

Greenhouse, Carol, and Davydd J. Greenwood. 1998. Introduction: The Ethnography of Democracy and Difference. In *Democracy and Ethnography: Constructing Identities in Multicultural Liberal States,* C. Greenhouse, ed., pp. 1–24. Albany: SUNY Press.

Greenhouse, Carol, Barbara Yngvesson, and David Engel. 1994. *Law and Community in Three American Towns.* Ithaca, N.Y.: Cornell University Press.

Gregory, Steven. 1992. The Changing Significance of Race and Class in an African-American Community. *American Ethnologist* 19(2): 255–274.

——. 1993. Race, Rubbish, and Resistance: Empowering Difference in Community. *Cultural Anthropology* 8(1): 24–48.

——. 1998. *Black Corona: Race and the Politics of Place in an Urban Community.* Princeton, N.J.: Princeton University Press.

Gregory, Steven, and Roger Sanjek, eds. 1994. *Race.* New Brunswick, N.J.: Rutgers University Press.

Grillo, Toni, and Stephanie M. Wildman. 1997. Obscuring the Importance of Race: The Implications of Making Comparisons Between Racism and Sexism (or Other Isms). In Adrien Katherine Wing, ed., *Critical Race Feminism: A Reader,* pp. 44–50. New York: New York University Press.

Griswold, Wendy. 2000. *Bearing Witness: Readers, Writers, and the Novel in Nigeria.* Princeton, N.J.: Princeton University Press.

Grossberg, Michael. 1997. The Politics of Professionalism: The Creation of Legal Aid and the Strains of Political Liberalism in America, 1900–1930. In Terence C. Halliday and Lucien Karpik, eds., *Lawyers and the Rise of Western Political Liberalism: Europe and North America from the 18th to the 20th Centuries,* pp. 305-347. Oxford: Oxford University Press.

Gunther, Gerald. 1985. *Constitutional Law,* 11th ed. Mineola, N.Y.: Foundation Press.

———. 1991. *Constitutional Law,* 12th ed. Mineola, N.Y.: Foundation Press.

Gupta, Akhil. 1998. *Postcolonial Developments: Agriculture in the Making of Modern India.* Durham, N.C.: Duke University Press.

Gupta, Akhil, and James Ferguson. 1997. Discipline and Practice: "The Field" as Site, Method, and Location in Anthropology. In A. Gupta and J. Ferguson, eds., *Anthropological Locations: Boundaries and Grounds of a Field Science,* pp. 1–46. Berkeley: University of California Press.

Guterson, David. 1995. *Snow Falling on Cedars: A Novel.* New York: Vintage.

Habermas, Jürgen. 1991. *The Structural Transformation of the Public Sphere: An Inquiry into a Category of Bourgeois Society.* Trans. Thomas Burger with the assistance of Frederick Lawrence. Cambridge, Mass.: Massachusetts Institute of Technology Press.

———. 1995. Citizenship and National Identity: Some Reflections in the Future of Europe. In R. Beiner, ed., *Theorizing Citizenship,* pp. 255–281. Albany: SUNY Press.

Hall, Kathleen D. 2005. Science, Globalization and Educational Governance: The Political Rationalities of the New Managerialism. *Indiana Journal of Global Legal Studies* 12(1): 153–182.

Hall, Stuart. 1985. Signification, Representation, Ideology: Althusser and Post-Structuralist Debates. *Critical Studies in Mass Communication* 2(2): 91–114.

———. 1992. The Question of Cultural Identity. In Stuart Hall, David Held, and Tony McGrew, eds., *Modernity and Its Futures,* pp. 273–326. The Open University. Cambridge: Polity Press.

Handler, Joel. 1995. *The Poverty of Welfare Reform.* New Haven, Conn.: Yale University Press.

Handler, Richard. 1995. Introduction: The Origin of the Dog. In Handler, ed., David M. Schneider as told to Richard Handler, *Schneider on Schneider: The Conversion of the Jews and Other Anthropological Stories,* pp. 1–15. Durham, N.C.: Duke University Press.

———. 1998. Raymond Williams, George Stocking and Fin-de-Siecle U.S. Anthropology. *Cultural Anthropology* 13(4): 447–463.

Haney, David Paul. 2008. *The Americanization of Social Science: Intellectuals and Public Responsibility in the Postwar United States.* Philadelphia: Temple University Press.

Hannerz, Ulf. 1969. *Soulside: Inquiries into Ghetto Culture and Community.* New York: Columbia University Press.

———. 1997. Borders. Special issue on Anthropology—Issues and Perspectives: II. Sounding Out New Possibilities, Michael Herzfeld, ed. *International Social Science Journal* 49(4): 537–548.

Harding, Susan Friend. 1994. Further Reflections. *Cultural Anthropology* 9(3): 276-278.

———. 2000. *The Book of Jerry Falwell: Fundamentalist Language and Politics.* Princeton, N.J.: Princeton University Press.

Harris, Angela. 1997. Race and Essentialism in Feminist Legal Theory. In Adrien Katherine Wing, ed., *Critical Race Feminism: A Reader,* pp. 11–18. New York: New York University Press.

Harrison, Faye V. 1995. The Persistent Power of "Race" in the Cultural and Political Economy of Racism. *Annual Review of Anthropology* 24: 47–74.

Hartigan, John. 1997. Forum: Establishing the Fact of Whiteness. *American Anthropologist* 99(3): 495–505.

Harvey, David. 2005. *A Brief History of Neoliberalism.* Oxford: Oxford University Press.

Heinzelman, Susan Sage, and Zipporah Batshaw Wiseman. 1994. Preface. In Heinzelman and Wiseman, eds., *Representing Women: Law, Literature and Feminism,* pp. vii–ix. Durham, N.C.: Duke University Press.

Held, David. 1992. Liberalism, Marxism and Democracy In Stuart Hall, David Held, and Tony McGrew, eds., *Modernity and Its Futures: Understanding Modern Societies,* pp. 14–60. Cambridge: Polity Press.

Held, David, and Anthony McGrew. 2000. The Great Globalization Debate: An Introduction. In Held and McGrew, eds., *The Global Transformations Reader: An Introduction to the Globalization Debate,* pp. 1–45. Cambridge: Polity Press.

Herbert, Steve. 1997. *Policing Space.* Minneapolis: University of Minnesota Press.

Hermann, Gretchen. 1997. Gift or Commodity? What Changes Hands in the U.S. Garage Sale? *American Ethnologist* 24(4): 910–930.

Herzfeld, Michael. 1996. *Cultural Intimacy: Social Poetics in the Nation-State.* New York: Routledge.

Heyman, Josiah McC. 1999. *States and Illegal Practices.* Oxford: Berg.

Holguín Cuádraz, Gloria. 2001. Lessons Learned from an Assistant Professor. In *Latina Feminist Group, Telling to Live: Latina Feminist Testimonios,* pp. 227–228. Durham, N.C.: Duke University Press.

Holland, Dorothy, Catherine Lutz, Donald M. Nonini, Lesley Bartlett, Marla Frederick-McGlathery, Thaddeus C. Guldbransen, and Enrique G. Murillo, Jr. 2007. *Local Democracy Under Siege: Activism, Public Interests, and Private Politics.* New York: New York University Press.

Hopper, Kim. 2003. *Reckoning with Homelessness.* Ithaca, N.Y.: Cornell University Press.

Horkheimer, Max, and Theodor C. Adorno. 1997. *The Dialectic of Enlightenment.* Trans. J. Cumming. New York: Continuum.

Jackson, John L. 2001. *Harlemworld: Doing Race and Class in Contemporary Black America.* Chicago: University of Chicago Press.

Jackson, John P., Jr. 2001. *Social Scientists for Social Justice: Making the Case Against Segregation.* New York: New York University Press.

Jameson, Fredric. 1981. *The Political Unconscious: Narrative as a Socially Symbolic Act.* Ithaca, N.Y.: Cornell University Press.

Jen, Gish. 1992. *Typical American.* New York: Plume.

Johnson, E. Patrick. 2003. *Appropriating Blackness: Performance and the Politics of Authenticity.* Durham, N.C.: Duke University Press.

Kaplan, Martha and John Kelly. 1999. On Discourse and Power: "Cults" and "Orientals" in Fiji. *American Ethnologist* 26(4): 843-863.

Kasinitz, Philip. 1992. *Caribbean New York: Black Immigrants and the Politics of Race.* Ithaca, N.Y.: Cornell University Press.

Kaufmann, Eric. 1999. American Exceptionalism Reconsidered: Anglo-Saxon Ethnogenesis in the "Universal" Nation, 1776–1850. *Journal of American Studies* 33(3): 437–457.

Kearney, Michael. 1995. The Local and the Global: The Anthropology of Globalization and Transnationalism. *Annual Review of Anthropology* 24: 547–565.

Keita, S. O. Y., and Rick A. Kittles. 1997. The Persistence of Racial Thinking and the Myth of Racial Divergence. *American Anthropologist* 99(3): 534–544.

Kluger, Richard. 1975. *Simple Justice.* New York: Alfred A. Knopf.

Kornbluh, Felicia. 2007. *The Battle for Welfare Rights: Politics and Poverty in Modern America.* Philadelphia: University of Pennsylvania Press.

Kourilsky-Augeven, Chantal, ed. 1997. *Socialisation juridique et conscience de droit.* Paris: Librairie Générale de Droit et de Jurisprudence.

Krasniewicz, Louise. 1992. *Nuclear Summer: The Clash of Communities at the Seneca Peace Encampment.* Ithaca, N.Y.: Cornell University Press.

Krupat, Arnold. 1993. *New Voices in Native American Literary Criticism.* Washington, D.C.: Smithsonian Institution Press.

Kymlicka, Will. 1995. *Multicultural Citizenship: A Liberal Theory of Minority Rights.* Oxford: Clarendon Press.

Laclau, Ernesto. 1996. A Universalism, Particularism, and the Question of Identity. In E. Wilmsen and P. McAllister, eds., *The Politics of Difference: Ethnic Premises in a World of Power,* pp. 45–58. Chicago: University of Chicago Press.

Laclau, Ernesto, and Chantal Mouffe. 1985. *Hegemony and Socialist Strategy: Towards a Radical Democratic Politics.* Trans. Winston Moore and Paul Cammack. London: Verso.

Laclau, Ernesto, and Lilian Zac. 1994. Minding the Gap: The Subject of Politics. In E. Laclau, ed., *The Making of Political Identities,* pp. 11–39. London: Verso.

Laguerre, Michel. 1984. *American Odyssey: Haitians in New York.* Ithaca, N.Y.: Cornell University Press.

Lamphere, Louise, Alex Stepick, and Guillermo J. Grenier, eds. 1994 *Newcomers in the Workplace: Immigrant and the Restructuring of the U.S. Economy.* Philadelphia: Temple University Press.

Lamphere, Louise, Patricia Zavella, and Felipe Gonzales, with Peter B. Evans. 1993. *Sunbelt Working Mothers: Reconciling Family and Factory.* Ithaca, N.Y.: Cornell University Press.

Lash, Scott, and John Urry. 1994. *Economies of Signs and Space.* London: Sage Publications.

Latina Anónima. 2001. "Don't You Like Being in the University?" In *Latina Feminist Group, Telling to Live: Latina Feminist Testimonios,* pp. 229–230. Durham, N.C.: Duke University Press.

Lawless, Elaine J. 1996. Review of *Blessed Assurance: Beliefs, Actions, and the Experience of Salvation in a Carolina Baptist Church,* by M. Jean Heriot. *American Anthropologist* 98(4): 907–908.

Lazarus-Black, Mindie, and Susan F. Hirsch. 1994. Performance and Paradox: Exploring

Law's Role in Hegemony and Resistance. In Lazarus-Black and Hirsch, eds., *Contested States: Law, Hegemony and Resistance*, pp. 1–31. New York: Routledge.

Lederman, Rena. 2004. Towards an Anthropology of Disciplinarity. *Critical Matrix* 15: 60–74.

———. 2007. Comparative "Research": A Modest Proposal Concerning the Object of Ethics Regulation. *Political and Legal Anthropology Review* 30(2): 305–327.

Leonard, Karen. 1992. *Making Ethnic Choices: California's Punjabi Mexican Americans*. Philadelphia: Temple University Press.

Lewin, Ellen. 1993. *Lesbian Mothers: Accounts of Gender in American Culture*. Ithaca, N.Y.: Cornell University Press.

———. 1996. Review of A Gay Synagogue in New York, by Moshe Shokeid. Ithaca, N.Y.: Cornell University Press. *American Ethnologist* 23(4): 932-933.

Lexis-Nexis. n.d. Welfare Reform Act of 1996. Electronic document: http://lexis-nexis.com/congcomp/document?_m=d1813eef81c5013152f502357bb4b0b&_docnum=95&wchp=dGLbV1b-zSkSA&_md5=885abe6fae2856011d545a91ec9 4ba79 (accessed December 15, 2006).

Library of Congress. n.d. THOMAS—Bill Summary and Status—H.R. 3610. Electronic document: http://hdl.loc.gov/loc.uscongress/legislation.104hr3610 (accessed May 21, 2010).

Lieberman, Leonard. 1997. Gender and the Deconstruction of the Race Concept. *American Anthropologist* 99(3): 545–588.

Lieberwitz, Risa L. 2005. Confronting the Privatization and Commercialization of Academic Research: An Analysis of Social Implications at the Local, National, and Global Levels. *Indiana Journal of Global Legal Studies* 12(1): 109–152.

Liebow, Elliot. 1967. *Tally's Corner: A Study of Negro Streetcorner Men*. Boston: Little, Brown.

———. 2003. *Tally's Corner: A Study of Negro Streetcorner Men*, 2nd ed. Lanham, Md.: Rowman, Littlefield.

Lin, Jan. 1998. *Reconstructing Chinatown: Ethnic Enclave, Global Change*. Minneapolis: University of Minnesota Press.

LiPuma, Edward, and Sarah Keene Meltzoff. 1997. The Crosscurrents of Ethnicity and Class in the Construction of Public Policy. *American Ethnologist* 24(1): 114–131.

Liss, Julia. 1998. Diasporic Identities: The Science and Politics of Race in the Work of Franz Boas and W. E. B. DuBois, 1894–1919. *Cultural Anthropology* 13(2): 127–166.

Loewen, James C. 1988. *Mississippi Chinese: Between Black and White*, 2nd ed. Long Grove, Ill.: Waveland Press.

Louie, David Wong. 1992. *Pangs of Love*. New York: Plume.

Loury, Glenn C. 2001. Politics, Race, and Poverty Research. In Sheldon H. Danziger and Robert H. Haveman, eds., *Understanding Poverty*, pp. 447–453. New York: Russell Sage Foundation and Cambridge, Mass.: Harvard University Press.

Low, Setha M. 1996. The Anthropology of Cities: Imagining and Theorizing the City. *Annual Review of Anthropology* 25: 383–409.

Lowe, Lisa. 1998. The Power of Culture. *Journal of Asian American Studies* 1(1): 5–29.

Lowi, Theodore. 1979 [1969]. *The End of Liberalism: The Second Republic of the United States,* 2nd ed. New York: Norton.

Lugo, Alejandro. 1990. Cultural Production and Reproduction in Ciudad Juarez, Mexico: Tropes at Play Among Maquiladoro Workers. *Cultural Anthropology* 5(2): 173–196.

———. 1994. Review of Ethnic Identity: Formation and Transmission Among Hispanics and Other Minorities, ed. Martha E. Bernal and George P. Knight. *American Anthropologist* 96(2): 462.

Lukács, Georg. 1971. *History and Class Consciousness: Studies in Marxist Dialectics.* Trans. Rodney Livingstone. London: Merlin Press.

Lutz, Catherine. 1990. The Erasure of Women's Writing in Sociocultural Anthropology. *American Ethnologist* 17(4): 611–627.

———. 2001. *Homefront: A Military City and the American Twentieth Century.* Boston: Beacon Press.

McMillan, Terry. 1989. *Disappearing Acts.* New York: Viking.

Mahler, Sarah J. 1995. *American Dreaming: Immigrant Life on the Margins.* Princeton, N.J.: Princeton University Press.

Maira, Sunaina. 1999. Identity Dub: The Paradoxes of an Indian American Youth Subculture (New York Mix). *Cultural Anthropology* 14(1): 29–60.

Marable, Manning. 1980. Black Nationalism in the 1970s: Through the Prism of Race and Class. *Socialist Review* 50–51: 57–108.

Marcus, George E. 1991a. American Academic Journal Editing in the Great Bourgeois Cultural Revolution of Late 20th-Century Postmodernity: The Case of *Cultural Anthropology. Cultural Anthropology* 6(1): 121–127.

———. 1991b. A Broad(er)side to the Canon: Being a Partial Account of a Year of Travel Among Textual Communities in the Realm of Humanities Centers and Including a Collection of Artificial Curiosities. *Cultural Anthropology* 6(3): 385–405.

———. 1995. Ethnography of/in the World System: The Emergence of Multi-Sited Ethnography. *Annual Review of Anthropology* 24: 95–117.

Marcus, George E., and Michael Fischer. 1986. *Anthropology as Cultural Critique: An Experimental Moment in the Human Sciences.* Chicago: University of Chicago Press.

Margolis, Maxine L. 1994. *Little Brazil: An Ethnography of Brazilian Immigrants in New York City.* Princeton, N.J.: Princeton University Press.

Marquand, John P. 1949. *Point of No Return.* Boston: Little, Brown.

Marshall, Paule. 1992 [1969]. *The Chosen Place, the Timeless People.* New York: Vintage.

Martinez, Samuel. 1996. Indifference Within Indignation: Anthropology, Human Rights, and the Haitian Bracero. *American Anthropologist* 98(1): 17–25.

Marx, Karl. 1975a. Excerpts from James Mill's *Elements of Political Economy.* In Karl Marx, *Early Writings,* trans. Rodney Livingstone and Gregor Benton, pp. 259–278. Harmondsworth, UK: Penguin Books.

———. 1975b. Critique of Hegel's *Doctrine of the State.* In Karl Marx, *Early Writings,* trans. Rodney Livingstone and Gregor Benton, pp. 57–198. Harmondsworth, UK: Penguin Books.

Mascia-Lees, Frances E., Patricia Sharpe, and Colleen Ballerino Cohen. 1989. The Postmodernist Turn in Anthropology: Cautions from a Feminist Perspective. *Signs: Journal of Women in Culture and Society* 15(1): 7–33.

Massey, Douglas, and Nancy Denton. 1993. *American Apartheid: Segregation and the Making of the Underclass.* Cambridge, Mass.: Harvard University Press.

Matsuda, Mari. 1996. *Where Is Your Body? and Other Essays on Race, Gender and the Law.* Boston: Beacon Press.

Maurer, William. 1998. Cyberspatial Sovereignties: Offshore Finance, Digital Cash, and the Limits of Liberalism. *Indiana Journal of Global Legal Studies* 5(2): 493–519.

Mauss, Marcel. 1967 [1924]. *The Gift: Forms and Functions of Exchange in Archaic Societies.* New York: W. W. Norton.

McKeever, Robert J. 1999. Race and Representation in the United States: The Constitutional Validity of Majority-Minority Congressional Districts. *Journal of American Studies* 33(3): 491–507.

Menchú, Rigoberta, and Elisabeth Burgos-Debray. 1984. *I, Rigoberta Menchú: An Indian Woman from Guatemala.* Trans. and ed. Ann Wright. London: Verso.

Merry, Sally Engle. 1990. *Getting Justice and Getting Even.* Chicago: University of Chicago Press.

_____. 1992. Anthropology, Law, and Transnational Processes. *Annual Review of Anthropology* 21: 347–369.

Mertz, Elizabeth. 1994. Legal Loci and Places in the Heart: Community and Identity in Sociolegal Studies. *Law & Society Review* 28: 971–992.

———. 2002. The Perfidy of Gaze and the Pain of Uncertainty: Anthropological Theory and the Search for Closure. In C. Greenhouse, E. Mertz, and K. Warren, eds., *Ethnography in Unstable Places: Everyday Lives in Contexts of Dramatic Political Change,* pp. 355–378. Durham, N.C.: Duke University Press.

Michaelsen, Scott, and David E. Johnson. 2009. *Anthropology's Wake: Attending to the End of Culture.* New York: Fordham University Press.

Mitchell, Angelyn. 1994. Introduction: Voices Within the Circle—A Historical Overview of African American Literary Criticism. In Mitchell, ed., *Within the Circle: An Anthology of African American Criticism from the Harlem Renaissance to the Present,* pp. 1–18. Durham, N.C.: Duke University Press.

Miyazaki, Hirokazu. 2004. *The Method of Hope: Anthropology, Philosophy, and Fijian Knowledge.* Stanford: Stanford University Press.

Moens, Gabriel. 1976. *Equality for Freedom: A Critical Study of Unresolved Problems of School Desegregation Cases in the United States.* Vienna: Universitats-Verlagsbuchhandung.

Moffatt, Michael. 1990. Do We Really Need Postmodernism to Understand *Ferris Bueller's Day Off? Cultural Anthropology* 5(4): 367–373.

———. 1992. Ethnographic Writing About American Culture. *Annual Review of Anthropology* 21: 205–229.

Moore, Sally Falk. 1980. *Social Facts and Fabrications: "Customary" Law on Kilimanjaro, 1880–1980.* Cambridge: Cambridge University Press.

———. 1987. Explaining the Present: Theoretical Dilemmas in Processual Anthropology. *American Ethnologist* 14 (4): 727–736.

Moraga, Cherríe, and Gloria Anzaldúa, eds. 1983 [1981]. *This Bridge Called My Back: Writings by Radical Women of Color.* Latham, N.Y.: Kitchen Table, Women of Color Press.

Moreiras, Alberto. 2001. *The Exhaustion of Difference: The Politics of Latin American Cultural Studies.* Durham, N.C.: Duke University Press.

Morgen, Sandra. 2001. The Agency of Welfare Workers: Negotiating Devolution, Privatization, and the Meaning of Self-Sufficiency. *American Anthropologist* 103(3): 747–761.

Morgen, Sandra, and Jeff Maskovsky. 2003. The Anthropology of Welfare "Reform": New Perspectives on U.S. Urban Poverty in the Post-Welfare Era. *Annual Review of Anthropology* 32: 315–338.

Morrison, Toni. 1972 [1970]. *The Bluest Eye.* New York: Washington Square Press.

———. 1987. *Beloved: A Novel.* New York: Knopf.

———. 1992. *Jazz.* New York: Knopf.

Mostern, Kenneth. 1999. *Autobiography and Black Identity Politics: Racialization in Twentieth-Century America.* Cambridge: Cambridge University Press.

Moynihan, Daniel Patrick. ["The Moynihan Report"]. *See* United States Department of Labor 1965.

Mukhopadhyay, Carol C., and Yolanda T. Moses. 1997. Reestablishing "Race" in Anthropological Discourse. *American Anthropologist* 99(3): 517–533.

Mullings, Leith. 1997. *On Our Own Terms: Race, Class, and Gender in the Lives of African American Women.* New York: Routledge.

———. 2001. Households Headed By Women: The Politics of Class, Race, and Gender. In Judith Goode and Jeff Maskovsky, eds., *The Ethnography of Power, Politics, and Impoverished People in the United States,* pp. 37–56. New York: New York University Press.

Murphy, Robert F. 1990. The Dialectics of Deeds and Words: Or Anti-the-antis (and the Anti-antis). *Cultural Anthropology* 5(3): 331–337.

Myrdal, Gunnar. 1995 [1945]. *An American Dilemma: The Negro Problem and Modern Democracy.* New Brunswick, N.J.: Transaction.

Nader, Laura, ed. 1980. *No Access to Law: Alternatives to the American Justice System.* New York: Academic Press.

Narayan, Kirin. 1993. How Native is a "Native" Anthropologist? *American Anthropologist* 95(3): 671–686.

Nassy-Brown, Jacqueline. 2000. Enslaving History: Narratives on Local Whiteness in a Black Atlantic Port. *American Ethnologist* 27(2): 340–370.

Newman, Katherine S. 1999. *Falling from Grace: Downward Mobility in the Age of Affluence.* Berkeley: University of California Press.

Nugent, David. 2002. *Locating Capitalism in Time and Space: Global Restructurings, Politics, and Identity.* Stanford: Stanford University Press.

Nussbaum, Martha C. 1995. *Poetic Justice: The Literary Imagination and Public Life.* Boston: Beacon Press.

Omi, Michael, and Howard Winant. 1994. *Racial Formation in the United States: From the 1960s to the 1990s,* 2nd ed. New York: Routledge.

Ong, Aihwa. 1999. *Flexible Citizenship: The Cultural Logics of Transnationality.* Durham, N.C.: Duke University Press.

Ortner, Sherry. 1998. Generation X: Anthropology in a Media-Saturated World. *Cultural Anthropology* 13(3): 414-440.

———. 2005. *New Jersey Dreaming: Capitalism, Culture and the Class of '58.* Durham, N.C.: Duke University Press.

Page, Hélan E. 1997. "Black Male" Imagery and Media Containment of African American Men. *American Anthropologist* 99(1): 99–111.

Paley, Julia. 2001. *Marketing Democracy: Power and Social Movements in Post-Dictatorship Chile.* Berkeley: University of California Press.

Park, Kyeyoung. 1996. Review of Blue Dreams: Korean Americans and the Los Angeles Riots, by Nancy Abelmann and John Lie. *American Anthropologist* 98(2): 449–450.

———. 1997. *The Korean American Dream: Immigrants and Small Business in New York City.* Ithaca, N.Y.: Cornell University Press.

Passel, Jeffrey S., and Michael Fix. 1994. U.S. Immigration in the Global Context: Past, Present, and Future. *Indiana Journal of Global Legal Studies* 2(1): 5–20.

Peacock, James. 1997. The Future of Anthropology. *American Anthropologist* 99(1): 1–21.

Peirano, Mariza G. S. 1998. When Anthropology Is at Home: The Different Contexts of a Single Discipline. *Annual Review of Anthropology* 27: 105–128.

Pels, Peter. 1997. The Anthropology of Colonialism: Culture, History, and the Emergence of Western Governmentality. *Annual Review of Anthropology* 26: 163–183.

Peshkin, Alan. 1991. *The Color of Strangers, the Color of Friends: The Play of Ethnicity in School and Community.* Chicago: University of Chicago Press.

Peutz, Nathalie. 2006. Embarking on an Anthropology of Removal. *Current Anthropology* 47(2): 217–241.

Pinckney, Darryl. 1992. *High Cotton.* New York: Farrar, Straus and Giroux.

Polanyi, Karl. 1957[1944] *The Great Transformation.* Boston: Beacon Press.

Pollack, David. 1992. *Reading Against Culture: Ideology and Narrative in the Japanese Novel.* Ithaca, N.Y.: Cornell University Press.

Posner, Richard. 1995. *Overcoming Law.* Cambridge, Mass.: Harvard University Press.

Poulantzas, Nicos. 1975. The Present Phase of Imperialism and the Domination of the USA. In Nicos Poulantzas, *Classes in Contemporary Capitalism,* trans. David Fernbach, pp. 42–88. London: NLB.

Powdermaker, Hortense. 1966. *Stranger and Friend: The Way of an Anthropologist.* New York: W. W. Norton.

Proschan, Frank. 1995. Review of Beyond the Killing Fields: Voices of Nine Cambodian Survivors in America, by Usha Welaratna. *American Ethnologist* 22(3): 652–653.

Ramos, Alcida. 1990. Ethnology Brazilian Style. *Cultural Anthropology* 5(4): 452–472.

Reams, Bernard D., Jr., Peter J. McGovern, and John S. Schultz. 1992. *Disability Law in the United States: A Legislative History of the Americans with Disabilities Act of 1990, Public Law 101-336*, 6 volumes. Buffalo: William S. Hein.

Reddy, William M. 1993. Postmodernism and the Public Sphere: Implications for an Historical Ethnography. *Cultural Anthropology* 7(2): 135–168.

Richards, David. 1994. *Masks of Difference: Cultural Representations in Literature, Anthropology and Art*. Cambridge: Cambridge University Press.

Richland, Justin B. 2009. On Neoliberalism and Other Social Diseases: The 2009 Sociocultural Anthropology Year in Review. *American Anthropologist* 111(2): 170–176.

Riles, Annelise. 1998. Infinity Within the Brackets. *American Ethnologist* 25(3): 378–398.

———. 2001. *The Network Inside Out*. Ann Arbor: University of Michigan Press.

Rodgers, Robert, and Stephen Macedo. 2009. Local Political Geography and American Political Identity. In Carol Greenhouse, ed. *Ethnographies of Neoliberalism*, pp. 77–95. Philadelphia: University of Pennsylvania Press.

Rose, Dan. 1989. *Patterns of American Culture: Ethnography and Estrangement*. Philadelphia: University of Pennsylvania Press.

Rouse, Roger. 1995. Thinking Through Transnationalism: Notes on the Cultural Politics of Class Relations in the Contemporary United States. *Public Culture* 7: 353–402.

Rutherford, Danilyn. 2000. The White Edge of the Margin: Textuality and Authority in Biak, Irian Jaya, Indonesia. *American Ethnologist* 27(2): 312–339.

Ryan, Mary P. 1997. *Civic Wars: Democracy and Public Life in the American City During the Nineteenth Century*. Berkeley: University of California Press.

Said, Edward W. 1978. *Orientalism*. New York: Vintage.

Saldívar, José David. 1991. *The Dialectics of Our America: Genealogy, Cultural Critique, and Literary History*. Durham, N.C.: Duke University Press.

Saldívar, Ramón. 1990. *Chicano Narrative: The Dialectics of Difference*. Madison: University of Wisconsin Press.

———. 1991. Narrative, Ideology, and the Reconstruction of American Literary History. In Héctor Calderón and José David Saldívar, eds., *Criticism in the Borderlands: Studies in Chicano Literature, Culture, and Ideology*, pp. 11–20. Durham, N.C.: Duke University Press.

Saldívar-Hull, Sonia. 1991. Feminism on the Border: From Gender Politics to Geopolitics. In Héctor Calderón and José David Saldívar, eds., *Criticism in the Borderlands: Studies in Chicano Literature, Culture, and Ideology*, pp. 203–220. Durham, N.C.: Duke University Press.

Salecl, Renata, and Slavoj Žižek, eds. 1996. *Gaze and Voice as Love Objects*. Durham, N.C.: Duke University Press.

Sandel, Michael. 1995. *Democracy's Discontents: America in Search of a Public Philosophy*. Cambridge, Mass.: Harvard University Press.

Sangren, P. Steven. 1995. "Power" Against Ideology: A Critique of Foucaultian Usage. *Cultural Anthropology* 10(1): 3-40.

Sanjek, Roger. 1990. Urban Anthropology in the 1980s: A World View. *Annual Review of Anthropology* 19: 151–186.

———. 1992. Review of Reading Ethnography, by David Jacobson. *American Anthropologist* 94(4): 999.

———. 1998. *The Future of Us All: Race and Neighborhood Politics in New York City.* Ithaca, N.Y.: Cornell University Press.

Santiago-Irizarry, Vilma. 1996. Culture as Cure. *Cultural Anthropology* 11(1): 3–24.

Sartre, Jean-Paul. 1988. *"What Is Literature?" and Other Essays.* Cambridge, Mass.: Harvard University Press.

Sassen, Saskia. 1988. *The Mobility of Labor and Capital.* Cambridge: Cambridge University Press.

———. 1991. *The Global City: New York, London, Tokyo.* Princeton, N.J.: Princeton University Press.

Sawhill, Isabel V., R. Kent Weaver, Ron Haskins, and Andrea Kane, eds. 2002. *Welfare Reform and Beyond: The Future of the Safety Net.* Washington, D.C.: Brookings Institution.

Schmidt, Nancy. 1994. Review of Anthropology and Literature, by Paul Benson. *American Anthropologist* 96(2): 459.

Schneider, David. 1968. *American Kinship: A Cultural Account.* Englewood Cliffs, N.J.: Prentice-Hall.

Schneider, Dorothee. 1998. "I Know All About Emma Lazarus": Nationalism and Its Contradictions in Congressional Rhetoric of Immigration Restriction. *Cultural Anthropology* 1998 13(1): 82–99.

Schneider, Jo Anne. 1999. And How Are We Supposed to Pay for Health Care? Views of the Poor and the Near Poor on Welfare Reform. *American Anthropologist* 101(4): 761–782.

Schultz, Vicki. 1990. Telling Stories About Women and Work: Judicial Interpretations of Sex Segregation in the Workplace in Title VII Cases Raising the Lack of Interest Argument. *Harvard Law Review* 103(8): 1749–1843.

Scott, James C. 1998. *Seeing Like a State: How Certain Schemes to Improve the Human Condition Have Failed.* New Haven: Yale University Press.

Scott, Joan Wallach. 1988. The Sears Case. In J. Scott, ed., *Gender and the Politics of History,* pp. 167–177. New York: Columbia University Press.

Segal, Daniel. 1996. Resisting Identities: A Found Theme. *Cultural Anthropology* 11(4): 431-434.

Shankman, Paul. 1996. Review of Not Even Wrong: Margaret Mead, Derek Freeman, and the Samoans, by Martin Orans. *American Anthropologist* 98(4): 889.

Shapiro, Ian, and Will Kymlicka, eds. 1997. Ethnicity and Group Rights (*Nomos* xxxix). New York: New York University Press.

Shokeid, Moshe. 1988. *Children of Circumstance: Israeli Emigrants in New York.* Ithaca, N.Y.: Cornell University Press.

Silbey, Susan. 2005. After Legal Consciousness. *Annual Review of Law and Social Science* 1:323-368.

Silko, Leslie Marmon. 1996 [1977]. *Ceremony.* New York: Penguin.

Singh, Nikhil Pal. 1998. Culture/Wars: Recoding Empire in an Age of Democracy. *American Quarterly* 50(3): 471–522.

Skočpol, Theda. 1995. *Social Policy in the United States: Future Possibilities in Historical Perspective.* Princeton, N.J.: Princeton University Press.

Small, Cathy A. 1997. *Voyages: From Tongan Villages to American Suburbs.* Ithaca, N.Y.: Cornell University Press.

Smart, Carol. 1989. *Feminism and the Power of Law.* London: Routledge.

Smith, Rogers M. 1997. *Civic Ideals: Conflicting Visions of Citizenship in U.S. History.* New Haven, Conn.: Yale University Press.

Smith, Sedonie, and Julia Watson, eds. 1992. *De/Colonizing the Subject: The Politics of Gender in Women's Autobiography.* Minneapolis: University of Minnesota Press.

Sollors, Werner. 1986. *Beyond Ethnicity: Consent and Descent in American Culture.* New York: Oxford University Press.

———. 1989. Introduction: The Invention of Ethnicity. In Werner Sollors, ed., *The Invention of Ethnicity,* pp. ix–xx. New York: Oxford University Press.

Spillers, Hortense J. 1991. *Comparative American Identities: Race, Sex, and Nationality in the Modern Text.* New York: Routledge.

Stack, Carol. 1974. *All Our Kin: Strategies for Survival in a Black Community.* New York: Harper and Row.

Steedly, Mary Margaret. 1999. The State of Culture Theory in the Anthropology of Southeast Asia. *Annual Review of Anthropology* 28: 431–454.

Stepick, Alex. 1994. Miami: Capital of Latin America. In Louise Lamphere, Alex Stepick, and Guillermo Grenier, eds., *Newcomers in the Workplace: Immigrants and the Restructuring of the U.S. Economy,* pp.129-144. Philadelphia: Temple University Press.

———. 2006. "There Is More to Life than a Glass of Water": Immigration in the Contemporary United States. *American Anthropologist* 108(2): 392–396.

Stewart, Kathleen, and Susan Harding. 1999. Bad Endings: American Apocalypse. *Annual Review of Anthropology* 28: 285–310.

Stoller, Paul. 1992. Review of Anthropological Poetics, by Ivan Brady. *American Anthropologist* 94(2): 508–509.

———. 1994. Ethnographies as Texts / Ethnographers as Griots. *American Ethnologist* 21(2): 353–366.

———. 2002. *Money Has No Small: The Africanization of New York City.* Chicago: University of Chicago Press.

Stone, Geoffrey R., Louis M. Seidman, Cass R. Sunstein, and Mark V. Tushnet. 1991. *Constitutional Law,* 2nd ed. Boston: Little, Brown.

Strathern, Marilyn. 1987. Introduction. In Marilyn Strathern, ed. *Dealing with Inequality: Analysing Gender Relations in Melanesia and Beyond,* pp. 1–32. Cambridge: Cambridge University Press.

———. 1988. *The Gender of the Gift: Problems with Women and Problems with Society in Melanesia.* Berkeley: University of California Press.

Strathern, Marilyn, ed. 1995. *Shifting Contexts: Transformations in Anthropological Knowledge.* London: Routledge.

———. 2000. *Audit Cultures: Anthropological Studies in Accountability, Ethics and the Academy.* London: Routledge.

Strauss, Claudia. 1990. Who Gets Ahead? Cognitive Responses to Heteroglossia in American Political Culture. *American Ethnologist* 17(2): 312–329.

———. 1997. Partly Fragmented, Partly Integrated: An Anthropological Examination of "Postmodern Fragmented Subjects." *Cultural Anthropology* 23(3): 362–404.

Sullivan, Mercer L. 1989. *"Getting Paid": Youth Crime and Work in the Inner City.* Ithaca, N.Y.: Cornell University Press.

Susser, Ida. 1996. The Construction of Poverty and Homeless in U.S. Cities. *Annual Review of Anthropology* 25: 411–435.

———. 1998. Inequality, Violence, and Gender Relations in a Global City: New York, 1986–1996. *American Ethnologist* 29(4): 981–1002.

Takezawa, Yasuko I. 1995. *Breaking the Silence: Redress and Japanese American Ethnicity.* Ithaca, N.Y.: Cornell University Press.

Tan, Amy. 1989. *The Joy Luck Club.* New York: Ivy Books.

———. 1991. *The Kitchen God's Wife.* New York: Penguin.

Taylor, Charles. 1994. The Politics of Recognition. In A. Gutman, ed., *Multiculturalism: Examining the Politics of Recognition,* pp. 25–73. Princeton, N.J.: Princeton University Press.

Thomas, Nicholas. 1991. Against Ethnography. *Cultural Anthropology* 6(3): 306–322.

Tocqueville, Alexis de. 1945. *Democracy in America,* 2 vols. trans. Henry Reeve, rev. Francis Bowen, ed. Phillips Bradley. New York: Vintage Books.

Toniatti, Roberto. 1995. Minorities and Protected Minorities: Constitutional Models Compared. In M. Dunne and T. Bonazzi, eds., *Citizenship and Rights in Multicultural Societies,* pp. 195–219. Keele: Keele University Press.

Traube, Elizabeth G. 1990. Reply to Moffatt. *Cultural Anthropology* 5(4): 374–379.

———. 1992. *Dreaming Identities: Class, Gender, and Generation in 1980s Hollywood Movies.* Boulder, Colo.: Westview Press.

———. 1996. "The Popular" in American Culture. *Annual Review of Anthropology* 25: 127–151.

Trix, Frances, and Andrea Sankar. 1998. Women's Voices and Experiences of the Hill-Thomas Hearings. *American Anthropologist* 100(1): 32–40.

Tsing, Anna Lowenhaupt. 1993. *In the Realm of the Diamond Queen: Marginality in an Out-of-the-Way Place.* Princeton, N.J.: Princeton University Press.

———. 1994. From the Margins. *Cultural Anthropology* 9(3): 279–297.

———. 2000. The Global Situation. *Cultural Anthropology* 15(3): 327–360.

Turner, Bryan S. 1993. Contemporary Problems in the Theory of Citizenship. In B. S. Turner, ed., *Citizenship and Social Theory,* pp. 1–18. London: Sage.

Turner, Terence. 1993. Anthropology and Multiculturalism: What Is Anthropology That Multiculturalists Should Be Mindful of It? *Cultural Anthropology* 8(4): 411–429.

United States Congress. 1988a. Civil Liberties Act of 1988. 100th Cong., 2nd sess. (H.R. 442).

———. 1988b. Americans with Disabilities Act of 1988. Joint Hearing before the Subcommittee on the Handicapped of the Committee on Labor and Human Resources, United States Senate, and the Subcommittee on Education and Labor, House of Representatives, on S. 2345 to establish a clear and comprehensive prohibition of discrimination on the basis of handicap. 100th Congress, 2nd session. September 27, 1988. Washington, D.C.: United States Government Printing Office.

———. 1996. Personal Responsibility and Work Opportunity Reconciliation Act of 1996. 104th Cong., 2nd sess. (H.R. 3734).

United States Department of Commerce. 1990. Census of Population: Social and Economic Characteristics, United States. Economics and Statistics Administration, Bureau of the Census. Electronic document: http://www.census.gov/prod/cen1990/cp2/cp-2-1.pdf (accessed November 4, 2009).

———. 1993. We the American . . . Foreign Born. Economics and Statistics Administration, Bureau of the Census. Electronic document: http://www.census.gov/apsd/wepeople/we-7.pdf (accessed November 4, 2009).

United States Department of Health and Human Services. 1997. Major Provisions of the Personal Responsibility and Work Opportunity Reconciliation Act of 1996 (P.L. 104-193). Electronic document: http://www.acf.hhs.gov/programs/ofa/law-reg/fin alrule/aspesum.htm (accessed December 21, 2010).

United States Department of Labor, Office of Policy Planning and Research. 1965. The Negro Family: The Case for National Action. Electronic document: http://www.dol .gov/oasam/programs/history/webid-meynihan.htm (accessed October 29, 2009).

United States House of Representatives. 1987. Committee on Education and Labor. Hearing on Discrimination against Cancer Victims and the Handicapped. Hearing before the Subcommittee on Employment Opportunities. Washington, D.C., June 17, 1987. Serial no. 100-31. Washington, D.C.: United States Government Printing Office.

———. 1989a. Joint Hearing on H.R. 2273, The Americans with Disabilities Act of 1989. Joint Hearing before the Subcommittees on Select Education and Employment Opportunities of the Committee on Education and Labor. 101st Congress. 1st session. July 18, 1989. Serial 101-37. Washington, D.C.: United States Government Printing Office.

———. 1989b. American With Disabilities Act. Hearing before the Committee on Small Business. 101st Congress. 2nd session. Serial no. 101-45. Washington, D.C.: United States Government Printing Office.

———. 1990. Hearings before the Committee on the Judiciary and the Subcommittee on Civil and Constitutional Rights of the Committee on the Judiciary on H.R. 2273, Americans with Disabilities Act of 1989. 101st Congress. 1st session. August 3, October 11 and 12, 1989. Serial no. 58. Washington, D.C.: United States Government Printing Office.

———. 1996a. Committee on the Judiciary, Immigration in the National Interest Act of 1995 (H.R. 1915), Hearing before the Subcommittee on Immigration and Claims. 104th Cong., 1st sess., June 29, 1995. Washington, D.C.: United States Government Printing Office.

———. 1996b. Contract with America—Welfare Reform. Hearing before the Subcommittee on Human Resources of the Committee on Ways and Means, 104th Cong., 1st sess., January 13, 20, 23, 27, and 30, 1995. Part 1. Serial 104-43. Washington, D.C.: United States Government Printing Office.

———. 1996c. Contract with America—Welfare Reform. Hearing before the Subcommittee on Human Resources of the Committee on Ways and Means. 104th Cong., 1st sess., February 2, 1995. Part 2. Serial 104-44. Washington, D.C.: United States Government Printing Office.

United States Senate. 1990. Civil Rights Act of 1990. Hearing before the Committee on Labor and Human Resources. 101st Cong., 1st sess., February 23, 27, March 1, and 7, 1989. Washington, D.C.: United States Government Printing Office.

———. 1991. Judiciary Committee, Nomination of Judge Clarence Thomas to be an Associate Justice of the Supreme Court of the United States: Hearings before the Committee on the Judiciary. 102nd Cong., 1st sess., September 10, 11, 12, 13, and 16, 1991.

———. 1995. Welfare Reform Wrap-Up. Hearing before the Committee on Finance. 104th Cong., 1st sess., April 27, 1995. Washington, D.C.: United States Government Printing Office.

———. n.d. Roll Call Votes. 101st Congress. 2nd session. Electronic document: http://www.senate.gov/legislative/LIS/roll_call_cfm.cfm?congress=101&session=2&vote=00304 (accessed May 2, 2010).

———. n.d. Public Law 104-208. Vote summary. Electronic document: http://www.senate.gov/legislative/CIS/roll_call_lists/roll_call_vote_cfm.cfm?congress=104&session=2&vote=00200#position (accessed May 21, 2010).

United States Social Security Administration. n.d. Social Security Online. History – Vote Tallies – 1996 Welfare Amendments. Electronic document: http://www.ssa.gov/history/tally1996.html (accessed May 2, 2010).

Urban Institute. 1998. A Comparison of Selected Key Provisions of the Welfare Reform Reconciliation Act of 1996 with Current Law. Washington, D.C.: Urban Institute. Electronic document: http://www.urban.org/url/cfm?ID=410327 (accessed October 29, 2009).

Urciuoli, Bonnie. 1994. Acceptable Difference: The Cultural Evolution of the Model Ethnic American Citizen. *Political and Legal Anthropology Review* 17(2): 19–36.

———. 1996. *Exposing Prejudice: Puerto Rican Experiences of Language, Race, and Class.* Boulder, Colo.: Westview Press.

———. 1998. Acceptable Difference: The Cultural Evolution of the Model Ethnic American Citizen. In C. Greenhouse, ed., *Ethnography and Democracy: Constructing Identities in Multicultural Liberal States,* pp. 178–195. Albany: SUNY Press.

———. 2005. The Language of Higher Education Assessment: Legislative Concerns in a Global Context. *Indiana Journal of Global Legal Studies* 12(1): 183–204.

van Steenbergen, Bart, ed. 1994. *The Condition of Citizenship.* London: Sage.

Varenne, Hervé. 1977. *Americans Together: Structured Diversity in a Midwestern Town.* New York City: Teachers College Press.

———. 1984. Collective Representation in American Anthropological Conversations: Individual and Culture. *Current Anthropology* 25(3): 281–300.

———. 1986. Drop in Anytime: Community and Authenticity in American Everyday Life. In H. Varenne, ed., *Symbolizing America,* pp. 209–228. Lincoln: University of Nebraska Press.

———. 1998. Diversity as American Cultural Category. In C. Greenhouse, ed., *Democracy and Ethnography: Constructing Identities in Multicultural Liberal States,* pp. 27–49. Albany: SUNY Press.

Varenne, Hervé, ed. 1986. *Symbolizing America.* Lincoln: University of Nebraska Press.

Verdery, Kathryn. 1996. *What Was Socialism, and What Comes Next?* Princeton, N.J.: Princeton University Press.

Visweswaran, Kamala. 1994. *Fictions of Feminist Anthropology.* Minneapolis: University of Minnesota Press.

———. 1997. Histories of Feminist Anthropology. *Annual Review of Anthropology* 26: 591–621.

———. 1998. Race and the Culture of Anthropology. *American Anthropologist* 100(1): 70–83.

Von Eschen, Penny M. 1997. *Race Against Empire: Black Americans and Anticolonialism, 1937–1957.* Ithaca, N.Y.: Cornell University Press.

Wacquant, Loïc. 2009. *Punishing the Poor: The Neoliberal Government of Social Insecurity.* Durham, N.C.: Duke University Press.

Wagner-Pacifici, Robin. 1994. *Discourse and Destruction: The City of Philadelphia Versus MOVE.* Chicago: University of Chicago Press.

Wagoner, Paula L. 1997. Surveying Justice: The Problematics of Overlapping Jurisdictions in Indian Country. *Droit et Cultures* 33(1): 21–52.

Walker, Alice. 1992. *Possessing the Secret of Joy.* New York: Pocket Books.

Warner, Lloyd. 1949. *Democracy in Jonesville: A Study in Quality and Inequality.* New York: Harper and Row.

———. 1959. *The Living and the Dead.* New Haven, Conn.: Yale University Press.

———. 1962. *American Life: Dream and Reality.* Chicago: University of Chicago Press.

Warren, Kenneth W. 1993. *Black and White Strangers: Race and American Literary Realism.* Chicago: University of Chicago Press.

Wax, Murray. 1997. Forum: On Negating Positivism. *American Anthropologist* 99(1): 17–23.

Wax, Rosalie H. 1971. *Doing Fieldwork: Warnings and Advice.* Chicago: University of Chicago Press.

Weber, Max. 1954. *Max Weber on Law in Economy, and Society.* Max Rheinstein, ed., Edward Shils and Max Rheinstein, trans. Cambridge: Harvard University Press.

Weiner, Annette B. 1995. Culture and Our Discontents. *American Anthropologist* 97(1): 14–21.

Welaratna, Usha. 1993. *Beyond the Killing Fields: Voices of Nine Cambodian Survivors in America.* Stanford: Stanford University Press.

Wells, Miriam. 1996. *Strawberry Fields: Politics, Class and Work in California.* Ithaca, N.Y.: Cornell University Press.

West, Cornel. 2001. *Race Matters.* New York: Vintage.

West, Robin. 1993. *Narrative, Authority and Law.* Ann Arbor: University of Michigan Press.

Weston, Kath. 1998. *Long Slow Burn: Sexuality and Social Science.* New York: Routledge.

White, Robert Boyd. 1990. *Justice as Translation: An Essay in Cultural and Legal Criticism.* Chicago: University of Chicago Press.

Whitman, Mark. 1993. *Removing a Badge of Slavery: The Record of Brown v. Board of Education.* Princeton, N.J.: Markus Wiener Publishing.

Wilkinson, J. Harvie, III. 1979. *From Brown to Bakke: The Supreme Court and School Integration 1954–1978.* New York: Oxford University Press.

Williams, Brett. 1988. *Upscaling Downtown: Stalled Gentrification in Washington, D.C.* Ithaca, N.Y.: Cornell University Press.

Williams, Susan H. 1997. A Feminist Reassessment of Civil Society. *Indiana Law Journal* 72(2): 417–462.

———. 2004. *Truth, Autonomy and Speech: Feminist Theory and the First Amendment.* New York: New York University Press.

Williams, Walter L. 1993. Review of Gay Culture in America: Essays from the Field, by Gilbert Herdt. *American Anthropologist* 95(1): 222–223.

Wilmsen, E., and P. McAllister, eds. 1996. *The Politics of Difference: Ethnic Premises in a World of Power.* Chicago: University of Chicago Press.

Wilson, William Julius. 1987. *The Truly Disadvantaged: The Inner City, the Underclass, and Public Policy.* Chicago: University of Chicago Press.

Wing, Adrien Katherine. 1997. Introduction. In *Critical Race Feminism: A Reader,* pp. 1–6. New York: New York University Press.

Wing, Adrien Katherine, ed. 1997. *Critical Race Feminism: A Reader.* New York: New York University Press.

———. 2000. *Global Critical Race Feminism: An International Reader.* New York: New York University Press.

Wright, Richard. 1993 [1940]. *Native Son.* New York: Harper Collins.

Yanagisako, Sylvia Junko. 1985. *Transforming the Past: Tradition and Kinship Among Japanese Americans.* Stanford: Stanford University Press.

Yeates, Nicola. 1996. Appeals to Citizenship in the Unification of Europe: The Political and Social Context of the EC's Third Programme to Combat Poverty. In V. Ruggiero, ed., *Citizenship, Human Rights and Minorities: Rethinking Social Control in the New Europe.* XX conference of the European Group for the Study of Deviance and Social Control. Athens/Komotini: Ant. N. Sakkoulas Publishers.

Yngvesson, Barbara. 1993. *Virtuous Citizens, Disruptive Subjects.* New York: Routledge.

———. 1997. Negotiating Motherhood: Identity and Difference in "Open" Adoptions. *Law & Society Review* 31(1): 31–80.

Young, Iris Marion. 1995. Polity and Group Difference: A Critique of the Ideal of Universal Citizenship. In R. Beiner, ed., *Theorizing Citizenship*, pp. 175–207. Albany: SUNY Press.

Zabusky, Stacia E. 1995. *Launching Europe: An Ethnography of European Cooperation in Space Science.* Princeton, N.J.: Princeton University Press.

Žižek, Slavoj. 1996a. "I Hear You with My Eyes": or, The Invisible Master. In R. Salecl and S. Žižek, eds., *Gaze and Voice as Love Objects,* pp. 90–126. Durham, N.C.: Duke University Press.

———. 1996b. "There Is No Sexual Relationship." In R. Salecl and S. Žižek, eds., *Gaze and Voice as Love Objects,* pp. 209–249. Durham, N.C.: Duke University Press.

Law Cases Cited

Brown v. Board of Education, 387 U.S. 483 (1954).

Cayuga Nation of New York v. Pataki, 413 F. 3rd 266 (2005).

Griggs v. Duke Power Company, 401 U.S. 424 (1971).

Grutter v. Bollinger, 539 U.S. 306 (2003).

Korematsu v. United States, 323 U.S. 214 (1944).

Oneida County v. Oneida Indian Nation, 470 U.S. 226 (1985).

Oneida Indian Nation v. County of Oneida, 414 U.S. 661 (1974).

Plessy v. Ferguson, 163 U.S. 537 (1896).

Wards Cove Packing Company v. Atonio, 490 U.S. 642 (1989).

Public Laws Cited

Alaska Native Community Settlement Act (ANCSA), 43 USC 1601-1624.

Americans with Disabilities Act of 1990, P.L. 101-336; 42 USC 12101, 104 Stat 327.

Illegal Immigration Reform and Immigrant Responsibility Act (IIRAIRA) of 1996, P.L. 104-208, Div 3; 110 Stat 3009-546.

Civil Liberties Act of 1988, H.R. 442

Civil Rights Act of 1991, P.L. 102-166, 42 USC 1988.

INDEX

ACKNOWLEDGMENTS

I am indebted to Princeton University and Indiana University for their generous support of this project. Without their funds for faculty research and writing in the humanities and social sciences, this work would not have been possible. I benefited greatly, too, from the support of several other institutions: a residency at the Rockefeller Foundation's Study Center at Bellagio, a short period in residence at the International Institute for the Sociology of Law at Oñati, and a year in Paris under the auspices of the French-American Foundation's chair in American civilization. There, I had an ideal base at the Centre d'Etudes Nord-Américains at the École des Hautes Etudes en Sciences Sociales, thanks to the extraordinary collegial generosity of its director, Jean Heffer, and colleagues François Weil and Pap Ndiaye. Subsequently, the project benefited from a further period of teaching in the Faculté du Droit at the University of Paris II, and collegial exchanges with my academic host, Elisabeth Zoller. A brief guest instructorship at a summer seminar on the rule of law, sponsored by the National Endowment for the Humanities and the University of New England, was exceptionally helpful, thanks to the engagement of the seminar leaders, Cathrine Frank and Matthew Anderson—and the remarkable collegial circle they gathered in Portland, Maine. I completed the manuscript during a sabbatical year at the Maurer School of Law at Indiana University–Bloomington as a visiting scholar; I am very grateful to Dean Lauren Robel.

This book had several starting points, but from the beginning, it was a study of the discourse of race as a critical feature in the hermeneutics of federalism and transnationalism in ethnography, law and literature in the United States. The book is about the 1990s but very much from the perspective of the present—that is, in the aftermath of the security crisis that followed the events of the fall, 2001, as well as the legitimacy crisis that followed the election of President Obama in 2008, and the intensification of political contests over market discourse in relation to social security in 2010. I do not discuss those developments as such, but it was in their light that periodicity became a more pressing question, not only in relation to highly public events, but also relative to the specifics of disciplinary and interdisciplinary exchanges and their imaginative demands. Along the way, at home and abroad, the book evolved in the classroom. My experiments (and enjoyments) in reading were sustained and enriched in conversations with undergraduate and graduate students in seminar, and in the context of their own ethnographic commitments – the latter being abundant evidence of anthropology's flourishing creativity and determined relevance. I acknowledge those exchanges gratefully. It is also a pleasure to acknowledge family, friends and faculty colleagues at my own institution and elsewhere whose insights helped shape the project at critical junctures (which is not to claim their endorsement of the result): Louis Assier-Andrieu, Marc Abélès, Judith Allen, Emma Amos, Jesús Azcona, Richard Bauman, João Biehl, James Boon, Constance Borde, John Borneman, Amy Borovoy, Don Brenneis, Jessica Cattelino, Isabelle Clarke-Décès, John Comaroff, Marianne Constable, Susan Coutin, Elizabeth Davis, David Engel, Nicola Evans, José-Antonio Fernández de Rota, Eugene Fidell, Hannah Fidell, Rebecca French, Wynne Furth, Bryant Garth, Ilana Gershon, Jane Goodman, Linda Greenhouse, Kathleen Hall, Abdellah Hammoudi, Mary Harper, Dirk Hartog, Sue Hirsch, Linda Hutcheon, Michael Hutcheon, Robert Ivy, Stephanie Kane, Roshanak Kheshti, Chantal Kourilsky-Augeven, Mindie Lazarus-Black, Rena Lederman, Brad Levinson, Sheila Malovany-Chevalier, Alan Mann, Bill Maurer, Sally Merry, Elizabeth Mertz, Frank Munger, Susana Navotzky, Grey Osterud, Serguei Oushakine, Phil Parnell, Andrew Parker, Adriana Petryna, Jesús Prieto de Pedro, Nancy Ries, Annelise Riles, Lawrence Rosen, Carolyn Rouse, Austin Sarat, Kim Scheppele, Gene Shreve, Marguerite Shreve, Sandhya Shukla, Peter Skafish, Robert J. Smith, Valerie Smith, Beverly Stoeltje, Patricia Sullivan, Ignazi Terradas, David Williams, Sam Williams, Susan Williams, Gordon Wood, Louise Wood, Hervé Varenne, Honorio Velasco, Kamala Visweswaran, Barbara Yngvesson, and Frances Zimmerman. Grey Osterud read an early version of the manuscript– an ideal and timely interlocutor. Peter Agree brought his own deep understanding of the period to the project. I am grateful for his reading, as well as for providing me with two exceptionally constructive reports from anonymous readers. Gabriela Drinovan undertook the enormous labor of checking and updating my bibliography; I am greatly in her debt. My warm thanks go, too, to Noreen O'Connor-Abel and all the superb team at Penn Press, as well as to Twin Oaks Indexing. My greatest debt, as always, is to Fred Aman. This project has been so much a part of our shared time that its dedication feels co-authored: to my mother—born on the day women won the right to vote in the United States.

Several elements of this book involve revisions and recontextualizations of material that originally appeared elsewhere. "Identity, Law and the Dream of Time" in *Looking Back at Law's Century,* Austin Sarat, Bryant Garth and Robert Kagan, editors. Pp. 184-209. Ithaca: Cornell University Press (2002); "Ethnography and Democracy: Texts and Contexts in the United States in the 1990s" in *Cultural Analysis, Cultural Studies and the Law: Moving Beyond Legal Realism*, Austin Sarat and Jonathan Simon, editors. Pp. 191-219. Durham: Duke University Press (2003); "Burdens of Proof" *Cambridge Journal of Anthropology* 28(3):113-126 (2008/09); "Life Stories, Law's Stories: Subjectivity and Responsibility in the Politicization of the Discourse of 'Identity' " *Political and Legal Anthropology Review (PoLAR)* 31(1): 79-95 (2008). Excerpts from my chapter "A Federal Life" in *Race, Law and Culture*, Austin Sarat, editor. Pp. 170-189 (1997) are used with the kind permission of Oxford University Press.